COTTON AND FAMINE IN BERAR
1850–1900

Cotton and Famine in Berar
1850–1900

LAXMAN D. SATYA

MANOHAR
2026

First published 1997
Reprinted 2021, 2023, 2024, 2026

ISBN 978-81-7304-160-0

Published by
Ajay Kumar Jain *for*
Manohar Publishers & Distributors
4753/23 Ansari Road, Daryaganj
New Delhi 110 002

Printed at
Replika Press Pvt. Ltd.

TO
MY PARENTS
SATYAWADA MANIKYAM DEVI
SATYAWADA VEERA RAJU

Contents

List of Tables

Foreword

IT IS WITH MUCH pleasure that I write these few words of introduction and appreciation of Dr. Laxman Dass Satya's study of cotton and famine in Berar in the latter half of the nineteenth century. This book is an important and original contribution to the social and economic history of modern India. Dr. Satya has gleaned a fascinating set of materials from archives in London, New Delhi and Central India. His work focuses on an important cotton-growing region of Central India which has been curiously neglected by agrarian historians. Soon after being annexed by the British, Berar experienced a cotton boom during the American Civil War. Dr. Satya explores and explains Berar's shift to commodity production for a capitalist world market and the absence of any significant developmental impact of agricultural commercialization under conditions of colonial capitalism.

In a very substantial chapter on the land revenue settlement between 1861 and 1877 Dr. Satya skilfully unravels the ways in which the colonial state sought to settle and sedenterize Indian rural society. While most agrarian historians have used cadastral survey and settlement reports to collect information on landholding and agrarian social structure, Dr. Satya is able to show how modern technology used in the settlement operations was deployed to achieve the aim of standardizing local social and cultural practices. He probes the balance between forests and agricultural plains to make important points about the reduction of rural mobility and its environmental consequences.

Dr. Satya's chapter on the cotton economy will be a very useful addition not only to South Asian history but also work done as far afield as Egypt and American South. While concerned primarily with Berar, this work also addresses broader issues concerning technology and comparative labour history. The chapter on balutedars, khatedars, banias and banjaras illuminates key changes in rural social relations in colonial India. Readers should be particularly interested in everyday forms of resistance by bhagindars (sharecroppers) to the khatedari system introduced by the British. Dr. Satya's analysis of the late nineteenth century famines shows that subsistence crises even in that relatively early period were not Malthusian disasters but were brought about by sharp declines in entitlements.

Dr. Satya has done a major service to the historical profession and to the working people of Berar.

Professor of History and Diplomacy SUGATA BOSE
Tufts University

Acknowledgements

THE SPECIAL STATUS of Berar within the British colonial empire in India in the nineteenth century in itself reveals its importance to the contemporary world economy. The dramatic takeover and the linkup of the region to world market and the consequent socio-economic change the region underwent is the story which had waited long to be told. This work retrieves Berar from the colonial documents of the nineteenth century and critically places it in the historiography of South Asia.

The book was originally conceived as a doctoral dissertation under the supervision of Dr. Sugata Bose and Dr. David Dapice. This work owes a great deal to their energy, patience, time, and thought. Dean Robert Guertin's solid financial and moral support during my graduate days at Tufts is remembered here with gratitude. Dr. Steve Marrone's friendship and kind sympathetic gestures during the trying times were a source of tremendous inspiration in every step of the writing process. Dr. Gary Leupp and his family and home always provided a comforting relief from the monotonous routine of academic life.

The research work for this book was conducted at India Office Library and Records, London; British Museum and Library, London; National Archives of India, Central Secretariat Library, and Nehru Memorial Museum and Library, New Delhi; Andhra Pradesh State Archives, Hyderabad; The Smithsonian Institution, The Library of Congress, and The National Archives, Washington, D.C.; Harvard University Library, Cambridge; Columbia University Library, New York City; and The University of Wisconsin Library, Madison.

The Smithsonian Institution was generous in supporting the early stages of research with a pre-doctoral fellowship. Special thanks to Dr. Pete Daniel and Dr. Terry Sharrer for providing encouragement by commenting on the very early drafts of the manuscript. Their warm friendship ever since has been a source of great inspiration.

The author also wishes to thank Dr. John Rogers and Dr. Doug Haynes for taking the time out of their own work to read the draft and provide useful suggestions. Ana and Odysseus Chairetakis in Florida, Neal and his parents Eve and Jacob Bernstein in Long Island, and Sherri West and family in New Jersey readily provided the comfort of home and are remembered here with gratitude.

This book is dedicated to my parents whose love and affection sustained me during the challenging years of my schooling in the United States. The affection of my sister Jyothi Devi, and brothers Vishwanath anaya, Ramdass anaya, and Vishnu are immense.

LAXMAN D. SATYA

Lock Haven,
Pennsylvania
1995

Introduction

IN THE NINETEENTH century cotton was in great demand in the world market as a cash crop. The need for raw cotton during the industrial revolution motivated Great Britain to colonize the rich cotton growing lands in Egypt and India, besides engaging in trade with the slave plantations of the American south. From the beginning of the nineteenth century, cotton was thus associated with colonialism and slavery. This connection played a major role in shaping and reshaping the economy and society of the areas engaged in cotton production throughout the world. Karl Marx in the mid-nineteenth century noted this process happening on a global scale:

> The discovery of America, the rounding of the Cape, opened up fresh ground for the rising bourgeoisie. The East-Indian and Chinese markets, the colo-nizationof America, trade with the colonies, the increase in the means of exchange and in commodities generally, gave to commerce, to navigation, to industry, an impulse never before known. . . .
>
> Subjection of nature's forces to man, machinery, application of chemistry to industry and agriculture, steam-navigation, railways, electric telegraphs, clearing of whole continents for cultivation, canalization of rivers, whole populations conjured out of the ground—what earlier century had even a presentiment that such productive forces slumbered in the lap of social labor?[1]

As a major supplier of cotton, India's role was crucial to the survival of British textile industry. After the outbreak of American Civil War (1861), Indian cotton acquired an even greater significance in the world market. The rich black soil of western India and the Deccan had traditionally produced the best cotton in the country. Hidden in the navel of India, Berar had all the right conditions for large scale production of cotton. Berar's position at the centre of

[1] Karl Marx and Friedrich Engels, *The Communist Manifesto*, Samuel H. Beer, ed., Arlington Heights, Illinois, 1955, pp. 10, 14.

overland trade routes connecting all parts of India was exceptional.

As one of the richest *subahs* of the Mughal empire, Berar had provided for Mughal armies when Aurangzeb campaigned in the Deccan against Marathas. Even after the devastating factional wars between the Nizam and the Marathas in the eighteenth century, Berar's position remained strategically important. As the shadow of East India Company lengthened on the land, the military significance of Berar could not remain unnoticed. Furthermore, no other province of colonial India had the capacity to engage 30 per cent of its best agricultural lands to single cash crop cotton. Surrounded by British colonial possessions, Berar did not have much chance of escaping colonization. The colonization of Berar became necessary to guarantee continued supplies of raw cotton to Britain.

The political drama of the annexation of Berar in 1853 marked a hight point of Dalhousie's administration. Located in the centre of colonial India, Berar was a major base of British political and economic power. The transformation of Berar under the impact of the nineteenth century capitalist world economy is a fascinating story yet to be told. This dissertation attempts to tell that story within the broader framework of India's colonial experience and its links to the world economy.

There has been an ongoing debate in Indian historiography on the impact of British colonial rule on Indian economy. Colonial theoreticians in the nineteenth and early twentieth century like James Mill, William Digby, Vera Anstey, Strachey brothers and modern writers like Morris D. Morris, Michelle McAlphin and Peter Harnetty have argued that India under British rule was politically stable and economically prosperous. The new law and order brought security to life and property. The rise in cultivated acreage, irrigation, trade and commerce, railways, roads, canals, telegraph, post-office and an organized market economy brought about a general prosperity in the region leading to the development of a manufacturing sector in India.

The early Indian nationalists of the late nineteenth century like R. C. Dutt, Dadabhai Naoroji, and Mahadeo Gobind Ranade and contemporary writers like Bipin Chandra, Tapan Raychaudhuri, and Amiya Bagchi have presented a critique of colonialism. The Indian economy served British interests by producing revenues for the state and cash crops for the world market. The drain of wealth funneled through India's export surplus led to the impoverishment of the country. Therefore disease, famine, poverty and economic backwardness was the eventual outcome of British colonialism in India.[2]

The reflections of the observations made in the colonial and nationalist/Marxist debate can be noticed in the works of modern day scholars who are writing on the theme of continuity and change under colonial rule. Over the past two decades a more sophisticated debate has developed on whether the Indian social and economic structure remained unaltered or whether there was a qualitative change taking place under colonial conditions.[3] Some scholars have observed that the British rule in India did not penetrate deep enough and that the basic structural features of the society and economy remained unchanged.[4] Other scholars have

[2] For an entire debate on this issue see: 'The Indian Economy in the Nineteenth Century: A Symposium', *Indian Economic and Social History Review*, IX, No. 1 (March 1972).

[3] For recent works on the theme of continuity and change see: Himadri Banerjee, *Agrarian Society of Punjab, 1849-1901*, New Delhi, 1982; Dipesh Chakrabarti, *Rethinking Working-Class History: Bengal, 1890-1940*, Princeton, 1989; Partha Chatterjee, *Bengal: The Land Question, 1920-1947*, Calcutta, 1984; Sumit Guha, *The Agrarian Economy of Bombay Deccan, 1818-1941*, Delhi, 1985; David Ludden, *Peasant History in South India*, Princeton, 1985; Gyan Prakash, *Bonded Histories: Genealogies of Labour Servitude in Colonial India*, Cambridge, 1990; C. A. Bayly, *Rulers, Townsmen and Bazaars: North Indian Society in the Age of British Expansion, 1770-1870*, Cambridge, 1983; Eric Stokes, *The Peasant and the Raj: Studies in Agrarian Society and Peasant Rebellion in Colonial India*, Cambridge, 1978; Dharma Kumar, *Land and Caste in South India: Agricultural Labour in Madras Presidency in the Nineteenth Century*, Cambridge, 1965; Rajat and Ratna Ray, 'The Dynamics of Continuity in Rural Bengal under the British Imperium', in *Indian Economic and Social History Review*, 10, 2 (1973), pp. 103-28; Ratnalekha Ray, *Change in Bengal Agrarian Society, 1750-1850*, Delhi, 1979; Asok Sen, Partha Chatterjee and Saugata Mukherji, *Perspectives in Social Science 2: Three Studies on the Agrarian Structure in Bengal, 1850-1947*, Delhi, 1982; Asiya Siddiqi, *Agrarian Change in a North Indian State: Uttar Pradesh, 1819-1833*, Oxford, 1973; Elizabeth Whitcombe, *Agrarian Conditions in Northern India: The United Provinces under British Rule, 1860-1900*, Berkeley, 1972.

[4] See the works of Anand Yang, *The Limited Raj: Agrarian Conditions in Colonial India, Saran District, 1793-1920*, Berkeley, 1989; Rajat and Ratna Ray, 'The Dynamics of Continuity in Rural Bengal under the British Imperium', *Indian Economic and Social History Review*, 10, 2 (1973), pp. 103-28; Michelle McAlpin, *Subject to Famine: Food Crisis and Economic Change in Western India, 1860-1920*, Princeton, 1983; Robert E. Frykenberg, *Land Control and Social Structure in Indian History*, Madison, 1969; Neil Charlesworth, *Peasants and Imperial Rule: Agriculture and Agrarian Society in the Bombay Presidency, 1850-1935*, Cambridge, 1985.

made 'an attempt to ferret out the elements of qualitative change in an agrarian scenario where many social structural features appeared to remain unaltered'.[5] A number of scholars in different ways have identified the elements of qualitative change under colonial rule.[6] My research has also observed several such elements of qualitative change in Berar. For example, in one instance it is noted (Chapter 3) that the forcing up of labour intensity within peasant household led to increased exploitation of unpaid and underpaid women and childrens labour in the countryside.

The Subaltern Studies collection in Indian historiography, Ranajit Guha (ed.), *Subaltern Studies,* Vols 1 to 6, Delhi, 1982-91, has come out with new ways of studying subordinated social classes.The subaltern school has emphasized the culture and consciousness of the people rather than the material factors. While taking the cultural dimension into account, my research on the Berar evidence suggests that there were strong links between resistance, colonial control and the material condition of the people.

The Berar evidence also suggests that there was indeed qualitative change taking place in the structure of society and economy under colonial rule. My study attempts to precisely show what those changes were and what impact those changes had on society and economy. No substantial work has been done on Berar's experience under colonial rule. The arguments presented by scholars studying the region surrounding Berar, i.e. Central Provinces and Bombay Presidency, fall short of explaining the qualitative change taking place in Berar. Therefore this study has been undertaken to fill a major lacuna in the historiography of colonial India.

No significant work has been done on Berar despite its being a leading cotton producing region of India. Some studies have been undertaken on the agrarian history of the regions around Berar.

[5] Sugata Bose, *Peasant Labour and Colonial Capital: Rural Bengal since 1770*, Cambridge, 1993, p. 2.

[6] See the works of Shahid Amin, *Sugarcane and Sugar in Gorakhpur*, Delhi, 1984; C. J. Baker, *An Indian Rural Economy: The Tamilnad Countryside, 1885-1955*, Oxford, 1984; Crispin Bates, 'Regional Dependence and Rural Development in Central India: The Pivotal Role of Migrant Labour', *Modern Asian Studies*, 19, 3 (1985), pp. 573-92; Neeladri Bhattacharya, 'The Logic of Tenancy Cultivation: Central and South-east Punjab', *Indian Economic and Social History Review*, 20, 2 (1983), pp. 121-70; Jan Breman, *Of Peasants, Migrants and Paupers: Rural Labour Circulation and Capitalist Production in West India*, Delhi, 1985; Binay Bhushan Chaudhuri, 'The Process of Depeasantization in Bengal and Bihar, 1885-1947', *Indian Historical Review*, II, 1 (1975), pp. 105-65.

Sumit Guha's work on the agrarian economy of Bombay Deccan has excluded Berar as being 'environmentally and linguistically' similar to Hyderabad State and Central Provinces rather than Bombay Presidency. But, his overall observation that agricultural '. . . techniques changed little during the colonial period' can also be applied to Berar. But his observation that in Bombay Presidency 'property and taxation, from being central to the economy [under Marathas]' became peripheral to it [under British]' does not capture the historical experience of Berar.[7] In Berar, the khatedars were created as an agrarian class of government registered tenants whose property rights were conditional on revenue payment.

Similarly the works of Crispin Bates and David Baker on Central Provinces concern themselves primarily with wheat and rice cultivation and domestic trade and markets.[8] They have devoted considerable attention to the malguzari system of large landholdings in the Narmada valley. Although the condition of subtenants labouring for the malguzars was similar to that of the bhagindars of Berar, yet khatedars as a class were very different from malguzars of Central Provinces. The works of Bharati Ray and Karen Leonard deal with various aspects of the Hyderabad State. Ray has presented some hard facts on the colonial political economy by quite correctly pointing out that Berar '. . . provided employment for British people in high positions; it also kept the Lancashire textile industry supplied with raw materials when its existence was threatened by the American Civil War'. Similarly she also observed the standardization of Berar's economy by stating that 'roads were constructed connecting the railways with important trade centres in the interior of Berar, and commerce developed rapidly. Paper currency replaced the multiplicity of coins in use and helped create a uniform standard exchange and in avoiding troublesome fluctuations in value. Mines were explored and exploited thoroughly. . . .'[9] Despite such sharp

[7] Sumit Guha, *The Agrarian Economy of the Bombay Deccan: 1818-1941*, Delhi, 1985, pp. 2-3.

[8] Crispin Bates, 'Class and Economic Change in Central India: The Narmada Valley 1820-1930', in Clive Dewey, ed., *Arrested Development in India: The Historical Dimension*, Maryland, 1988; 'Regional Dependence and Rural Development in Central India: The Pivotal Role of Migrant Labour', *Modern Asian Studies*, 19, No. 3 (1985), pp. 573-92; David E. U. Baker, *Changing Political Leadership in an Indian Province: The Central Provinces and Berar, 1919-1939*, Delhi, 1979.

[9] Bharati Ray, *Hyderabad and British Paramountcy, 1858-1883*, Delhi, 1988, p. 107.

observations, Ray's study focuses primarily on the political and diplomatic history of British colonialism and falls short of analysing the agrarian society.

Karen Leonard's work on Hyderabad State makes passing references to Berar in relation to the banking operations of the 'kayasth caste'. Leonard's primary concern is with the financial politics at the court of Hyderabad and Berar's position in it.[10] The internal dynamics of Berar's political economy is never analysed. Tara Sethia's doctoral dissertation on the railway and mining enterprises in Hyderabad State in the 1870s and 1880s devotes some attention to Prime Minister Salar Jung's life-long effort to regain Berar from the British:

> The main reason behind Salar Jung's persistent attempts to extend the Nizam's State Railway with capital raised in England was his belief that Berar would soon be restored to Hyderabad. The revenues of that Province, according to Salar Jung, would have enabled the Hyderabad Government to pay the guaranteed interest on the money raised.[11]

Sethia's analysis is basically limited to political and diplomatic conflict between the Nizam and the British over the possession and restoration of Berar. It does not tell us anything about the economy and society of Berar.

Peter Harnetty has done work on cotton production in the surrounding areas of Godavari, Dharwar, and Khandesh. His work has also devoted some attention to British cotton trade with India during the American Civil War.[12] He has concluded that weavers all

[10] Karen Isaksen Leonard, 'The Hyderabad Political System and its Participants', *Journal of Asian Studies*, 30, No. 3 (May 1971), pp. 569-82; *Social History of an Indian Caste: The Kayasths of Hyderabad*, Berkeley, 1978.

[11] Tara Sethia, *The Railway and Mining Enterprises in Hyderabad State under the British Raj during 1870s and 1880s*, unpublished Doctoral Dissertation, UCLA, 1986, p. 96.

[12] Peter Harnetty, *Imperialism and Free Trade: Lancashire and India in the mid-Nineteenth Century*, Vancouver, 1972; 'India and British Commercial Enterprise: The Case of Manchester Cotton Company, 1860-64', *Indian Economic and Social History Review*, Vol. III, No. 4 (Dec. 1966), p. 396; 'Crop Trends in Central Provinces of India, 1861-1921', *Modern Asian Studies*, Vol. II (1977), pp. 341-78; 'Cotton Exports and Indian Agriculture, 1861-70', *Economic History Review*, Series 2, Vol. XXIV, 3 (1971), pp. 414-29; 'The Landlords and the Raj: The Malguzars of the Central Provinces, 1861-1921', *Studies in History*, Vol. 3, No. 3 (July-Dec. 1987), pp. 187-210; 'The Indian Cotton Duties Controversey, 1894-1896', *English Historical Review*, Vol. LXXVII (1962), pp. 684-702; 'The Cotton Improvement Program in India, 1865-1875', *Agricultural History*, Vol. XLIV (1970), pp. 379-92.

over India gave up their traditional occupation in favour of agriculture due to the rise in wages. Accordingly:

> The increased demand for labour on the land and on public works . . . attracted many weavers from their traditional occupations. . . . The general increase in the cultivated area, itself greatly stimulated by the demand for cotton, created a demand for agricultural labour and at enhanced wages. From all parts of India came reports that weavers were turning to the land where they found work as day labourers, thereby sharing to some extent in the prosperity created by the demand for cotton.[13]

This study uses data from Berar to question Harnetty's argument. The wage-price exchange rate indicates that the wages of unskilled labourers failed to keep up with prices (see Chapter 7). It was therefore not the attraction of high wages but the pressure of colonial cotton economy and the large-scale imports of British manufactured cloth that pushed the native spinners and weavers out of their traditional occupation. Tim Dyson has done some work on demography and famines in Berar. His argument that population growth and declining yields were the cause of famines is also misleading.[14] In fact Berar was exporting foodgrains to the rest of India during famines (see Chapter 7).

A review of the available literature suggests that an indepth study of Berar is immediately needed to fill a major gap in the historiography of modern India. All the above scholars in one way or another agree that Berar is a distinctive case which needs to be studied not only in the context of itself and surrounding areas but in the wider context of colonialism, the world market and its impact on local society.

There are four related parts to this study. The first maps out the pre-colonial scenario of the region (Chapter 1). The second deals with the problem of political and economic transformation under colonialism (Chapters 2 and 3). The third grapples with the issue of

[13] Peter Harnetty, 'Cotton Exports and Indian Agriculture, 1861-1870', *The Economic History Review*, Vol. XXIV (1971), p. 423.

[14] Tim Dyson, 'The Population History of Berar since 1881 and its Potential Wider Significance', *The Indian Economic and Social History Review*, Vol. XXVI, No. 2 (April-June 1989), pp. 167-203; 'On the Demography of South Asian Famines', *Population Studies*, Vol. 45 (1991), pp. 5-25; ed., *India's Historical Demography: Studies in Famine, Disease, and Society*, London, 1989.

the impact of colonialism on local society (Chapters 4-6). The fourth analyses the material condition of people at the turn of the century (Chapter 7). The conflict between the local society and the colonial state is a constantly reccurring theme throughout the book.

The pre-colonial scenario of Berar is the subject of Chapter 1. The *balutedari* was a socio-economic system based on the provision of labour services provided by the lower caste people to the upper caste people in villages. It also involved the distribution rights exercised by the upper caste people on the produce of land rather than land ownership. The dynamics of landownership and produce distribution was closely linked to social status, political and economic control. How did *balutedari* function as a system of social, political and economic control and why did the colonial state find it necessary to dismantle it? How was the rural society reorganized after the demise of the *balutedari* system? These are some of the problems analysed in the opening chapter.

The British takeover in 1853 was a turning point in the history of Berar. For the first time Berar received a modern administrative system run by a highly trained European bureaucracy, i.e. the 'Berar Commission'. Similar to any other newly acquired territory, the Raj maintained an efficient military and police force to back the Berar Commission officers. It was definitely not a 'limited raj' as Anand Yang has suggested for British colonial control of Saran district of Bihar.[15] It is beyond doubt that the colonial control over Berar was thorough. Building a cotton economy on such an enormous scale and linking it to the world market would have been impossible under a 'limited raj'. There is ample evidence to suggest that the state played a major role in fashioning colonial capitalism in Berar. The introduction of railways, telegraph, metalled roads and the post office provided a dynamic technological force in transforming Berar's subsistence agriculture to a major cotton producing economy.

The first act of the colonial state after takeover was to conduct extensive survey and settlement operations to determine the extent of land under cultivation and the revenue base of the state (Chapter 2). What kind of change did the survey operations bring about in the countryside? What was the role of technology in bringing about this change and how permanent was the change? What impact did the 'boundary marks' have on pastures and forests? What was the

[15] Anand Yang, *The Limited Raj: Agrarian Relations in Colonial India, Saran District: 1793-1920*, Berkeley, 1988.

people's response to the creation of property rights in land? What type of a social change did the new class of government registered tenants (*khatedars*) bring about in Berar? The answers to these queries leads the discussion to an analysis of the *khatedari* system.The colonial *khatedari* system, which replaced pre-colonial balutedari, created an awareness of private property rights in land. This not only guaranteed ownership but also guaranteed revenues to the state. In Berar caste and class were closely inter-linked. The *khatedars* and agricultural labourers often came from the same caste but formed two distinct classes of landholders and primary producers. However, the definition of agricultural labourers is very ambiguous. The top castes owned land but never touched the plough. They either leased land or cultivated through hired labour. Similarly the mahars and mangs formed the lowest strata of society and seldom owned land. They mostly worked as agricultural labourers and provided services to the upper castes in the village. However, the majority of cultivating peasants were lower caste kunbis. They cultivated land with their own or family labour. Some among them were government-registered *khatedars*. But a large number of them were subtenants who leased land from *khatedars* and were permanently indebted to the moneylenders. The latter provided credit on interest to cover the operating cost and rental demand. This firmly tied the primary producer to moneylenders and *khatedars*. Nearly 25-30 per cent of the smaller *khatedars* were themselves primary producers. Therefore the definition of peasant labourers in Berar is applied to a very broad spectrum of the agrarian population. The landowners were mostly upper caste. The untouchables were mostly agricultural labourers.

The position of kunbis as a caste and class was very critical. Although ranked low in the caste hierarchy, they were not untouchables. The majority of them rented land and worked it with family labour. They mostly produced for the *khatedar* and the moneylender in addition to their own subsistence. Although they did not own land yet they had the satisfaction of living on it and considered themselves better off than landless agricultural labourers. Some of the kunbis did move up from being rent paying tenants to acquire partial or full khatedari rights. But most of them were indebted cultivators. The majority of the kunbis who rented land were in fact peasant labourers surviving on the margin of subsistence and producing for those who were registered tenants of the government. Their position was only slightly better than that of landless agricultural labourers. They were attached to the land through rent contracts and debt bondage while landless agricultural labourers wandered all over Berar selling their labour and hiring themselves as day labourers, daily wage earners, seasonal labourers, or hired on a permanent basis by the month or year. Labourers on the land therefore encompassed a broad section of agrarian society.

Women played a very significant role in Berar agriculture. They constituted nearly half the agrarian labour force. Their role in cotton cultivation was particularly crucial. This study devotes some attention to their position in the society and role in the economy. All lower caste and tribal women worked as wage labourers and contributed to family income. Women often commuted their cotton wages to cash and used it to purchase daily domestic necessities. Thus a million Berari women engaging in this process everyday created an economic system of their own. How did this economic system work? An attempt is made to recreate the social and economic world of women in Berar. In addition some interesting questions are raised. What was the composition of the new khatedari class? Did *khatedari* system also guarantee loyalty as the colonial state envisioned? What was the nature of relationship between the *khatedars* and *bhagindars* (subtenants)? The extent of social and economic mobility within the khatedari system is also analysed.

The development of a cotton economy (Chapter 4) is a facinating story of the economic transformation of Berar. It was cotton which was instrumental in drawing the latest European technology to the region. The railway, telegraph, post office, metalled roads, the market towns, agricultural experiment stations, etc., brought irreversible changes in the lives of people. What was the nature of this change and what impact did it have on the quality of life? What did modernization mean to people? What was the role of cotton market towns in the political economy of Berar? Were the cotton markets free or controlled? How was life in the market towns different from life in the countryside of Berar? Who made the profit from cotton trade and how much of it percolated down to the masses? Did Berar register any environmental change as a result of the introduction of western technology? The answers to these questions draw Berar into the framework of the global cotton economy.

The introduction of the *khatedari* system and the rise in demand for Indian cotton in the world market during the American Civil War opened enormous opportunities for investment in Berar. It attracted all kinds of people and one of the many types was the moneylender. While all others conducted their business in cotton towns, the moneylender moved in villages and set up a kirana sundry store along with petty cash moneylending. Who were these moneylenders and what was their caste and class background? Why did they choose to move in the countryside rather than operate in large market towns? Why were they not interested in acquiring land? Who borrowed from the moneylender and what was the nature of creditor-debtor relationship? How did the state and society look at the moneylender's role in the economy? Was there any resistance to moneylender activity? The causes of indebtedness in an agrarian society and other related aspects form the subject matter of Chapter 5.

The theme which runs uniformly throughout the book is the theme of standardization and sedentarization of Berar. The diversity and mobility, which was the characteristic feature of pre-colonial Berar, began to gradually erode during the colonial period. The case of banjaras is especially poignant (Chapter 6). In pre-colonial times the banjaras were carriers of goods and services from one place to another. They also owned carts and beasts of burden. They spoke many different languages and followed many different customs. Their social organization was different from the Hindu and Muslim society around them. In what way was it different and what was the position of women in banjara society? How did the settled Hindu/ Muslim landlords and peasants and the colonial state look at a mobile and fluid community like the banjaras? Why did they give up their traditional occupation and become agriculural labourers? What happened to banjaras under colonialism? The study of banjaras is a colourful but a sad chapter in the history of Berar.

There has been a raging debate between colonialists and nationalists as well as different schools of historians and economists on the causes of famine. Colonial officials claimed that the chief cause of famine was the failure of rains leading to crop failure and scarcity. The nationalists put forth the thesis that famines were man-made and that British colonial rule was responsible for the deteriorating material condition of the people.

The problem of famine and scarcity is tackled in the last chapter. The causes of famine and related problems of disease and mortality are analysed. Were the famines in Berar caused by human error or climatic factors or both? As mentioned earlier, there is enough evidence to show that the region exported foodgrains during the famine decade of 1890s. Was there an aggregate food availability decline or a failure of exchange entitlements? How did the low purchasing power of cash wages and the export of foodgrains during famines contribute to the crisis? The material condition of the people during half a century of colonial rule is the subject of this chapter. There is no doubt that the famine intensified poverty, but how was the material life of people in non-famine years? A detailed analysis of the wages, prices and the movement of peasant labour is undertaken to scrutinize the impact of famine and the failure of famine relief. Why was it that prices kept rising but the wages were relatively immobile? Did the wage-price exchange rate of jawari show a tendency to decline or rise? How did Berar compare with other provinces in terms of nourishment, disease and mortality? Was the application of Bombay Famine Relief Code suitable to the conditions in Berar? The story of the famine relief measures is finally capped with people's reaction to the state and government during famine years.

This book begins with a discussion of pre-colonial society and economy of Berar and proceeds to systematically trace the changes taking place under colonial rule. The interest of the colonial state in cotton and the reorganization of society and economy brought in new technology and led to the rise of new socio-economic classes in the region. The role of these new class of moneylenders and *khatedars* and their collaboration with the colonial state brought in a new vigour in the countryside. What was the connection between this new vigour in the society and economy with the devastating famines of the late nineteenth century? Within this story is embedded the more powerful story of reaction and resistance of peasant labourers and wandering groups to the colonial state and the new social classes. How did the will and consciousness of the working people survive and manage to find expression even in the face of the combined onslaught of the capitalist world economy, the colonial state, the moneylender, and the *khatedar*? The human element of resistance is a tale of survival and forms the other side of the grim story of colonial oppression in the nineteenth-century Berar.

CHAPTER 1

Pre-Colonial Berar: The *Balutedari* System

ONE HUNDRED and fifty million years ago dinosaurs are reported to have roamed on the plains of Gondwanaland.[1] They were the original inhabitants of this vast region, the central part of which came to be known as Berar.

After the disappearance of dinosaurs, Berar was largely inhabited by Gonds and Korku tribes.[2] In addition to fishing and hunting the Gonds and Korkus practised slash and burn agriculture similar to the native inhabitants of North America.[3] In fact it is the prejudice of the human species that the region is named after Gonds rather than after dinosaurs.

Pre-Colonial Rural Society

The Gonds roamed freely on the Deccan plateau hunting animals and birds, burning trees and plants and at times destroying each other in internecine warfare. Their life style however was rudely

[1] G. V. R. Prasad and Ashok Sahni, 'First Cretaceous Mammal from India', *Nature*, Vol. 332 (No. 14), 14 April 1988; also see: S. K. Srivastava, *Proceedings of Symposium on Cretaceous of India*, Lucknow, 1983.

[2] Baden-Powell, *Land-Systems of British India; Being a Manual of the Land-Tenures and of the Systems of Land-revenue Administration Prevalent in Several Provinces*, Oxford, 1892, p. 366.

[3] For aspects of Native American Agriculture see: Richard I Ford, ed., *Prehistoric Food Production in North America*, Ann Arbor, 1985; 'Gardening and Farming Before AD 1000: Patterns of Prehistoric Culture North of Mexico', *Journal of Ethnobiology*, 1 (1), pp. 6-7; Donald W. Lathrap, 'The Introduction of Maize in Prehistoric Eastern North America: The View from Amazonia and the Santa Elena Peninsula', in William F. Keegan, ed., *The Emergent Horticultural Economies of the Eastern Woodlands*, Carbondale, Il (1987), Illinois, Occasional Paper 7.

interrupted by 'civilized' people who conquered Berar and introduced settled agriculture. The sedentarization of the region began with the break up of the Gupta empire in the late fifth century and continued till twelfth century[4] during which period northern India was controlled by local chieftains and warlords known as *ranas* and *ranakas*. The Delhi Sultans captured power in the early twelfth century and behaved like the 'civilized' rulers with a mission to introduce order on unruly tribes.[5]

The authority of the Sultans was based on the Turkish army, a tightly-knit and highly disciplined military force. This force was employed to maintain control over Delhi and its vicinity but was ineffective in launching long-range military campaigns.[6] However by the late fourteenth century Alauddin Khilji menacingly marched his army over the Deccan and passed through Berar on his way to capture Deogiri.[7] In general the Delhi Sultans were *looteras*[8] (looters) like the European adventurers several centuries later. They were content with extracting tributes rather then systematically settling the land revenue.

The first systematic settlement of land revenue in Berar was made by Raja Todar Mal after its acquisition by emperor Akbar in c. AD 1596. Todar Mal organized a separate revenue department which measured all the arable land and estimated its produce. The revenue rate was fixed at one-quarter of the estimated produce. The sum total of the demand for a village or group of villages was calculated and called the 'tankhwa' or standard rent-roll. All barren, virgin, and waste lands were excluded from the 'tankhwa'. The

[4] R. S. Sharma, *Indian Feudalism, c. A.D. 300-1200*, Delhi, 1980.

[5] On this subject see: Irfan Habib, 'Economic History of the Delhi Sultanate', *Indian Historical Review*, Vol. IV, No. 2 (1981); Andre Wink, *Al-Hind, the Making of the Indo-Islamic World*, New York, 1990; Burton Stein, *Peasant State and Society in Medieval South India*, New York, 1980; Clifford Edmund Bosworth, *The Later Ghaznavids: Splendor and Decay: The Dynasty in Afghanistan and Northern India, 1040-1186*, New York, 1977.

[6] On aspects of Sultanate military force see: Mohammad Habib, *Some Aspects of the Foundation of the Delhi Sultanate*, Delhi, 1968; L. S. Chandel, *Early Medieval State: A Study of Delhi Sultanate*, New Delhi, 1989; Agha Hussain Hamadani, *The Frontier Policy of the Delhi Sultans*, Islamabad, 1986.

[7] See Syama Prasad Basu, *Rise and Fall of Khilji Imperialism*, Calcutta, 1963; Kishori Lal Saran, *Twilight of the Sultanate: A Political, Social and Cultural History of the Sultanate from the Invasion of Timur to the Conquest of Babur, 1398-1526*, New York, 1963.

[8] *Lootera* is a native term for looters, hoodlums and hooligans.

revenue was levied field by field on the land under cultivation each year. Tankhwa was the standard average and the actual receipt fluctuated around it. But from time to time the actual tankhwa itself was revised.[9]

The tankhwa rate was based on the fertility of the soil. The soil of Berar being unique was divided into three types according to its quality and colour. *Ainkali* was the deep black soil, *Miankalas* was when black soil began to mingle with lighter soil, and *Kalaspati* was the classified light soil lying towards the hills. For each of these categories, a general rate was estimated and fixed. Within this general rate the actual demand varied according to the crops grown. Cash revenue replaced grain revenue and tankhwa rates were fixed *dahsala* (for 10 years).[10] The grain had to be commuted to cash to make the payment of land revenue possible. This gave rise to the development of regular grain markets in Berar as it did in the rest of Mughal empire.[11] Thus the Mughal land revenue system was directly linked to the marketplace.[12]

Berar was an important *subah* (province) of the Mughal empire. The Mughal provincial administration was based on the *mansabdari* system. The *mansabdars* were directly appointed by the emperor on the basis of rank *(zat)* and responsibility *(sawar)*. There were approximately two dozen *mansabdars* at the height of Mughal power. Each *mansabdar* was responsible for maintaining a certain number of troops in a *subah* for the exclusive use of the emperor. The payment of *mansabdars* was made by allocating the revenues of alienated villages known as jagirs. The revenue from the *subah* was remitted directly to the imperial treasury. The early *mansabdari* was based on medieval meritocracy rather than heredity. This is not to argue that almost every *mansabdar* belonged either to the nobility or the aristocracy. The *mansabdars* were often transferred from one *subah* to another depending upon their loyalty, service, experience, ability and influence. This system was devised to ensure the loyalty of troops to the emperor. The troops throughout the empire were paid from the imperial treasury located at the

[9] *Amraoti Gazetteer*, Bombay, 1911, p. 292.

[10] See Irfan Habib, *The Agrarian System of Mughal India, 1556-1707*, Bombay, 1963. Also see *Amraoti Gazetteer*, Bombay, 1911, p. 292.

[11] *Central Provinces and Berar: A Review of the Administration of the Provinces*, Vol. II, Nagpur, 1923, p. 207.

[12] A. C. Lyall, *Gazetteer of the Haidarabad Assigned Districts Commonly called Berar*, 1870, pp. 246-53.

capital city of Fatehpur Sikri. The system of transfer kept the power of *mansabdars* in check.[13]

This system of military and fiscal arrangement was quite different from the feudal system of medieval Europe. Under feudalism the feudal lords maintained troops and the troops were loyal to the lord. The lord supplied troops to the king and the king depended on feudal lords for support.[14] This system was similar to medieval Japan where the *shogun* (feudal monarch) and *daimyo* (feudal barons) exercised power with the assistance of a military class known as the *samurai*.[15]

In the late seventeenth century, the mansabdari system acquired a hereditary character. Serious internal revolts weakened the military-bureaucratic structure and cracked open the mighty Mughal empire.[16]

The *subahs* and the *subahdars* (provincial heads) were a Mughal creation. Each *subah* (like the *subah* Berar) was divided into several parganas each under a deshmukh (pargana head) and a deshpandya (pargana accountant). At the break up of the Mughal empire in the early eighteenth century, the deshmukhs and deshpandyas mobilized local resources to resist the authority of the *subahdars*.

The system of cash revenue demand under Emperor Akbar (1556-1605) gradually deteriorated into grain rent. Under emperor Aurangzeb (1658-1707) the oppressive Mughal army campaigned

[13] See Athar Ali M., *The Mughal Nobility under Aurangazeb*, New York, 1966; 'The Passing of Empire: The Mughal Case', *Modern Asian Studies*, 11, No. 3 (July 1975), pp. 385-96.

[14] Maurice Herbert Dobb, *Studies in the Development of Capitalism*, New York, 1964; Paul Marlor Sweezy, *Transition from Feudalism to Capitalism*, London, 1976; Marc L'eopold Benjamin Bloch, *French Rural Society: An Essay on its Basic Characteristics*, Berkeley, 1966; Rodney Howard Hilton, *English and French Towns in Feudal Society: A Comparative Study*, Cambridge, 1992; Robert Brenner, 'Agrarian Class Structure and Economic Development in Pre-Industrial Europe', *Past and Present*, No. 70 (February 1976).

[15] See Peter Duus, *Feudalism in Japan*, Random House, 1976; John Whitney Hall and Marius Janson, ed., *Studies in the Institutional History of Early Modern Japan*, Princeton, 1968; Archibald Lewis, *Knights and Samurai: Feudalism in Northern France and Japan*, London, 1974; Kan'ichi Asakawa, *The Documents of Iriki*, Tokyo, 1955.

[16] Muzaffar Alam, *The Crisis of the Empire in Mughal North India: Awadh and the Punjab, 1707-1748*, New Delhi, 1986; 'Sikh Uprising Under Banda Bahadur, 1708-1715', *Studies in History* 1, No. 2 (July-Dec. 1979). Also see Irfan Habib, *The Agrarian System of Mughal India, 1556-1707*, Bombay, 1963.

against the Marathas and Sikhs in the Deccan and randomly foraged, extorted, and billeted Berar. 'The subah of Berar was rich in natural resources. It formed the base center of the Mughal expansion further. It was used not only as a starting point for the campaigns but also it was battle field among the contending Mughal-Maratta nobles.'[17]

A brief interregnum from 1605-28 saw the development of a mysteriously unique system of land revenue unparalleled in the history of India and the Deccan. This was the Malik Ambar's system. Malik Ambar was a powerful prime minister under the Nizam Shahi kings of the Deccan. He introduced private property rights in land through systematic survey and settlement. This was contrary to the Mughal system in which all land theoretically belonged to the state and simply measured instead of surveyed. Ambar developed a regular market in land by transforming it into a commodity of purchase and sale. The price of land for the first time was based on the fertility of soil and its capacity to grow a variety of crops whose value was deter-mined by the marketplace. The government share was based on the estimated produce per *bhiga* commuted to cash value.[18] Thus in 1610, 'he first made a regular assessment by fixing the government share in the estimated produce, commuted to money value'.[19] This also triggered some manufacturing in the Deccan. But Malik Ambar's system was short lived. It soon eroded after his death (1628) and completely disappeared when the Mughal army appeared in the Deccan under Aurangzeb.

'Long wasting wars, bloody feuds, revolts, massacres, assassinations, cruel and barbarous punishments, sad stories of the death. . . .'[20]

[17] Mohammed Yaseen Quddusi, *Berar Under the Mughals, 1595-1724*, Ph.D Thesis, 1973, in microfilm at National Archives of India, Acc. No. 1891, p. 165.

[18] A *bigha* is equivalent to approximately 1.75 acres. For more see: H. H. Wilson, *A Glossary of Judicial and Revenue Terms of British India*, Calcutta, 1885; A revised edition with case notes by A. C. Ganguli and N. D. Basu, eds., Calcutta, 1940; H. Yule and A. C. Burnell, *Hobson-Jobson: A Glossary of Colloquial Anglo-Indian Words and Phrases*, London, 1886; G. A. Watt, *Dictionary of the Economic Products in India*, 6 Vols., Calcutta, 1889-93.

[19] Extract from Dr. W. W. Hunter's *Imperial Gazetteer's of India*, Vol. III, pp. 517-26 in *Hyderabad Affairs*, Vol. 1, Moulvie Syed Mahdi Ali, ed., pp. 359-65; *Hyderabad Affairs* is an eight volume set compiled by Moulvie Syed Mahdi Ali, Bombay, 1883-6; also see *Central Provinces and Berar: A Review of the Administration of the Province*, Vol. II, Nagpur, 1923, p. 207; A. C. Lyall, *Gazetteers for the Haidarabad Assigned Districts, Commonly called Berar*, 1870, p. 120.

[20] *Amraoti Gazetteers*, 1911, p. 290.

TABLE 1

Taluka	AD *1707*			AD *1869*		
	Rs.	*a.*	*p.*	*Rs.*	*a.*	*p.*
Dongargaon	1	2	1	1	8	5
Matargaon	1	5	0	1	8	11
Jalam	1	2	4	1	4	5
Malkapur	1	2	2	1	6	0
Ridhora	1	3	8	1	8	7
Wiala	1	3	2	1	5	1

Note: Early colonial rental rates were based on the revenue rates of the later Mughal period. So the value of Indian rupee is assumed to be similar.

which fill the chronicles of Plantagenets and Valois in medieval Europe was also true of medieval India. But most of the agricultural activity took place off the high roads of armies and at a distance from the royal capitals. The state fed on the revenues and resources from the country. The British colonial documents often charge the Mughal state as being too extortionate. But a comparative analysis of the Mughal and the colonial period reveals that the rental rate in Berar at the time of Aurangzeb's death (1707) was in fact lower than under the British in *c.* 1869. Table 1 gives the rental rate in some selected talukas of Berar for which data is available.[21]

Within a decade after Aurangzeb's death another unique system of revenue collection developed in Berar known as *do amli.*

In *c.* AD 1717 the Mughal emperor granted the revenues of Berar to the Nizam and the Marathas. This gave rise to a rapacious system known as '*do amli*' or double government. By this system the Nizam and the Marathas divided the revenues of Berar between themselves. The Nizam controlled Berar politically and paid to the Marathas a *chauth* (one-quarter) and *sardeshmukhi* (one-tenth) of the revenue in addition to the regular '*ghas dana*' (horse-fodder) levy. In case of failure the latter raided the territory and appropriated the revenue. The Nizam made every effort to avoid inviting Maratha raids. Thus both the Nizam and the Marathas became rapacious plunderers of Berar.[22]

[21] A. C. Lyall, *Gazetteer of the Haidarabad Assigned Districts,* 1870, pp. 151, 246. Source for *c.* AD 1707 from Balapur Deshpandia's registers as quoted in Lyall *Gazetteer.*

[22] *Central Provinces and Berar: A Review of the Administration of the Province,* 1923,

The reign of Raja Chandulal, Prime Minister at the court of the Nizam of Hyderabad, was notorious. He dominated the politics of Hyderabad for two decades (1820-40) with Machiavellian manipulation, bribery, trickery and deceit. With full underhanded support from the British Resident at Hyderabad, Chandulal introduced and managed the system of indiscriminate 'revenue farming' which brought ruin and disaster to Berar. Under this system the revenues of villages were auctioned off to the highest bidder on advances.[23] The revenue farmer then proceeded to the village and extracted at will to make good the amount paid at the auction bid in Hyderabad. Chandulal often farmed the same villages to several farmers simultaneously. This created a situation of total extortion leading to a drastic reduction in cultivated acreage. The people simply abandoned the fields and fled to escape repression. The system of revenue farming reduced Berar to chaos. The revenue farmers fought in the countryside to establish their right to extortion. Amraoti Gazetteer records an interesting anecdote:

There is a story told of one of these contractors that he rode out of Hyderabad after the auction with his face to the horse's tail. His followers approached him and asked 'Why this undignified pose?' I am on the look out, said he, for my successors to overtake me.[24]

William Palmer, an English investment banker and an 'unscrupulous adventurer', made a fortune advancing loans to revenue farmers to pay off Chandulal and plunder Berar.[25]

The Balutedari System

All the above-mentioned varieties of revenue extraction from thirteenth to the nineteenth century devastated Berar but did not

p. 208; also see A. C. Lyall, *Gazetteers for the Haidarabad Assigned Districts*, 1870, pp. 125-6; Surendra Nath Sen, *The Military System of the Marathas*, Calcutta, 1979; *Twilight of the Marathas, 1818:* Queries from Mr. Montstuart Elphinstone, Commissioner of the Deccan to the Collectors in the Deccan and Political Agent, Satara (Peshwa Daftar), R. D. Choksey, ed., Poona, 1976.

[23] See Karen Leonard Isakson, *Social History of an Indian Caste: The Kayasthas of Hyderabad*, Berkeley, 1978.

[24] *Central Provinces District Gazetteers: Amraoti Gazetteer*, Bombay, 1911, p. 295.

[25] See Zubaida Yazdani, *Hyderabad During the Residency of Henry Russell, 1811-1820*, Oxford, 1976; Karen Leonard, 'Banking Firms in Nineteenth Century Hyderabad Politics', *Modern Asian Studies*, Vol. 15 (1981), pp. 177-202.

alter the system of organizing production within the village. The system known as the *balutedari* remained pervasive and unchanged despite the rapacious extraction of the state and government. What was the *balutedari* system and how did it function? In a nutshell it was a system of organizing agrarian production by means of social and political control exercised by the dominant family, clan or caste in the village. The dominant family was almost invariably from the upper caste. This meant the enforcement of caste rule and *balutedari* became the instrument of caste and class control. In pre-colonial Berar the caste and class interpenetrated. The upper caste exercised managerial power and supervisory control over all agrarian production in the village. They enforced their social status and political power by laying claim on the annual yield and appropriating the surplus produce. They also formed the wealthier class of Berarian society. The lower caste, in addition to serving the upper caste, generally worked the land as agricultural labourers. They were the primary producers and also formed the lower class of the agrarian society. The share of the produce was determined by the upper caste according to the ranking of a given caste in social hierarchy. In order to understand the *balutedari* system it is essential to understand the relationship between the *asạmi* (lower caste labourer/producer) and the *balutedar* (upper caste appropriator).

The relationship between the *asami* and the *balutedar* was that of master-servant. The *asami* as the servant produced goods and services for the master. The term *baluta* literally meant 'share of the produce'. Technically anyone who received a share of the produce was a *balutedar*. But the upper castes had absolute rights over the distribution of the produce and demanded loyal service from the lower caste. The entire *balutedari* system was based on the master-servant relationship of social status in the caste hierarchy. The control of rights over the produce of land was the key factor in the operation of this system. The obedience of the lower caste was required for the smooth functioning of the entire system. The lower caste provided free service to the upper caste *balutedars* in exchange for a share of the grain during harvest time. This share was decided by the *balutedars*.

Mr. Furdoonji Jamshedji, the Superintendent of Revenue Survey and Assessment has provided us with a detailed glimpse of the functioning of the *balutedari* system in Aurangabad district which except for the artificial colonial demarcation had a social and

TABLE 2

Service Balutedars	*Grain in seers per annum*
Mahar (menial labourer)	110
Sutar (carpenter)	65
Chambar (cobbler)	60
Lohar (blacksmith)	35
Dhobi (washerman)	15
Navi (barber)	35
Kumbhar (potter)	35
Mang (drum beater)	15
Koli (water carrier)	15
Mulani (butcher)	15
Bhutt (astrologer)	15
TOTAL	415 seers

cultural affinity with Berar. The remuneration paid by the *balutedars* to the services of the lower caste is given in Table 2.

The dominant family in the village was usually from the Brahmin, Maratha, Rajput, Kunbi, and/or Bania caste. In general each village in Berar had one dominant family. Sometimes a single family was dominant in several villages. However, instances of more than a single dominant family in a village were very rare. As already stated the dominant family had rights over the distribution of *baluta*. This right was exercised to appropriate more than 95 per cent of the produce. For instance with four bullocks and fifty acres of land the average out-turn at 6 maunds (480 lbs) per acre would be 300 maunds or 12,000 seers (24,000 lbs). Out of this produce the *asamis* were given only 415 seers of grain which constituted only 4 per cent of the total produce. The remaining 96 per cent was appropriated by the upper caste *balutedars*.[26]

The extraction of such a large surplus left the *asamis* in a constant state of want and dependency. The *asamis* were also coerced to provide mandatory services to the upper castes. Generally the *asamis* constituted twelve service castes. The following list gives the names of the *asami* caste and the services they provided:

[26] *Note on the Agriculturists of the District of Aurangabad, H. H. the Nizam's Dominion*, by Furdoonji Jamshedji, Superintendent Revenue Survey and Assessment, North West Division, in *Hyderabad Affairs*, Vol. I, Moulvie Syed Mahdi Ali, ed., Bombay, pp. 801-33.

Mahar – served as a menial labourer, buried dead animals, rubbed the horses of the master, served as a messenger and guide.

Sutar – carpenter, repaired and built agricultural implements, carts, houses and furniture.

Chambar – dealt with the skin of dead animals, repaired shoes and *mhote* (leather buckets for lift irrigation), supplied a new whip to the master which was sometimes used on him.

Lohar – blacksmith, made all iron parts for the agricultural implements, shoe for the masters horses and bullocks.

Dhobi – washed dirty clothes of the masters family, provided clean linen during marriage ceremonies and festivities.

Navi – barber, actively participated in hair-shaving ceremony.

Kumbhar – supplied earthen vessels and pots.

Mang – drum-beater and horn-blower in the village chowdi and temple.

Koli – water carrier and sweeper of village streets.

Mulani – butcher and leather supplier.

Bhutt – astrologer, conducted marriage ceremonies and read *panchang* (future).

Bhangi – cleaned latrines, swept human and animal waste.

There was no separate caste of agricultural labourers. The members of all the above castes worked as agricultural labourers in village lands. Their wives and children worked as domestic servants in the *balutedari* household. During the sowing, weeding, and harvest season the labour of women and children was also demanded.

During the marriage ceremony in the *balutedari* household, the dominant clan demanded service from all *asamis*. The barber's duty was to walk the groom's horse while other members of his caste had to wave a fan over the mounted groom's head. The *mangs* had to beat the drums and blow horns before the marriage procession. The *dhobi* carried a milk-white sheet and spread it for the groom to walk to the bride's house. The *sutar* attended the procession with a *chaorung* or wooden stool made by himself. He had to place the *chaorung* at the feet of the groom to alight the horse in front of bride's house. The *kumbhar* supplied the bride's family with all the earthen vessels for the marriage feast. The *koli* supplied fresh water and swept the floor in preparation for the feast. *Mahar* women attended to the bridegroom's needs and carried lights at night to show the way to the procession. Generally the upper castes preferred dancing girls and nautch to accompany the marriage procession. The *bhutt* performed the marriage ceremony. Finally the *bhangi* had to clean up all the mess made by the marriage party. No wonder the upper caste loved and cherished the institution of *balutedari*.[27]

In the American south during the 'reconstruction' period, the planter class used legal and political institutions as instruments of race control by denying equal rights to the freedman.[28] Similarly, *balutedari* was an oppressive weapon by which the clan dominance was guaranteed at the cost of the subjugation of large groups of people of the lower caste. The labour of these groups was essential for the maintenance of *balutedari* domination. Thus the lower caste *asamis* also formed the lower class of Berarian society which worked as agricultural labourer in the field and provided services in the village.

Balutedari as a System of Control

The *balutedari* was a self-sufficient system in which all the wants of the village were produced in the village. The labour and production was organized in a regime similar to the plantations of American south. The plantation economy and *balutedari* system had many features in common. In both cases the slaveowner and the *balutedar* had absolute rights over the produce and labour of the plantation and the village. Both literally owned and controlled the labour and leisure of the primary producer.[29] The only difference was that the slaves were owned by the plantation master as a piece of property, while the lower caste peasant labourers were only socially obligated to provide free labour services to the *balutedars*.

The process of caste and class control was essential to the survival of *balutedari* system. Agriculture was in fact organized to realize the

[27] 'Peasant life in North-Western Deccan: Aurangabad: A Review of Furdoonji Jamshedji's Notes on the Agriculturists of the District of Aurangabad', in *Hyderabad Affairs*, Vol. 4 (n.d.), pp. 371-7.

[28] Michael Wayne, *The Reshaping of Plantation Society: The Natchez District, 1860-1880*, Baton Rouge, 1983. Also see Jay Mandle, *The Roots of Black Poverty: The Southern Plantation Economy after the Civil War*, Durham, 1978.

[29] Jacob Metzer, 'Rational Management, Modern Business Practices, and Economics of Scale in the Ante-Bellum Southern Plantation', *Exploration in Economic History*, Vol. 12 (1975), pp. 123-50; also see Robert E. Gallman, 'Self-sufficiency and Cotton Economy of the Antebellum South', *Agricultural History*, Vol. XLIV, No. 1 (January 1970), pp. 5-23.

objective of caste and class control. The dominant caste controlled power through the medium of village *panchayats*.[30] Theoretically the *panchayat* was a council of village elders from every caste. Its function was to ensure the day-to-day administration of the village. It also performed judicial functions and implemented social laws, customs and conventions. The eldest male of the dominant family was generally the head of the village panchayat. Theoretically decisions had to be made by the consent of each member of the *panchayat*. But in practice the dominant clan always prevailed. The village lands were divided into *khels* (estates) and controlled by the extended family of the dominant clan. The head of the *khel* was a member of the *panchayat*. The decision-making was invariably manipulated in favour of the dominant clan. In fact the will of the dominant clan was imposed on the whole village through the medium of the *panchayat* raj. It was truly a *raj* as it had unquestionable authority over each caste and individual.

Balutedari as a system of caste and class control manifested itself in many different forms. The right of planting fruit trees for example was exclusively held by the upper caste. While the lower castes were prevented from planting them, they were however forced to tend those planted by the upper caste. The settlement officer of Ellichpur mentions in 1870 that, 'this systematic oppression, which . . . dates back as far as the very existence of caste in India, seems at last to have made the very idea of planting a tree by a common ryot to have been looked upon, as a kind of sacrilege.'[31] The lower caste tended the trees but the fruits of their labour was owned and enjoyed by the upper caste and temples. The temples also extracted unpaid labour from the lower caste by summoning the whole locality to congregate with ploughs to sow temple lands even though the brahmans prohibited temple entry to the lower caste untouchables. This system of free labour which came to be known as *atari* [32] was similar to the *corvee* labour extracted from the serfs in feudal Europe.[33]

The control and management of water was yet another mode of caste and class control adopted by the upper caste. Pre-colonial Berar had a well-organized irrigation system of dams and catchment basins

[30] B. H. Powell, *The Land-Systems of British India*, 1892, p. 370.

[31] *Oomrawuttee and Ellichpur Settlement Report*, No. 444 of 1870, para 4, p. 1.

[32] A. C. Lyall, *Gazetteer for the Haidarabad Assigned Districts, Commonly called Berar*, 1870, p. 66.

[33] Emmanuel Le Roy Ladurie, *Tithe and Agrarian History from the Fourteenth to the Nineteenth Centuries: An Essay in Comparative History*, New York, 1982;

which supported a self-sufficient rainfed agriculture. The colonial gazetteers and settlement reports mention the existence of ruins of permanent dams and anicuts from bygone centuries scattered all over Berar. The settlement officer of Mehkur taluka has left us a graphic description of one such reservoir of the bygone era. Writing in 1868 he narrates:

Judging from the style of its architecture it must have been built about 400 years ago and it is still in an almost perfect state. This dam connects the extremities of two spurs, which run down from the higher ground in the neighbourhood, and thus a large basin is formed for the accumulation of water. The construction of this wall, which contains in its interior numerous steps and passages, is well worth a close examination. Nothing in modern Indian masonry can, in my opinion, approach, both in solidity and perfection of construction, this unique specimen of ancient art.[34]

Balutedars either destroyed these permanent dams and reservoirs or simply neglected its repair. Instead they organized the *asami* labour to construct temporary dams and catchment basins. What forced the *balutedars* to resort to this practice? This important question will be discussed later. It will be appropriate here to describe the temporary dams which replaced the permanent masonry dams and reservoirs. One survey officer in 1871 presented an eye-witness account of these temporary structures which he was fortunate enough to observe: 'These dams are merely earthen structures which have to be renewed yearly, as the monsoon floods wash them clean away. . . .'[35] Similarly Harry Rivett-Carnac touring Berar in the late 1860s observed: 'In old days, . . . a temporary anicut used to be built, towards the end of the rains. . . . By the custom of the village, every man at the appointed time lent a hand at this good work. . . . The labour being thus found by the villagers, the expense of the work was inconsiderable.'[36] The temporary nature of these dams and anicuts suggest that the *balutedars* effectively used water as an instrument of political control. By controlling water the growth of crops and labour was effectively monitored.

Times of Feast, Times of Famine: A History of Climate Since the Year 1000, Doubleday, 1971; *The French Peasantry, 1450-1660*, Berkeley, 1987.

[34] *Mehkur Taluka Settlement Report*, No. 1098 of 1868, para 10, pp. 8-9.

[35] *Morsi Taluka Settlement Report*, No. 563 of 1871, para 10, p. 3.

[36] *Report on the Cotton Department for the Year 1868-69*, by Harry Rivett-Carnac, 1869, para 11.

Karl Wittfogel in his thesis on 'oriental despotism' has drawn a connection between water management and political power in agrarian based hydraulic societies.[37] Wittfogel only referred to large empires and thus overlooked its functioning at the local level. In pre-colonial Berar such a connection can be noticed at the local level. The *balutedari* class exercised power and authority by controlling rights over the distribution of water. The temporary and seasonal nature of dams and catchment basins suggest that the *balutedars* deliberately thwarted the construction of permanent irrigation works for the fear of erosion of their power over labour. Permanent dams and anicuts would seize the need to organize labour and with it the *balutedar's* power of decision-making on crop share would seize to exist.

It is now feasible to argue that *balutedari* as an institution came into existence by destroying the permanent irrigation works which had existed in Berar for centuries. Such an argument would suggest that the *balutedari* system was a more recent historical phenomenon in Berar. Its origins can be placed in the late seventeenth and early eighteenth century coinciding with the decline of the Mughal empire and the rise of successor states in central India.

Why was it necessary for the *balutedars* to destroy and neglect these permanent dams and catchment basins? Due to the rise in trade and commerce, banking and manufacture, wars and famines, the eighteenth-century India experienced a general shortage of labour.[38] In order to keep labour on the land and control their migratory habits, the dominant clan in villages resorted to impose the caste factor. Though caste was only a lever of control, in reality the dominant family could not survive economically without extortion. The service of *asami* labour was essential for the survival of the dominant clan although the *asami* labour could easily survive without the dominant family. The *balutedari* system originated and maintained itself through the combination of caste and class exploitation.

[37] Karl Wittfogel, *Oriental Despotism: A Comparative Study of Total Power*, New Haven, 1957. For a critique of the concept of 'Oriental Despotism' see: Edward W. Said, *Orientalism*, New York, 1978.

[38] K. N. Chaudhuri, *Asia Before Europe: Economy and Civilization of the Indian Ocean from the Rise of Islam to 1750*, Cambridge, 1990; also see C. A. Bailey, *The Imperial Meridian: The British Empire and the World, 1780-1830*, London, 1989; *Rulers, Townsmen, and Bazaars: North Indian Society in the Age of British Expansion, 1770-1870*, Cambridge, 1983.

It is therefore necessary now to narrate the story of how the *baluta* family maintained its power and authority.

The dominant clan exercised its authority by means of four relative factors, namely, *dimmat, watan, khel, and ghurry.*[39] As mentioned earlier, every village had a dominant family which exercised its decision-making right over the division of agricultural produce. It thus decided on the exact quantity of grain each service caste was to be granted. Exercise of this right was crucial for the continued domination of the primary clan. The primary clan or the parent family in local lingo was called the *dimmat*. The head of the *dimmat* served as the head of the village. The power behind the dimmat were the *khels*. The sub-division of a village into several units and each unit under the extended family of the *dimmat* was called *khel*. The dominant family exercised its power and authority by the strength of its *khels*. The *khel* then was simply an extended family of the *dimmat*. It was the division of a *dimmat* into several branches forming a network of kinship groups.

The power of the *dimmat* depended upon the number of *khels* it could summon in times of crisis. The strong villages and weak villages really implied the strength commanded by each *dimmat* clan. The loyalty of the *khels* denoted the strength of the *dimmat* while indifference or disloyalty denoted its weakness. Since each *khel* received its material income from the distribution of the *baluta*, the *balutedar* (the head of the *khel*) extracted as much out of the land as the labour could bear and sometimes even more. In fact the *dimmat* was a *khel* in itself and self-sufficient in terms of its material income. Often times the head of the *dimmat* demanded contribution from *khel balutedars*. In fact the *khel balutedars* exercised their authority on behalf of the head of the

[39] The information for discussion of *dimmat, khel, watan,* and *ghurry* is taken from the following sources: *Amraoti Gazetteer,* Bombay, 1911; Baden-Powell, *The Land-Systems of British India,* 1891; *The Berar Patels and Patwari's Law, 1900,* D. V. Shiddore, ed., Amraoti, 1935; *Central Provinces and Berar: A Review of the Administration of the Province,* Vol. II, Nagpur, 1923; *General Administration Report on the Hyderabad Assigned Districts for the Year 1855-56,* Calcutta, 1857; A. C. Lyall, *Gazetteer for the Haidarabad Assigned Districts, Commonly called Berar,* 1870; Note on the Proposals in Revenue Department No. 1543/180-2, dated 9 July 1897, for Revision of the Berar Patel and Patwari Law, 1886, by Chichele-Plowden, Resident at Hyderabad, in *Proceedings of the Hyderabad Administration on Matters of Routine for the Month of July 1898,* submitted to the Revenue and Agricultural Department, No. 206, 19 July 1898; *Observations on the State and Administration of Hyderabad Assigned District,* by Sir Richard Temple, dated 14 December 1867; *Yeotmal District Gazetteer,* Calcutta, 1908.

dimmat. The head of the *dimmat* had the power to replace the *khel balutedar* if necessary in order to implement the loyalty of the *khel* to the *dimmat*. But this was the internal problem of the dominant family. The conflict between *khel* and *dimmat* hardly ever manifested itself. The authority of the *dimmat* always prevailed. *Dimmat* was therefore the sum total of the *baluta* right of each *khel*.

Sometimes but only rarely the *khels* extended into several villages where the loyalty of the *khel* was to the parent village or the original centre of the first location of clan family. There are no records of internecine wars or conflict between various *dimmats*. Although it seemed highly unlikely considering the disturbed political situation of the eighteenth century. It is also likely that the *dimmats* and *khels* entered into matrimonial alliances with other *dimmats* and *khels* to form an even wider feudal network. Since the *khel* was a revenue unit between a village and a *pargana*, the deshmukhs and deshpandias (pargana heads) had to constantly deal with the *balutedars*. For *pargana* officials, a *khel* usually signified merely a distinct share in a *watan*.

Theoretically the term *watan* signified a geographical area or territory of affinity. The upper caste claimed a village or province as their *watan* over which they exercised their political power and social authority. The territory of the *watan* was however very ambiguously defined. It had a tendency to expand in proportion to the power and strength of the *dimmat*. In practice however a *watan* merely meant the hereditary right of the dominant clan to extract land revenue in a given geographical area or territory. So control over land itself did not mean anything. A claim over the produce of the land and the labour which produced it was the crux of the landholding structure in pre-colonial Berar. This ambiguity between theory and practice confused the British who came generations later. In south Asia in general and Berar in particular land control was really not the issue. The main issue was control over the produce. It was through the exercise of this right that the *balutedars* were able to subdue and control the labour of the *asami*. Therefore it was necessary to check the movement of labour and prevent them from freely migrating.

How were the *balutedars* able to control the mobility of labour? Enforcement of caste rules and social sanctions was in itself insufficient. Therefore the *balutedars* built fortification around their houses and armed themselves. These fortifications which came up all over Berar in the late seventeenth and early eighteenth century were only a partial response to the political disturbances of the time. Its real purpose was to contain labour within the bounds of the village and to coerce labour to serve the dominant clan.

The fortification mentioned above were popularly known as the *ghurry*. It literally meant a mud-walled fort. It was generally 10 to 15 feet high with an approximate length of 150 feet. The *khel* clan built this structure around its house. The clan family resided within these walls. The huts of the villages generally clustered around this mud-walled fort. Often times these walls were built with solid granite stones locally available in abundance. Although the dominant family did not encourage the use of solid stones to construct permanent dams but for its own defense it built stone walls. The walls were built with the free labour of the *asamis*. Within these walls the children of the *balutedars* practised wrestling, horse-riding, archery, muscat practice, shooting, lathi-charge, and such other forms of martial arts. The *ghurry* was usually para-military in nature. The *khel* family often accumulated swords, guns, and sometimes cannons to mount on the turrets of these fortified walls. The *balutedars* rode out of these walls to punish and subdue a peasant family or ward off a Maratha, Sikh, Mughal, or a tribal raid on the village. It must be noted that it was not so much to protect the village but its own interest that the *balutedari* household acquired a semi-military character. The forts also symbolized power, authority and repression. Any challenge to its authority was ruthlessly crushed. The *ghurry* also served as a prison to discipline an *asami* who tried to escape the *balutedari* jurisdiction. In the face of an external attack the unprotected *asami* huts formed the first line of defense while the *balutedari* family stayed within the safe protection of the *ghurry*. The clan family was basically dysfunctional without the free labour of the *asami*. Along with the temporary dams, the fortification walls were also repaired every year. In 1853 the British were terrified at the extent of these fortified walls in Berar. Their fear was not unfounded when in 1857 many *khel* families supported the rebellion. In fact Tantia Topi sent his appeals to the *balutedars* rather than to the *asamis*. Had he appealed to the latter, the course of his rebellion would have been different. However, after the retreat of Topi, an obscure tribal leader named himself Tantia Bhil and conducted the struggle in the surrounding countryside.[40]

[40] *Amraoti Gazetteer*, Bombay, 1911, p. 350.

British Takeover and the Destruction of Balutedari System

Systematic dismantling of the fortifications became the first political act of the British in Berar. With an enormous show of raw colonial power, the system of *khel* was suspended and *balutedars* retired. The families which took part in the revolt of 1857 were excluded from colonial favours and patronage. The village officials like the *patel* and *patwari* were appointed from the families which were loyal to the colonial state and were legally made subservient to the authority of the colonial government.[41] The transition of *balutedari* system to the colonial system is an interesting story. It could not have been achieved without the destruction of the *balutedari* system. How was it achieved? Let us now turn to this question.

The destruction of the *balutedari* system commenced immediately after the takeover in 1853. The first attack was launched on *ghurrys* and citadels. Tearing down of these fortifications was an effective way of attacking the pre-colonial system.[42] The demilitarization of Berar was essential to prevent counteraction against British power. The militarized and semi-militarized tribes like the Banjaras, Rhatores, and Musulmans were also neutralized.[43] Similarly the *panchayats* were abolished since they were autocratic bodies representing the power of *khels* and *dimmats*. Though *panchayats* were as authoritarian as the colonial state itself yet it posed a threat by providing an alternative form of government.[44] The *panchayats* also had its own legal code which resisted the imposition of colonial laws and rules at the local level. Therefore the *panchayat raj* had to be replaced by British raj.

[41] Note on the Proposals in Revenue Department, No. 1543/180-2, dated 9 July 1897, for Revision of the Berar Patels and Patwaris Law, 1886, by T. Chichele-Plowden, Resident at Hyderabad, in *Proceedings of the Hyderabad Administration on Matters of Routine for the Month of July 1898,* submitted to the Revenue and Agricultural Department, No. 206, 19 July 1898. For a similar comparison in Oudh and North-Western Provinces see Eric Stokes, *The Peasant and the Raj: Studies in Agrarian Society and Peasant Rebellion in Colonial India,* Cambridge, 1980; *The Peasant Armed,* Oxford, 1986.

[42] *Hyderabad Affairs,* Vol. I (n.d.), p. 275 (at Andhra Pradesh State Archives, Hyderabad).

[43] *Hyderabad Affairs,* Vol. II, p. 201.

[44] From: J. H. Bullock, Deputy Commissioner, North Berar To: Major L. Davidson, Ist Assistant Resident at Hyderabad, 31 July 1854, No. 303, in *Foreign Department Political Proceedings,* 28 March 1856.

The revolt of 1857 slowed down the dismantling process. The threat of encirclement and annihilation similar to the 'Great Fear' experienced in France during the revolution of 1789[45] was expe-rienced by the colonial officials in Berar at the start of the Great Rebellion in May 1857. As *balutedars* threatened to join the rebel forces, the threat came from all directions. Meadows Taylor, the Deputy Commissioner of Berar, in his moments of fear writes the story of his life thus in October 1857:

> I received many anonymous letters, . . . warning me of contemplated assassination, and stating that when I was disposed of the native troops at Ellichpur were prepared to rise, and aided by the military and predatory classes of the district, would plunder the chief towns, and join the rebel forces beyond the Satpoora range, which constituted my whole northern frontier.[46]

Nana Sahib and Tantia Topi's name haunted the colonial officials long after the revolt was suppressed. But when the revolt was current the shudder was registered from the southern and the western frontiers of Berar as well. The General Administration Report of 1857-58 reports:

> During the past year all along the Bombay frontier reports have been very rife about the coming of some great man from the north at the head of a large army . . . similar reports have been also equally current throughout the Nizam's Territory, and Nana's name has often been connected with these reports.[47]

Similarly the General Administration Report of 1858-9 also referred to the 'utmost dread at the approach of the rebels'.[48] When similar threats arrived from the east, Major Meadows Taylor in great anxiety supplied 600 to 1000 Berar draught cattle to General Whitlock's force at Nagpur. Taylor did this partly from fear and partly out of a desire to later lay claim over the booty of rebel treasury.[49]

[45] See Georges Lefebvre, *The Great Fear of 1789: Rural Panic in Revolutionary France*, New York, 1973; Albert Soboul, *Sans-culottes: The Popular Movement and Revolutionary Government, 1793-1794*, New York, 1972.

[46] In *Hyderabad Affairs*, Vol. 2, 1883, p. 725.

[47] *General Administration Report on the Hyderabad Assigned Districts for the year 1857-58*, Calcutta, 1859, para 399.

[48] *General Administration Report on the Hyderabad Assigned Districts for the Year, 1858-59*, Calcutta, 1859, p. 188.

[49] In *Hyderabad Affairs*, Vol. 2, Bombay, 1883, p. 728.

The revolt slowed down the dismantling process but by no means did it stop. The first decade of the colonial rule saw a simultaneous attack on the *hoondakuri* system as well. The *hoondakurs* were a group of Indian merchants and bankers who controlled cotton routes and collected tolls on Berar highways.[50] Now if the colonial government wanted to develop a cotton economy in Berar the *hoondakurs* had to be disposed and cotton roads freed and made available for colonial trade. Therefore the colonial attack on *balutedari* and *hoondakuri* commenced simul-taneously.

In fact the dismissal of the *balutedars* and the *hoondakurs* was not an easy task. The settlement officer in 1872 writes: 'Their influence among the people, however, is still more or less great, in proportion to the means of which they are possessed, but the deprivation of their former powers rankles deeply in their mind. . . .'[51] The colonial state was aware of the discontentment of the demobilized elites. Breaking their power caused a great deal of 'heartburning and disloyalty' says Elphinstone the settlement officer of Darwa taluk. He further states that '. . . our annihilation of the time-honoured and much-cherished village system, under which the heads of villages possessed considerable power and influence. . . . I am inclined to think that if we had grafted our present Municipal system on the former, instead of destroying it entirely, a more satisfactory state of things than at present exists might have been brought about.' He then goes on to suggest an alternative colonial system to diffuse the effect of 'annihilation', by stating 'we should then very soon have at least one man in every village fit to be entrusted with subordinate magisterial powers, and we should thus obtain a valuable machinery at a small cost'.[52] The disposal of *dimmat* chiefs automatically disposed the heads of all the *khels*. Even the pre-colonial division of Berar into *parganas* and *turruffs* were declared null and void as new boundaries were drawn out.[53]

Some of the *dimmat*, deshmukh, and deshpandya family chiefs were given honorary positions in colonial municipal committees.[54] Most of them however were retired on pension under the Pension Act. The

[50] A. C. Lyall, *Gazetteer of the Haidarabad Assigned Districts*, 1870, p. 136.

[51] *Darwa Taluka Settlement Report*, No. 420 of 1872, para 7.

[52] *Darwa Taluka Settlement Report*, No. 420 of 1872, para 6.

[53] *The Berar Inam Rules, 1859*, in the *Berar Code*, Nagpur, 1931, p. 64.

[54] *Observation on the State and Administration of Hyderabad Assigned Districts*, by Richard Temple, 1867, p. 3.

remuneration generally was merely 3 per cent of the revenue of the village.[55]

The power of the *balutedar* to annually summon *asamis* to construct temporary dams and anicuts was the main pillar on which the *balutedari* system rested. In pre-colonial times the Mughal and the Maratha governments had even allotted a small grant for the maintenance of these dams and anicuts. It was partly through the control of water resources that the *balutedars* had grown rich and powerful. The colonial state stopped financing the dams and anicuts and took over the rights of water management. This hit the *balutedari* system at its root. The British surmised that cotton did not need much water as it was a rainfed arid crop.[56] Therefore the state did not feel any need to finance irrigation.

Another major source of income for the *balutedars* was from the fruit trees of the village. Although the *asamis* tended the trees with their sweat and labour, the upper caste *balutedars* had enjoyed all the fruits of the village trees by robbing the *asamis* of their share and labour. With one stroke of colonial law the *balutedars* were disposed of this right and the fruit trees passed out into the jurisdiction of the colonial state. The Berar Land Revenue Code specifically stated: 'trees, brushwood, jungle, and other natural products shall be disposed of from time to time under the orders of the Deputy Commissioner by public auction'.[57] The colonial state and the *balutedars* competed for the resources of Berar. The lot of the *asamis* could not have been any worse in either of the two systems.

The final nail in the coffin of *balutedari* system went in with the creation of private property rights in land and the introduction of boundary marks to delineate plots. With one stroke of 'Chanakyan' duplicity,[58] the British buried the *balutedari system* and the *balutedars* in the same coffin. The orders issued in 1856 clearly stated: '. . . it shall put

[55] *Central Provinces and Berar: A Review of the Administration of the Province*, Vol. II, 1923.

[56] *Report on the Cotton Department for the Year 1868-69*, by Harry Rivett-Carnac, 1869, p. 11.

[57] *Rules Under the Berar Land Revenue Code, 1896*, Nagpur, 1907, p. 100.

[58] Chanakya or Kautilya was the dubious prime minister at the Mauryan court in fourth century BC. He wrote a treatise on government called the *Arthashastra* in which he suggests that any possible means is justifiable to achieve ends. It was

an end to all unlicensed exemptions and privileges and shall secure a fair revenue to the state, shall, by the recognition of a proprietary right, in those who can establish a hereditary or prescriptive title. . . .'[59] The introduction of boundary marks finally destroyed the whole theoretical idea of the *watan* by giving a rude jolt to the centuries old ambiguity in proprietary rights and launching a new course in which Berar was to remain throughout the colonial period. This new course was the replacement of the *balutedari* with the *khatedari* system of private ownership in land. This pronounced the end of the organic unity of the self-sufficient villages. It tore down the fabric of the old order by creating a *khatedar* or the government registered tenant supervised by the government and paying revenue directly to the government.[60] The khatedari system of landholding will be analysed in greater detail in the following chapter. However it is essential to trace the origins of this system.

Colonial Reorganization of Berar

When the British annexed Berar they found the villages under the control of dominant families organized into *khels* and *dimmats*. The representatives of the dominant family acted as patels (village headman) and patwaris (village accountant). Naturally the patels and patwaris manipulated the crop share and village income to appropriate most of it for themselves. If the British were to establish their power over crops and revenue, the institution of *khels* and *dimmats* had to be overthrown along with the power and influence of the dominant family. Therefore the overthrow of the *balutedari* could not have been achieved without the reorganization of the entire administrative structure. The services of patel and patwari families loyal to the British in 1857 were retained. However, the power of such families was made subservient to the colonial bureaucracy.

originally written in Sanskrit. But its English translation is now available in print. See: Thomas Trautman, *Kautilya and the Arthashastra: A Statistical Investigation of the Authorship and Evolution of the Text,* Leiden, 1971; Kautilya, *Arthashastra,* tr. by R. Shamasastry, 5th edn., Mysore, 1956; *Essentials of Indian Statecraft: Kautilya's Arthasastra for Contemporary Readers,* tr. by T. N. Ramaswamy, Bombay, 1962.

[59] *Central Provinces and Berar: A Review of the Administration of the Province,* Vol. II, 1923, p. 214.

[60] *Akote Taluka Settlement Report,* No. 268 of 1867, para 23, p. 9.

The patels and patwaris joined the lower ranks of colonial bureaucracy and were made answerable to the government instead of to their own class. Their task was to collect revenue for the government for which they received a fixed payment. The whole province was divided into districts and sub-districts each under a British bureaucrat. The colonial officials claimed absolute authority over the province and districts. The Deputy Commissioner incharge of the district was virtually a monarch with the power to appoint and dismiss patels and patwaris. The village officials who tried to agitate or subvert the government were dismissed and punished. Total loyalty to the government was the criterion for the appointment of lower-level Indian officials. All women were disqualified by the colonial law to serve as patels or patwaris on grounds of questionable loyalty, efficiency, and inferior status.[61] In this the colonial law took its source from the Hindu law codes of Manu known as the *Dharmashastra* [62] which denied property rights to women on grounds of inferior status.

The offices of patels and patwaris were subjected to renewal every ten years. Absentee, inefficiency, and neglect of duty were the common grounds for dismissal. When there was more than one dominant family in a village, the patelship was usually rotated. This was also done to maintain the loyalty of the dominant families who collaborated with the colonial state. Continued loyalty of the dominant families was the main pillar of strength of the colonial state. Therefore in order to keep the dominant family in line, the office of the *patel* and *patwari* was rotated. This was also done to minimize the conflict among the dominant families. However, rival claims and competition for patelship as a rule was discouraged. All claims to the possession of patelship was very narrowly scrutinized. The family history of every dominant clan was kept on record and any discrepancy in the loyalty of a member disqualified the entire family from the office of patel and patwariship. The whole family was made responsible for the activity of the individual who was to acquire the office of patel or patwari. It was

[61] See *The Berar Patels and Patwaris Law, 1900*, by D. V. Shiddore, Amravati, 1935, Chapter 7, sec. 30.

[62] *Dharmashastra* was the text written in second century BC justifying the caste system, slavery, and the inferior status of woman. See Manu, *The Laws of Manu*, translated with extracts from seven commentaries by George Buhler, New York, 1969; Haran C. Chaladar, *Social Life in Ancient India*, 2nd rev. edn., Calcutta, 1954.

legally stated that 'the foundation of the law is that the watan belongs rather to the family than to any individual of it.... In case of forfeiture of watan rights ... the family which is subject to forfeiture ... includes every member of the watan family ... by their exclusion there is an end of the watan altogether.'[63] The local Indian officials were also made responsible for the security of the village in addition to revenue duties. The government virtually did nothing in the villages except hiring and firing Indian officials. The labour of the hitherto dominant family was thus exploited by the colonial government almost free of charge. The institution of patel and patwari was an effective colonial instrument of revenue extraction and maintenance of law and order in the countryside.[64]

The local aristocracy was so thoroughly eliminated that by 1895 the *balutedari* system was a thing of the past. The Deputy Commissioner of Akola in that year did not even acknowledge the existence of *balutedari* in some bygone times. R. D. Hare writes: 'There never has been a local aristocracy, and there are no families which are respected by the people as those of their leaders in the past, or whose disappearance could cause the slightest regret to those outside their own kindred.'[65] The colonial official, Mr. R. D. Hare, was correct in observing that the cultivators had no regrets about the disappearance of their exploiters—the *balutedars*. But Mr. Hare overlooked the fact that colonialism in turn created a *khatedari* class which survived at the mercy of the colonial state. It is therefore only appropriate to turn to *khatedars* and analyse their role in Berarian society.

But before we turn to the *khatedars*, it is essential to analyse the process by which the *khatedari* system came into existence. There is no doubt that *khatedars* were a colonial creation associated with the creation of private property rights in land. How did property in land come into existence in Berar? Immediately after colonial takeover, extensive land survey and settlement operations were

[63] *The Berar Patels and Patwaris Law, 1900,* D. V. Shiddore, ed., Amraoti, 1935, p. 21.

[64] The material for the above discussion of the *patel* and *patwari* is taken from *The Berar Patels and Patwaris Law, 1900,* D. V. Shiddore, ed., Amraoti, 1935.

[65] From: R. D. Hare, Deputy Commissioner, Akola, To: The Commissioner, Hyderabad Assigned Districts, dated 27 July 1895, in *Proceedings of the Hyderabad Administration on Matters of routine for' the month of September 1895,* submitted to the Revenue and Agricultural Department, No. 337, 28 September 1895.

conducted with the aim of creating a landholding and a revenue structure. The survey and settlement was the basis for consolidating the political power of the state and in turn laying the foundation for the development of a cotton economy. Therefore it is essential to analyse in detail the early colonial land settlements and survey operations in Berar.

CHAPTER 2

The Colonial State and Land Settlements in Berar: 1861-77

The Motives for Colonial Conquest

WHY DID THE British take over Berar in 1853? There were two main reasons. Firstly, the colonial state in India needed revenues to pay for the costs of administering its expanding empire. Under the Governor-Generalship of Lord Dalhousie (1845-55) it had reached its territorial apogee. Threats to the colonial state from internal rebellions and mutinies were draining the exchequer. The colonial army had developed into a huge machine accounting for a large chunk of the budgetary expenditure. Berar was seen to be an attractive field for expansion and a source for additional revenue. Secondly, the overwhelming monopoly of American cotton in the London market had been a cause of some concern to the Manchester Chamber of Commerce. As the contradiction between 'Slave States' and 'Free States' sharpened in North America, the British manufacturers began to feel a threat to their cotton supplies. It was but natural for them to look for an alternative source. A 'Cotton Supply Association' (1857) was organized specially for this purpose. Egypt and India were chosen as possible sites for the development of cotton culture suitable to the needs of British textile manufacturers. Berar in central India possessed the most suitable climate and soil for cotton cultivation. The annexation of Berar therefore became imperative.

The British takeover of Berar is a fascinating tale of skilful skulduggery. Historically, Berar was an important *Subah* of the Mughal Empire. After the breakup of the empire in early eighteenth century, Berar was contested between the Marathas and the Nizam of Hyderabad. When the Marathas were defeated (1818) Berar was given to the Nizam for his obedience and loyalty. Constant pressure was maintained on the Government of India by Manchester Chamber of Commerce in response to dramatic political developments in North America.[1] Dalhousie as Governor General was sent to India at the right moment to satisfy Great Britain's appetite for raw cotton. The annexation of Berar was the high point of Dalhousie's administration. Edwin Arnolds in his biography of Dalhousie quite dramatically captures the spirit of the times in the following manner:

> It was in the end of 1853, then, when the Burmese war was well settled and, the vast machine of the empire was falling again into brief regularity of peace, that the eye of the Marquise of Dalhousie, traversing the map of India, lighted on the central portion of it named 'the Nizam's dominions'. In that day there included the rich red and black soil about Omrawattee the metropolis of the cotton fields which have since rescued Manchester from her shameful partnership with the slavedrivers. It included Berar and Pal Ghaut, the fattest and most fertile tract, perhaps, in central Hindostan, where poppy-heads and cotton-pods may be grown bigger than anywhere in the world.[2]

Revenues of the cotton-rich Berar became a bone of contention between the British and Nizam. The British tied the Nizam with all kinds of treaties and stipulations before outright annexation. A dubious military force known as the 'Hyderabad Contingent' was organized under the pretext of providing protection to the Nizam. The revenues of Berar were supposedly assigned for maintenance of this force. The British Resident at Hyderabad made sure that all treaty stipulations regarding Berar were strictly observed. Blatant threats were issued whenever the Nizam raised the issue of Berar's restoration. Factions were created in the Nizam's court to prevent him from consolidating his forces against the British. Angered by resistance to annexation, Lord Dalhousie in a letter warned the Nizam, 'that the Government of India could crush him under its

[1] For details of political manipulations of the Manchester Chamber of Commerce see the following works: Arthur Silver, *Manchester Men and Indian Cotton, 1847-1872* and 'Manchester Administration of British India', in *Hyderabad Affairs,* Vol. 2, 1883, p. 401. *Hyderabad Affairs* is an eight-volume set compiled by Moulvie Syed Mahdi Ali, Bombay, 1883-6.

[2] Extract from Chapter 18 of Edwin Arnold's 'Marquis of Dalhousie's Administration of British India', in *Hyderabad Affairs,* Vol. 2, 1883, p. 401.

feet, so that neither name nor trace of him should remain'.[3] But the Nizam under his persistent Prime Minister Nawab Sir Salar Jung continued to campaign for the restoration of Berar. Salar Jung even made a trip to England to meet Queen Victoria and represent the case of Berar.[4] But Berar was too precious to be returned. Bharati Ray argues that 'for the British, regardless of any legal connotation, the annexation and retention of Berar came to be symbolized with imperial power and glory'.[5] This may well be true but it was more than just a matter of imperial power and glory. It was a matter of economics and politics. In addition to being economically rich Berar was strategically important. It was a junction point of trade routes from all parts of India—'navel of India'.

Historically Berar had always been an important transit point between Mirzapur (Bengal Presidency) and Bombay. The junction of routes from all directions made Berar a very important entrepot of inland trade and commerce. Traditionally it was known for its 'up-country' cotton trade. An elaborate system of metalled roads was planned and executed in order to maintain a strong military and political control over the region. The military garrison at Ellichpur was quite successfully used to maintain relative control over south India during the disturbances of 1857. It was therefore a combination of economic and political motives that determined the annexation of Berar.

The Early Colonial State in Berar

The period from 1853 to 1861 can be conveniently marked off as the early period of colonialism in Berar. It was during this time that the foundation of the local arm of colonial state was laid. The

[3] 'The History of the Assignment of the Berar Provinces in Trust for the Maintenance of the Hyderabad Contingent', *The Statesman* of July 1881, p. 17. This article traces the history of Hyderabad Contingent and details how the British by their clever manipulation reduced the Nizam to a puppet client.

[4] For a detailed analysis of Nawab Salar Jung's activity, see Bharati Ray, *Hyderabad and British Paramountcy: 1858-1883*, Delhi, 1988; and Tara Sethia, *The Railway and Mining Enterprises in Hyderabad State under the British Raj during 1870s and 1880s*, Doctoral Dissertation, UCLA, 1986.

[5] Bharati Ray, *Hyderabad and British Paramountcy*, Delhi, 1988, p. 107. This is a good political history of Hyderabad State and Ray devotes a chapter on Berar. The author analyses British manoeuvres of playing one faction against the other at the Nizam's court. The most corrupt methods were employed to keep the Nizam in a state of bankruptcy and maintain control over Berar.

colonial state was formed in Berar with two main purpose, i.e. revenue and cotton. The early colonizers found that the already existing system of 'revenue farming' was a great obstacle to the realization of land revenue and development of cotton cultivation. Under revenue farming 'the village was let to the highest bidder often yearly, to the head of the village, or to a stranger, a contractor'.[6] Under revenue farming the local village officials in collaboration with revenue farmers had exercised a great deal of power and authority over revenue collection. The first act of colonial government was to do away with the system of revenue farming and curb the power of local authority. This was a sensitive matter and needed to be done in a very strategic manner.

The taking over of Berar entailed a great display of raw colonial power and strength. A show of military might was necessary even though it was a peaceful transfer. The early colonial government moved in very swiftly to establish itself. Summary settlements were introduced to replace revenue farming. On the spot assessments were made with strongmen of the village. The responsibility of revenue payment was taken away from the village as a whole and imposed on individuals living in the village. By this act the power of decision-making was taken away from the local officials and vested in the colonial government. It was made clear that 'the carcoon who makes the Patwa Putruk [village rent rolls] ought not to have any power whatever over the assessment. He merely registers the land under cultivation. . . .'[7]

But before elaborating the question of summary settlements it is important here to look at the development of colonial state itself. The abolition of revenue farming would not have been possible without first demilitarizing Berar. Gawilghur fortress in Melghat taluk had historically been a strong citadel of the Mughals against Marathas. It was from this fortress and out of the revenues of Berar that Aurangazeb had conducted his wars against the Marathas in the

[6] *General Administration Report on the Hyderabad Assigned Districts, 1856-57*, Calcutta, 1858, para X, published annually from 1855-6 to 1866-7 by John Gray, Calcutta. Thereafter the title and the publisher changed to *Report on the Administration of the Hyderabad Assigned Districts*, Residency Government Press, Hyderabad.

[7] From: S. H. Bullock, Deputy Commissioner in Charge of Commissioner's Office, To: J. Allardyce, Office of Deputy Commissioner, East Berar Ellichpur, 2 May 1859, in *India Political Consultations*, No. 109, 8 July 1859.

late seventeenth century. This frontier outpost in the Deccan was manned by Arabs and Rohillas. Immediately following the annexation this fortress was systematically liquidated.[8] The region surrounding this citadel was a beautiful country of hills and forests inhabited by ancient Gond and Korku tribes. The colonial state from its inception looked at the tribal people with suspicion and alarm. Therefore a large military cantonment was established in the heart of the tribal country in Ellichpur and a strong cavalry, artillery, and infantry force was stationed. In addition to Ellichpur, cantonments were built in Amraoti and Akola.[9] Troops from these garrisons were furnished to guard jails. In order to display its power the colonial state built huge and distinct Orwellian structures as symbols of authority. For the first time the people of Berar saw cantonments, jails, barracks, courthouses, government executive buildings and bungalows mushrooming everywhere. These colonial structures were plain, dull and monotonous and stood as symbols of awe and fear.

In a way these structures represented the bureaucratic machine unleashed on the people soon after annexation. It was organized under the pseudonym of 'Berar Commission'.[10] The Berar Commission was an all European institution manned by British civil and military officers. It was a tightly organized body based on hierarchy of patronage and service. During the early period except at the lowest echelons of village headmen (patel) and accountants (patwari), there were practically no Indians in this bureaucracy. For

[8] Lord Dalhousie's 'Minute on his Indian Administration—Hyderabad', *Madras Spectator*, 2 August 1856, in *Hyderabad Affairs*, Vol. II, 1883, p. 200.

[9] *General Administration Report on the Hyderabad Assigned Districts for the Year 1861-62*, Calcutta, 1863, para 96.

[10] 'Memorandum on the Special Features of the Hyderabad Assigned Districts Bearing on their Administration', *Proceedings of the Hyderabad Administration for the Month of April 1887*, submitted to the Foreign Department, No. 1025-R, dated 25 April 1887. This memorandum provides a detailed description of the hierarchy of bureaucratic and administrative structure. It also provides information on jails and military garrisons in Berar. Also see *General Administration Report on the Hyderabad Assigned Districts for the Year 1861-62*, Calcutta, 1863, para 96; *General Administration Report on the Hyderabad Assigned Districts for the Year 1856-57*, Calcutta, 1858, Appendix A; *General Administration Report on the Hyderabad Assigned Districts for the Year 1858-59*, Calcutta, 1860, Appendix IV.

administrative convenience the province was divided into divisions and sub-divisions of districts, talukas and villages. The colonial administrative structures and bungalows rose in the towns and its suburbs. The land had to be cleared and the wild animals executed.[11] But the colonizers lived in the valley only during the winter months (November-March).

There was a proposal to settle Europeans for cotton farming in Berar. This was similar in nature to indigo cultivation in Bengal and Bihar and tea gardens in Assam.[12] But the intense heat from March to June drove Europeans from the plains of the Poorna valley to the hill stations of Berar.[13] A hill resort was built in Chikalda specially for this purpose. The Sanitary Commissioner writes thus about this hill station: 'This small hill plateau, 3,656 feet above sea level, is hot weather resort of the Commissioner and the several heads of departments, and is an agreeable refuge from the intense heat of the plains during April and May.'[14] The Europeans never ventured into Berar countryside and villages in the hot summer months. They stayed specially away from Melghat and considered the general mass of people as wild and uncivilized.[15]

In addition to establishing their authority, the early activity of the colonial state was targeted towards opening the country to external

[11] Rates for the execution of wild animals were as follows:

	Rs. for each animal
Tiger	20
Panthers	15
Bears	5
Hyenas	5
Wolves	7

Half rates for the cubs of above animals. *Book Circular No. XXXV* of 1889, in *Proceedings of the Hyderabad Administration on Matters of Routine for the Month of December 1889*, submitted to the Home Department, No. XXXV, 23 December 1889.

[12] Blair Kling, *The Blue Mutiny: The Indigo Disturbances in Bengal, 1859-1862*, London, 1966. Also see Sugata Bose, 'Peasant Labour and Colonial Capital: Rural Bengal Since 1770' in the *New Cambridge History of India*, Cambridge, 1993.

[13] *Times of India*, 21 August 1867, in *Hyderabad Affairs*, Vol. I, compiled by Moulvie Syed Mahdi Ali, Bombay, 1883-6, p. 13.

[14] *Report of the Sanitary Commissioner, Hyderabad Assigned Districts for the Year 1894*, Hyderabad, 1895, para 55.

[15] Appendix to the *Report of the Indian Famine Commission, 1898, Being Minutes of Evidence*, etc., Vol. IV: 'Central Provinces and Berar', London, 1899, p. 51.

market. As already mentioned, the extraction of revenue and profits from cotton were the main aims of the state. 'When we interfered and took Berar in 1853 it was solely in order to realize our own extortionate claim . . . and not in any degree on behalf of a downtrodden and oppressed people',[16] was how a British correspondent of the *Times of India* reported in June 1882 on the motives of the colonial state. All other cotton tracts in the neighborhood were already a part of British India. These included the rich areas of Khandesh in the west of Berar; Hingunghat in the east; Dharwar in the south; and Central Provinces in the north. 'In the possession of Berar and the neighboring districts of Nagpore the British Government, it deserves to be remembered,' wrote Dalhousie 'has secured the finest cotton tracts which are known to exist in all the continent of India, and thus has opened up a great additional channel of supply, through which to make good a felt deficiency in the staple of one great branch of its manufacturing industry.'[17] Early reports of colonial officials covetously mention large tracts of waste lands which could be successfully planted with cotton.[18] Berar had tremendous potential to grow this commodity. But this potential could not be realized without roads, railways, and capital. Early roads were therefore built with a dual purpose: (*a*) to open up the country and, (*b*) to serve as feeders to the railway in future. Unlike the railways, the roads were built with local cess and taxes. 'The road from Hingolee by Poosud to Woon on the banks of the Wurdah is being marked and opened out from the local funds of the Assigned Districts; this will run into the heart of the south-east part of the Assigned Districts, and will be of much benefit in opening up the country.'[19] In addition to opening the country the roads enabled rapid movement of colonial armies in times of need.

[16] From a correspondent writer for *Times of India*, 21 June 1882, in *Hyderabad Affairs*, Vol. 4, compiled by Moulvie Syed Mahdi Ali, Bombay, 1883-6, p. 387.

[17] 'Lord Dalhousie's Minute on his Indian Administration—Hyderabad', *Madras, Spectator*, 2 August 1856, in *Hyderabad Affairs*, Vol. 2, 1883.

[18] Walter R. Cassells, *Cotton: An Account of its Culture in the Bombay Presidency*, prepared from Government Records and other Authentic Sources, in Accordance with a Resolution of the Government of India, Bombay, 1862.

[19] *General Administration Report on the Hyderabad Assigned Districts for the Year 1861-62*, Calcutta, 1863, p. 100.

Land Survey and Settlement Operations in Berar

Early land revenue settlement under colonialism was a complex problem. The British had come to Berar with a pre-conceived European notion of private property rights in land. Land as private property was considered the best guarantee of ensuring state revenue. In pre-colonial times the *balutedari* system had existed and the question of private property right in land was left ambiguous. The produce of the soil (or crop yield) was divided according to social ranking in the caste hierarchy.[20] In other words, rights on land were defined not in terms of individual property, but as shares in the produce of the land.

The *balutedari* system created confusion in the colonial mind-set on the concept of private property rights in land. This confusion was sought to be cleared by the exercise of state power. Elaborate survey and settlement operations were conducted to carve out the cotton rich land into lots and assign it to individuals with responsibility to pay revenue directly to the state. It was the aim of the colonial state to account for every single piece of land in Berar. At the time of annexation the state took control of all land. Its early activity constantly reinforced the idea of private property right in land and all kinds of ways to generate revenue were experimented. For the first three years of cession, the revenue was collected strictly *mouzawur* from heads of villages or *muqquddums*. Settlement was executed summarily on whole villages, 'without regard to the actual quantity of land under cultivation, and in many places land not under cultivation was taxed'.[21] The *mouzawur* system was also found to be unsuitable because deshmukhs and deshpandias (local strongmen) in collaboration with patels and patwaris (village headman and accountant) had retained considerable power and influence in the villages. So the services of deshmukhs and desh-pandias were dispensed with but those of patels and patwaris were retained.

[20] For details on the *balutedari* system, see the excellent work by Furdoonjee Jamshedjee, *Notes on the Agriculturists of the Districts of Aurangabad*. Reviews of this work appeared in *Times of India*, 19 September 1879; and *Bombay Review*, 13 September 1879, in *Hyderabad Affairs*, Vol. 4, n.d., pp. 371-7, 461-6. The *balutedari* system is analysed in detail in Chapter 1.

[21] *General Administration Report on the Hyderabad Assigned Districts for the Year 1856-57*, Calcutta, 1858, para X.

By the late 1850s a crude form of land revenue settlement was beginning to emerge as the colonial state's shadow over Berar began to lengthen. In 1855 a new five-year settlement was initiated with an annually increasing *jama* (rent roll). The Deputy Commissioner of each district was bestowed with full authority to prepare annual *jamabandi* through the medium of *patels* and *patwaris*. It was soon discovered that the reason land revenue was not increasing was because inferior soils were highly assessed and rich soils were lightly assessed.[22] But there was yet another reason. The patels and patwaris were exercising some influence over the matters of land revenue administration in the villages. The government took immediate action. The jurisdiction of patels and patwaris over the business of revenue collection was done away with.[23] Another reason for the stagnation of revenue during the early colonial period was the existence of exemptions and privileges. During annexation there were a number of *inam* grants (revenue free) which were cutting into government revenue. The *inams* were revenue free patronage grants given by kings and nobles during the Mughal and pre-Mughal times. The colonial state through laws and regulations cautiously brought such holdings under government jurisdiction and subjected them to regular assessment. This also went well with the colonial idea of hereditary proprietary rights in land and fixity of tenure. 'The object aimed at has been so to conduct the years settlement that while it should put an end to all unlicensed exemptions and privileges, and should secure a fair revenue to the state, it should, by the recognition of proprietary right in those who can establish a hereditary or prescriptive title, and only by the protection of the interests of other cultivators of the soil, invest tenures of land with security and permanency under certain declared condition. . . .'[24]

The colonial state's obsession with private property rights in land was in a way a response to the intense pressure from the Manchester Chamber of Commerce to develop cotton cultivation.[25] This generated conflicts and controversies among colonial officials on the question of the most suitable system of landholding to be adopted in Berar.

[22] *Central Provinces and Berar: A Review of the Administration of the Province, 1921-1923*, Vol. II, Nagpur, 1923, pp. 155-7.

[23] *General Administration Report on the Hyderabad Assigned Districts for the Year 1856-57*, Calcutta, 1858, para X.

[24] Ibid., para 86.

[25] For details on this subject, see the work of Arthur Silver, *Manchester Men and Indian Cotton, 1847-1872*, Manchester, 1966.

Meadows Taylor and Mr. Bullock, the two colonial officials of the early period, were outright opposed to the idea of introducing the *zamindari* or *malguzari* system by which non-cultivating tenants owned land and relieved the government of the responsibility of rent collection.[26] They favoured the *ryotwari* model by which each cultivating peasant was registered with the government and supposedly paid revenue direct to the government. In fact this controversy was nothing new. It was a reincarnation of *zamindari-ryotwari* controversy in the early nineteenth century in Madras Presidency under the Governorship of Thomas Munroe (1792-1818).[27] The difference between *ryotwari, zamindari* or any other landholding system under colonialism was really only superficial. The colonial state was really not interested in reaching the primary producer. It was in fact at the head of several parasitic groups surviving on the produce of land and labour irrespective of the landholding system. However, the *ryotwari* system was adopted in Berar. In principle 'each cultivator [wa]s is to engage directly with the Government while the collections [we]re are to be made through the head men or representatives of the village'.[28] The government fixed the revenue demand on each cultivator separately and, 'the responsibility of the heads of villages for the whole rent was not insisted on, and each cultivator was made answerable only for the rent of his own holding'.[29] This system underwent drastic changes during and after the survey and settlement operations (1862-77).

The early colonial period in Berar was a time of trial and error. It was also a time of observation and planning for future colonial rule. Rooting out diversity and imposing standardization was the

[26] *Central Provinces and Berar: A Review of the Administration of the Province, 1921-1923*, Vol. II, Nagpur, 1923, pp. 155-7.

[27] For further details on this controversy, see T. H. Beaglehole, *Thomas Munro and the Development of Administrative Policy in Madras, 1792-1818: The Origins of the Munro System*, Cambridge, 1966; Burton Stein, 'Integration of the Agrarian System in South India' in Robert Frykenberg, ed., *Land Control and Social Structure in Indian History*, Madison, 1969; 'Privileged Landholding: The Concept Stretched to Cover the Case', in Robert Frykenberg, ed., *Land Tenure and Peasant in South Asia*, New Delhi, 1977.

[28] *General Administration Report on the Hyderabad Assigned Districts for the Year 1858-59*, Calcutta, 1860, para 99.

[29] *General Administration Report on the Hyderabad Assigned Districts for the Year 1856-57*, Calcutta, 1858, para X.

central creed of the colonial state. The colonizers knew that the state was losing revenue from a lot of unregistered land. If only all the hidden land could be exposed, a tremendous increase in revenue could be realized. Therefore all efforts of the early colonial state was directed towards this goal.

Proposals for the first systematic survey was made in 1857. The land revenue then was crudely defined as taxes derived from land, grazing, fruit trees and cess pertaining to every direct produce.[30] The system of *beegah*[31] which had existed at the time of annexation, was more of an assumption of area than a specific standard measurement. It is rather surprising that this caused confusion in the minds of survey officials, considering the fact the British society also operated on customs and conventions. However, this confusion was cleared by replacing the *beegah* with the standard English acre.[32] The acre became a standard measurement of land in Berar after annexation. Another indigenous practice which irritated the colonizers was the system of weights and measures. On the eve of annexation the colonizers found a diverse system of weights and measures in Berar. Every village had adopted its own system suited to local customs and practices. This posed enormous problems for the colonial state in realizing revenue and exercising control. So a standard British system of uniform weights and measures was introduced in 1862.[33] This enabled the government to exercise control over trade and markets. This also cleared the way for the development of a systematic survey procedure by which a step-by-step method was adopted. Accordingly:

Step I	The land was measured
Step II	The land was classified by soil condition
Step III	The land was tested for soil classification
Step IV	The land was broken up into survey fields
Step V	The assessment on land was fixed for thirty years

[30] *General Administration Report of the Hyderabad Assigned Districts for the Year 1857-58*, Calcutta, 1859, paras 292, 421.

[31] Approximately 1.75 acres or 19,173 sq. yards.

[32] From: Meadows Taylor, Deputy Commissioner, Western Districts, To: Major Davidson, First Assistant Resident, Hyderabad, dated 13 May 1854, in the *Proceedings of the Foreign Department*, 1854.

[33] *General Administration Report on the Hyderabad Assigned Districts for the Year 1862-63*, Calcutta, 1864, para 147.

This became a standard procedure for all the survey operations which began in 1861. 'The basis or unit of assessment is the survey number or plot of land of a size adapted for cultivation by a peasant with a pair of bullocks.'[34] The area of a survey number was ascertained by precise measurement. Each field was separately measured and entered in the field register with maps. The area of each holding was obtained by simple arithmetic and calculations were immediately recorded. The perimeter of each survey number did not exceed more than 20 to 30 acres. The fields were marked off from each other by a *dhura* (a narrow strip of fallow land) or by *warli* (earth mound) or by *gota pathar* (erected stone). The survey thus done, the classification of the soil began. Each field was divided temporarily into 12 parts of 2 acres each. Then three tests were conducted to detect the type of soil, the depth of soil, and defects in the soil. The classer then drew an outline of each field and indicated on it the result of each test. The full details of each field were entered in a *prati* or a field book which was kept at the headquarters of every district.

The rate of assessment was determined by dividing the land and villages into groups as described by Major Elphinstone (the survey chief from 1862-70) in the following manner:

> The first group contains the large market towns and adjoining villages. The second group contains the small market towns, the villages adjoining them, and all villages within a circle of four miles from the large markets. In the third group I have placed all the more remote villages, with the exception of a few villages lying within the spurs of the hills, and having an unhealthy climate, which I have placed in the fourth group.[35]

However the groupings were much more detailed and complex than the naive manner in which Elphinstone describes it. The villages were put into groups based on their physical characteristics such as climate, rainfall, fertility of the soil, nearness to communication lines, etc.[36] The prime criterion however was the proximity to the railway line. The villages nearest to the railway line paid higher rates than those farther away from it. It was on the basis of these

[34] *Central Provinces and Berar: A Review of the Administration of the Province, 1921-23*, Vol. II, Nagpur, 1923, para 218.

[35] *Basim Taluka Settlement Report*, Camp No. 203, Chikalda, dated 25 April 1900, p. 10.

[36] *Central Provinces and Berar: A Review of the Administration of the Province, 1921-23*, Vol. II, Nagpur, 1923, para 219.

groupings that the land revenue assessment was fixed. Therefore it is necessary to examine these groupings:[37]

Group I - Villages in this Group were situated parallel to railway line and around large market towns. These were fertile tracts of land with deep rich soil retentive of moisture. The soil had the capacity to grow two crops a year and cotton was the principal crop.

Group II - Villages in this Group were less favourably situated with regard to market and means of disposing off their produce. These villages were situated within a circle of six miles from large bazaars and small market towns. All the villages situated on high roads connecting the railways were classified into this Group. Hills mixed with rich strips along rivers were also categorized as Group II villages.

Group III - Foot hill villages and deserted villages inhabited by tribal people who were forced to adopt agriculture due to economic pressure. These villages were distant from bazaars and inconveniently situated for purposes of traffic. Remote and inaccessible villages lying in saline tracts with salt wells and badly supplied with water. Villages situated within a radius of 12 miles from the railway station.

Group IV - Deserted villages lying in the hills. Villages lying in unhealthy localities within the spurs of the hills. These villages had a very bad water supply and were distant from communication lines.

Garden lands were categorized separately. These were wet lands irrigated by wells, tanks, fresh water lakes, streams and *bandharras* (drains). Garden lands formed a very small percentage (less then 10 per cent) of total cultivated lands in Berar. These lands primarily grew rice, wheat, opium, chilies, sugarcane, turmeric, pan, vegetables, and fruits.

[37] This information is taken from the *Settlement Reports* of the following talukas: *Jalgaon*, No. 261 of 1865; *Malkapur*, No. 347 of 1866; *Chicklee*, No. 51 of 1866; *Akote*, No. 268 of 1867; *Mehkur*, No. 1098 of 1868; *Dariapur* and *Mortizapur*, No. 368 of 1869; *Oomrawuttee and Ellichpur*, No. 444 of 1870; *Morsi*, No. 563 of 1871; *Darwa*, No. 420 of 1872; *Chandur*, No. 470 of 1873; *Yeotmal*, No. 382 of 1874; *Wun*, No. 340 of 1875; *Basim*, No. 203 of 1900; *Mangrul*, No. 312 of 1900.

Modern Technology and Agrarian Society

The latest survey technology available in Europe was employed in Berar for conducting survey and settlement operations. The manual and crude method of chain and staff was replaced by theodolite and prismatic compass. When mounted on a plain table these instruments were most effective weapons for surveying and measuring the altitude and depression of horizontal surfaces.[38] This was vital because the scientific verifiability of land ownership was the primary criterion of all survey in Berar.[39] The theodolite gave speed to settlement operations and instantly doubled the area of survey. Speed and expansion were the two guiding principles of these operations. The rugged and mountainous tracts of Melghat in the North and Balaghat in the south obstructed the pace of survey operations. Therefore they were given over to the Forest Department for management. However, the waste lands were surveyed in blocks and disposed of with a guarantee to be brought under the plough.[40]

The survey and settlement operations began by concentrating on the rich plain talukas of the Purna valley in central Berar. The Purna valley districts gave speed and rapid mobility to survey parties. The Report of the Survey Department mentions in 1872 that, 'in a flat well cultivated and open district ten or twelve fields can be surveyed with greater facility in a morning's work than half that number in a hilly district like Woon and Pusad, where cultivation is in a backward state and the fields are but partially cleared of scrub and jungle'.[41] Trigonometrical survey stations were set up for conducting topographical surveys. The knowledge of local inhabitants was thoroughly exploited.[42] The purpose of trigonometrical survey was to carry out a series of triangulations covering a larger area of

[38] *Report on Survey and Settlement Operations in the Hyderabad Assigned Districts, for the Year ending 31st October 1872*, Hyderabad, 1873, p. 4.

[39] From: Captain Meadows Taylor, Deputy Commissioner of Western Districts, To: Major Davidson, First Assistant Resident, Hyderabad, in *Proceedings of the Foreign Department*, dated 13 May 1854.

[40] *Report on Survey and Settlement Operations in the Hyderabad Assigned Districts for the Year ending 31st October 1873*, Hyderabad, 1874, p. 1.

[41] *Report on the Survey and Settlement Operations in the Hyderabad Assigned Districts, for the Year ending 31st October 1872*, Hyderabad, 1873, p. 2.

[42] *Hyderabad Affairs*, Vol. 1, compiled by Moulvie Syed Mahdi Ali, Bombay, n.d. (approx. 1883), p. 54.

land in a single stretch.[43] The best available printing and mapping technology was introduced. Lithographs were prepared and detailed maps drawn up for every single village with positions of all the boundary marks. This facilitated a thorough annual boundary mark inspection.[44] A new system of *jamabandi* (rent roll) was introduced which showed a field by field record of each holder and the net amount of land revenue due to government along with the date on which it was due.[45] Receipt books were maintained to keep track of each cultivator's payment. Book Circulars (government orders) were constantly issued to regulate the revenue business. Thus continuous efforts were made to achieve greater efficiency of the revenue gathering machine.[46]

The survey and settlement was a huge operation conducted by a separate department of the government organized specifically for this purpose. At its peak there were six measuring establishments and three classing parties in addition to several small establishments and parties attached to the Department.[47] The Department was constantly reorganized as more land was measured and classified.[48] It took seventeen years (1861-77) to survey and settle the whole province with over 7000 villages and 10,458,980 culturable acres.[49] But although most villages were combed by 1877-8 and settled for thirty years, the settlement of scattered villages continued till the end of the century when extensive revision settlements were conducted.[50] The total cost of survey operations was only

[43] *Report on the Administration of the Hyderabad Assigned Districts, 1869-70*, Hyderabad, 1871, para 279.

[44] *Report on Survey and Settlement Operations in the Hyderabad Assigned Districts for the Year ending 31st October 1874*, Hyderabad, 1875, p. 5.

[45] *Report on the Administration of the Hyderabad Assigned Districts for the Year 1900-01*, Hyderabad, 1902, p. 53.

[46] *Report on the Revenue Administration of the Hyderabad Assigned Districts for the Year 1879-80*, Hyderabad, 1880, pp. 12, 17.

[47] *Report on Survey and Settlement Operations in the Hyderabad Assigned Districts, for the Year ending 31st October 1872*, Hyderabad, 1873, p. 9. Also see *General Administration Report on the Hyderabad Assigned Districts for the Year 1862-63*, Calcutta, paras 134, 135, 136, and 145.

[48] *Report on the Administration of the Hyderabad Assigned Districts, 1868-69*, Hyderabad, 1870, paras 64, 70.

[49] *Report on Survey and Settlement Operations in the Hyderabad Assigned Districts for the Year ending 31st October 1877*, Hyderabad, 1878, p. 1 and Appendix 2.

[50] Statement showing years of survey and settlement and the year in which the thirty-year settlement will expire, by the Director of Land Records and Agriculture,

Rs. 21,95,991 or less than 30 per cent of a single year's land revenue.[51] Most of this expense went towards the payment of colonial officials.

The colonial survey officials received huge salaries compared to Indian flagholders and villagers who worked for them. On average a British official conducting survey received Rs. 300/- per mensem or Rs. 3600/- per annum. An Indian survey labourer was paid 2 to 4 annas per day or Rs. 67/- per year.[52] While the colonial official sat under the shade of canopies and umbrellas supervising the operation, the Indian labourer worked in the sun without any insurance against sickness. One of the official writes: 'In inhabited villages we are able to obtain villagers at from 2 annas to 4 annas for the morning's work, and need only employ them day by day as required, so that a considerable saving is effected by not having to pay them on sundays, holidays, or when a measurer or classer is incapacitated by sickness from working in the field.'[53] Furthermore the colonial civil servants were given salaries, raises and bonuses according to the amount of revenue they helped to raise for the government. The higher the revenue yield in their district, the greater was their share of salary and bonus.[54] This led to intense competition among survey officials to appease their superiors on whose grace their careers depended.[55] Therefore every colonial official devoted his full energy to raise as much revenue as possible for the government coffers. This often resulted in the cultivators being subjected to exhortionate demands by the state officials.

Hyderabad Assigned Districts, Amraoti, dated 15 December 1894, in the *Proceedings of the Hyderabad Administration on Matters of Routine for the Month of December 1894*, submitted to the Revenue and Agriculture Department, Circular No. 5, 15 December 1894.

[51] *Report on Survey and Settlement Operations in the Hyderabad Assigned Districts for the Year ending 31st October 1877*, Hyderabad, 1878, Appendix 2.

[52] As compared to the pay scales of the British official, Karkun, a lower level Indian government official who registered goods of trade, was paid only Rs. 10 per month in salary. In *Report of the Trade of the Hyderabad Assigned Districts for the Year 1880-81*, Hyderabad, 1882. Also see *Report on Survey and Settlement Operations in the Hyderabad Assigned Districts, for the Years 1872-77*, published annually, Hyderabad.

[53] *Report on Survey and Settlement Operations in the Hyderabad Assigned Districts for the Year ending 31st October 1872*, Hyderabad, 1873, p. 8.

[54] Meadows Taylor, 'The Story of My Life, 1857' in *Hyderabad Affairs*, Vol. 2, compiled by Moulvie Syed Mahdi Ali, Bombay, 1883, p. 725.

[55] *Jalgaon Talooka Settlement Report*, No. 261 of 1865, para 53.

The survey officials were instructed by their superiors to keep an eye open for mineral resources of the Province. It was therefore the job of survey parties to look for minerals and recommend ways to exploit it. In 1855 iron ore was discovered in one of the peaks of Yeotmal range by one Mr. Mulheran who was appointed by Lord Dalhousie, the Governor General.[56] All minerals, forests, and land was declared as government property. In the event of a discovery of minerals, the proprietor lost all rights over the site. The location and sites of all mineral potential of Berar were carefully recorded and reported to higher authorities. In one of the reports Major Elphinstone, the Superintendent of Revenue Survey and Assessment, reports to his superiors in the following manner:

I ought not to omit drawing attention to some valuable iron ore which I noticed about one mile North of village Dabheri, at the side of a hillock, known under the name of the 'Goolal Tekri' or the purple mound. If fuel could be obtained cheaply, which it cannot at present, this ore could, I believe, be worked at a considerable profit.[57]

One of the primary reasons for the British annexation of Berar was its natural wealth. Hibernating in the midst of primeval volcanic ash, Berar had a tremendous potential to grow cotton and supply innumerable minerals and salts which could be profitably exploited with new technology. 'It possesses one of the richest and most extensive cotton fields in India; and several cotton marts of very first calibre. Its other products, especially millet and oilseeds, are also excellent. Altogether, it is one of the most promising tracts I have ever seen in India; and in respect to natural and material advantage, it surpasses any tract in either the Central Provinces or the Deccan', wrote the Commissioner in his annual administration report of 1867.[58] In yet another Settlement Report of the Mehkar district Major Elphinstone writes:

In one spot near Amrapur, there must have been quite a mine of Cornelians, as I found the surface of the ground, to the extent of about quarter of an acre, closely strewn with minute chips of this mineral. It

[56] *Hyderabad Affairs*, Vol. I (1885), p. 54, compiled by Moulvie Syed Mahdi Ali, Bombay, 1883-6.

[57] From: Major P. A. Elphinstone, Superintendent Revenue Survey and Assessment, Hyderabad Assigned Districts, To: The Second Assistant Resident, Hyderabad, From Superintendent's Office, Malligaum, 7 October 1871, in *Morsi Taluka Settlement Report*, 1871, No. 563 of 1871.

appears that some European had pitched his camp here, and after picking and chipping away for some time, to the mystification of the villagers, took with him baskets filled with fine Cornelians. Large crystals of the double refracting spar, the carbonate of lime, are often met with; I have not, however, found it in beds, or in sufficient quantity to be collected for the preparation of lime, for which it is eminently suitable.[59]

Searching for minerals was one of the many activities of survey parties. Their main purpose however was to achieve 'rationalization' of revenue rates. A widely differential rate from village to village was unacceptable. Uniformity and discipline were the guiding principles of all colonial activity. 'One of the great advantages of regular survey and assessment is equalization of rates, which from the circumstances of a long past time often vary exceedingly in adjoining villages of the same quality of soil.'[60] Uniformity and equalization was essential to ensure increasing returns of revenue. Uneven rates disturbed the regular process of revenue collection. Therefore, 'the principal object of the new settlement was to produce equality of incidence on land held. . . .'[61] Equalization of revenue rate was regarded as an improvement over the old rate. Equalization also had a political strategy behind it. Under differential rate the powerful families in the village paid relatively less revenue than the ordinary cultivator. With the introduction of equalized rates the government took away the power from the dominant families into its own jurisdiction. Equalized rates brought a great deal of discipline and made the people aware of the power of the state. In the old assessment the dominant families escaped paying the land revenue altogether by shifting the burden on general mass of cultivators. Under the iron hand of colonial rule, nobody escaped. Survey, settlement, and equalization were thus most effectively employed to account for and exploit Berar's land revenue.

[58] *Report on the Administration of the Hyderabad Assigned Districts for the Year 1866-67*, Hyderabad, 1867, p. 1.

[59] From: Major P. A. Elphinstone, Superintendent Revenue Survey and Assessment, Hyderabad Assigned Districts, To: Major C. J. Prescott, Acting Survey and Settlement Commissioner, Hyderabad Assigned Districts, dated 14 October 1869, in *Mehkar Taluka Settlement Report*, No. 426 of 1868, p. 6, para 6.

[60] *General Administration Report on the Hyderabad Assigned Districts for the Year 1862-63*, Calcutta, 1864, para 143.

[61] *Central Provinces District Gazetteers: Buldana District*, Vol. A: Descriptive, edited by A. E. Nelson, Calcutta, 1910, p. 356

Equalization was essential for strengthening private property rights in land. Its introduction completely changed the face of Berar. The whole country was marked off into plots and boundary marks were erected to delineate holdings.[62] The government-registered tenant was entered as a *khatedar*. The *khatedari* system put the occupant totally at the mercy of colonial government. The state became the supreme landlord and exercised the right to manipulate and revise land revenue rates. G. S. Khaparde, a High Court Vakil of Amraoti, writes thus in 1895:

> In British India Government is with very few exceptions the supreme landlord. Everybody else is more or less either its tenants or assignee of certain specified rights. These are greater or smaller according to the nature of holding, but the fact remains that nobody except Government can be said to be the proprietor of the soil. All others are either occupants or assignees of certain rights.[63]

Property and Occupancy: The State and the Khatedars

Every *khatedar's* right of occupancy was conditional on the payment of government land revenue demand. Default led to forfeiture not only of the right of occupancy but all rights connected with it, i.e. those over trees and buildings as well.[64] The land thus forfeited reverted back to the government and the right of occupancy was put up for auction after due notice. Even under occupancy the *khatedar* did not possess the right to divert his holding for non-agricultural purposes. He could sublet his holding by private engagement to subtenants on rack-rent.[65] The government had no qualms about it so long as the revenue was promptly paid. The state did not interfere between the *khatedar* and the *bhagindar* (subtenant).

[62] Meadows Taylor, 'The Story of My Life, 1857', in *Hyderabad Affairs.*, Vol. 2 (1883), p. 718, compiled by Moulvie Syed Mahdi Ali, Bombay, 1883-86. Also see *Chicklee Taluka Settlement Report*, No. 51 of 1866, para 23.

[63] From: G. S. Khaparde, High Court Vakil, Amraoti, To: The Commissioner, Hyderabad Assigned Districts, dated 19 July 1895, in *Proceedings of the Hyderabad Administration on Matters of Routine for the Month of September 1895*, submitted to the Revenue and Agriculture Department, No. 337, dated 28 September 1895.

[64] *Report on the Administration of Hyderabad Assigned Districts for the Year 1882-83*, Hyderabad, 1884, para 25.

[65] *Central Provinces and Berar: A Review of the Administration of the Province, 1921-23*, Vol. II, Nagpur, 1923, para 221.

The *khatedars* as a class were new to Berar. It was through them the colonial state was able to extend its control. Controlling them was therefore state's first priority. The power of the state depended upon *khatedari* loyalty. The state ruled over them more by threat than by persuasion. Their relationship to the government were defined by laws and decrees. Their collaboration was vital for the development of cotton economy. The *khatedars* were a colonial creation and their position was defined in the following manner:

> It must be borne in mind that the demand for land revenue from districts under Ryotwaree system is not fixed though the assessment may have been settled. The assessment is not on whole villages, but on fields, and the cultivating leases are for thirty years on the part of Government, but from year to year on cultivator's part. Thus the demand is made up every year on the actual rent roll of each village, and fluctuates with the yearly spread or diminution of cultivation. The assessed land tax of this Division, after all the cultivable land shall have been taken up, will be far beyond the demands now shown. During this year, the new assessment has operated by raising rates per acre, and by bringing concealed cultivation under revenue demand.[66]

Once the land was broken up into survey numbers, *sanads* (deeds) were issued granting pieces of land to *khatedars*.[67] The total number of *khatedars* at any given time is a good indicator of landholding activity in Berar. Table 3 registers fluctuations in the total number of occupants during the period under study.[68]

An increase in the total number of *khatedars* from 226,207 in 1870 to 394,644 in 1903 and decrease in per capita holdings from 23.7 to 18.2 acres during the same period suggests that fragmentation of landholding was taking place. The presence of indebtedness in

[66] *Report on the Administration of the Hyderabad Assigned Districts, 1868-69*, Hyderabad, 1870, para 53.

[67] From: T. Chichele Plowden, Commissioner, Hyderabad Assigned Districts, To: The Secretary for Berar to the Resident at Hyderabad, 31 January 1890, in *Proceedings of the Hyderabad Administration on Matters of Routine for the Month of October 1890*, submitted to the Foreign Department, No. 70-G, 4 March 1890.

[68] The data for this statement is taken from the following sources: *Gazetteer for the Haidarabad Assigned Districts Commonly called Berar*, edited by A. C. Lyall, Bombay, 1870, p. 109; *Report on the Revenue Administration in the Hyderabad Assigned Districts, 1880-81*, Hyderabad, 1882, p. 40; *Statistical Abstracts of British India from 1882-83 to 1891-92*, No. 27, London, 1893, p. 156; *Report on the Administration of the Hyderabad Assigned Districts for the Year 1902-3*, Hyderabad, 1904, p. 18.

TABLE 3

Year	No. of Khatedars	Area of Occupancy	Acres per Khatedar
1870	226,207	5,361,375 acres	23.7
1875	236,137	7,295,848 acres	30.8
1892	290,828	6,980,125 acres	24.0
1903	394,644	7,203,200 acres	18.2

Berar can be partly attributed to the fact that as the pressure on land increased, the acreage per capita shrank. The social transformation from *balutedari* to *khatedari* as well as the problem of indebtedness will be dealt in later chapters.

The Revenue Offensive: Land Revenue

The creation of *khatedari* had a major impact on the society and economy of Berar. It regularized and enhanced the government revenue. Revenue in every taluka increased dramatically during and after the survey. All unregistered and concealed land was taken

TABLE 4

Taluka	Comparative Years	% Increase in Occupied Area	% Increase in Land Revenue
Mehkur	1860-1 & 1867-8	31.4	38.3
Dariapur	1861-2 & 1868-9	3.1	16.5
Mortizapur	1861-2 & 1868-9	19.3	22.4
Oomrawuttee	1861-2 & 1869-70	26.6	42.7
Ellichpur	1861-2 & 1869-70	15.8	19.7
Morsi	1861-2 & 1870-1	30.0	37.4
Darwa	1861-2 & 1871-2	78.9	60.4
Chandur	1861-2 & 1872-3	145.9	71.6
Yeotmal	1861-2 & 1873-4	66.1	79.7
Wun	1865-6 & 1874-5	14.1	27.0
	Average Increase	43.1	41.5

[69] The data for this statement has been taken from the *Settlement Reports* of the following talukas: *Mehkar*, No. 1098 of 1869, para 13; *Dariapur and Mortizapur*, No. 368 of 1869, para 27 and 62; *Oomrawuttee and Ellichpur*, No. 444 of 1870, paras 26 and 53; *Morsi*, No. 563 of 1871, para 21; *Darwa*, No. 420 of 1872, para 22; *Chandur*, No. 470 of 1873, para 19; *Yeotmal*, No. 382 of 1874, para 24; *Wun*, No. 340 of 1875, para 28.

[70] *Darwa Taluka Settlement Report*, No. 420 of 1872, para 22.

over by the government and subjected to revenue payment. Table 4 shows percentage increases in area occupied and land revenue realized during the crucial decade of the 1860s and the early 1870s when survey and settlement operations were at its peak.[69]

While large increases in the land revenue and occupied area were being registered, famines were beginning to happen in Berar. Successive cycles of subsistence crisis hit the region in 1868-9 and 1871-2.[70] The situation became specially serious in talukas which registered large increases in government land revenue demand, i.e. Mehkur, Oomrawuttee, Morsi, Darwa, Chandur, Yeotmal, etc. The 'Survey and Settlement' laid the foundation for the development of cotton economy in Berar. The increasing rate of government revenue demand skimmed most of the surplus from people. The following statement provides data on percentage increases in land revenue in various groups of villages in selected talukas:[71]

Taluka	*Group I* %	*Group II* %	*Group III* %	*Group IV* %
Yeotmal	51	33	32	25
Wun	29	20	21	6
Mangrul	41	29	14	NA
Basim	33	31	18	NA
Average	38.5	28.2	21.2	15.5

The highest revenue increases were registered in the rich fertile tracts of central Berar. Here cotton occupied more than 40 per cent of the land and the rate of indebtedness was high. The total land revenue yield for Berar also showed a steady rise throughout the period under study. Table 5 shows the rate of total land revenue increase during the period of Settlement.[72]

[71] Data for this table has been taken from the *Settlement Reports* of the following talukas: *Wun*, No. 340 of 1875, para 40; *Yeotmal*, No. 282 of 1874, para 34; *Mangrul Settlement Report*, Camp No. 312, Chikalda, dated 13 July 1900, para 31; *Basim Settlement Report*, Camp No. 203, Chikalda, dated 25 April 1900, para 37.

[72] Figures for this statement is taken from the following sources: *Report on the Revenue Administration in the Hyderabad Assigned Districts*, Hyderabad, printed annually from 1877-8 to 1901-2; *Report on the Administration of the Hyderabad Assigned Districts*, Hyderabad, printed annually from 1860 to 1901.

In seventeen years of survey operations the revenue increased by 106.5 per cent from Rs. 29,83,415 to Rs. 61,63,485. The rate of increase being 6.2 per cent per annum.

TABLE 5

Year	*Rupees*[73]
1860-1	29,83,415
1861-2	32,24,718
1862-3	33,07,746
1863-4	35,54,976
1864-5	38,16,020
1865-6	39,72,442
1866-7	42,54,310
1867-8	44,43,798
1868-9	44,95,873
1869-70	45,81,356
1870-1	47,32,702
1871-2	49,37,847
1872-3	53,08,265
1873-4	53,56,311
1874-5	52,86,326
1875-6	67,09,723
1876-7	61,33,570
1877-8	61,63,485

The Revenue Offensive—Sources Other than Land Revenue

Land revenue was only a part of the total revenue collected from Berar. All kinds of taxes were levied to raise revenues. Table 6 gives a concise list of each item of government revenue demand.[74] A comparative analysis of three years is given in this table. According to the profile, on the eve of annexation (1853-4) the land revenue formed 74.5 per cent of the total revenue. But fifteen years later

[73] The currency exchange rate between Pound-Sterling and Rupees was as follows: 1 Pound-Sterling = 10 Rupees until 1873. The Rupee was devalued in 1873 to: 1 Pound-Sterling = 15 Rupees. Source: G.A. Watt, *Dictionary of Economic Products in India*, 6 vols. in 9 pts., Calcutta, 1889-93; H.H. Wilson, *A Glossary of Judicial and Revenue Terms of British India*, Calcutta: 1855, revd edn with case notes by A.C. Ganguli and N.D. Basu., eds., Calcutta, 1940; H. Yule and A.C. Burnell, *Hobson Jobson: A Glossary of Colloquial Anglo-Indian Words and Phrases*, London, 1886, rpt, 1968; *Encyclopedia Britannica*, Vol. XXIII, New York, 1911.

[74] A. C. Lyall, *Gazetteers of the Haidarabad Assigned Districts, Commonly called Berar*, Bombay, 1870, p. 263.

TABLE 6

Items of Land Revenue	1853-4 Rs.	1860-1 Rs.	1869-70 Rs.
I Land Revenue	19,15,372	29,61,722	45,73,430
II Abkari (liquor & opium)	90,349	2,98,933	11,45,139
III Salt Wells	19,281	32,628	6,500
IV Frontier & Transit Duties	1,95,357	Abolished	Abolished
V Sayer & Town Duties	71,144	NA	NA
VI Stamp Duty	NA	37,622	4,59,470
VII Forest Revenue	—	—	1,84,662
VIII Customs Duty on Salt			2,77,795
IX Village Tax, Watchman's Tax; Education Tax, Local Fund Tax	2,66,487	5,92,799	13,22,296
X Miscellaneous	22,717	81,122	3,94,135
GRAND TOTAL	25,80,707	40,04,826	83,63,387

(1869-70) it shrank to 54.6 per cent of the total. This shrinkage represented the introduction of several new taxes as indicated above. The revenues from liquor and opium increased tenfold from Rs. 90,349 to Rs.11,45,139 suggesting government encouragement of production and consumption of these intoxicants.

Berar had traditionally been an exporter of salt. The bed of lake *Lonar* in Buldana district was a natural source of pure primeval brine salt. The state imposed a heavy tax on the manufacture of this commodity which resulted in the closure of every salt well in Berar. From being a net exporter, it became an importer of this essential commodity. By 1870 the manufacture of salt had stopped completely and the net revenue from customs duty on salt was 46 times higher than taxes from indigenous salt wells (see Table 6: the rise from Rs.6,500 to Rs.2,77,795). After the annexation, the frontier and internal transit duties were abolished in order to facilitate the free movement of goods and services during the settlement operations. This also allowed the free extraction of cotton and minerals from Berar. Similarly a stamp duty was introduced in January 1857. In 1860-1 it stood at Rs.37,622 but in less than a decade it multiplied dramatically to net Rs.4,59,470, more than 1100 per cent. Immediately after the government takeover of forests during survey operations, a forest tax was imposed in 1869 which in its very first year netted Rs.1,84,622 in revenue (see Table 6).

In addition the colonial government imposed all kinds of nitty-gritty charges and fines to extract a handsome amount under miscellaneous heads. An illustration of one such charge will be appropriate here. Elphinstone (the survey boss), while operating in Ellichpur district in the 1870s, recommended an imposition of a poll-tax on all pilgrims attending fairs and festivals. Berar is a land of fairs and festivals. Since there is no official weekly holiday, the people participate in these fairs and festivals in colourful clothes. These fairs happen almost every month in addition to weekly markets in small and large villages. Besides providing an opportunity to exchange goods and services, these fairs offered a chance to relax and break away from the monotony of harsh agricultural life. Some of these fairs were huge gatherings attended by 150,000 to 200,000 people. The colonial government was always suspicious of these gatherings. The survey officers monitored these fairs and kept a watch over the people attending fairs. The state had a great fear of moving people specially the *banjaras*, the traditional carriers of goods and services in bullock carts. Therefore Major Elphinstone recommended an imposition of a poll-tax on all the people attending these fairs. Pointing at one such fair in Ellichpur called the *Bahiram*, he writes:

> By establishing a poll-tax of, say, 2 annas per head, during the fair, ample means for such a purpose could easily be collected. According to Tahsildar's account 200,000 people visit this fair yearly; a tax of 2 annas per head would not, I imagine, diminish the number of the people visiting the fair, as they resort to it chiefly to pay their devotions to the shrine of their favorite idol 'Bahiram,'in whose honour the fair is held.[75]

The survey and settlement operations left a devastating impact on the economy of Berar. As the revenue increased from year to year the colonial government congratulated itself. The officials competed to extract as much revenue as feasible in order to add colours to their rank and career. The result was the excessive fragmentation of holdings and the rise of subtenancy. The state dealt only with the registered occupant (*khatedar*). There are no returns to show the area cultivated under each of the occupancy tenures.[76] But if the *bhagindars* (subtenants) formed 44.9 per cent

[75] *Oomrawuttee and Ellichpur Settlement Report, 1870*, No. 444 of 1870, para 23.

[76] Mr. Dunlop's Report, in the *Report of the Famine Commission, 1881*, pp. 340-1.

of the total agrarian labour force, then it can be informally guestimated that more than half the *khatedari* held land was cultivated by *bhagindars*.[77]

The fragmentation of holdings started immediately after survey parties finished and moved to another village. In many villages the land was so minutely subdivided that the share of each cultivator barely sufficed for the support of his family.[78] Most of the *khatedari* land was sub-let on rack-rent at rates 3 to 4 times the government revenue demand. Table 7 shows the difference between revenue and rental rate[79] and the percentage of rack-rent to government revenue demand.[80]

On average the government registered tenant charged 54.3 per cent of rack-rent over the government revenue demand. The rate of revenue and rental demand had its toll on land. Mr. Bahmanji Jamasji in his report to the Famine Commission in 1881 provides the following description of soil exhaustion as a result of constant land use. He writes:

> The rapid succession on which crop succeeds crop in the present was not known in the bygone period of reference, and field land has therefore undergone an exhaustion of its fertile elements which the cultivator, in his constant need of means and his consequent avarice, has not been enabled to supply by the agricultural expedients which would have been possible of application were the soil given a period of rest and recuperation. Such periods of rest were of frequent intervals when the land was not surveyed nor measured, and portions of it set apart to cultivators, who used to take for their use as much land as they pleased for a nominal rent, thus

[77] A more detailed analysis of sub-tenancy in Berar is available in the chapter on *khatedars*. According to the census of 1891, the *bhagindars* outnumbered *khatedars* by a ratio of 2:1. See *Census of India, 1891: Berar or the Hyderabad Assigned Districts*, Calcutta, 1892, p. cxxxv; *Report on the Census of Berar, 1881*, p. 185.

[78] *Dariapur and Mortizapur Taluka Settlement Report, 1869*, No. 368 of 1869, p. 18.

[79] It is important to note the difference between revenue and rent. The revenue was the government demand per acre from the registered occupant or the *khatedar*. The rent was what the subtenant paid to the *khatedar* for subletting. So long as the *khatedar* paid the annual revenue demand, the government did not care how the *khatedar* dealt with the subtenants. Keeping the government revenue demand as a yardstick, the *khatedars* set the rental demand and oppressed the cultivators.

[80] *Report of the Census of Berar, 1881*, ed. Eustace J. Kitts, Bombay, 1882, p. 223, para 440.

TABLE 7

Taluka	Revenue Rate			Rental Rate			Rack-rent % to Govt. Demand
	Rs.	A.	P.	Rs.	A.	P.	
Amraoti	1	8	2	6	8	1	76.8
Morsi	1	5	2	1	12	2	52.0
Chandur	1	0	5	2	3	10	54.2
Akola	1	9	5	3	11	0	56.8
Akote	1	12	9	5	15	2	69.7
Balapur	1	2	9	2	12	6	57.8
Khamgaon	0	14	8	2	15	5	68.7
Jalgaum	1	5	2	2	13	8	65.6
Ellichpur	1	9	9	3	3	3	49.8
Daryapur	1	10	5	9	0	11	81.8
Melghat	0	6	4	0	11	2	31.7
Chikli	0	9	10	1	1	7	45.4
Malkapur	1	3	10	2	12	11	55.8
Mehkar	0	12	2	1	6	3	45.2
Yeotmal	0	7	9	0	13	10	43.4
Wun	0	9	3	1	0	1	42.5
Darwa	0	9	3	0	12	2	28.1
Kelapur	0	5	11	0	12	6	52.5
					Average		54.3

enabling themselves to allow rest alternately to portions of the land; whereas now it is different; all land has been surveyed, measured and duly apportioned between cultivators, who cannot now take an inch more than is allotted to them, and try to realize out of it as much crop as they can to defray Government demand, as also to satisfy their avarice, which has considerably increased on account of high prices.[81]

Table 8 gives the total area in acres and acreage under each description of crop in 1870.[82]

The Assault on Pastures and Forests

Due to the extension of private control over waste and culturable lands, the scarcity of firewood and grass was acute. The cultivators were forced to use manure from cattle dung as fuel. This led to the scarcity of manure for land. Therefore the means of restoring the

[81] Mr. Bahmanji Jamasji's Report, in the *Report of Famine Commission, 1881*, p. 299.

[82] A. C. Lyall, *Gazetteer of the Haidarabad Assigned Districts*, 1870, p. 226.

TABLE 8

Extent of description of culturable land	*Culturable land in acres*	*Percentage*
Rice land	33,706	0.3%
Irrigated *bagayat* (garden) land	63,660	0.6%
Dry crop land	2,574,763	24.4%
Total culturable	7,897,880	74.7%
Total area	10,570,009	

Note: The difference between the total culturable acreage and the total area constituted the waste lands, i.e. 2,672,129 acres (25.2 per cent) was given out on long leases (*izarah* tenure) to be brought under the plough.

fertility of the soil was lost.[83] Moreover the manure now had to be purchased. Mr. Bahmanji Jamasji, a native colonial official, provides a very sharp insight into the manure and cattle situation in the Famine Commission Report of 1881. He writes:

The manure the cultivator now uses has to be paid for by him both practically and dearly. The days when large areas of waste lands adjoining villages in Berar and afforded free and abundant pasture to village cattle have now departed, and in the present time the cultivator has to either pay the possessors of pasture lands for the privilege of grazing his cattle on them or to set apart a portion of his own land for the purpose — an alternative which represents loss on his part to the extent of the value of the crops that might have been raised on such land and the amount of revenue that has to be paid for it all the same. Thus the difficulties attending the keeping and rearing of large herds of cattle by the Berar agriculturist have increased so as to limit the number of head he now possesses to the actual requirements of tillage, and in this way the supply of the only description of manure used in Berar has been, in the cases of the mass of cultivators, so reduced as to be altogether insufficient to meet the demands of the soil for nourishment.[84]

The aim of survey and settlement operation was to push the land under plough so that an increasing rate of revenue returns can be realized. Lands were allocated under the condition that it would be brought under cultivation. The land containing rank grass and brushwood which was hitherto freely available was divided up, put

[83] *Oomrawuttee and Ellichpur Settlement Report, 1870*, No. 444 of 1870, para 45.

[84] Mr. Bahmanji Jamasji's Report in the *Report of Famine Commission, 1881*, p. 299.

under private control and taxed. The lessee had no other option but to clear the land and start cultivation.[85] 'The land is seldom or never set apart for grass and is invariably brought under tillage.'[86] This had a devastating toll on the health of cattle. Furthermore the colonial survey took away everything which was hitherto freely available. Now the people had to pay for everything and buy everything at a price. The following paragraph gives a graphic account of the scarcity and stringency experienced by the ordinary cultivator under colonial subjection:

> The cultivator is now put to expenses which in former times he did not know. His pecuniary wants are so pressing that often the whole produce of a crop is disposed of by him without provision being made from it for his own subsistence, and very often without his even reserving from it a sufficiency of seed grain for future sowing. He now pays more for his cattle than he did yore, and he can no longer fell a tree from any place he likes to provide him with a shaft for his plough, or a yoke for his oxen. He has now practically to expend coin where before he needed only to labour, and the grass with which he annually thatches his hut has now to be bought, and not merely cut and carried as it used to be.[87]

The percentage of annual remission of land revenue was negligible. Indebtedness of the peasantry was already occurring during the survey operation. Even though the government introduced two instalments for revenue payment (30 January and 15 March of each year), the land revenue was always paid in lumpsum.[88] This indicated the existence of indebtedness among the peasantry as the land revenue was paid by the moneylenders on behalf of the registered occupant. The government always demanded land revenue in cash and the peasantry was always short of cash. So the moneylenders and non-agricultural classes provided cash to the cultivators for the payment of land revenue and operating cost. The cultivators in turn often pledged their crops and entered into debt bondage. This story will be developed in the chapter on moneylenders. It will be appropriate here to mention that the survey

[85] *Yeotmal Taluka Settlement Report, 1874.*

[86] *Report of Famine Commission, 1880*, London, 1881, p. 141.

[87] Mr. Bahmanji Jamasji's Report, in the *Report of Famine Commission, 1881*, p. 299.

[88] From: A. Williams, Secretary for Berar to the Resident, To: The Secretary to the Government of India, Department of Revenue and Agriculture, Hyderabad Residency, dated 11 January 1896, in the *Proceedings of the Hyderabad Administration on Matter of Routine for the Month of January 1896*, submitted to the Revenue and Agricultural Department, No. 13, 11 January 1896.

and settlement operations paved the way for indebtedness in Berar.

Money poured into Berar from all quarters because of its cotton and mineral wealth. Intense poverty and destitution existed amidst superficial prosperity. While writing the Jalgaum Taluka Settlement Report during the American Civil War, Captain P. A. Elphinstone captured the poverty of Berar in the following manner:

> Money . . . poured into Berar since the rise in prices [caused by the Civil War], but it is strange that one should see so few outward indications of this influx of wealth. A better turban or 'doopatta' than previously worn is the only change perceptible in many of the ryots. They still occupy the same miserable, dirty, mud huts they lived in before; their villages are as filthy as ever—in fact they do not show signs of improvement in any tangible way.[89]

The poverty in Berar is directly related to the fate of culturable waste lands under survey. The state designated all the land with grass, brushwood and forest as culturable wastelands. These lands, on which the villagers grazed their cattle and used other produce for their own survival were given out on long leases for reclamation.[90] Shrinking waste lands meant lost opportunities of escape from poverty. Waste lands hitherto had provided cover during times of scarcity and famine. It provided food, fodder, and fuel in times of need. It also provided shelter to several species of birds and animals. The rapid depletion of wastes by survey operations had its impact on ecology. The ecological imbalance caused by clearing of waste lands led to increase in temperature and loss of moisture in the soil. The denudation of trees caused decreasing rainfall and drying up of rivers and wells under the impact of general warming in the region. There was not a single perennial river or stream left in Berar.[91] Lack of irrigation was one of the biggest problems of Berar agriculture. The colonial state was an efficient revenue collector but indifferent to public spending. The Berar Commission was popular in bureaucratic circles for its anti-irrigation argument which claimed that 'the soil of the region was naturally rich therefore there was no need to develop irrigation.' This argument was strongly adhered to throughout the colonial period. In the long-run this prevented

[89] *Jalgaum Taluka Settlement Report, 1865*, No. 261 of 1865, para 16.

[90] B. H. Baden-Powell, *The Land Systems of British India*, Vol. III, Oxford, 1891, pp. 380-3.

[91] *Oomrawauttee and Ellichpur Settlement Report, 1870*, No. 444 of 1870, para 19.

the economic growth of the region. (A detailed analysis of the anti-irrigation argument will be provided in the succeeding chapters.) It is befitting to mention here that during the high noon of colonialism, the irrigated area formed only 0.6 per cent of the total cultivated acreage.[92]

It is interesting to note that the percentage of waste to total area was quite disproportionate. While the cultivated acreage formed 71.7 per cent of the total area, the culturable waste formed only 17 per cent.[93] This proved fatal to both animal and human life forms in the region. As a consequence of scarcity of wastes there was very little land left for grazing, pasturage, threshing floors, storage, and standing room for cattle. In every taluka the cultivation had taken over the waste lands. In Jalgaum taluka report the settlement officer writes: 'There is very little waste land left in the district not more than 16,500 acres, and most of this constituted the threshing floors and standing places for cattle, or is used as grazing land, so that very little of this may be expected to be brought under cultivation.'[94] The precarious situation in Berar was reflected truly in Buldana district. Here the Deputy Commissioner unconcerned of its consequences, writes thus:

> The cultivation had extended during the settlement term so much that there was practically no culturable land left unoccupied. In 1869 when the original settlement was introduced into almost the whole taluk the area of culturable and assessed land lying unoccupied was about 67,100 acres. In 1896-97 the unoccupied area was only 11 acres.[95]

This had its impact on the health of cattle and people.

The survey and settlement operations triggered a great scramble for land in Berar. Large areas of land went under private control. The Amraoti settlement officer noted in 1870:

> In the first place, where the settlement approaches, every man endeavours to secure as much land as he can manage to pay for, knowing that this opportunity of securing land, having once passed away, will not occur again, and that he will have to pay very heavily to acquire it by private purchase. Land newly acquired is brought very gradually into cultivation: for the first year or two it may do little more than pay its expenses. The

[92] 'Irrigation as a Protection against Famine' by the Secretary, Public Works Department, in the *Report of Famine Commission, 1880*, London, 1881, p. 52.

[93] Ibid., p. 52.

[94] *Jalgaum Settlement Report*, No. 261 of 1865, para 52.

[95] *Central Provinces District Gazetteers: Buldana Gazetteer*, Calcutta, 1910, pp. 368-9.

eradication of the long straggling roots of the grass is a slow and laborious process, but till this is done nothing else will grow in perfection.[96]

In 1865 the Berar Waste Land Rules were promulgated.[97] Accordingly waste lands were given out for clearance on leases ranging from 10 to 30 years. These leases were known as *izara* tenures. Izarah rates were fixed on a gradually increasing scale of assessment.[98] Patelships were offered to ryots (cultivators) willing to clear waste lands and settle on it.[99] The lease holders were constantly pressured by the colonial government to extend cultivation into waste lands.[100] This had its impact on the valuable timber reserves. Commenting on the timber situation the Oomrawuttee Survey Officer writes thus in 1870: 'Eight years ago, when we were commencing settlements in Berar, a great part of the valley was overrun with dense thickets of Babool, including many trees of considerable size; these have nearly all disappeared, and been supplanted by cultivation. Some few reserved tracts alone remain.'[101]

Clifford Geertz in his study of the Indonesian island of Java has observed that the constant Dutch colonial demand for sugar in the nineteenth century created a 'hyper-intensive productive system'[102] whereby the limited land supply could not accommodate the rising population and labour pressure. This was also sited as the reason for the economic underdevelopment and prevalence of intense poverty in Java throughout the period of Dutch colonial rule. The situation of Berar under British colonial rule can be sited as a comparison wherein more than one-third of the acreage was under cotton culture. In the Poorna valley cotton exceeded more than 40 per cent of the acreage. Since cotton grew well on virgin soil, its encroachment over waste

[96] *Oomrawuttee and Ellichpur Settlement Report, 1870*, No. 444 of 1870, p. 24.

[97] *Report on the Administration of the Hyderabad Assigned Districts for the Year 1867-68*, Hyderabad, 1869, para 53.

[98] *Yeotmal Taluka Settlement Report, 1874*, No. 282 of 1874, para 42.

[99] *Chicklee Taluk Settlement Report, 1866*, para 36. Also see in this Report a *Memorandum* by the Survey Commissioner W. C. Anderson. See also *The General Administration Report on the Hyderabad Assigned Districts for the Year 1861-62*, Calcutta, 1863, para 146.

[100] *Darwa Settlement Report, 1872*, No. 420 of 1872, para 30.

[101] *Oomrawuttee and Ellichpur Settlement Report, 1870*, No. 444 of 1870, para 24.

[102] Clifford Geertz, *Agricultural Involution: The Processes of Ecological Change in Indonesia*, Berkeley, 1963, p. 95.

lands was rapid. 'The cultivated area averages per head of population only two-and-half acres. This is clearly insufficient for its support, especially when we take into account that nearly all the land is under dry culture, and that more than a third of the entire area is occupied by cotton. As there is now very little waste land available for cultivation, and what there is, is of inferior quality. . .'[103] was how one of the settlement officers reported as early as 1870. As a result of Berar's connection to the world market through cotton, there was an enormous increase in the demand for land. In general the land was parcelled out into minute holdings but capital at the disposal of each holder was extremely limited. The cotton crop guaranteed credit for working capital. So as the cotton acreage increased the debt increased and the grazing areas were curtailed.[104] A grazing tax of one anna per head of cattle per annum was levied on wastes (1865).[105]

Resistance to Survey and Settlement Operations

The survey and settlement was never a smooth operation. The survey parties headed by British officers appeared as suspicious characters in the countryside. The people looked upon them with distrust. The personal prodding and interrogation of the colonial data collectors elicited a great deal of resentment among the inhabitants.[106] Often times the harsh conditions in which the Indian surveyors had to work caused considerable hardship with which the British officers did not bother. Strikes occurred in measuring and classing establishments against oppressive superintendents under whom Indians refused to serve. Under such circumstances the Survey Department generally dismissed everyone.[107] Survey and settlement was a very sophisticated operation and any laxity was dealt with disciplinary action even if it involved British officers. A case of Mr. A. J. Guerin, a measuring party officer, is instructive. He was dismissed because of his laxity and liberal attitude towards local people working under his supervision.[108] Deserted places were considered dangerous for European life. Therefore renegade

[103] Ibid., para 43.

[104] *A Report on Cotton Growing in India*, by Arno Schmidt, Secretary, International Federation of Master Cotton Spinners and Manufacturers Association. This is a report of Secretary's visit to India, December 1911-January 1912, pp. 22-3.

[105] A. C. Lyall, *Gazetteer of the Hyderabad Assigned Districts*, Bombay, 1870, p. 258.

[106] *Chicklee Taluka Settlement Report, 1866*, No. 51 of 1866, para 11.

and loyal 'natives' were organized for protection.

The work of survey was temporarily disrupted by the uprising of 1857. The mutineers and the Rohillas attacked survey parties in Berar. The crossing of Narmada by Tantia Topi caused fear all over the Deccan. The survey officers were ordered to assist in the work of suppressing the mutiny.[109] The Survey Department received large number of anonymous petitions from influential landholders whose income was curtailed as a result of survey operations.[110] Interested parties among cultivators like patels, deshpandias, and deshmukhs often exerted their influence at the local level to obstruct survey operations and retard the progress of the settlement. This was a response to the demobilization of local power by the colonial state. This type of resistance often took the form of concealment of the actual cultivated acreage. It was precisely the job of survey parties to detect such cases. Whenever such cases were detected, the incumbents were severely dealt with.[111]

The most resistance to survey operations came from privatization of forest and waste lands and enhancement of revenue. The laws and rules to control forest and waste land were a constant source of irritation to the people dwelling and depending on it for survival. The survey officer of the Darwa taluka reports in 1872:

> In no part of Berar perhaps is the preservation of timber so much needed as here, but in one respect the forest rules appear to me to entail more hardship than there is any need for. The ryots have hitherto had the free use of all the firewood they required. This privilege has ceased to exist, and although the tax now levied is a just one, it is looked upon as a great grievance, not so much on account of its being a tax, and perhaps a rather heavy one, as on account of the numerous and occasionally serious annoyances inseparable from its levy.[112]

The people were resisting not so much the tax itself but the system which imposed it. The colonial system was curtailing the

[107] *Report on the Administration of the Hyderabad Assigned Districts for the Year 1866-67*, Hyderabad, 1867, para 61.

[108] *Report on Survey and Settlement Operations in the Hyderabad Assigned Districts for the Year ending 31st October 1872*, Hyderabad, p. 3.

[109] *Hyderabad Affairs*, Vol. I (1883), compiled by Moulvie Syed Mahdi Ali, Bombay, 1883-6, pp. 55, 57.

[110] *Report on Survey and Settlement Operations in the Hyderabad Assigned Districts for the Year ending 31st October 1872*, Hyderabad, p. 11.

[111] *Akote Taluka Settlement Report*, No. 268 of 1867, para 16.

[112] *Darwa Taluka Settlement Report*, No. 420 of 1872, para 8.

freedom of mobility and prohibiting the use of goods and services which were hitherto freely available. In yet another settlement report the survey chief writes:

The natives informed me that the wood traffic has considerably decreased since the introduction of the new taxes on wood and grass, which appear to be some what oppressive. The people complain loudly of the new taxation, perhaps even more of the system than of the actual weight of the tax. If I may be allowed to express an opinion on the subject, my belief is, that these direct and at the same time inquisitorial taxes will always be unpopular, as they must be attended in a country like India with a considerable amount of oppression.[113]

During the decade of the 1890s when the original settlement was coming under revision, the Indian National Congress (founded in 1885) had begun to irritate the government by openly discussing the land revenue system.[114] The 1890s was also a decade of severe famine. For the first time in Berar notices had to be issued for the collection of land revenue. Table 9 gives figures for the total number of land revenue notices issued in just one of the 20 talukas of Berar.[115]

Conclusion

To summarize, the survey and settlement operations transformed the face of Berar by completely overhauling its landholding and revenue structure. This feat was achieved scientifically by the application of the latest available technology. Sophisticated technology without the backing of force would have been ineffective. A great display of political and military power preceded the survey operations. The transformation besides being physical was also psychological. The colonial state influenced people's thinking by constantly injecting the idea of private property rights in land. The consequences of this approach were devastating. The rights of landlords and tenants were established

[113] *Morsi Taluka Settlement Report*. No. 563 of 1871, para 16.

[114] 'Note on the proposals in Revenue Department', Nos. 1543/180-2, dated 9 July 1897, for revision of the *Berar Patel and Patwari Law, 1886*, by T. Chichele-Plowden, Resident at Hyderabad, in *Proceedings of the Hyderabad Administration on Matters of Routine for the Month of July 1898*, submitted to the Revenue and Agriculture Department, No. 206, 9 July 1898.

[115] *Mangrul Settlement Report*, No. 312 of 1900, para 30.

TABLE 9

Year	*No. of Notices*
1893-4	309
1894-5	229
1895-6	169
1896-7	333
1897-8	210
1898-9	375
TOTAL	1625

and defined leading to sub-tenancy, rack-renting and indebtedness. Surveys accurately measured and defined estates paving the way for moneylenders to lend more freely on the security of ascertained interests in land. Railways and roads opened out new markets and brought Berar within the orbit of the world market. The cultivation expanded enormously at the expense of waste lands. The cultivator felt himself circumscribed in his miscellaneous perquisites of pasture and forest produce and his liberty of fallowing was curtailed as a result of pressure on land.[116] Trade was brisker and vast amounts of cotton was permanently leaving the region causing loss of surplus and shortages. The colonial state ensured the supply of raw cotton causing devastation to the economy and society. Cotton under colonialism became the curse of Berar. However, the most important outcome of the survey operation was the creation of a *khatedari* class attached to the land. The role of *khatedars* in the colonial political economy is the subject of the next chapter.

[116] 'Note on the Economic Condition of the Agricultural Population of India', by J. B. Piele, in the *Report of Famine Commission, 1880*, London, 1881, p. 162.

CHAPTER 3

Changes in Berar Rural Social Relations under Colonialism: The *Khatedari* System

BERAR IN THE mid-nineteenth century came to be ruled by the book. Dozens of laws, acts, codes, decrees, circulars, and orders were prepared to empower colonial officials with maximum authority and control over those they ruled (Indians). It succeeded in acquiring a position as close to a totalitarian state any government could achieve in the nineteenth century. This manifested itself in transformation of the *balutedari* into the *khatedari* system of landholding. Colonialism reordered pre-existing forms of social organization and production. A. C. Lyall in his gazetteer (1870) compares the *khatedari* system with the feudal system of copyhold estates in the reservations of English manor lords.[1] Here the colonial state was the manor lord and government registered tenant (*khatedar*) was the copyholder. The *khatedars* were coined in the image of the farmers and graziers of England before the enclosure movement of the sixteenth and seventeenth century.[2] He (*khatedar*) was at the mercy of the government and his right existed only so long as he paid the government land revenue demand. Default of revenue payment automatically led to the seizure of all rights over the land and its produce.

By definition a *khatedar* then was a registered occupancy tenant who accepted state as a superior landlord. He entered into a contract with the state. This contractual bond was executed after an

[1] A. C. Lyall, *Gazetteers for the Haidarabad Assigned Districts, Commonly called Berar*, Bombay, 1870, p. 96.

[2] *Report of the Census of Berar, 1881*, Bombay, 1882, p. 177.

elaborate survey and settlement operation. The revenue rate was fixed on the land based on its proximity to the railway line, the market town and the metalled road. Theoretically the *khatedar* held land directly from the state, subject to revision at the termination of thirty years. But in reality he held the land from year to year subject to the payment of land revenue. The holding of la nd was therefore conditional on revenue payment. The Famine Commission of 1880 defined *khatedar* as '. . . the agriculturist . . . possesses only right of occupancy, which . . . is declared to be a transferable and heritable property, and the occupant is not deprived of it so long as he continues to pay the assessment due upon his land . . .'[3] The colonial government was the owner of all land in Berar. During Mughal times also the state was the owner of all lands but it had not strictly enforced this law and the state ownership existed largely in the realm of customs and conventions. But the colonial government took this law from the realm of theory to reality. It strictly enforced its proprietary right by laying claim over forests, waste lands and grazing grounds. The state ownership in pre-colonial Berar had been a very loosely understood concept. The villages then had enjoyed some degree of autonomy as the dominant clan exercised its authority at the local level. The village cultivators had felt the whip of the dominant family much more strongly than the oppression of the Mughal state. But under colonialism the state replaced the clan power with its own power.

The state was equally merciless on the *khatedars*. Many of the government registered tenants lived in a precarious state. Mr. Bahmanji Jamasji, a colonial official, describes their pathetic state in the following manner:

> . . . they [*khatedars*] really live in the most precarious manner, that their income in most cases meets, and barely meets, their necessities, and while of them a favored few may have enough to spare, their number is more than counterbalanced by those who really have not a sufficiency to meet their most ordinary wants, and whose state is practically an endless bondage of indebtedness.[4]

Indebtedness was a chronic problem of the *khatedars*. They had land but no capital to work it. The only source to obtain capital was

[3] *Report of Famine Commission, 1880,* London, 1881, p. 296.
[4] *Report of Famine Commission, 1880,* London, 1881, p. 299.

through the services of the moneylender at exorbitant rates of interest. Irrespective of whether the land was under cultivation or not, every *khatedar* was obligated to pay the government land revenue demand. In pre-colonial times all lands not under cultivation was exempt from land revenue payment. But under colonialism the remissions were refused even during crop failure and famine. This left no choice for the *khatedar* but to fall into the cycle of debt.

The *khatedari* holding in Berar ranged from 5 to 45 acres with an average of 20 acres per *khatedar*.[5] The land revenue itself was charged at the rate of Rs.1-5-0 per acre. At a conservative estimate, the cost of cultivation per acre with all the miscellaneous expenses came to about Rs.20/- per acre.[6] This excluded the expenses on basic necessities of food, clothing, and shelter. On average a *khatedar* borrowed Rs.100/- to cover for all the expenses and immediately went into debt by mortgaging his crop. The whiff of cotton and private property in land lured moneylenders into Berar.

The state defined land to incorporate almost everything which could be taxed. Its definition of land was so elaborate that nothing escaped. The Berar Land Revenue Code described land in the following manner:

> All public roads, lanes and paths, the bridges, ditches, dykes and fences on or beside the same, the beds or rivers, streams, nalas, lakes and tanks, and all canals and water-courses, and all standing and flowing water, and all lands whereever situated, . . . are, and are hereby declared to be, . . . the property of the Government. . . .[7]

The same document also claimed the fruit on the tree and even the juice in the fruit to be a part of the land and hence government property.

[5] From: T. Chichele Plowden, Commissioner, Hyderabad Assigned Districts, To: The Secretary for Berar to the Resident at Hyderabad, Amraoti, 31 January 1890, in the *Proceedings of the Hyderabad Administration on Matters of Routine for the Month of October 1890*, submitted to Foreign Department, No. 70-G, 4 March 1890.

[6] From: R. D. Hare, Assistant Commissioner on Special Duty, To: The Commissioner, Hyderabad Assigned Districts, Bulgaon, 14 April 1887, in the *Proceedings of the Hyderabad Administration for the Month of January 1888*, submitted to the Revenue and Agriculture Department, No. 9-R, 3 January 1888.

[7] *The Berar Land Revenue Code, 1896*, in *British Enactments in Force in Berar*, 1916, p. 112.

> 'Land' includes the sites of villages, towns and cities; it also includes trees, growing crops and grass, fruit upon, and juice in, trees, rights of way, ferries, fisheries, and all other benefits to arise out of land and things attached to the earth, or permanently fastened to things attached to the earth, and also shares in, or charges on, the revenue or rent of villages, or other defined portions of territory.[8]

On failure to pay the land revenue, the occupant automatically lost all rights over trees and buildings. And whenever the land was auctioned, the trees and buildings had to be bought separately.[9]

Although legally the government granted proprietary rights to the *khatedars* but in practice no sale, lease, or mortgage could be executed without the permission of the government. Such a stringent government supervision prevented the development of land market in Berar. Out of the total cultivated acreage of 5,410,435 acres in 1870 and 7,677,914 in 1895, only 1,762 acres traded hands in 1877-8 and 543 acres in 1878-9.[10] The proprietary rights in land was really very superficial. The bond placed the government property (land) under the care of the *khatedar* and *khatedar* in turn was placed under the care of the government.[11] This prodded the government to depute the Survey Department and prepare detailed maps and rent-rolls on all *khatedars*. It showed field by field occupancy along with the name of each and every field holder in every single village of Berar. It showed the net amount of land revenue due to government together with cesses thereon. It also showed the number of instalments in which the revenue was to be paid, along with the amount of each and the date on which they were due.[12]

[8] *The Berar Land Revenue Code, 1896,* p. 102.

[9] *Central Provinces and Berar: A Review of the Administration of the Province,* Vol. II, Nagpur, 1923, p. 221.

[10] This data is taken from the following sources: *Report on the Revenue Administration of the Hyderabad Assigned Districts for the Year, 1878-79,* Hyderabad, 1879, p. 31; A. C. Lyall, *Gazetteers for the Haidarabad Assigned Districts, commonly called Berar,* 1870, pp. 108-10; *Proceedings of the Hyderabad Administration on Matters of Routine for the Month of September 1895,* submitted to the Revenue and Agriculture Department, No. 337, 28 September 1895.

[11] *The Berar Land Revenue Code, 1896,* 1916, p. 163.

[12] *Report on the Administration of the Hyderabad Assigned Districts for the Year 1900-1,* Hyderabad, 1902, p. 53.

Drawing Boundaries to Define Property

The single most effective weapon which did maximum damage to the pre-existing *balutedari* system was the introduction of boundary marks in Berar. The creation of private property rights in land could not be guaranteed without delineation. The boundary marks represented the operation which guaranteed land revenue. The centuries-old natural geography of Berar was thus broken into bits and pieces of scattered land. But the purpose was achieved. The entire province registered a net increase of 32.1 per cent in land revenue collection. Table 10 shows a marked increase in rates between the original settlement (1861) and the revision settlement (1892).[13]

TABLE 10

Old Rate Rs.	A.	P.	*No. of Villages*	*Final Rate* Rs.	A.	P.	*% Increase*
			Group I				
1	8	0	29	1	12	0	16.7
1	4	0	77	1	12	0	36.0
1	1	0	117	1	12	0	36.4
0	14	0	22	1	12	0	76.7
			Group II				
1	8	0	1	1	8	0	0.0
1	4	0	9	1	8	0	21.7
1	1	0	43	1	8	0	37.9
			Group III				
1	4	0	1	1	2	0	-7.1
1	1	0	3	1	2	0	3.4
0	14	0	16	1	2	0	17.8
			Average % Increase				32.1 %

A one per cent average revenue increase per annum in addition to causing hardship caught the *khatedars* in the vice grip of colonial maps and lithographs. The latest European mapping and printing technology was employed to thoroughly demarcate boundaries. Each and every village was separated and the holdings of every

[13] *Basim Taluka Settlement Report*, No. 203 of 1900, para 37, pp. 12-13.

single *khatedar* was mapped to the last detail so that no village or *khatedar* escaped the payment of revenue demand. By this method the government also kept a strong vigil over the activities of the *khatedar* class. The villages and holdings were transferred unceremoniously between districts and taluks without any regard to the social situation of the people. Many *khatedars* found themselves caught in the artificial boundary markings as the identities of villages was being wiped out by these boundaries.[14] The boundary marks and private property rights in land broke down the organic unity of the self-sufficient villages. This breaking of the atomic unity was necessary for the development of cotton market and Berar's linkage to world trade.[15]

This revolutionary transformation from *balutedari* to *khatedari* introduced in Berar an institutionalized form of private property in land. The boundary marks challenged and laid to rest the traditional Indian notions of proprietorship. It constantly reminded the people of the coming into existence of a new power whose authority demanded unquestioned loyalty. In fact loyalty was a pre-condition for obtaining *khatedari* rights. Disloyalty resulted in the forfeiture of the claims of not only the *khatedar* but his entire family for generations. So it was in the interest of the *khatedars* to submit to colonial authority for the fear of being ousted. Therefore the colonial government poured enormous effort to maintain these boundary marks in good order. The Government of India proclaimed the following order as the prime responsibility of every colonial official:

> It is the primary duty of the Deputy Commissioners to maintain the field boundary marks erected at the survey, and to see that they are preserved with the greatest care and repaired when necessary.[16]

[14] *Report on Survey and Settlement Operations in the Hyderabad Assigned Districts for the Year ending 31st October 1871*, Hyderabad, 1875, p. 56.

[15] Karl Marx in his *Asiatic Mode of Production* has developed this thesis in greater detail. See Marian Sawer, *Marxism and the Question of the Asiatic Mode of Production*, Nijhoff, 1977; Stephen Porter Dunn, *The Fall and Rise of the Asiatic Mode of Production*, 1982; also see A. R. Desai, *Social Background of Indian Nationalism*, Bombay, 1966; Irfan Habib, 'Problems of Marxist Historical Analysis', *Enquiry*, Vol. 3, No. 2 (1968); 'Colonization of the Indian Economy, 1757-1900', *Social Scientist*, March (1975).

[16] *Rules under the Berar Land Revenue Code, 1896*, Nagpur, 1907, p. 125.

Thus the entire cultivated land was divided into plots and each *khatedar* was allotted a survey number. The survey numbers were more or less of equivalent size whose boundaries could not be altered during the term of the settlement which was normally fixed for thirty years. Each survey number was separated by a boundary line known as *dhura*.[17] At the junction of these boundary lines a *warali* or an earthen mound was built. It was every *khatedar's* responsibility to keep the *waralis* and *dhuras* in good shape. The holders of culturable land could transfer their holdings with government permission. But the *khatedars* holding waste lands could not transfer their fields until it was brought under the plough.[18]

While British officials did only the most comfortable and supervisory jobs, the Indian officials had to do the most labourious task of the actual inspection of the boundary marks on the ground. Between 1 November and 15 December of each year the patels and patwaris inspected the boundary marks of each survey number in every village. There were strict rules for monitoring this work:

> Early in October the Tahsildar will issue . . . a general notice at each village calling on all occupants and other interested persons to repair their boundary marks by the end of October, warning them that if after that date any boundary marks are found in a state of disrepair, such boundary marks will be liable to be repaired by hired labour and the cost recovered from the defaulters as an arrear of land-revenue.[19]

Any default of boundary strip or encroachment on government land was immediately reported for legal action. Often times the government hired private contractors to erect boundary marks to demarcate waste lands from cultivated lands. The rate charged was 9.5 annas for each earthen mound and 5.5 annas for the stone marker. The stone marker known as *gota pathar*[20] was more

[17] A *dhura* was a narrow strip of fallow land 4.5 feet in breadth and 3 feet in height. For more detail see *Central Provinces and Berar: A Review of the Administration of the Province*, Vol. II, Nagpur, 1923, para 218.

[18] *Yeotmal District Gazetteer,* Calcutta, 1908, p. 78.

[19] *Rules under the Berar Land Revenue Code, 1896,* 1907, p. 126.

[20] A *gota pathar* was a rectangular stone slab of an approximate length of 2.5 to 3 feet and a width of one feet sunk in the ground at a 90 degree angle. For detail see: *Central Provinces and Berar: A Review of the Administration of the Province,* Vol. II, Nagpur, 1923, para 218.

popular than the earthen mound which had the tendency to be washed away by monsoon rain. The charges of erecting these boundary marks were recovered from the *khatedars*.[21] But in general the *khatedars* maintained these boundary marks out of their own expense which was equivalent to the amount of land revenue itself. This further added the pressure of revenue and debt on the *khatedars*. Even the cost of preparation of the record of rights and annual measurement of boundaries was recovered from *khatedars*. The negligent *khatedars* were asked to demarcate boundaries, build and maintain fences.[22] The colonial government really did not incur any expenditure.[23] Its main purpose was to generate income from every source possible and boundary- marking was one such vital source.

Structure of Landholding and Cultivation

The structure of landholding in Berar although primarily *khatedari* was also based on sharecropping and tenancy. The actual cultivation was done in many different ways. The following were the several ways in which the land was cultivated:[24]

1. *Metaire* tenure in which the *khatedar* sublet in return for half the produce and paid government rent. The subholder incurred all the expenses including the operating cost.
2. In addition to paying half the produce, the subholder also paid 1/3rd of government rent.
3. The sub-renter paid 1/4th of the produce and half the government rent.
4. *Ang bail ki* tenure by which the *khatedar* took partners and shares were divided according to the labour provided by each partner. Each pair of bullock and one man was treated as one unit share.
5. Often times moneylenders and large *khatedars* possessed bullocks and rented them out on loan.

[21] *Report on Survey and Settlement Operations in the Hyderabad Assigned Districts for the Year ending 31st October 1873*, Hyderabad, 1874, p. 10.

[22] *The Berar Land Revenue Code, 1896*, 1916, p. 133.

[23] *The Berar Land Revenue Code, 1896*, 1916, p. 130.

[24] A. C. Lyall, *Gazetteer for the Haidarabad Assigned Districts*, 1870, p. 165.

6. Some cultivators cultivated another cultivator's holding under special contract on a limited period of occupancy.
7. A subtenant paying cash rent and cultivating from year to year. Such tenants obtained occupancy rights after twelve years of continuous cultivation.

Mr. Furdoonji Jamshedji, a colonial official and a shrewd observer of agrarian society in Aurangabad, has provided us with a very graphic class categorization of Berar peasantry. He divides the agrarian society into four classes in the following manner:[25]

1. The upper caste who also formed the upper class of the agrarian order comprised of mostly brahmans, well-to-do marattas, rajputs, and prosperous artisans. This class had a sprinkling of kunbis also. This class did not work the land and considered touching the plough as a social taboo. Most of their land was worked by lower caste cultivators. The holdings ranged on average from 50 to 60 acres.
2. This class indulged in garden cultivation comprising of mostly fruits and vegetables. They also raised milch cattle and dairy stock. They did not work in the field but supervised farm families and labourers. The caste composition of this class was mostly kunbis, telis, and malis.
3. This class laboured full-time in the field along with their families and solely depended upon land for subsistence. They indulged in mostly dry crop cultivation like wheat, millets, and cotton. This class was not very prosperous and lived on the margin of subsistence.
4. This class worked mostly as hired labourers or co-sharers. They practically did not own any land and lived from hand to mouth and their children were employed as cattle herders and crop watchers. They provided services to the upper caste and in return received remuneration in cash and kind. Almost everyone of them was from the untouchable caste of mahars, mangs, chambars, dhobis, dhungurs, kumhars, etc.

The upper caste and the garden cultivators were all government registered *khatedars* and seldom cultivated the land themselves.

[25] *Notes on the Agriculturists of the District of Aurangabad. H. H. The Nizam's Dominion*, by Furdoonji Jamshedji, Superintendent, Revenue Survey and Assessment, N.W. Division, in *Hyderabad Affairs*, Vol. I (n.d.), pp. 801-33.

But the majority of the *khatedars* were full-time farmers who laboured on the land along with their entire families. They acquired land through distempered biddings[26] and borrowed to start cultivation. They also sublet their holdings. But cultivation occupancy and indebtedness was a compatible feature of the *khatedari* system. It also divorced *khatedari* from the *balutedari* system.

Women labour was freely employed by all classes except the upper class who preferred their womenfolk to be within the bounds of the household. Majority of the *khatedars* were men. However, a small per centage of them were also women.[27] Out of a total of 162,540 *khatedars* recorded by the census of 1881, 8,585 or 5.2 per cent were women. Most of the female *khatedars* were either from the upper caste or kunbis.[28] The disappearance of *balutedari* by no means weakened the caste system or the oppression of women. Women in lower caste families generated some income through field labour. The women in upper caste families wholely depended upon men for subsistence.

The upper caste followed other trades and profession in addition to agriculture. The brahmins, rajputs, and marwaris often worked for the colonial government. In fact this gave them a better leverage over society. The colonial state used them as an instrument of social control. It was with the assistance of Maratha brahmins and Bengali baboos that the colonial state had subjugated Berar. Due to the existence of general illiteracy hardly many Beraris could work for the colonial government. Writing about the brahmins, A. C. Lyall narrates:

> They rarely take to any profession requiring manual labour or skill, to the plough, or still more rarely, to the sword. They had monopolized the education of the country . . . they had absorbed all literate work, and are still dominant in every Government office.[29]

Far from weakening the caste system as the colonizers argued, the *khatedari* system further enhanced the oppression of the lower

[26] After every survey the colonial government auctioned land to the highest bidder. The purchaser borrowed the capital to pay for the purchase, the rental demand, and the operating cost. This type of transaction was known as 'distempered bidding'. For more detail see *Proceedings of the Hyderabad Administration for the Month of October 1874,* submitted to the Home Department, No. 99, 26 October 1874.

[27] *Report of the Famine Commission in India, 1880,* London, 1881, p. 162.

[28] *Report on the Census of Berar, 1881,* 1882, pp. 184-5.

[29] A. C. Lyall, *Gazetteer of the Haidarabad Assigned Districts,* 1870, p. 183.

TABLE 11

Year	*Total No. of Khatedars*	*Total Cultivated Area in Acres*	*Cultivated Acreage Per Khatedar*
1870	226,207	5,410,435	23.9
1875	279,731	NA	NA
1881	162,540	NA	NA
1891	222,180	NA	NA
1893	290,828	8,168,592	28.0
1895	162,500	7,677,914	47.2
Average	223,997	7,085,647	33.0

Sources: Statistical Abstracts Relating to British India from 1882-83 to 1891-92, No. 27, London, 1893; *Census of 1901*; *Report on the Census of Berar, 1881*, Bombay, 1882; *Proceedings of the Hyderabad Administration on Matters of Routine for the Month of September, 1895*, submitted to the Revenue and Agricultural Department, No. 337, 28 September 1895; A. C. Lyall, *Gazetteer of the Haidarabad Assigned Districts, Commonly called Berar*, 1870; *Census of 1891; Report on the Census of 1881*, Bombay, 1882; *Report of Famine Commission, 1880*, London, 1881; *Report on the Cotton Department for the Year 1868-69*, by Harry Rivett-Carnac, Bombay, 1869.

caste. The upper caste still exercised priority rights over temples, festivals, and worship. In majority of the temples in Berar the lower caste were not permitted to enter. Furthermore, no untouchable group was even allowed to light the *holi* fire before the upper caste lit their own fire.[30]

Data on the total number of *khatedars* and the area held by them are scattered and far from complete. Yet it is not very difficult to formulate a statistical picture of Berar *khatedars*. Table 11 gives the total number of *khatedars* in Berar during the period under study.

This Table shows that on average there were a quarter of million *khatedars* in Berar at any given point in time between 1870 and 1900. Each *khatedar* on average held 33 cultivated acres. An average *khatedari* family constituted about 5 to 8 members and cultivated approximately 20 acres and the rest was leased on subtenancy in various ways mentioned above. Before moving on to analyse the extent of subtenancy and rack-renting it is essential to show the extent of *khatedari* holdings in proportion to all other types of land tenures. Table 12 presents a

[30] A. C. Lyall, *Gazetteer of the Haidarabad Assigned Districts*, 1870, p. 218.

TABLE 12

Nature of Tenure	*No. of Estates* %	*No. of Villages* %	*No. of Holders or Shareholders* %	*Gross Area in Acres* %
Khatedari	94.5	86.6	96.6	85.4
Revenue free	3.8	5.8	2.8	4.4
Waste lands	0.7	0.8	0.02	0.8
Redeemed Revenue	0.09	0.05	0.001	0.06
Zamindars paying Rs.1000 to 100 Revenue	0.05	3.0	0.08	6.2
Small zamindars paying less than Rs.100	0.04	2.6	0.06	2.3

profile in per centages of various tenures in the year 1891-2 in the following manner.[31]

The above statement clearly shows that the predominant form of land tenure in Berar was *khatedari*. All other forms of landholdings were basically marginalized under colonialism. While the gross cropped area and the number of villages under *khatedari* exceeded 85 per cent, the overwhelming majority of landholders were *khatedars*. But these government registered tenants did not cultivate all the lands in Berar. Although the colonial state did not recognize the existence of undertenants, there was in fact a large underclass of subtenants in Berar. As mentioned earlier, there is no data available on their numbers. Although the data is scanty yet there is plenty of evidence that reveals the existence of subtenancy. It is estimated that more than half the cultivated land was leased out to untouchables on oral contract or bonded labour. They also formed more than half the cultivating labour force.[32]

Before analysing subtenancy let us look at the caste composition of *khatedars*. In 1881-2 caste composition (per centages in descending order) of the *khatedars* in Berar is given in Table 13.[33] From this table it can be gauged that *khatedari* was a multi-caste system. It

[31] *Statistical Abstracts Relating to British India from 1882-83 to 1891-92*, No. 27, London, 1893, p. 156.

[32] *Census of India, 1891, Berar or the Hyderabad Assigned Districts*, Calcutta, 1892, p. cxxxv.

[33] *Report on the Census of Berar, 1881*, 1882, pp. 184-5.

TABLE 13

Khatedars	%
Kunbi	55.0
Mali (gardeners)	14.6
Musalman	4.2
Teli (oiler)	3.4
Mahar (sweeper)	3.1
Rajput	2.6
Dhangar (herder)	2.5
Brahmins	2.3
Andh (tribal)	1.9
Korku (tribal)	1.9
Wani	1.7
Bari	1.5
Gond (tribal)	1.3
Koli	1.3
Wanjari	1.3
Mahali	0.8
TOTAL	100

constituted both the lower and the upper caste. The kunbis and malis formed over 60 per cent of the *khatedars* of Berar. From the above list only brahmins, rajputs, and malis can be classed as the upper caste. While all the rest formed the lower caste yet the kunbis, telis, wanis, and baris ranked higher than the rest in terms of social status.

The caste system was subjugated to service the colonial state. The loyalty of *khatedar* class was guaranteed through the system of land proprietorship. The colonial government and the colonizers patronized the caste system. Throughout Indian history the upper castes had tended to collaborate with the conquerors. After the military subjugation of India the colonial state enlisted the support of loyal brahmins, rajputs, and such 'well-bred' men to act as peons of the colonial state. Under the patronage of their European masters the arrogance of the upper caste did not diminish. The upper caste themselves were victims of colonial racism as the European rulers looked down upon Indians in general irrespective of caste. The colonial documents of the nineteenth century are full of pejorative terms used to address Indian people. Terms such as native-niggers, idol-worshippers, animistic barbarians, low-born natives, etc., were not only used freely in these documents but also in their day-to-day speech and language. Colonialism in India and Berar represented violence and oppression of the people of non-European descent by the Europeans. Several English philosophers and thinkers of the nineteenth century in fact justified British colonial and paternalist attitude towards Indian people.[34]

Although much revered in Europe, the English philosophers and thinkers like James Mill, John Stuart Mill, Jeremy Bentham, and Macaulay regarded India as inferior on the scale of civilization compared to Europe. They recommended colonialism as a way to lift India from the depths of darkness and ignorance to the light of knowledge and enlightenment represented by Europe. James Mill wrote eighteen volumes on the history of India to prove that India was below Europe on the scale of civilization. It took nearly two decades for Mill to write these volumes but like his other contemporaries never did he ever visit India in his life time and nor did he know any Indian language. In the early nineteenth century there was hardly any translation of Indian literature available in Europe. Therefore Mill's volumes on the history of India was primarily based on his philosophical intuition, Euro-centric and racist notions of societies and cultures outside Europe.[35] In fact most of the European philosophers writing about India in the nineteenth century were approaching India from their Euro-centric prejudices. The colonizers who came to India as rulers, administrators, traders, bureaucrats and missionaries were in fact much less intellectually inclined than these philosophers from whom they took ideas and inspiration.

Therefore it is not surprising at all that the colonizers looked at Indians from their pre-conceived prejudices and divided the people on the basis of race, colour, caste, religion, and such other racial categories. Large numbers of people who did not fit into the prejudicial categories of the colonial mind were excluded from the official documents. One such large group was that of the subtenants of Berar. Only by recreating these subordinated groups can we now successfully challenge the Euro-centric racism perpetrated by colonialism not only in Berar but throughout the world. Whereever the colonial trade spread, racism followed in its trail. The rise of racism in the world can be appropriately associated with the rise of

[34] See Eric Stokes, *The English Utilitarians and India*, Oxford, 1959.
[35] See James Mill, *The History of British India*, abridged, Chicago, 1975.

colonialism. It is in this context that the exploitation of *khatedars* and subtenants can be better understood.

The Buldana District Gazetteer mentions that 'changes of dynasties and chronicles of wars attract the historian, but the uneventful lives of the patient masses are passed by in silence'.[36] This is a perceptive observation as it challenges the present-day investigators and urges us to recreate the lives of the patient masses. But by no means were the lives of these patient masses uneventful. The colonial government did not take any interest in registering things which did not generate revenue and income for the state. Obfuscation of subtenancy information is the characteristic feature of colonial documents pertaining to Berar. However, bits and pieces of information on subtenants lies scattered in half a century of colonial documents. It is therefore not impossible to recreate the life and times of subtenants under colonialism.

Subtenancy in Berar

The subtenants or *bhagindars* worked for the *khatedars* in return for a share of the crop. The term *bhagindar* literally meant a sharecropper. The system of subtenancy therefore was based on sharecropping. The subtenants in most cases were landless. In general there were two types of sharecroppers in Berar, i.e. co-sharers and co-occupants. The former were partners of the *khatedar* and worked for him on a joint stock principle. Under this system of cultivation the stocks were pooled together and shares of the produce were divided according to the units of stock provided by each family. The units were counted as *ang* and *bail* or 'body' and 'bullock'. Two bullocks were counted as one body unit. *Ang* was the share of labour power and *bail* was the share of bullock power. The generic word for these two types of sharecroppers was *ang-bhagindar* and *bail-bhagindar*. *Ang-bhagindars* were very poor and possessed nothing except their body and labour. *Bail-bhagindar* were also very poor and possessed nothing except a pair of bullocks to supplement their labour.[37]

[36] *Buldana District Gazetteer*, Calcutta, 1910, p. 230.

[37] *Report on the Census of Berar, 1881*, Bombay, 1882, p. 185.

TABLE 14

Year	*Total No. of Khatedars*	*Approximate No. of Bhagindars*
1870	226,207	452,414
1875	279,731	559,462
1881	162,540	325,080
1891	222,180	444,360
1893	290,828	581,656
1895	162,500	325,000
Average	223,997	447,995

Co-occupants on the other hand rented whole fields from the *khatedar* in exchange for either a fixed cash or grain rent. They usually borrowed bullocks and implements on loan. They cultivated the land as independent cultivators on oral contract and were not registered with the government. Their contracts ran from year to year and renewal was at the pleasure of the *khatedar*. While co-sharers were usually people of the same caste, the co-occupancy extended beyond caste. In the rich cotton belt of the Poorna valley co-sharing was more prominent. The co-occupancy persisted in the less fertile areas of the hills and ghats.[38] In the Poorna valley it was common for a single family to open a survey number and cultivate it as co-sharing with extended family units. In the hill region independent subtenancies existed alongside *khatedari* households. Irrespective of whether it was a co-sharing or co-occupancy, the tenancy law defined subtenant as '. . . a person who holds land of another person and is, or, but for a contract, would be, liable to pay rent for such land to such other person . . . '.[39] The Famine Commission Report of 1880 observed that the 'Government deals only with the registered occupant or khatedar, and we have no returns to show the area cultivated under each of the occupancy tenures . . .'.[40]

Although we have the actual number of *khatedars*, we do not have the numbers for *bhagindars*. But with the available data it is feasible to form a reasonable estimate of their numbers. The census of 1891 states

[38] *Report of the Census of Berar, 1881,* Bombay, 1882, p.186.

[39] *The Berar Alienated Villages Tenancy Law, 1921,* in *The Berar Code,* Nagpur, 1931, p. 89.

[40] *Report of Famine Commission, 1880,* p. 341.

that the *bhagindars* outnumbered *khatedars* by a ratio of 2:1.[41] At this ratio the total number of *bhagindars* is given in Table 14.

The census of 1891 also states the total number of persons with direct interest in land to be at 997,602. So the total number of *bhagindars* on average constituted 44.9 per cent of the total agrarian labour force (the total population of Berar according to the census of 1891 was 2,897,491). The caste composition of *bhagindars* coincided with the *khatedars*. Table 15 lists *bhagindari* and *khatedari* castes in percentages.[42]

TABLE 15

Caste and Communal Composition	*Bhagindari %*	*Khatedari %*
Kunbi	57.9	55.0
Mali	14.1	14.6
Mahar	4.6	3.1
Musulman	4.1	4.2
Dhangars	3.2	2.5
Telis	2.9	3.4
Rajputs	2.0	2.6
Andhs	1.8	1.9
Gonds	1.6	1.3
Kolis	1.4	1.3
Baris	1.4	1.5
Banjaras	1.3	1.3

It is interesting to note that the *bhagindars* like the *khatedars* came from all different castes suggesting that the *khatedari* system cut across caste lines and polarized along class lines. However, the majority of *khatedars* and *bhagindars* were kunbis. The *khatedars* as registered tenants of the government had their tenures secured so long as they complied with the government revenue demand. The *bhagindars* did not have any tenures but the difference between them and the *khatedars* was very slender. Mr. G. S. Khaparde, a High Court vakil of Amraoti, writes in 1895 thus about *bhagindars* and *khatedars*:

> . . . in principle the distinction between the one class and the other is so slender as to vanish altogether if minutely examined. Everybody else is more or less

[41] *Census of India, 1891, Berar or the Hyderabad Assigned Districts,* Calcutta, 1892, p. cxxxv.

[42] *Report on the Census of Berar,* 1881, pp. 184-5.

either its tenants or assignee of certain specified rights. These are greater or smaller according to the nature of holding, but the fact remains that nobody except Government can be said to be the proprietor of the soil. All others are either occupants or assignees of certain rights.[43]

The high rate of indebtedness among the *khatedars* pushed the rental demand to as much as five times the government revenue demand. The rack-renting racket further elbowed the *bhagindars* to the margin of subsistence. Contrary to the colonial indifference and outright denial of the existence of subtenancy, the practice of rack-rent is yet another indicator of the existence of subtenancy in Berar. Rack-rent is a phenomenon when a *khatedar* sublets the land to the *bhagindar* at an appreciated rate of rental demand compared to the rate of government revenue demand. It is important here to stress the difference between revenue and rent. Revenue was the rate which the *khatedar* paid to the colonial state while rent was the rate which the *bhagindar* paid to the *khatedar*. The rental rate was fixed on the basis of government revenue demand. So the rental rate was approximately 5 times higher than the survey assessment rate.[44] This also suggests increased intensification of labour exploitation of unpaid and underpaid women and children's labour within the peasant household. Table 16 shows the rack-rent per centage to government revenue demand in various districts of Berar.[45]

TABLE 16

District	%
Amraoti	61.0
Akola	63.8
Ellichpur	54.4
Buldana	48.8
Wun	41.7
Average	53.94

The existence of such a high per centage of rack-renting suggests a state of intense indebtedness of *khatedars*. The *khatedar*, who was

[43] From: G. S. Khaparde, High Court Vakil, Amraoti, To: The Commissioner, Hyderabad Assigned District, Amraoti, dated 19 July 1895, submitted to the Revenue and Agricultural Department, No. 337, 28 September 1895.

[44] *Basim Taluk Settlement Report,* No. 203 of 1900, paras 18-23, p. 6.

[45] *Report on the Census of Berar, 1881,* p. 223.

also a government registered tenant, was a free target of the moneylender as the latter thrived under the legal and institutional protection of the colonial state. The moneylenders on average charged 24 to 50 per cent interest on *khatedari* loans. In this state of indebtedness the *khatedars* simply shifted the burden of debt over to the *bhagindars*. However most of the *bhagindars* were in bondage to the *khatedars* and the *khatedars* were indebt to the moneylenders. The *khatedars* and *bhagindars* together formed the total agrarian labour force of Berar. Both this class of cultivators were indebted to the moneylender. The moneylenders however preferred government registered tenants over *bhagindars*. But since the *khatedars* shifted the burden of debt over to *bhagindars*, it was the latter who bore the brunt of the socio-economic oppression in the countryside.

Mr. Trimbuk Rao, the Tahsildar of Malkapur, after prolonged and careful enquiries found that 'in this taluk the owners of land let out their fields in no less than 28 ways, receiving in return from nil to five times as much as the land revenue of the fields let out in cases of cash, and from 1/21 to 1/2 of the produce of the soil let out with or without proportionate assessment of the fields'.[46] This observation shows the complexity of the land-renting pattern and how the government revenue demand became the yardstick of exorbitant rental demand. Subletting and rack-renting in addition to moneylending and indebtedness was the characteristic feature of the *khatedari* system in Berar. The colonial laws generally favoured the moneylenders and the *khatedars* viz-a-viz subtenants. The threat of legal action was often employed to keep the subtenants in a state of perpetual subjection.[47] Furthermore the *bhagindars* had no claim over the land they cultivated. Baden-Powell, the colonial authority on the question of land-systems, writes thus: 'Co-sharers in Berar, . . . can, under no circumstances, claim, under the revenue law, to have their shares demarcated or separately registered.'[48]

[46] *Report on the Revenue Administration of Hyderabad Assigned Districts for the Year 1879-80*, Hyderabad, 1880, p. 22.

[47] For the detailed clauses of one of the agrarian laws, see 'The Berar Alienated Villages Tenancy Law, 1921', in the *Berar Code*, Nagpur, 1931.

[48] Baden-Powell, *The Land-Systems of British India*, Vol. III, London, 1891, p. 353.

Even if the subtenants wanted to appeal, the courts were not open to them. In case of grievances they had nowhere to go. They were left to the mercy of the moneylenders and *khatedars*. The subtenancy situation described in the revenue report (1877-8) for the Ellichpur taluk can be fairly applied to the rest of Berar:

> numerous co-sharers not recorded at the settlement . . . are being ousted daily, . . . the civil courts are not open to them, and the revenue courts do not take up their complaints.[49]

In the absence of any legal protection, the *bhagindars* entered into oral contracts. The absence of written leases put the subtenants in a position of disadvantage as they could not prove their point in case of disputes. This problem seems to have been quite banal in Berar. It is confirmed by the following observation of the revenue report of 1877-8:

> Almost all subtenants are, as is well known, entirely in the hands of those from whom they hold their lands . . . the need khatedars have of their services is their protection that written leases are uncommon. . . .[50]

In order to keep the subtenants in bondage, the *khatedars* and moneylenders avoided giving receipts of the exorbitant rents paid by the subtenants.

Therefore it was said that the cultivators of Berar 'sowed their crops in sorrow and tended them in fear . . .'.[51]

The right of pre-emption did develop in Berar towards the close of the period under study. By this right, when a *khatedar* relinquished his position, the co-sharers and co-occupants were given the option to takeover the survey number under their own name. But unless the land was retaken within a year of relinquishment, the subtenants were demobilized and the state took possession of it.[52] The relinquishments were rare and in most cases the *bhagindars* were unable to organize enough capital to finance the purchase of a

[49] *Report on the Revenue Administration of the Hyderabad Assigned Districts for the Year 1877-78*, Hyderabad, 1878, p. 31.

[50] *Report on the Revenue Administration of the Hyderabad Assigned Districts for the Year 1877-78*, p. 30.

[51] *Buldana District Gazetteer*, Calcutta, 1910, p. 230.

[52] See *The Berar Land Revenue Code, 1896*, in the *British Enactments in Force in Berar*, 1916, p. 156; *Report on the Revenue Administration of the Hyderabad Assigned Districts for the Year 1877-78*, p. 31.

survey number. Moreover the system of oral contract and sub-tenure differed from taluka to taluka and according to the Deputy Commissioner of Akola (1881) it even differed from village to village and it can even be presumed to vary from *khatedar* to *khatedar*.[53] Under such a system the fragmentation of land was only natural. The Dariapur settlement officer reported as early as 1869 that 'in many villages the land is so minutely subdivided that the share of each cultivator barely suffices for his support'.[54] So the fragmentation of holdings in Berar began immediately after the survey and settlement operation. The fragmentation of holding is also an indicator of the existence of poverty in Berar. The sanitary commissioner's reports, the gazetteers, the census reports, general administration reports, revenue reports and all the colonial reports of the nineteenth century tell us that majority of the people of Berar lived in huts and tenements.

Except for the bungalows and houses of colonial officials and European merchants, Berar gave the appearance of abject poverty both in the cotton towns and the countryside. Government permission was needed for the people to build houses on the land. This was seldom given for the fear that the buildings cut into agricultural land and jeopardized the government revenue.[55] All illegal constructions were confiscated and the culprits were brought to court for trial. It was the duty of the patels (village headman) to report such activities in the countryside. The fact that such illegal activities were taking place in the countryside was a manifestation of the discontentment of the people towards the colonial control of land.

Poverty, Discontent and Everyday Forms of Resistance in Berar

James Scott in his book, *Weapons of the Weak*, has made a case for every day forms of peasant resistance in pre-industrial and colonial societies.[56] There is plenty of evidence of such forms of resistance in early colonial Berar even though the state took elaborate legal and institutional measures to prevent crop robbing, smuggling,

[53] *Report on the Census of Berar, 1881*, p. 185.

[54] *Dariapur Taluka Settlement Report*, No. 368 of 1869, para 16, p. 7.

[55] B. H. Baden-Powell, *The Land-systems of British India*, 1891, p. 370.

[56] James C. Scott, *Weapons of the Weak: Everyday Forms of Peasant Resistance*, New Haven, 1985.

illegal sale of cotton, trespassing, unauthorized occupancy, illegal cultivation, unauthorized cutting of grass and wood from government wastelands, felling of trees, etc. The colonial documents do not tell us how the peasants did this. However, the law codes and rules governing the conduct of colonial officials give us some information on the subversive activities of the agrarian population. The legal codes in colonial Berar were formed in response to popular resistance which the state dubbed as crime. The Berar Patel and Patwaris Law was one of the collection of laws which was compiled in a volume known as *British Enactments in Force in Berar.* The language used in this law profoundly suggests that the state was determined to wipe out any form of resistance to its authority. Therefore the Berar Patel and Patwaris Law stated that 'the strongest and fittest man in the village was needed to put down the evil doer within the gate or marauder without . . .'.[57] The musclemen and bullies were appointed as patels and patwaris to maintain colonial order in the villages. The jaglia or the uniformed village guard was appointed as an enforcer of patel's order. Why were such tough men appointed and why were such tough laws enacted prescribing in detail the duties and responsibilities of the village officials?

The high incidence of crop-robbing in the villages was countered by hiring thugs as local government officials. Whenever the government or the moneylender seized crops on the default of revenue the instances of crop-robbing became prominent. In addition to this, the government also had to deal with raids on grass, trees, and government controlled wastelands.[58] It should be noted that in Berar default generally followed occupancy, which according to government was unauthorized and illegal. The government then unleashed the patels and jaglias on such trespassers and forcibly evicted them by levying penalties and fines. The crops on defaulters lands were appropriated and disposed as the government deemed fit. Buildings and other structures constructed without government permission were forfeited.[59]

[57] *The Berar Patels and Patwaris Law, 1900,* D. V. Shidore, ed., Amraoti, 1935, p. 106.

[58] See *Rules Under the Berar Land Revenue Code, 1896,* pp. 85-6.

[59] *The Berar Land Revenue Code,* in *British Enactments in Force in Berar,* 1916, p. 118.

The illegal grazing on the officially designated wastelands and woodlands was a common problem for the government. This type of activity generally happened at night when the *khatedars* let loose their animals to freely graze in these lands. The government countered this type of illegal grazing by establishing 'cattle-pounds' in every village under the supervision of patels. Stray cattle found grazing on government lands were impounded and brought to these cattle prisons. The owners were then notified and heavy fines were levied. A new system of 'cattle-passes' was devised by which every single head of cattle in Berar was taxed. Similarly Pound Acts and Grazing Laws prohibited *khatedars* from letting their cattle freely roam in the fields without passes. Exhibiting pride in this power, the Deputy Commissioner of Wun District, writes:

> The Pound Act gives me ample power, and if I found that any particular . . . cowherd took his cattle into Government grazing grounds unprotected by passes, and if he had on former occasions similarly transgressed, I could proceed against him in extreme cases under the Penal Code (section 147).[60]

The European firms, the moneylenders, and the government were faced with a very strange problem dealing with the cultivation of cotton. Since most of the cotton was on contracts at pre-fixed prices, the cultivators resisted tending the cotton crop the same way as they did the grain crop.[61] Sometimes even the growth of cotton was disrupted reminiscent of the activities of 'luddites' in England during the industrial revolution.[62] The high rate of indebtedness gave rise to the attitude of indifference towards the cash crop. Often then the cotton was '. . . left for days lying in heaps exposed to both

[60] Memorandum by Lieutenant Colonel J. Fitzgerald, Deputy Commissioner, Wun District, dated 13 March 1886, in *Proceedings of the Hyderabad Administration for the Month of October 1887*, submitted to the Foreign Department, No. 445-G, 31 October 1887.

[61] *Report of the Cotton Department for the Year 1868-69*, by Harry Rivett-Carnac, 1869, para 65.

[62] See E. P. Thomson, *The Making of the English Working Class*, New York, 1964; Frank Ongley Darval, *Popular Disturbances and Public Order in Regency England: Being an Account of the Luddite and other Disorders in England During the Years 1811-1817, and of the Attitude and Activity of the Authorities*, New York, 1969; Robert William Reid, *The Land of Lost Content: The Luddist Revolt, 1812*, London, 1986; Thomas Malcolm, *The Luddites: Machine Breaking in Regency England*, England, 1970.

dust and rain . . . and unprotected against the clamancy of weather, sometimes for weeks, until it is cleaned from its seed. . .',[63] lamented the settlement officer of the Mortizapur taluka in central Berar. The similarity of this form of protest with the southern sharecroppers during the contemporary post-bellum period is striking. Ransom and Sutch have argued with great force and brilliance that the freed men after the demise of slavery withdrew their labour in protest and in exercise of their freedom.[64]

Even after its appropriation the cotton was not safe. The appropriators had to guard it from the primary producers. Mr. E. A. Hobson, a colonial cotton expert, has left us a very interesting glimpse of the cotton fever in the countryside. He observed that when the cotton is picked:

> . . . it is carried to the threshing floors, or enclosures specially prepared, and placed in long stacks; when the stack is completed, the owner spreads ashes long ways and crossways, over the stack, in order to detect whether the stack has been tampered with. . . .[65]

Now this observation tells us something about the existence of the problem of crop-robbing in the countryside but it does not tell us as to who was doing it. Furthermore, petty dealing in cotton went on throughout the province despite 'The Cotton and Grain Markets Law' which banned the sale and purchase of cotton outside the government designated markets. The main reason for introducing a fee for stall space in hitherto free weekly bazars and markets was to curb the illegal trade of cotton in Berar.[66] This was similar to the 'Sunset Laws' in American south in the 1870s which banned the country storekeepers in blackbelt Alabama from purchasing cotton from the blacks between sunset and sunrise.[67]

[63] *Mortizapur Taluka Settlement Report*, No. 368 of 1869, para 52, p. 21.

[64] See Roger L. Ransom and Richard Sutch, *One Kind of Freedom: The Economic Consequences of Emancipation*, Cambridge, 1977.

[65] *Note on Cotton in Berar*, by E. A. Hobson, Survey and Settlement Officer, Berar, Hyderabad, 1887, in the *Proceedings of the Department of Revenue and Agriculture*, Fibre and Silk Branch (November 1887), Nos. 22-3.

[66] *Yeotmal District Gazetteer*, Calcutta, 1908, p. 80.

[67] See, Jonathan M. Weiner, *Social Origins of the New South: Alabama, 1860-1885*, Baton Rouge, 1978; Michael Wayne, *The Reshaping of Plantation Society: The Natchez District, 1860-1880*, Baton Rouge, 1983.

After the disappearance of *balutedari* system the Public Works Department took control of water management in Berar. Then all cultivating tenants were subjected to water rates varying according to the crops cultivated. The revenue rate on *patasthal bagait* or lands irrigated by channels, streams, or wells was 10 to 15 time the assessment rate on *motasthal bagait* (rain irrigated lands).[68] This exorbitant rate forced the *khatedars* to raise garden crops in sheltered places in the hills and on the banks of the tributaries of the Poorna by means of a simple and quick mode of irrigation:

> A triangle is constructed of sticks eight feet long, to which is suspended a flat basket, called a 'sop', fastened to a pole. With this the water is shovelled from the river on to the land.[69]

This type of unauthorized contraband agriculture was resorted to cultivate short-term high-value cash crops like opium, flowers, plantains, pan, spices, aromatic nuts, etc.[70] When cotton destroyed the diversity in agriculture, the cultivators had no other course left for survival othar then to resort to contraband agriculture. The beautiful valley of Berar with its tremendous diversity of flora and fauna was permanently destroyed as a result of the colonial pressure of cotton cultivation.

In some villages on *palampat* tenure the cultivators, in desperation to avoid payment of land revenue, recorded the returns of cultivated area as wastelands even though the latter had been brought under the plough. The purpose of colonial survey and settlement (1862-77) and revision settlement (1892-1900) was precisely to detect all unauthorized cultivation in the province and punish the wrong doers by settling the rate much higher than what it was supposed to be originally.[71]

Since railway was the lifeline of the colonial cotton trade the land surrounding half a mile of the railway line was given only to cultivators most loyal to the state. The family of the patels and *khatedars* in villages surrounding the railway line was carefully scrutinized. A family with questionable loyalty to the state or

[68] *Basim Taluka Settlement Report,* No. 203 of 1900, para 40, p. 13.

[69] *Jalgaum Taluka Settlement Report,* No. 261 of 1865, para 13, p. 5.

[70] *Report on the Cotton Department for the Year 1868-69,* by Harry Rivett-Carnac, 1869, para 5; A. C. Lyall, *Gazetteers of the Haidarabad Assigned Districts,* 1870, p. 257.

[71] *Rules under the Berar Land Revenue Code, 1896,* p. 123

government was considered a threat to the colonial lifeline. No permanent proprietary right was granted in this half a mile radius. Only temporary occupancy rights were given and government retained the right of eviction from these lands.[72] This indicates that the railways were in danger of being attacked and therefore necessary precautions had to be undertaken.

In 1872 the colonial government expressed great alarm at the spread of a foreign variety of cotton in Berar. In fact this cotton known as *khandeshi* or *kati vilayati* had been under cultivation for sometime before government detection. The cultivators took to *khandeshi* in order to counter the existing *bani* and *jari* which was basically an export crop. The *khandeshi* was locally consumed and had a market even outside Berar. The Bombay mills which were always short of supplies readily bought *khandeshi* grown in Berar. Further the *khandeshi* was a hardy and fast-growing crop which came up for early picking than *bani* and *jari* and therefore served well to counter debt. *Khandeshi* could be grown with little expense and minimal labour compared to *bani* and *jari* which demanded intensive care and labour for its growth with little returns to the cultivator. *Khandeshi* was also underselling 'Oomra' (*bani* and *jari*) and therefore posed a threat to the colonial cotton trade. Therefore the colonial state took series of measures to counter the spread of *khandeshi*. An attack on *khandeshi* became an attack on the *khatedars* who grew it.

In 1872 the colonial government legally banned the cultivation of *khandeshi* in Berar. The Secretary to the Bombay Chamber of Commerce expressed his concern by stating, 'that it would be nothing short of a calamity to the cotton trade of western India to introduce into the Berars the old khandeshi cotton which was known as the most worthless cotton exported from Bombay'.[73] When despite the government ban the cultivators of Akola and Amraoti sowed *khandeshi*, the government send for all the cultivators who had sown *khandeshi* and issued a warning. The cotton report of 1880-1 states:

[72] *Rules under the Berar Land Revenue Code, 1896*, pp. 93-8.

[73] See Mr. A. J. Dunlop's Memorandum on 'Cotton Prospects in the Berar', in the *Proceedings of the Revenue and Agricultural Department*, Fibre and Silk Branch (October 1883), No. 122.

These men were sent for, and it was explained to them by the Tahsildar what would be the effect of this kind of cotton being common, and they were asked to discontinue the sowing of this description of cotton seed.[74]

The suppression of *khandeshi* became the oppression of the peasantry. The *khatedars* countered it by adopting a new method of agriculture known as 'intercultivation' by which rows of *khandeshi* were grown hidden within the rows of *bani* and *jari*.[75] This *khatedari* persistence provoked the colonial state to adopt even more stringent measures. The Chief Commissioner of Berar S. O. B. Risdale wrote the following note to the Resident at Hyderabad in 1883:

> . . . stringent measures were adopted in 1874, to eradicate this cotton [Khandeshi] from the Province. A circular was widely circulated in May 1874, forbidding the use of the seed. Copies of the circular were posted up at every public office, market and bazaar, and the village officers were held responsible that the orders were rigidly obeyed.[76]

Every colonial official from the Deputy Commissioner of the district to the village watchman was activated to prevent the distribution of *khandeshi* seeds in Berar. But mysteriously the *khandeshi* had a way of distributing itself much to the dismay of the colonizers and merchants. One cotton merchant expressing his disgust at the situation states:

> The cotton trade has become deteriorated past renovation, under a number of years . . . unless some very high-handed measures can be enforced before the coming monsoon with reference to cotton, . . . the next season will see the end of the prosperous times in Berar.[77]

When *khandeshi* thus threatened the 'prosperous times' of European merchants and traders, the colonial government invented a yet another instrument to achieve the final 'elimination of the vilayati

[74] *Cotton Report of the Hyderabad Assigned Districts for the Year 1880-81*, Hyderabad (n.d.), in the *Proceedings of the Department of Revenue, Agriculture and Commerce*, Fibre and Silk Branch (August 1882), Nos.12-18.

[75] *Cotton Seed Adulteration*, in the *Proceedings of the Department of Revenue and Agriculture*, Fibre and Silk Branch (November 1884), Nos. 1 and 2.

[76] *Cotton Report on the Hyderabad Assigned Districts, 1882-83*, Hyderabad, 1883, in the *Proceedings of the Department of Revenue and Agriculture*, Agriculture Branch (December 1883), No. 7.

[77] *Cotton Prospects in the Berars: A Memorandum*, by Surgeon T. Hume, in the *Proceedings of the Revenue and Agriculture Department*, Fibre and Silk Branch (October 1883), Nos. 1 and 2.

from Berar'.[78] By the order of the Chief Commissioner, the *khandeshi* cotton was banned and steps were taken to 'exclude this description of cotton from all the markets' of Berar.[79] In fact often this order went even further. Anyone found in possession of *khandeshi* was in danger of persecution.

How was this 'final elimination' of vilayati attempted? All the European merchants and traders ganged up against *khandeshi* by outrightly refusing to deal in it. This was done under the sponsorship of the colonial government. The railways even refused to carry cotton which was not for export. The cotton report of 1882-3 gives a graphic description of this colonial conspiracy in the following manner:

> In this state of affairs the aid of all the European merchants was called in, and they were asked to reject all cotton of the khandesh variety that might be brought to them for sale . . . , this was agreed to, and it was then announced that the European merchants at every market in Berar have agreed among themselves to reject all cotton of that variety which may be brought for sale. Several small lots which were brought in during that season for sale were rejected in the Amraoti market; and it was anticipated that the effect of this measure would be to entirely stop the growth of khandesh cotton in time.[80]

Yet *khandeshi* prevailed despite the oppression and suppression. Mr. D. Fitzpatrick, the Resident at Hyderabad, deliberately concealing the cruel oppression perpetrated on the *khatedars* rather modestly made it appear as if it was a naive mischief. He wrote thus in July 1890, 'we could do little or nothing towards altering the course things have taken, and I may add that, if we only succeeded in altering it to a limited extent, the immediate result would certainly be mischievous'.[81]

[78] *Cotton Prospects in the Berars*, in the *Proceedings of the Revenue and Agriculture Department*, Fibre and Silk Branch (October 1883), Nos. 1 and 2.

[79] *Cotton Report on the Hyderabad Assigned Districts for the Year 1880-81*, Hyderabad (n.d.), in the *Proceedings of the Department of Revenue, Agriculture and Commerce*, Fibres and Silk Branch (August 1882), Nos. 12-18.

[80] *Cotton Report on the Hyderabad Assigned Districts for the Year 1882-83*, Hyderabad, 1883, in the *Proceedings of the Department of Revenue and Agriculture*, Agriculture Branch (December 1883), No. 7.

[81] 'On the proposed measures in connection with cotton cultivation in Berar', a note by D. Fitzpatrick, Resident at Hyderabad, in *Foreign Department Proceedings* (July 1890), No. 328.

The resistance of *khatedars* symbolized by the persistence of *khandeshi* indicates a total failure of the colonial state in achieving its goal of the 'final elimination' of *khandeshi*.[82] The arrogance of Commissioner S. O. B. Risdale was a little more sophisticated than D. Fitzpatrick's crude response. While accepting the total failure of the colonial government in eliminating *khandeshi* from Berar, he unabashedly states:

> It is sufficient here to state that all those measures, though persecuted with the greatest vigour and determination, and with neither stint in regard to money nor hesitation in enforcing the orders issued, resulted in total admitted failures, and the inferior variety continued to hold its own, and to increase in favor with the cultivators.[83]

When the original settlement (1862-77) came up for revision in the 1890s, the Indian National Congress (founded in 1885) began taking an active interest in the debates and discussions much to the discomfort of colonial authorities in Berar. The issue of the material condition of people was brought up in the light of British colonialism

[82] For more on *khandeshi* see following references:

Note on Indian Cotton, in the *Proceedings of the Department of Revenue and Agriculture*, Fibre and Silk Branch (May 1889), No. 25/27; *Cotton Report of the Hyderabad Assigned Districts for the Year 1879-80*, Hyderabad, 1881; Report written by Lt. Col. J. G. Bell, Officiating Commissioner, Hyderabad Assigned Districts, to the Secretary for Berar to the Resident at Hyderabad, Amraoti (23 December 1880), in the *Proceedings of the Department of Revenue, Agriculture and Commerce*, Fibre and Silk Branch (August 1882), Nos. 12-18; Memorandum on the improvement of the quality of cotton grown in Berar by Mr. E. C. Ozanne, Director of Land Records and Agriculture, Bombay, in the *Proceedings of the Department of Revenue and Agriculture*, Fibre and Silk Branch (July 1890), No. 11; *Report on the Cotton Trading Season in Central Provinces and Berar*, 19 June 1874, in the *Proceedings of the Department of Revenue, Agriculture and Commerce*, Fibre and Silk Branch (June 1874), Nos. 41-42; *Cotton Prospects in Central Provinces and Berar*, in the *Proceedings of the Department of Revenue, Agriculture, and Commerce*, Fibre and Silk Branch (November 1874), No. 5; Agricultural Ledger Series, Hyderabad Assigned Districts, No. 2; *Cotton Cultivation in Berar or the Hyderabad Assigned Districts*, in the *Proceedings of the Department of Revenue and Agriculture*, Fibre and Silk Branch (December 1898), No. 19; From: A. J. Dunlop, Assistant Commissioner, Akola District to Secretary, Chamber of Commerce, Bombay, dated 11 June 1874, in *Foreign Department Proceedings of the Government of India*, Nos. 6-10, dated January 1874; *Central Provinces and Berar District Gazetteer—Akola District*, Calcutta, 1910; *Chicklee Taluka Settlement Report*, No. 51 of 1866.

[83] *Cotton Seed Adulteration in Berar*, in the *Proceedings of the Department of Revenue and Agriculture*, Fibre and Silk Branch (November 1884), Nos. 1 and 2.

in India. Although the early Congress was conservative in its politics but its stalwarts like Naoroji, R. C. Dutt, Ranadey, Tilak, and Gokhale had put forward a radical programme of economic nationalism criticizing the British rule and holding it responsible for the poverty of India.[84] According to them the British rule was draining wealth from India in the form of raw material and the people were loosing their purchasing power to British finished goods. So on both counts India was being bled white and this was the prime reason for its depressed material condition. This thesis which became famous as the 'drain theory of poverty and unBritish rule' was the central creed around which the early Congress rallied its programme of economic nationalism.[85]

The early activists of the Congress from Berar came from the leading families of the demobilized *balutedari* clans. Many patels and patwaris in the villages were also early Congress sympathizers. The colonial state in the late nineteenth century was very much concerned about the spread of Congress influence in the countryside. In order to counter this influence the colonial state introduced the system of rotation of patels and patwaris by which families with Congress sympathies were rotated in favour of loyalists. But the colonizers were constantly haunted by the prospect of the leading men of the villages joining the Congress camp. Mr. Chichele-Plowden writing at the height of famine in 1898, was more concerned about the Congress influence than relief measures: 'I conceive no measure which would be more certain to throw the influential men in the villages on the side of the agitators and create in their minds distrust and dislike against [the] Government.'[86] It was during the

[84] See Bipin Chandra, *The Rise and Growth of Economic Nationalism in India: Economic Policies of Indian Nationalist Leadership, 1885-1905*, New Delhi, 1966; John R. McLane, *Indian Nationalism and the Early Congress*, New Jersey, 1977; Briton Martin Jr., *New India 1885: British Official Policy and the Emergence of the Indian National Congress*, Berkeley, 1969; A. R. Desai, *Social Background of Indian Nationalism*, Bombay, 1966.

[85] See R.C. Dutt, *The Economic History of India under the early British Rule, from the Rise of the British power in 1757 to the Accession of Queen Victoria in 1837*, Vol. I, London, 1906; *The Economic History of India in the Victorian Age, from Accession of Queen Victoria in 1837 to the Commencement of the 20th Century*, Vol II, London, 1906; Dadabhai Naoroji, *Poverty and Un-British Rule in India*, London, 1901.

[86] Note on the Proposals in Revenue Department, Nos. 1543/180-2, dated 9 July 1897, for revision of the *Berar Patels and Patwaris Law, 1886*, by T. Chichele-

great famines of the 1890s and the early twentieth century that the British created *khatedars* came back to haunt the colonizers as Indian nationalists.

The Colonial Invention of Tradition and the Berar Peasantry

When colonial census was first introduced in Berar on the night of 16 May 1867, for the first time the people were systematically divided on the basis of caste, religion, race, and language. All forms of prejudice and bigotry with which the colonial mind was afflicted was introduced in Berar through the colonial census. The 'Inquisition of the Enumerators' caused enormous psychological violence on the generally secular nature of the Berari people. The crudeness and cruelty of the census operations is depicted in the observation of the Deputy Commissioner of the Akola district who writes thus while addressing the people:

> The object of Government in taking census is not yet thoroughly understood by the people, especially by the ignorant and superstitious who make it a point to refrain from giving information on some plea or other, such as the musalmans who dislikes the idea of the names and ages of the female relatives being known by another.[87]

In order to counter such resistance a Census Act was passed on 16 October 1890 which specified that any person refusing to give information to the census enumerators was liable to legal action. Consequently many Berarians refused to act as enumerators. The government then brought in Bengali-baboos, Punjabi bureaucrats, and Maratha brahmins to act as enumerators and question people. Every decade these 'suspicious characters' came to Berar and gathered information and reported to government about the situation in villages. Census was thus used by the colonial state as an instrument of social and political control.[88]

Although differences of caste and language did not generally cause conflict among people, the colonial census planted 'antagonistic consciousness' by differential distribution of official favours. The

---

Plowden, Resident at Hyderabad, in *Proceedings of the Hyderabad Administration on Matter of Routine for the Month of July 1898,* submitted to the Revenue and Agriculture Department, No. 206, 19 July 1898.

[87] *Census of India 1891, Berar or the Hyderabad Assigned Districts,* 1892, p. clxxi.

[88] *Census of India, 1891*, p. lxxiv.

people often reacted sharply on being inquired about the language they spoke in the following manner: 'My language is what I speak; how do I know what language it is?'[89]

David Washbrook writing about Madras Presidency stated that the consciousness of 'caste' was a colonial creation.[90] His argument can also be used to understand the operation of the caste system in Berar under colonialism. The colonial census divided the *khatedars* on the basis of castes of good social standing and castes of bad social standing.

According to this categorization those who collaborated with the British were designated as castes of good social standing and those who resisted obedience were branded as castes of bad social standing. Therefore in all colonial documents in general and census reports in particular we see upper castes (brahmins, kshatriyas, and vaishyas) categorized as castes of good social standing while the lower caste categorized as castes of bad social standing. Those groups of people who were outside the framework of caste, i.e. the tribal people, were outrightly branded as 'criminal castes and tribes'.[91] Once such a categorization was made, the groups met their fate according to the category in which they fell. Therefore we see a systematic persecution of the lower caste and tribals under colonialism just because the census branded them as criminal.

Every successive generation of British colonial officials was trained and indoctrinated in the documents created by earlier generation of colonizers. Thus racism and pejorative ways of looking at Indians was perpetuated by generation after generation of British colonizers in Berar. Often times the services of the upper castes was used in the persecution of the colonial designated 'criminal class', i.e. lower castes and tribals. Historical research has proved that the Indian upper caste had collaborated with the colonizers in manning the lower echelons of colonial bureaucracy and imitating the colonizers by being as oppressive on the people as their colonial masters.[92] When the rate of oppression became

[89] *Census of India, 1891*, p. lxxxi.

[90] David A. Washbrook, 'Progress and Problems: South Asian Economic and Social History, c. 1720-1860', *Modern Asian Studies* 22, pt. 1 (1988), 57-96; *The Emergence of Provincial Politics, 1880-1920*, Delhi, 1977.

[91] *Census of India, 1891, Berar or the Hyderabad Assigned Districts*, 1892, p. 101.

[92] See Eugene F. Irschick, *Politics and Social Conflict in South India: The Non-Brahman Movement and Tamil Separatism, 1916-1929*, Bombay, 1969.

unbearable the lower castes struck work against the upper caste and refused to provide them with essential services in the villages. This method of protest was often adopted by the menial service castes like the chamars (leather workers), dhobis (washerman), nais (barbers), mangs, mahars (sweepers), sutars (carpenters), etc.[93] In fact there was very little difference between the way upper castes treated the lower castes and the way colonizers treated Indians. Whenever the lower castes showed signs of economic well being, the upper caste denounced them and even used physical violence against them. Due to a sudden spurt in cash wages during the American Civil War when the *khatedars* and *bhagindars* acquired some purchasing power to expend on food and clothing, the brahmins, deshmukhs, and deshpandias denounced them by exclaiming: 'every cooly took to dressing himself like a Brahmin'.[94]

The process of sanskritization which M. N. Srinivas mentions in his study of caste in modern India actually begins in Berar with the introduction of colonial census operations.[95] According to this process, the lower castes blur their caste identity by minor alterations to their family names. This was done not only to resist colonial persecution but also strive to achieve higher social status.

As an illustration let us take the example of the kunbis of Berar who formed 18 to 41 per cent of the population. Although the colonial state categorized them as lower caste Hindus yet they practised a diverse range of professions.[96] Some were teli kunbis

[93] Harry Rivett-Carnac, *Report on the Cotton Department for the Year 1868-69.* 1869, p. 145. A similar type of protest became the political strategy of the Kisan Sabha movement in the twentieth century. The strategy of 'nai-dhobi band' was adopted against the upper caste oppression in the villages. For more see: Majid Hayat Siddiqi, *The Agrarian Unrest in North India, 1918-22,* New Delhi, 1978; Gyanendra Pandey, 'A View of the Observable: A Positivist "Understanding" of Agrarian Society and Political Protest in Colonial India', *Journal of Peasant Studies,* Vol. 7, No. 3 (April 1980); *The Ascendancy of the Congress in Uttar Pradesh, 1926-34: A Study in Imperfect Mobilization,* Delhi, 1978; Walter Hauser, *The Bihar Provincial Kisan Sabha, 1929-1949: A Study of an Indian Peasant Movement,* Doctoral Thesis, Chicago, 1961.

[94] Harry Rivett-Carnac, *Report on the Cotton Department for the Year 1868-69,* 1869, p. 145.

[95] See M. N. Srinivas, *Caste in Modern India and Other Essays,* New York, 1962; *Social Change in Modern India,* Los Angeles, 1962.

[96] *Notes on the Agriculturists of the District of Aurangabad, H. H. Nizam's Dominion,* by Furdoonji Jamshedji, Superintendent, Revenue Survey and Assessment, N. W. Division, in *Hyderabad Affairs,* Vol. I (n.d.), 801-33.

(oilpressers), some were mali kunbis (garden cultivators), some were nai kunbis (barbers), some claimed brahmanical status by referring to themselves as manbhav kunbis, and some even buried their dead like the Muslims.[97] This was the method adopted by the people to resist a straight jacket categorization of them by the colonial state with utter disregard for the centuries-old social, cultural and occupational diversity. The colonial state was not only incapable of recognizing such a rich diversity of culture and creed but it also prevented the healthy growth of such a diversity in Berar. Consequently when the census enumerators appeared in Berar every ten years with prepared questionnaires, the people were left perplexed. The census of 1891 notes this state of discomfort and anxiety in the following manner: 'A large proportion of the people have very indefinite ideas as to the nomenclature of their caste, and comparatively few possess fixed notions as to the subdivision to which they belong'.[98]

Ali Asani in his work on the *sufi* tradition of India has brilliantly argued that the majority of the Muslims of India who lived in the countryside were no doubt practising Islam but were secular by nature. According to him 'Islam in the popular tradition of South Asia' gradually blended with the local culture yet successfully maintained its distinctness. This type of popular Islam was different from the orthodox Islam practised by the ruling class elite.[99] In Berar too, the majority of people were secular in their approach to religion. The inquisition of census enumerators about religion put the people in a very uncomfortable position. They were forced to adopt and declare a single identity despite the multiplicity of identities and the general secular nature of the society. This deliberate insensitivity to popular beliefs was yet another form of violence by which the colonial state controlled the lives of the people in Berar.

The secular culture of Berar had come under attack with the decline of fairs and bazars in the villages as a result of the rise of cotton trade and the development of cotton market towns. Originally

[97] *Yeotmal District Gazetteer*, Calcutta, 1908, p. 66.

Census of India, 1891, Berar or the Hyderabad Assigned Districts, 1892, p. xciii.

[98] *Census of India, 1891, Berar or the Hyderabad Assigned Districts*, 1892, p. xcii.

[99] See Ali Sultan Ali Asani, *The Bujh Niranjan: An Ismaili Mystical Poem*, Cambridge, 1991.

the fairs and bazars were held around shrines in which people of all creeds congregated. These shrines had existed in Berar long before the arrival of colonizers. These shrines were also centres to which people looked for relief in times of crisis. The shrines of Shah Dawal at Dariapur and Khaki Shah Wala at Malegaon were revered and adored by Hindus and Muslims alike.[100] A. C. Lyall in his Gazetteer records this secular trend which not too many colonial documents observe:

> The kunbis practice to a very great extent mahomedan shrine worship and vows. On these occasions the musalman fakir and mujawar officiates as priest, and encourages ceremonials forbidden by the koran.[101]

Similarly when the colonial officials appeared once in a decade to gather information, the *khatedars* encountered them with a barrage of complaints. One oftenly aired public complaint was that:

> Government tax us for public investment and yet we see nothing come of it. Why do they not build Chowrees and Durumsallas for us. . . .[102]

Colonial Intervention in Berar Agrarian Society

The discontentment of the people stated above was intrinsically related to the impact of *khatedari* system on Berar. Therefore it is important to critically analyse colonial activities in the region. It used to be said in pre-colonial times that 'a man travelling in this part of Berar requires but a short string to his lotah' to draw fresh water anywhere in the wells.[103] Since Berar is geologically placed in the centre of Deccan plateau, the common source of fresh water was through tanks and wells. Under *balutedari* system the numerous tanks and wells were freely utilized although the dominant clan had 'first-rights' over them. But with the privatization of land the free use of these wells was restricted. For the first time in Berar water scarcity became a problem and this caused enormous hardship to the people and cattle alike. The Akote taluka settlement report draws attention to this problem in the following manner:

[100] A. C. Lyall, *Gazetteer for the Haidarabad Assigned Districts,* 1870, pp. 123, 151 and 190.

[101] A. C. Lyall, *Gazetteer for the Haidarabad Assigned Districts,* 1870, p. 214.

[102] *Chicklee Taluk Settlement Report,* No. 51 of 1866, para 24, p. 9, by Chowrees and Durumsallas is meant the village squares and rest houses.

> . . . during a great portion of the year fresh water is not procurable in the villages, and the expense of cultivation is materially enhanced by the distance the cultivators have to traverse with their bullocks in proceeding to, and returning from the places where the cattle are watered, which in some villages must occupy several hours, and diminish correspondingly the amount of work the bullocks would otherwise be capable of performing.[104]

This also depreciated the number of hours the *khatedar* put to cultivation thus greatly stagnating the per acre yield. In some talukas like Wun the cultivators had to travel a round-journey of six miles everyday to fetch water from the stream. This caused enormous hardships to the inhabitants especially during the sowing and harvest season.[105]

During times of scarcity and famine under *balutedari*, the dominant clan shirked all the responsibility of protection even though they appropriated 95 per cent of the agricultural produce. But then at least the cultivators had the option to abandon the village till such time as the calamity passed. Under *khatedari*, due to the requirement of a registered tenant, the *khatedars* clung to their land and preferred to suffer and perish rather than to abandon and lose their lands.[106] This was also the reason for high mortality not only during the famine years but even during non-famine years.

The intensity of water scarcity was in fact related to a novel system of tenure devised by the colonial government to bring waste lands under cultivation. Merely alienating the waste and woodlands would be of no use to the government. If the land had to be made to generate revenue it had to be brought under the plough. The colonial government therefore devised a scheme to bring wastelands under the plough and this scheme was known as the *izaradari* system. What was this scheme and what was *izara*?

> They were leases for thirty, twenty or fifteen years of waste or wholly or partly uncultivated 'villages' beginning at a low rent, which was gradually to rise with spread of cultivation.[107]

[103] *Lotah* was a small metal pot popularly carried for storing water, see *Report of the Cotton Department for the Year 1868-69,* by Harry Rivet-Carnac, 1869, para 5.

[104] *Akote Taluka Settlement Report,* No. 268 of 1867, para 13.

[105] *Wun Taluka Settlement Report,* No. 340 of 1875, para 11.

[106] *Akote Taluka Settlement Report,* No. 268 of 1867, para 30.

[107] B. H. Baden-Powell, *The Land-systems of British India,* 1891, pp. 380-1.

No sooner after the allotment, the government exerted pressure on *izaradars* to bring the wastelands under cultivation. The *izaradars* normally paid a lumpsum amount annually for tracts of land ranging from 500 plus acres. These tracts of land were purchased on distempered biddings financed by the moneylenders on behalf of *izaradars*. The latter gradually cleared these tracts and brought it under the plough by working the subtenants on it.[108] The combined pressure of government demand and moneylender's interest coupled with leasers' greed, converted *izaradari* into one of the most oppressive systems ever to operate in Berar. The subtenants had no right of appeal in the law courts and their condition under *izaradari* was even worse than what it was under *khatedari*. After the expiry of *izaradari* leases, the *izaradars* were registered as regular government tenants and settled as *khatedars*. The position of subtenants who were the actual cultivators of the soil remained unchanged.

It should be noted that the purpose of clearing waste lands was also to suppress the tribes who lived in these lands. The tribal people whom the colonizers regarded as wild and unruly were branded under the category of 'criminal castes and tribes' by the colonial census. However the first census operation (1867) took its cue from the 'Waste Land Rules of 1865' specifically formulated to achieve this purpose. The rule clearly stated that:

> In order to encourage the occupation of certain wild and hilly tracts, and to provide land for settling certain wandering and semi-criminal tribes, a scheme of izara tenure was drawn up under the title of the 'Waste Land Rules of 1865'.[109]

Izaradari became the most oppressive institution of colonial exploitation unparalleled to any previous governments in Berar's history. Major P. A. Elphinstone had very sharply envisioned the destruction of wastes and trees in 1875:

> . . . as the lease-holders are constantly making new clearances for the purpose of cultivation, and most of the timber will most probably entirely disappear in the course of a few years.[110]

[108] *Wun Taluka Settlement Report,* No. 340 of 1875, para 47, p. 15.

[109] *Central Provinces and Berar: A Review of the Administration of the Province,* Vol. II, Nagpur, 1923, para 225.

[110] *Darwa Taluka Settlement Report,* No. 420 of 1872, para 30.

The *izaradari* was a transition system leading to the establishment of full *khatedari* rights. Once the waste lands were cleared and *khatedari* rights established, the government strictly enforced land revenue collection. The policy stated:

> The Government rent shall be paid yearly in not more than two instalments, and on failure to pay any one instalment, within three months after it is due, the lease shall be forfeited and the village resumed . . . . No failure of crops or other excuse will be held to exempt him from payment of rent, and failure to pay the full amount will entail the attachment or sale of his estate.[111]

The 'Gaothan' or the common village sites for threshing and winnowing were also auctioned by the patels under government authority. Although under *balutedari* the dominant clan reserved primary rights over the village sights and public places, its free use was not restricted to the people. But under *khatedari* such sights and places were privatized and no longer freely available.[112]

Jay R. Mandle in his short book on *The Roots of Black Poverty* in American south has asserted that the south remained backward because cotton cultivation prevented technological change and labour diversification.[113] This hypothesis is very useful in studying the relationship between cotton cultivation and economic backwardness of Berar under colonialism.

Cotton in the nineteenth century was a labour-intensive crop and demanded large number of hands during the picking season. In a situation of labour abundance and capital scarcity it was but normal for the technology to stagnate. Stagnant technology is one of the prime indicators of the economic backwardness under *khatedari*. In fact the *khatedari* system and cotton cultivation were inward-looking and kept the agricultural technology from changing. *The Report of the Famine Commission of 1880* noted that 'there has been no change in agricultural implements in Berar'.[114] The bulk of the land in Berar was done by *nagar* and *bukhur* which were two types of light and heavy ploughs commonly used for breaking the

[111] *The Berar Patels and Patwaris Law, 1900,* D. V. Shiddore, ed., Amraoti, 1935, p. 88.

[112] *Rules under the Berar Land Revenue Code, 1896,* Calcutta, 1907.

[113] Jay R. Mandle, *The Roots of Black Poverty: The Southern Plantation Economy After the Civil War,* Durham, 1978, Chapter 5, p. 52.

[114] *Report of the Famine Commission, 1880,* London, 1881, p. 196.

hard pre-monsoon black soil.[115] Although a wide variety of trees grew in Berar, i.e. teak, babool, dhaman, tiwas, dhowra, anjan, jambhool, tamarind, etc., the ploughs and carts were made from dhaman and babool because the wood from these trees had the strength and elasticity to bear the pressure of Berari soil and weather.[116] The attack on trees which the *izara* system brought and the government alienation of woodlands caused a general shortage of wood availability for the construction of agricultural implements and carts. In a situation of general shortage of wood the *khatedars* used the same wood for both carts and implements.

The reason why the native carts vanished with the onset of the monsoon was that the *khatedars* disassembled the carts and reassembled the wood into *nagar* and *bukhur* (ploughs). Then when the cultivation was done the ploughs were disjoined and reassembled as carts. This was resorted not only due to the general scarcity of wood but also due to the prevalence of general poverty in the country. The repeated use of wood in this manner often broke the bridge of ploughs and axles of carts. The cultivators had no other way than to resort to the moneylender for capital to fix it. In general the agricultural implements in Berar were old, broken, and in a constant state of repair and idleness. In such a state the agricultural technology was hardly expected to change. The Jalgaum settlement officer rightly pointed out in 1865, 'that any improvement will, for some time to come, take place in the construction of these implements, we hardly can expect . . .'.[117] It was often noted:

> In Berar the soil during the ploughing season is as hard as rock. The native plough was designed to work as a wedge. It is heavy and made of wood. It works well when heavily loaded and pressed hard. But since there is no iron in it, its penetrating capacity is greatly reduced. Even the wooden joints need to be constantly maintained by tightening and prevented from breaking . . . services of the carpenter into the field is constantly needed.[118]

[115] *Annual Report of the Cotton Department for 1870-71,* by Harry Rivett-Carnac, in the *Proceedings of the Department of Agriculture, Revenue and Commerce.* No. 8/11, dated February 1873, para 7. Also see *Report on the Cotton Department for the Year 1868-69,* by Harry Rivett-Carnac, 1868, paras 119-20.

[116] *Mortizapur Taluka Settlement Report,* No. 368 of 1869, para 54.

[117] *Jalgaum Taluka settlement Report,* No. 261 of 1865, para 19.

[118] *Hyderabad Affairs,* Vol. I, compiled by Moulvie Syed Mahdi Ali, Bombay (n.d.), p. 10.

Often times the moneylenders and European firms owned and loaned carts and ploughs to keep the cultivators in debt bondage. They also imported lighter and speedier carts from Madras and Nagpur which gradually led to the disappearance of local cart-making skills.[119] Technologically the Berari carts were heavier and slower and consumed too much wood and had no demand in a state of general destitution.

The absence of the technology for shoeing the bullocks knocked the non-cotton carts off the metalled roads. The moneylenders and European firms then resorted to acquiring and loaning bullocks with metal shoes. Most of the *khatedari* bullocks had no shoes and could not be used for transportation as the metalled roads cut their hoofs to pieces. And those who accompanied the carts with bullocks without metal shoes had much walking to do in the hot hard road which was equally unmerciful to their feet as well.[120]

Several years ago Barrington Moore had argued that when an agrarian class of landholders dominate the society, then the industry and the urban centres become subservient to agriculture. This prevents the society from industrializing and keeps it agricultural. Under such a society most of the surplus is consumed by the landlord class which also prevents its full reinvestment into the economy. Unless the landlord class is overthrown the society continues to remain agrarian and inward-looking. Such a system of production ties the labour to land and prevents the development of a free market economy. Every unit of production is geared to serve the 'Junker class' which keeps the society entrenched on the 'Prussian Road'.[121]

The case of Berar goes further then Barrington Moore's hypothesis. In Berar the *khatedari* class was created and reduced to serve the interest of the colonial state. The colonial state was the supreme landlord and through its rule kept Berar on the 'Prussian Road'. It was not the landlord class but the state which kept Berar pinned to agriculture. The state also prevented the growth of industries in the

[119] *Report on the Cotton Department for the Year 1868-69,* by Harry Rivett-Carnac, paras 119-20.

[120] *Report of the Cotton Department for the Year 1868-69,* by Harry Rivett-Carnac, para 119.

[121] See Barrington Moore, *Social Origins of Dictatorship and Democracy: Lords and Peasants in the Making of the Modern World,* Boston, 1966.

region by linking it to the world market. Furthermore no building could be constructed without the permission of the colonial state. This was because the colonial government feared that encroachment over agricultural land would threaten the revenue and disrupt the cotton trade. So in order to keep Berar on the 'Prussian Road' it was absolutely essential for the state to assert its rights over all lands, mines, and mineral resources of the province. Therefore policies were implemented to prevent economic diversification and keep Berar agrarian. Heavy fines were levied on all classes of land 'appropriated to any purpose unconnected with agriculture, and at the same rate in proportion for fractions of an acre'.[122] Table 17 lists the rate of fines.

TABLE 17

Land	*Fine in Rs. per acre*
Class I	Rs. 2,500
Class II	Rs. 1,500
Class III	Rs. 1,000
Class IV	Rs. 500
Class V	Rs. 100

The absence of avenues for diversification led to the rapid exhaustion of soil as crop succeeded crop in quick succession. The *khatedari* system locked the *khatedar* in a situation where the pressure of world market, the colonial state, and the moneylender forced the *khatedar* to grow cotton. The Mehkur district settlement officer as early as 1868 noted that the *khatedar* had no other course left but 'to exhaust his land, by repeating his cotton crop too often or to grow it over too large a surface to the almost entire exclusion of cereals'.[123] Similarly Amraoti settlement officer also noted:

> The land will deteriorate as well as the staple, . . . manuring the field would to some extent stave off the evil day, even under this too rapid system of rotation; but while firewood is so scarce, and the ryots have to use manure in the place of fuel, this means of restoring fertility to the soil can only be adopted exceptionally.[124]

[122] *Rules under the Berar Land Revenue Code, 1896,* Nagpur, 1907, p. 109.

[123] *Mehkur District Settlement Report,* No. 1098 of 1868, para 8.

[124] *Oomrawuttee and Ellichpur Taluka Settlement Report,* No. 444 of 1870, para 45.

Under *khatedari* all the local skills of Berar were threatened. The skills of pottery, bricktile making, salt making, glass, soap, ghur and cane sugar making came under attack as permission to obtain mud, sand, stone, kankar, gravel, and murum had to be acquired from the tahsildar.[125] The *khatedari* and the privatization of land prevented the free use of resources so vital for the preservation of local skills. In England the skills which were acquired under the 'putting out' system came in handy at the dawn of industrial revolution although in both cases the journeyman and labourer suffered intense oppression.[126] In Berar also similar skills were present prior to colonialism. But before these skills had a chance to grow, the colonial interruption prevented its development. The raw materials locally produced were exported rather than made available for the development of local skill and industry. Thus the *khatedari* system suppressed all the local skills of manufacturing and prevented Berar's economic transformation from agriculture to industry. Consequently the region remained economically and socially backward. The region also lost the capacity to absorb shocks like famine and disease which were to follow.

The *khatedari* system created a class of corrupt and oppressive government officials at the local level known as patels and patwaris. As mentioned already these were lumpen elements who collected revenue on behalf of the colonial government. They summoned cultivators to the village chowries for the purpose of revenue payment.[127] This class was similar to the renegade class of black overseers whom the white planters in the American south freely employed to supervise the slave labour force.[128] This class was also synonymous with the character U Po Kyin immortalized by George Orwell in his novel the *Burmese Days*.[129] They were the eyes and ears of the colonial state and reported every activity of the people in the village. They were also granted the right to search any dwelling at any time of the day and under any pretext or suspicion.

[125] *Rules under the Berar Land Revenue Code, 1896*, 1907, p. 100.

[126] See Peter Laslett, *The World We Have Lost: England Before the Industrial Age*, 1984; E. P. Thompson, *The Making of the English Working Class*, 1964.

[127] *The Berar Patels and Patwaris Law, 1900*, D. V. Shiddore, ed., 1935, p. 130.

[128] See Robert W. Fogeland Stanley L. Engerman, *Time on the Cross: The Economics of American Negro Slavery*, 2 Vols, Boston, 1974.

[129] George Orwell, *Burmese Days*, San Diego, 1974.

The patels and patwaris had existed in pre-colonial times also but they had never worn a uniform. For the first time under *khatedari*, the visible presence of the colonial officials warned people of the existence of a new power from whose authority no one could escape. The patels normally wore *kala angarkhi* or the long black coat while the patwari wore *lal angarkhi* or the long red coat. Similarly jaglia (the village watchman) wore a thick leather belt, a badge, blue *pagri* (headgear), and a coat edged with yellow band. These local-level colonial officials also carried small arms.[130]

Despite their status as colonial officials the patels and patwaris were really very low paid commission agents. According to the rule:

> The rule throughout Berar is that the patel and patwari each receive as personal remuneration 5 per cent on the first Rs.1000 of land revenue collected 4 per cent on the second 3 on the third, so on to a final rate of 1 per cent per Rs.1000.[131]

Such a low pay naturally forced the patels to resort to corrupt and exploitative practices through the means of colonial office. As the Yeotmal Gazetteer noted that 'some patels also added considerably to their income by irregular means, taking money especially from poor and ignorant cultivator for doing their duty in some respects and for not doing it in others'.[132] A heavy security deposit was demanded when the Indians accepted government positions. Table 18 gives the amount of security deposit demanded.[133]

TABLE 18

Position	*Deposit in Rs.*
Tahsildar	5,000
Naib Tahsildar	2,500
Head Accountant	2,500
Treasurer	5,000
Potdars	500
Stamp store clerk	5,000
Revenue head copyist	200

[130] *Amraoti Gazetteer*, Bombay, 1911, p. 323.
[131] *Yeotmal District Gazetteer*, 1908, p. 187.
[132] *Yeotmal District Gazetteer*, 1908, p. 187.
[133] *Rules under the Berar Land Revenue Code*, Nagpur, 1907, p. 20.

It was the general tendency among the colonial officials to use their position to make good the amount paid as deposit. The figures for deposits made by patels is not available. But by using the position and power of the office, the patels often extracted *manpan* from everyone during festivals and marriages in the village. Since the patels were mostly from the upper caste, it made it all the more easy for them to employ government pressure of extraction to compensate for their low pay.

But however dominant the patels may have been, they were in turn exploited as a group by the colonial government. They were hostages in their own village. The Berar Patels and Patwaris Law stubbornly forbade them from physically moving about without the written permission of the Deputy Commissioner. This rule was in fact also applied to the people in general. The patel's duty was to report the movement of the people in and out of the village. He was also responsible for questioning such a mobility. The people of Berar were strictly monitored with colonial rules and regulations.[134] They had no freedom to move and this was serious especially in a depressed state of their material condition. Furthermore the most mundane, tedious, and physically demanding work of day-to-day administration was assigned to Indian officials while all the decision-making and managerial powers were exercised by the British officials.[135]

While every possible law was devised to persecute Indians, the European officials were immune from any complaint or grievance Indians might have against them. The government was immune from even court appeal by the laity. The Berar Land Revenue Code of 1896 clearly stated:

> No Revenue-officer shall be liable to be sued in any Civil Court for any act done, or ordered to be done, by him as such in pursuance, or execution, or intended execution, or the provisions of this Law or of any law, rule or order for the time being in force.[136]

The people in general were threatened by the presence of colonial courts and laws with awe. The upper castes and the

[134] *The Berar·Patels and Patwaris Law, 1900,* D. V. Shiddore, ed., 1935, p. 103.

[135] *Rules under the Berar Land Revenue Code, 1896,* Nagpur, 1907, p. 90.

[136] *The Berar Land Revenue Code, 1896,* in British Enactment in Force in Berar, 1916, p. 150.

moneylenders often made use of these courts and laws to extract labour and services from the illiterate populace. In this particular regard Chapter XI of the Berar Land Revenue Code caused fear in Berar. Whenever people heard the beat of drums at the village *chowri*, a terror ran through the entire populace. Twice a year the *khatedars* were summoned in every village by the beat of the drum for revenue collection. In cases of default, the government sold crops, moveable, and immoveable property of the defaulter *khatedar* in public auction. Under Chapter XI the beat of the drum was followed by the court decree leading to the arrest, imprisonment, detention, and attachment of *khatedari* belonging. The *khatedari* lands and belongings were then publicly auctioned in front of his person causing total shame, degradation, humiliation, and disgrace to himself and his entire family.[137]

Colonialism and the Problem of Literacy and Alcohol

At the time of first settlement (1862-77) Major Elphinstone had visualized the ideal of a school for every village combined with compulsory primary education.[138] The existence of mass illiteracy in 1900 goes to show that the *khatedari* system was incapable of investing in the education of people. Figures given in Table 19 shows a very low rate of literacy in Berar.[139]

TABLE 19

Year	*Total Population*	*Total Literate Population*	*Literacy Percentage*
1891	2,897,491	93,586	3.2
1901	2,764,016	123,316	4.5

On average only 3.8 per cent of the population was literate. Most of the literate population were either government servants or upper castes. Even among them literacy was minimally stressed. The patels and government clerks normally had just enough knowledge to run the

[137] *The Berar Land Revenue Code, 1896,* in British Enactment in Force in Berar, 1916, pp. 134-245.

[138] *Basim Taluka Settlement Report,* No. 203 of 1900, para 17.

[139] *Census of India 1901, Berar,* Part II, *Imperial Tables,* Allahabad, 1902, p. 126.

day-to-day business of administration and revenue collection. The shortage of teachers was a chronic problem. Table 20 shows the magnitude of this problem.[140]

TABLE 20

Census Year	*Total Population*	*Total No. of Teachers*	*No. of Persons per Teacher*
1881	2,672,673	1,451	1,841
1891	2,897,491	2,306	1,265

In the districts and talukas the situation was even more precarious. In Wun taluka in 1875 only 1 per cent of the population was literate.[141] Similarly in Amraoti Taluka out of 108,936 males only 2,749 persons (2.5 per cent) were literate and out of 51,674 females only 89 (0.1 per cent) could read and write.[142] Chandur Taluka also showed the same pattern of 1.5 per cent literacy rate. In a state of general poverty and material want, the necessity to employ children to work was more acute than the incentive to send them to school. This aspect of illiteracy was very sharply observed by the Chandur Taluka settlement officer and can also be conveniently applied to the whole of Berar. Writing in 1873 he states:

> Boys can be usefully employed at such an early age in tending cattle and numerous other duties, that it is a matter of great difficulty to induce a ryot to send his sons to the school. . . .[143]

The prevalence of general poverty and illiteracy naturally led to alcohol and opium indulgence. 'The ryots are as a rule, greatly addicted to drinking',[144] stated the Jalgaum settlement officer in 1865. The colonial government in fact encouraged consumption as it fetched revenue to the state. This is revealed in the following statement by supposedly one of the most enlightened colonial official of Berar and also of British India. Major P. E. A. Elphinstone wrote thus in his report of the Jalgaum Taluka:

[140] See *Census of India, 1891, Berar or the Hyderabad Assigned Districts*, Calcutta, 1892, p. cxlvii.

[141] *Wun Taluka Settlement Report*, No. 340 of 1875, para 25.

[142] *Oomrawuttee and Ellichpur Taluka Settlement Report*, No. 444 of 1870.

[143] *Chandur Taluka Settlement Report*, No. 470 of 1873, para 15.

[144] *Jalgaum Taluka Settlement Report*, No. 261 of 1865, para 17.

Both the mhowra and the toddy trees are very numerous all over the district, and I cannot help thinking that it would repay European enterprise to engage in arrack distillation in these parts. I suggest this in the interest of the Government as well as of public, as the former would, by extended competition, obtain a greater Abkaree revenue, and the latter, by a better mode of distillation, a more wholesome liquor.[145]

A yet another devastating impact of *khatedari* on Berar was the general shortage of capital and resources in the economy. The skimming of surplus in the form of revenues and raw materials left very little in the countryside. The settlement officer of the Mehkur taluka noted the state of general capital depletion in the following manner:

Want of capital among the agricultural population, as well as of the knowledge how to employ it, are, I imagine, two of the principal causes why farming is less profitable in India than it is in any other part of the world.[146]

This simple observation in fact tells only half the story. It is true that illiteracy and general capital shortage were the twin causes of Berar's backwardness. But it would be an exaggeration to state them as 'principal causes'. It was the settlement officer's inability to critically look at the role of colonial trade and government. Capital shortage and illiteracy were only the consequences revealing a state of backwardness. The real cause of Berar's backwardness was the colonial state itself.

Conclusion

It is argued in this chapter that the *khatedars* as a class of government registered tenants were created by the colonial state to ensure land revenue and political loyalty. The creation of private property rights in land conditional to revenue payment, guaranteed state control over the population. This had several ramifications. The development of subtenancy, rack-renting and indebtedness were the major consequences of the *khatedari* system. Landed property attracted moneylenders into the region. The brunt of the burden was borne by subtenants who rented land on oral contract and had no institutional protection either from the state or the government. State as the supreme landlord kept Berar tied to agriculture and prevented

[145] *Jalgaum Taluka Settlement Report,* No. 261 of 1865, para 31.
[146] *Mehkar Taluka Settlement Report,* No. 1098 of 1868, para 19.

the development of local entrepreneurial skills. Privatization of land, state control over forests, and the prevention of free use of available resources kept the region socially and economically backward. The population was pinned to the land through legal bonds and contracts. The upper castes formed the bulk of the *khatedars* and collaborated with the colonial state in exercising social and political control. The vast majority of the agrarian labour force resorted to resistance for survival. The agrarian discontentment to the *khatedari* system manifested itself in the form of crop robbing, illegal sale of cotton, trespassing, unauthorized occupancy, illegal cultivation, unauthorized cutting of grass and wood from government lands, smuggling, etc. The threat to secular social culture posed by colonial census was countered by people's refusal to give information to census inquisitors. The determination of *khatedars* to grow *khandeshi* cotton despite government ban was a clear manifestation of general discontentment of the population towards the colonial trade.

The state was primarily interested in developing a cotton economy to service the demands of powerful commercial interests in England. The development of cotton economy and its impact on local society is the story of next chapter.

CHAPTER 4

The Development of Cotton Economy and its Impact on Local Society

The Pre-colonial Background

FOR CENTURIES before the colonial takeover, cotton and cloth had been the prized commodities of Berar. The travellers passing through the valley never failed to notice the endless fields of cotton like lumps of fresh snow on the plants. It was in contrast to the thick black soil on which it grew and which enveloped the region throughout its length and breadth. It was also in contrast to the dark bodies of labourers who struggled in the fields under the bright sun of Deccan plateau. The scene was overwhelming and no traveller could have failed to notice it. The long trails of *banjara* carts originated from Purna valley and traversed in all directions carrying the famed *Oomra* cotton on their back. The ponies and packed bullocks herded by little boys and men were also commonly seen throughout the region from *kartik* (November) to *vaisak* (May) of every year. Then when monsoons began in June, the mundane rhythm of agricultural cycle year after year created a culture of its own which was quite unique to Berar.[1]

The first recorded export of cotton in modern times was made by a couple of Parsi merchants from Bombay and Hyderabad. In the season of 1825-6 Messrs. Vikaji and Pestonji, the great revenue farmers, made the first export of Berar cotton direct to Bombay. They took

[1] The earliest colonial accounts of Berar were recorded by British travellers Captain Meadows Taylor and Sir Richard Temple in the following works:

Meadows Taylor, 'The Story of My Life, 1857', in *Hyderabad Affairs*, Vol. 2, compiled by Moulvie Syed Mahdi Ali, Bombay, 1883, p. 725, at Andhra Pradesh State Archives, Hyderabad.

Sir Richard Temple, *Observation on the State and Administration of Hyderabad Assigned Districts*, dated 14 December 1867.

120,000 lbs of raw cotton worth 25,000 rupees in 500 bullocks. The same firm also opened the first cotton press in 1836.[2] Berar cotton was consumed in central India and also exported to the Princely State of Hyderabad. In fact revenues from Berar had maintained the despotic monarchy of the Nizam of Hyderabad in the eighteenth and early nineteenth century. Berar cotton went as far as Mirzapur in Awadh on its way to Calcutta at the mouth of river Ganges. This was a much longer and adventurous route covering 500 miles on bullocks to Mirzapore and then loading in boats on the holy Ganges and floating it down 450 miles to Calcutta. The whole journey took nearly hundred days. The journey on pack oxen from Berar to Bombay —a distance of 450 miles—normally took 60 days.[3] Most of the cotton was transported before the commencement of monsoon in June. A sufficient amount of lint was locally consumed. The pre-colonial Berar had a very large number of specialized castes, i.e. ginners, spinners, weavers and dyers. Together they had formed a manufacturing base in the region. Berar cloth competed in the neighbouring regions of Dharwar, Nagpur, central, and north India.

Under the Marathas and the Nizam, much of the cotton tracts were subjected to revenue farming. Since Berar was a principal *subah* of the Mughal Empire in Deccan, the emperors had taken special interest in developing roads and internal communication network. In the late seventeenth century the revenues from Berar had financed Aurangzeb's disastrous campaign against Marathas in the Deccan.[4] In spite of disturbed political condition of the eighteenth century, cotton trade of Berar continued to flourish. Its control became the bone of contention between Nizam and Marathas. The revenue farming system had come into existence during the late eighteenth century under *do amli* or double government of the Marathas and the Nizam.[5] When Marathas were defeated in 1818 by a combined force of the Nizam and British, Berar was unceremoniously mortgaged to Nizam. It was

[2] *Amraoti District Gazetteers*, Bombay, 1911, p. 248. Also see: 'Note on Indian Cotton', in the *Proceedings of the Department of Revenue and Agriculture*, Fibre and Silk Branch (May 1889), No. 25/27, New Delhi.

[3] *Report on the Cotton Department for the Year 1868-69*, by Harry Rivett-Carnac, Cotton Commissioner for the Central Provinces and the Berar, Bombay, 1869, p. 127.

[4] Mohammed Yaseen Quddusie, *Berar under the Mughals, 1595-1724 A.D.*, Ph.D Thesis, Nagpur, 1973, p. 145, in microfilm at NAI.

[5] *Central Provinces and Berar: A Review of the Administration of the Province, 1921-1923*, Nagpur, 1923, p. 151.

during this period that a unique system of revenue farming developed which came to be known as the *hoondakuri* system.

The precise origins of the *hoondakuri* system is unknown. It can be speculated that the expediency of raising revenues to counter the Maratha threat and the outright greed of Nizam's court at Hyderabad, gave rise to the system of tax farming of cotton routes. The internal roads through which raw cotton moved were auctioned off to the highest bidders known as *hoondakurs*. The *hoondakurs* generally constituted bankers and merchants based in Hyderabad and Bombay. They purchased cotton routes on an annual tax-farm basis and assumed control over these routes by appointing their agents. The agents then set up checkposts for collecting transit duties. The traders and merchants who purchased cotton in Berar paid transit tolls to take cotton out of the region. Since all the roads were auctioned off to *hoondakurs*, the merchants had to find the shortest possible route to trek their goods without paying too much in tolls. The process was slow and corrupt. The system which was initially meant to raise revenues (by taxing only cotton carts) was extended to all other commodities.

J. Forbes Royle, a colonial official travelling in Berar observed the *hoondakuri* system in the following manner: 'The routes selected by the carriers of the cotton, depends more upon the bargains made with the farmers of the transit duties, than upon the roads.'[6] Once the route has been farmed out, every carrier had to strike an average of what he has to pay for every description of the produce for the rest of the year.

The *hoondakuri* contracts usually ran from year to year. Since *hoondakurs* controlled the roads, the carriers did not have much choice. They had to traverse their cotton on the route defined by *hoondakurs*.[7] But there were several routes and several *hoondakurs* and the carrier had the choice to go from one to the other depending upon the rate of contract. For instance, on the road to Bombay, a man started from Amraoti and went to the first district transit duty contractor and said, 'I shall have the means of passing 500,000 bullock-loads of produce through your district during the next twelve months; at what rate will you levy *sayer* duties on the various commodities?' If

[6] J. Forbes Royle, *Review of the Measures which have been adopted in India for the Improved Culture of Cotton*, London, 1857, p. 49.

[7] J. Forbes Royle, *On the Culture and Commerce of Cotton in India and Elsewhere*, London, 1851, p. 327.

the terms were satisfactory a bargain was at once struck. If the terms were unsatisfactory, he tried contractors in neighbouring districts. And ultimately an agreement was reached with one or the other *hoondakur*. The cotton usually arrived at Bombay either by a direct route or a circuitous route. The rate charged by *hoondakurs* had no reference to the time occupied in transit. The time of transit was regulated by *banjaras*, 'who alone have the carrying trade in their hands, and who undertake to deliver to Bombay as many bullock-loads of cotton as may be made over to their custody; but they will never allow themselves to be restricted to time; they restrict themselves to the road, because they are obliged to adopt roads that the *hoondakurs* have previously established',[8] observed Walter L. Cassels as early as 1862.

The system made rapid transportation of cotton at low rates virtually impossible. The carts were taxed at every point and this kept the price of cotton high although the producers benefited little from the *hoondakuri* system.

TECHNOLOGY AND SOCIO-ECONOMIC CHANGE

The Development of Cotton Economy

However inefficient or corrupt the *hoondakuri* system may have been, a large amount of cotton stayed within Berar for either domestic consumption or for the production of value added manufactured cloth. An average Berari was adequately clothed. The *hoondakuri* system indirectly helped in retaining raw cotton within Berar. The transportation was expensive and *hoondakuri* system further added to the expense.

With the beginning of tension between American North and South in the 1850s, the European merchants and manufacturers in Manchester and Liverpool began to be concerned about cotton supplies.[9] This was

[8] Walter R. Cassels, *Cotton: An Account of its Culture in the Bombay Presidency*, Bombay, 1862, p. 203.

[9] See Gavin Wright, *The Political Economy of the Cotton South: Households, Markets, and Wealth in the Nineteenth Century*, New York, 1978; Peter Harnetty, *Imperialism and Free Trade: Lancashire and India in the mid-Ninteenth Century*, Vancouver, 1972; 'India and British Commercial Enterprise: The Case of Manchester Cotton Company, 1860-64', *Indian Economic and Social History Review*, Vol. III, No. 4 (Dec. 1966), p. 396.

one of the reasons for the British takeover of Berar in 1853. The *hoondakuri* system presented too many obstacles for the smooth transhipment of cotton out of Berar. As the colonial state began consolidating power, its political and economic interest increasingly came in conflict with that of the *hoondakurs*. The latter not only controlled the economy but also posed a political threat by creating local bases of power. Furthermore, the *hoondakuri* system was intimately connected with the prevailing system of revenue farming.

The revenue farmers and *hoondakurs* had dominated the politics and revenues of Berar from the turn of the nineteenth century. Governor General Lord Wellesley (1798-1805) almost broke the power of Marathas by granting Berar to the Nizam of Hyderabad for his loyalty to the British power.[10] The revenue farmers were freebooters and agents who purchased revenue collecting rights over different regions of the province by paying a fixed cash sum to the Nizam's treasury in Hyderabad. These rights were sold annually in auction to the highest bidder. The revenue farmers then went to their respective districts and looted peasants and villages by employing force, violence, and oppression. Since revenue contracts ran for one year, the rate of appropriation was maximized. This devastated the countryside.

If the British were to establish their power and authority, then revenue farming and the *hoondakuri* system needed to be dismantled. This was precisely what the colonial state did after the takeover. The *hoondakurs* and revenue farmers were dismissed without compensation. Transit duties and tolls were done away with and a modern bureaucratic structure was put in its place. The revenue system was regularized and standardized. Modern technology was introduced to facilitate smooth and rapid movement of cotton in and out of Berar. The development of colonial cotton economy would not have been possible without the destruction of *hoondakuri* system.

While extraction of revenue was the primary aim of colonial land survey and settlement operations, the extraction of cotton was the principal motive behind the introduction of European technology. Therefore the planning and immediate execution of railroads and metalled roads was the first priority of the Government of India and its cronies in Berar. This was a very strategic operation and carried

[10] See C. U. A. Aitchison, *Collection of Treaties Engagements and Sanads Relating to Indian and Neighbouring Countries*, Vol. II, Delhi, 1930.

out with great speed. An efficient coordination of railroads and roads with telegraph and post office was essential for the success of cotton trade. In 1866 Harry Rivett-Carnac (an agent of the Manchester Chamber of Commerce) was appointed as the 'Cotton Commissioner for Central Provinces and Berar' by the order of the Government of India. It was his 'duty to watch over all affairs relating to cotton, and to further, so far as might be legitimately possible all interests connected therewith'.[11] With the aid of colonial district officers and cooperation of European merchants, he exercised a powerful influence and was a law unto himself. His job was to keep a strict supervisory eye on the cotton and act as a quality control enforcer. He was paid to make sure that Berar exported the best cotton to England.[12] But the general mass of people looked at the Cotton Commissioner with suspicion and distrust. He usually operated through local collaborators, i.e. landlords and strongmen of the villages.[13]

The Railways and Roads in Cotton Territory

On the eve of the inauguration of Khamgaon branch line in 1870, Lord Mayo, the then Governor General, openly declared that 'the mills of Manchester are, I fear still working at very short time, and we know that they can take a great deal more cotton then they get . . . that being the case, our object ought to be to strain every nerve both to improve quality and increase quantity.' He further elaborated by stating: 'This puts me in mind of a remark made by a well-known bon vivant, who used to say that "the best thing in the world is good wine, that the next best thing in the world is bad wine; but whatever it is, good or bad, let us have enough of it". Now I think that this is very much what the Manchester people are saying with regard to cotton. They say "give us good cotton if you can, but give us any sort

[11] *Report on the Operations of the Cotton Department for the Year 1867,* by Harry Rivett-Carnac, Cotton Commissioner, Central Provinces and Berar, Bomaby, 1869, p. 23.

[12] Note by Mr. H.E.M. James, Bombay Civil Service, On Cotton Trade Frauds and Deterioration of Staples, in the *Proceedings of the Revenue and Agricultural Department,* Fibre and silk Branch (November 1891), pp. 1-13.

[13] *Report on the Operations of the Cotton Department for the Year 1867,* by Harry Rivett-Carnac, Cotton Commissioner, Central Provinces and Berar, Bombay, 1869, pp. 29-31.

rather than none. Whatever it is we get we will find the way to spin it"; and they are right, for what they most dread is the idle mill.'[14]

The above statement was made well after the railways were firmly established in Berar. All through the nineteenth century the Manchester Chamber of Commerce had openly collaborated with slaveholders of the American south. The development of a cotton economy in colonial India was in a way an escape from the shameful union of Manchester with the ante-bellum southern planters. 'The Berar country about Oomrawattee is the center of the cotton cultivation, and, by the advancing line of the Great India Peninsular Railway, Manchester has already drawn from these provinces the bales which saved her from sharing the penalty, as she once shared the crime of the southern states of America.'[15] Berar especially became vulnerable to colonial exploitation during and after the American Civil War when Indian cotton prevailed in the London market.[16]

By 1870, one hundred and fifty miles of railroad were laid connecting Berar to Bombay in the west and Nagpur in the east. Fourteen stations were built on this line which came to be known as the Nagpur branch of the Great Indian Peninsular Railway. Metalled roads were built to connect with railways and fair-weather roads were built connecting villages.[17] Immediately after its invention in England, the railway was introduced in India and ultimately in Berar. In 1853 on the recommendation of the Governor General Lord Dalhousie, the Board of Directors of the East India Company gave immediate approval for the construction of Nagpur branch line. The main purpose of course was the extraction of upcountry cotton. 'This recommendation has our approval, and we shall make immediate arrangements in view of the survey of the valley of the Taptee and that of the Syhadrée range. In conducting the necessary operation, for deciding this question, we should wish that ready access to the great cotton Districts of Berar be kept in view as the great object of this line of Railway,'[18] wrote the

[14] *Hyderabad Affairs*, Vol. 4, compiled by Moulvie Syed Mahdi Ali, Bombay (n.d.), p. 196.

[15] *Hyderabad Affairs*, Vol. 2, compiled by Moulvie Syed Mahdi Ali, Bombay, 1883, p. 405.

[16] Frenise A. Logan, 'India - Britain's Substitute for American Cotton, 1861-1865', *The Journal of Southern History*, XXIV, No. 4 (November 1958), pp. 472-80.

[17] A. C. Lyall, *Gazetteer of the Haidarabad Assigned Districts, Commonly called Berar*, Bombay, 1870, p. 239.

[18] *India and Bengal Despatches*, Vol. 82, 17 August 1853, pp. 1140-2, from Board of Directors, EIC (London), to Financial/Railway Dept., Government of India.

Board of Director to the Governor General in Calcutta on the eve of Berar's takeover. The colonial state, while being sluggish about extending irrigation or public works, never showed any inhibition in the extension of the branch railway line. Indeed the railway was the backbone of cotton trade and no stone was to be left unturned in its development.[19] The GIP railway was to run through the heart of Berar like a knife to 'carry off the greater part of its cotton'.[20] The cotton trains ran the entire length of the Berar valley carrying huge bales on its back. All cotton from Berar then was destined for England. It was the first priority of colonial government to maintain this cotton line because this was the main artery of traffic between cotton producing districts and the ports of shipment. 'It is the desire of the Government of India that measures be at once taken to have such lines of traffic examined and reported on by a competent officer.'[21] The cost of the maintenance of cotton line was defrayed from local funds and taxes.[22]

William Cronon, in his recent work on the nineteenth, century American mid-west, has argued that technological innovations like the railroads and grain elevators drew natural resources from its surrounding areas and transformed the face of the mid-western countryside. It also made possible the rise of large metropolis like Chicago. He has forcefully presented an argument demonstrating the power of technology to bring about change like a 'sorcerer wielding a magic wand'.[23] Such an analysis exhibits traits of 'technological determinism' and has its limitations when applied to developments in colonial societies like Berar. Here colonial technological innovations like railways and steam gins and presses did bring about a revolution in processing and shipping of cotton but failed to trigger the growth of

[19] *Report of the Operations of the Cotton Department for the Year 1867,* by Harry Rivett-Carnac, Cotton Commissioner, Central Provinces and Berar, Bombay, 1869, p. 46.

[20] Walter R. Cassels, *Cotton: An Account of its Culture in the Bombay Presidency,* Bombay, 1862, p. 225.

[21] From: M. J. Shaw Stewart, Under Secretary to Government, To: W. C. Anderson, Superintendent Revenue Survey and Assessment, Southern Mahratta Country and Berar, in the *Proceedings of the Revenue Department,* No. 1977 of 1861, in *British Parliamentary Papers,* Vol. 44, 1863, p. 392.

[22] Walter R. Cassels, *Cotton: An Account of its Culture in the Bombay Presidency,* 1862, p. 221.

[23] See William Cronon, *Nature's Metropolis: Chicago and the Great West,* New York, 1991.

large metropolis like Chicago in the Great West. Instead it brought environmental degradation and altered the social relationship between capital and labour leading to the exploitation and impoverishment of the latter.

The revolt of 1857 gave a rude shock to the colonial state. It was then realized that unless control was tightened, India would also slip out of the colonial grasp as North America had done a century earlier. Therefore the internal communications had to be developed with a dual purpose of facilitating the rapid movement of trade and troops. 'The roads from Akote and Akolah, and from Morsee to Budnaira, are probably the most important as feeders to the railway; but in a military point of view, those connecting the troops at Ellichpur and Hingolee with the railway would appear to be the most consequence.'[24] Metalled roads were built to feed the railways with cotton. Whenever a railway station was built, a feeder road was simultaneously constructed. The covering cost for the feeders was collected by the imposition of a 1 per cent income tax on merchants and moneylenders who eventually passed it on to the cultivators. The construction of road network was designed to serve as feeders to the railway. This was done with a colonial foresight of developing an 'uninterrupted communication between the railway and the principal marts in Berar, which are at any distance from the line'.[25]

The feeders did an excellent job of transporting cotton from deep inside villages and marts to the railway line. But cotton arrived and glutted railway stations and obstructed traffic. The colonial state was then faced with the problem of the smooth loading of cotton bales into the railway bogies. The Manchester men were getting upset about this bottleneck in the cotton flow. In 1865, Mr. Cordery, the Deputy Commissioner of Akola, developed a unique system for solving this problem. Huge yards were built in every railway station and stocks of cotton were taken in. These yards were owned and operated

[24] From: Captain W. Cadell, Assistant Commissioner in Charge of Commissioner's office, To: First Assistant Resident at Hyderabad, Nos. 2059-301, dated 19 September 1861, in *The British Parliamentary Papers*, Vol. 44, 1863; Correspondence from 1 January 1861 to the present time between the Secretary of State for India and the Governor General or other persons in India, on the subject of Cotton Cultivation in India, and the Prospects of Supplies of that Article to this country during the Present Year 1864, p. 176 (IOLR).

[25] *General Administration Report on the Hyderabad Assigned Districts for the Year 1861-62*, Calcutta, 1863, para 114.

by the government and the railway company. The principal aim of the 'Cordery System' was: (a) the safety of the cotton detained, and (b) the prevention of unfair practice in the dispatch of cotton. 'The system of stack-yards for cotton in immediate proximity to the railway stations, which met the approval of the Supreme Government in 1864, has been extended to all the new stations, and been excellently worked by the Cotton Commissioner. By these means an independent registration of all bales is ensured immediately after their arrival within 200 yards of the station.'[26] The system of cotton yards was a very efficient operation. The bales were stacked in rows and cleared in the order received. The yards were provided with fire-engines, buckets, tanks of water, police guards and dogs. The Cotton Commissioner periodically visited these yards with an inspector to oversee the entire operation. In order to enable easy loading of bales from the yards to railway bogies, 'sidings were run into the yards from the main line of railway, which materially assisted the loading of the cotton'.[27] While the Cotton Commissioner and other colonial officials stood on the side in their jackboots, jungle hats, khaki uniforms holding stiff leather canes, the Berar *coolies* ran up and down the sidings carrying bales of precious cotton from the yards into the railway wagons. This was a common sight in every railway station of Berar in the nineteenth century. The belching chimney of the railway engine carried hundreds and thousands of bales of cotton out of Berar year after year.

A marked improvement in the 'carrying off' traffic was achieved with the erection of cotton presses in government yards. This marked improvement to a considerable extent was owing to the increase in rolling stocks, the construction of new crossing stations, through trains and such other arrangements of detail. 'I must also mention', wrote the Cotton Commissioner in 1867, 'that not only were the arrangements of the railway company such as that the cotton was never detained in the yards through any fault of theirs, but that, thanks to the improved traffic arrangements, the cotton trains were pushed on to Bombay with much fewer stoppages, and much less delay than in former years'.[28]

One marked feature which sharply distinguished the colonial state

[26] *Report on the Operations of the Cotton Department for the Year 1867*, by Harry Rivett-Carnac, p. 49.

[27] Ibid., p. 48.

[28] *Report on the Operations of the Cotton Department for the Year 1867*, by Harry Rivett-Carnac, p. 53.

from pre-colonial Berar was that the colonial state constantly struggled to achieve maximum efficiency from its instruments of exploitation. The railway was one such crucial instrument. Within four years after the introduction of the 'Cordery System' (1865), the cotton yards became obsolete. In 1869 a further improvement was brought about in the existing system of delivering cotton: 'There is, in fact, no cotton now to guard and watch. The consignments are generally loaded up a few hours after their arrival; and the establishment of clerks, police guards, men to fill the water-tanks and work the fire-engines, are no longer necessary. . . . In like manner, . . . the cotton now merely passes through the yards and is no longer stacked there. . . .'[29] The Cotton Commissioner did an excellent job in detecting and clearing glitches in the cotton flow. He personally went up and down the line checking the arrangements made at each and every station. In 1870 no cotton was to be found stacked near the stations. In Khamgaon and Amraoti, the two great cotton marts of Berar, the bales were taken straight to the waiting railway wagons.[30]

While in Great Britain the railways accelerated the pace of industrialization,[31] in Berar it became the instrument of extraction. Contrary to triggering industrialization, the accelerated pace of trade brought by the railway reduced the region to a producer and supplier of raw material. The chief articles of exports were raw cotton and oil-seeds. The chief articles of imports were cotton piece-goods and salt.[32] Thus within a decade (1860-70), the railway had succeeded in linking the region to world market. Consequently Berar ended up as the supplier of raw cotton and consumer of finished cloth. The process of deskilling and deindustrialization transformed Berar into a full-fledged agrarian society. The demobilized weavers, spinners, and ginners fell on the land for livelihood. The impact on the *banjaras* was much more dramatic. They were traditionally the owners of carts and

[29] *Report on the Cotton Department for the Year 1868-69*, by Harry Rivett-Carnac, para 107.

[30] From: H. Rivett-Carnac, Cotton Commissioner, Central Provinces and Berar, To: Lieutenant G. H. Trevor, Officiating Ist Assistant Resident, Hyderabad, No. 50, dated 13 February 1869, in *Foreign Department Proceedings*, May 1869, Nos. 49-51.

[31] See David Landes, *The Unbound Prometheus: Technological Change and Industrial Development in Western Europe from 1750 to the Present*, Cambridge, 1979.

[32] *Report of the Famine Commission, 1880*, Appendix V: Irrigation as a Protection against Famine, London, 1881, p. 481.

carriers of cotton. With the full impact of railways, they had to give up their old trade and become agricultural labourers.[33]

The construction of railways was not a very expensive operation. Mostly famine labour was utilized in building railroads.[34] During times of famine and scarcity the labour was cheaper and available in abundance. The railways primarily served two functions: (1) The imperial function of moving troops and military hardware, and (2) The colonial function of exporting cotton and importing cloth. There is no evidence of any passenger traffic on this line. It was neither designed to serve the people nor did the people have the means to avail its services. The railways were therefore solely serving the imperial and colonial interest. The total number of employees working for the Nagpur branch of the Great Indian Peninsula Railway was also minuscule compared to the total population of Berar. Of the total population of 2,897,491 in 1891 only 3,410 persons were employed in the railways.[35] Furthermore the hiring practices of the railway company stank of racial and caste prejudice. Both the colonial state and European firms systematically used race and caste in their hiring practices. As soon as the colonial census (introduced in 1871) and gazetteers categorized people on the basis of caste and race, the practice of reserving certain types of jobs exclusively for certain castes and races came into being. For instance, in railway service the driving of the engine and its maintenance was assigned to the upper caste while the tracks and signals were worked by the lower caste. The Railway Order VII read: 'It will be seen that the Railway obtains its employees from among Christians, Parsis and Brahmans for the upper posts, and from Musalmans, Kunbis, Mahars and others for the lower posts.'[36]

Dividing people on the basis of race and caste was the standard practice of colonial state in Berar. The imposition of order and discipline was in fact a truly modern characteristic of the colonial state. A centralized bureaucratic structure brought about a uniformity necessary for the regimentation of labour and resources. Colonialism in a way represented modernism in its organization and categorization of people and by encroaching over their political, economic, and

[33] *Census of India, 1891*, Vol.VI, *Berar or the Hyderabad Assigned Districts*, Calcutta, 1892, p. cxlvi.

[34] *Basim Settlement Report*, No. 203 of 1900, para 38, p. 13.

[35] *Census of India-1891*, Vol. VI, *Berar or the Hyderabad Assigned Districts*, p. cxlvi.

[36] *Report on the Census of Berar, 1881*, Bombay, 1882, p. 182.

social freedom. Colonial modernism also represented itself in the visible infrastructure it created. The arrangement of rows of cotton in yards by the railway stations, and the meeting of railways and roads at right angle intersection was directly related to the colonial order and hierarchy. The colonial state therefore made stern efforts to achieve a high degree of uniformity by its intense hostility to all forms of diversity and mobility. It was precisely this type of a modern state that Berar represented in the late nineteenth century.

In Berar all roads led to the railway station. At the height of the cotton trade, 'the Great Indian Peninsula Line, which almost bisects the province, is, with the subsidiary state line running to Khamgaon and Amraoti, the one main artery of trade in the province. All other lines of trade are subsidiary to it, and every road constructed is valuable chiefly as leading to the railway.'[37] While the railways connected Berar to the world market, the roads connected cotton villages to the railway line.

It was the colonial thesis from the earliest times that the absence of good metalled roads was an obstacle in the development of cotton cultivation in India.[38] This was particularly true of the region like Berar where the topography made carriage expensive. This was one of the reasons that in pre-colonial times cotton was a staple crop like any other crop. Its use was mostly for home consumption.

Under the Mughal administration the *subah* Berar had a well-maintained system of roads which were used mostly for political and military purposes.[39] But these had since the early eighteenth century fallen into disrepair. The *hoondakurs* in the nineteenth century revived these roads for the purpose of farming cotton routes. Since Berari cotton had an enormous internal market, the *hoondakuri* system had developed an elaborate scheme of local tolls and taxes. With the colonial takeover the basic structure of *hoondakuri* cotton roads were retained but internal tolls and taxes were done away with. It was soon realized that the *hoondakuri* roads were slow and circuitous and unusable during the monsoon season. A replanning of major roads was undertaken under the colonial aegis. A need to build all weather metalled roads was felt for the first time. The newly built metalled

[37] *Report on the Trade of the Hyderabad Assigned Districts for the Year 1878-79*, Hyderabad, 1880, p. 3.

[38] J. Forbes Royle, *On the Culture and Commerce of Cotton in India, and Elsewhere*, London, 1851, p. 5.

[39] See Irfan Habib, *An Atlas of the Mughal Empire*, Delhi, 1982.

roads also interconnected railway lines at right angle. Colonial transportation network in a way personified the orderly and disciplined colonial state itself.

In 1861 the Government of India appointed a committee to suggest a system of roads for Berar. The committee recommended fourteen full metal roads which 'in their opinion, will be the most useful for conveying the produce of the country to the railway stations'. It further asserted that 'it appears to be admitted that roads which cannot be used throughout the year would be of little or no use as feeders to the railway, and the Committee have therefore recommended that any roads which may be made should allow of traffic passing over them during the monsoon'.[40] Free government land was allocated for the purpose of roads and railway construction. The recommendation was made for the roads to be built connecting cotton marts with the cotton, growing villages deep inside Berar. It was specified that these roads were to be built for the use of 'trade and troops'.[41] The work was immediately commenced and by 1884 Berar had no less than 3,016 miles[42] of roads of which 1500 miles were excellent full metalled *pucca* roads and 197.5 miles of railroads.[43] 'The system of communication in Berar and in this District [Amraoti] in particular may be roughly compared to the human anatomy. The Great Indian Peninsula Railway running the whole length of the central valley is the backbone: on it converges a network of roads, metalled and unmetalled, communicating with most of the important towns and centres of trade.'[44] The railway line passed through the centre of Purna valley and connected all important cotton marts of the region like 'pearls in a necklace'. Instructions were issued to all the officiating Commissioners to throw open roads on both sides of the valley as feeders to the railway.[45] Consequently all the metalled roads were

[40] *The British Parliamentary Papers,* Vol. 44 (1863), p. 176.

[41] From: G. V. Yule, Esq., C.B., Resident at Hyderabad to Secretary, To: The Government of Bombay in the Public Works Department, No. 185, dated 23 January 1865, in *Hyderabad Affairs,* Vol. IV, compiled by Moulvie Syed Mahdi Ali, Bombay, [apprx. 1884], pp. 206-8.

[42] *Report on the Trade of the Hyderabad Administration for the Year 1883-84,* Hyderabad, 1884, p. 6.

[43] *Proceedings of the Hyderabad Administration for the Month of April 1887,* submitted to the Foreign Department, No. 1025-R, dated 25 April 1887.

[44] *Amraoti District Gazetteer,* ed. by S. V. Fitzgerald, Bombay, 1911, p. 254.

[45] *General Administration Report on the Hyderabad Assigned District for the Year 1858-59,* Calcutta, 1860, para 161.

built connecting the railway line and the cotton trade obediently gravitated towards the railway. As already mentioned, the roads and railway lines were laid out in a perfectly planned right angle intersection resembling order and hierarchy which the colonial state had imposed on Berar. These were first class modern roads available for traffic at all seasons of the year.[46] The roads were provided with bridges and causeways for through traffic. The average width of the road was 10 to 12 feet and was built with hard indurated basalt obtained from the local trap.[47]

The toll-free roads were a great envy to some of the colonial officials who felt that revenues could be raised by taxing the cotton carts plying on these roads. But the external market and the Manchester Chamber of Commerce preferred to keep the price as low as possible at the source of its primary production. So even though the colonial officials tried to appease the government by trying to raise the revenue, it could not be done because the colonial government itself tried to appease their Manchester masters. The frustration of the colonial officials was undeniable. As early as 1868, one of them wrote:

> I have not noticed toll-bars anywhere in Berar. It seems to me a pity that so simple and suitable a means for collecting funds for the repair of the roads should not be adopted. Such a mode of taxation the natives are accustomed to, it would therefore be more welcome to them then any other with which they are less familiar, and I do not think that we need fear any evil effect from it on the trade of the country. . . . I would recommend cotton carts being taxed much more heavily than carts conveying other produce. . . .[48]

Bulk of the cotton passed during the months from November to April. During this period the interior roads connected the villages to the metalled roads. The colonial state did not find it necessary to construct metalled roads in the interior of Berar. Transforming country-roads to metalled roads was considered more expensive then building light railways.[49] Moreover there was no traffic during the monsoon season anyway. Once the land revenue was paid and cotton delivered, there was no need for the government to bother with villages. So

[46] *General Administration Report on the Hyderabad Assigned Districts for the Year 1865-66*, Calcutta, 1867, paras 111-12.

[47] *Buldana District Gazetteer*, Calcutta, 1910, p. 280.

[48] *Mehkur Taluka Settlement Report*, No. 1098 of 1868, p. 2, para 11 (NMML).

[49] *Report of the Cotton Department for the Year 1868-69*, by Harry Rivett-Carnac, p. 118.

villages remained isolated from market towns until the next cotton season. The village roads and conditions in villages remained in an absolute state of neglect. The cart-tracks which came alive during non-rainy season became useless with the onset of monsoons. The showers gutted the ruts with slush and broke axles and wheels which were generally made of wood. As mentioned earlier the peasants during the monsoon months from June to September took their carts to pieces and hung them in the out-houses. 'As soon as the rains set in, it appears to be the almost universal practice to take the carts to pieces and stow them away in the houses till the monsoon is over,'[50] wrote the settlement officer of the Wun Taluka in 1869.

The instruments of modernization, i.e. the metalled roads and the railway, hardly touched the villages. It helped in carrying the cotton away and was mostly used by merchants, traders, and the colonial state. Even by the end of the nineteenth century the villages were still connected with useless ruts.[51] In fact as the ruts became deeper and deeper, the communication became slower and slower. But it did not in any way affect the cotton trade. The fairs and country markets shifted from the villages to metalled roads along which the goods flowed.

Other Instruments for the Colonial Extraction of Cotton

Another major step in the development of cotton economy was the introduction of post and telegraph in Berar. These so- called new instruments of change also performed the same function as the roads and railway. While roads had connected the internal markets of Berar, the railway succeeded in connecting Berar to the world market. Similarly the postal system connected markets from Amraoti to Khamgaon while telegraph connected Berar to Manchester and

[50] *Wun Taluka Settlement Report,* No. 340 of 1875, para 15. Also see *Report on the Cotton Department for the Year 1868-69,* by Harry Rivett-Carnac, para 120.

[51] The ruts were tracks made by the wheels of the slow moving country bullock carts. It consisted of two parallel ruts situated at about 3 feet apart, varying in depth from a few inches to 1.5 feet. The rain water usually collected in these ruts and struck the wheels and broke the axles. Cart drivers usually carried several spare axles at the bow of their carts for emergency. Most of the internal communication of Berar outside the metalled roads and railway was conducted on these ruts. For more see *Report on the Cotton Department for the Year 1868-69,* by Harry Rivett-Carnac, Cotton Commissioner for the Central Provinces and the Berars, Bombay, 1869, p. 119.

Liverpool. Cotton messages could now be delivered directly from Manchester to Khamgaon and Amraoti to Liverpool without any delay.

The first electric telegraph was built in 1862-3 at Sheagaon which was a major railway station on the Nagpur-Bombay branch line. It was but natural for the railway company to undertake the construction of telegraph line. Every telegraph line originated from the railway station and connected other railway stations where cotton marts were located.[52] The wires of the telegraph lines suspended from the wooden poles ran along the streaks of the thick black smoke emitted by the railway engines. The view of the clear sky was obstructed by these poles on which often the country birds rested and nested. The government controlled all the land. So, free land was given to the railway company for building railway and telegraph. By 1868 all cotton markets of Berar were connected to Bombay and Lancashire. A cotton merchant sitting in Manchester could sent quotations of prices at which the cotton was to be purchased in Berar and have the consignment delivered to him within four to six weeks. The telegraph made instant communication of 'cotton messages' a reality.[53]

With the perfection of telegraph, the postal system was also geared into action. Imperial mail during Mughal times was carried by runners with spears and bags. Under colonialism, the system of runners was done away with and 'tanga daks' were introduced. These were horse-drawn carriages which carried bulk mail faster than the runners. The railways were also used for the delivery of mail. Special railway mail bogies were attached to the cotton trains for prompt delivery of letters and parcels. By 1870-71 the postal system was perfected to such an extent that the Bombay letters reached Khamgaon at 8 a.m. in the morning and the outward mail closed at 3:30 p.m. the same day.[54] The Nagpur Dak Line ran through Berar—a distance of 165 mile connecting all the stations on the way to Bombay.[55] 'The post-offices in Berar are treated as Imperial, not as provincial establishments; that is, the

[52] *General Administration Report on the Hyderabad Assigned Districts for the Year 1862-63*, Calcutta, 1864, para 97.

[53] *Report on the Cotton Department for the Year 1868-69*, by Harry Rivett-Carnac, pp. 112-14.

[54] *Report on the Cotton Experiments in West Berar during the Season 1869-70.*

[55] *General Administration Report on the Hyderabad Assigned Districts for the Year 1861-62*, para 95.

receipts and expenditure connected with them are credited and debited to the revenues of British India.'[56] Whether Imperial or Provincial, the post offices were hardly ever used by the general masses. Most of the letters were either official government correspondence or the letters of merchants and traders doing business in cotton. The post office was neither designed nor structured for use of general public. The clutter and clang of the post office and telegraph was a nonsensical nuisance so far as the people were concerned. Even the volume of the letters was insignificant to be of any worth to the people. For example, for the whole of Wun taluka with a population of 83,000 people, only 200 letters were received in the year 1908.[57] In addition to railways, telegraph, post office, and metalled roads, there were several minor but equally significant instruments employed for the development of cotton economy in Berar. One such instrument was the 'pluviometer' for the accurate measurement of rainfall in the region.[58] Keeping accurate record of the weather was top priority of the colonial government. Absence of an organized irrigation system threw agriculture at the mercy of climate. Almost every colonial document of the nineteenth century has devoted a considerable amount of time and energy to compiling weather data. Manchester men were kept well informed by their agent (the Cotton Commissioner) about the state of supplies. During the cotton season the Cotton Commissioner sent fortnightly reports to the Chamber of Commerce on the state of the weather and the state of supplies.[59] The development of an unfavourable weather condition or major disturbances in weather pattern were immediately reported so that precautionary measures could be taken by cotton interests in England. Agent's fortnightly 'Report on the State of Weather and the Condition of Cotton Crop' was followed with great interest in Bombay and Liverpool. Advance warnings were sounded on any unfavourable cotton season. The Cotton Commissioner wrote in 1867: 'The weather reports periodically submitted by me, and published by permission of Government, for

[56] *Report on the Administration of the Hyderabad Assigned Districts for the Year 1869-70*, Hyderabad, 1871, para 266.

[57] *Yeotmal District Gazetteer*, Calcutta, 1908, p. 142.

[58] A. C. Lyall, *Gazetteer of the Haidarabad Assigned Districts, Commonly called Berar*, 1870, p. 51.

[59] From: Cotton Commissioner, Central Provinces and Berars, To: Secretary Chamber of Commerce, Bombay, dated 12 February 1868, in *Foreign Department Proceedings*, March 1868, Nos. 124-5.

the information of those interested in the cotton trade, will, I think, have prepared the Chief Commissioner to bear of an unfavorable cotton season.'[60] There is no evidence of these weather reports being made available to the cultivators.

Stations of Another Kind: Agricultural Experiments

The two main types of cotton grown in Berar were *bani* and *jari*. Both varieties were medium to long stapled and were popularly known in the Liverpool market as the great 'Oomra' taking the name from Amraoti, the principal cotton mart in Berar. Traditionally indigenous to the region, the *bani* grew in rugged but rich black terrain of the south known as *Balaghat.* The *jari* grew in the dark alluvial plain of the north and around the Purna river valley known as *Payanghat.*[61]

Irrespective of the quality, the Manchester cotton men had always looked down upon Indian cotton vis-a-vis American strain. The cotton mills in Britain were designed to process American staple and the Manchester men were unwilling to invest in redesigning the machinery to accommodate any other cotton. In any case, elaborate experimental stations were set up all over India and the cultivation of exotic varieties of cotton seeds was undertaken. Berar became the front rank colonial possession for conducting these experiments. Large experimental stations were opened in Sheagaon and Amraoti in 1867-8.[62] The seeds from New Orleans, Sea Island, Upland Georgian, Egyptian, Brazilian, Peruvian and all possible varieties were tried.[63] The Cotton Commissioner had pronounced in 1867: 'The most important question connected with cotton cultivation seemed to be this:- Whether, in the matter of improving the cotton staple for the home market, a greater degree of success could be obtained in this part of India by introducing exotic seed, or by improving the indigenous cotton of the country.'[64] Hybridization of plants was also attempted. This was done by impregnating the flowers of native varieties with

[60] *Report on the Operations of the Cotton Department for the Year 1867,* by Harry Rivett-Carnac, p. 13.

[61] *The British Parliamentary Papers,* Vol. 44, 1863, p. 6.

[62] *Report on the Cotton Department for the Year 1868-69,* by Harry Rivett-Carnac, p. 48.

[63] *The British Parliamentary Papers,* Vol. 44, 1863, p. 2.

[64] *Report on the Operations of the Cotton Department for the Year 1867,* by Harry Rivett-Carnac, p. 38.

pollen from the foreign kinds.[65] Similarly, experiments with European wheat were also tried alongside cotton. The much-needed seed was provided by Messrs Oakshott and Co., the Seed Corn Growers of Reading in Berkshire.[66]

The motives behind these experimental ventures was to encourage the growth of cotton varieties better suited for the machines of Manchester cotton textile mills. Whether indigenous or foreign, Manchester succeeded in extracting the necessary cotton from Berar but the experimental farms were an enormous waste of money. As Mr. R. D. Hare, the survey and settlement officer, stated in 1890:

> Experimental farms have never been anything but a pure waste of money in Berar, and it is to my mind very doubtful whether it would be possible to teach the kunbis any improved processes of agriculture that would be suited to their circumstances. Such improvements all seem to run in the direction of machinery to save labour or methods of restoring the productive power of the land by chemical manures. They all require capital, and are thoroughly unsuited to a country broken up into very small holdings, the owners of which live from hand to mouth.[67]

The experimental farms became a mockery in a country of poverty and indebtedness. Similarly, the Cotton Commissioner in cahoots with the Manchester Chamber of Commerce organized a cotton exhibition at Akola in 1867. 'For the Akola Exhibition I had more time to prepare', writes the Commissioner, 'and as it was held in the centre of the field of my labours and in one of the most important cotton growing tracts in India, an attempt was made to render the cotton department of the exhibition interesting and instructive.'[68]

[65] From: The Commissioner, West Berar, To: First Assistant Resident, Hyderabad, Akolah, dated 13 May 1871, in the *Proceedings of the Department of Agriculture, Revenue, and Commerce*, No. 8/11, dated February, 1873, para 17 (NAI).

[66] From: Lt. W. H. Cornish, Officiating Secretary for Berar to the Resident at Hyderabad, To: Secretary to Government of India Revenue Department, Bombay, No. 178-G, dated 19 May 1887, Hyderabad Residency, in *Proceedings of the Hyderabad Administration for the Month of May 1887*, submitted to the Revenue and Agriculture Department, No. 178-G, dated 19 May 1887 (IOLR).

[67] From: R. D. Hare, Survey and Settlement Officer, Hyderabad Assigned Districts, To: The Commissioner, Hyderabad Assigned Districts, Yeotmal, dated 12 June 1890, in *Proceedings of the Hyderabad Administration on Matters of Routine for the Month of October 1890*, submitted to the Revenue and Agriculture Department, No. 351, 6 October 1890 (IOLR).

[68] *Report on the Operations of the Cotton Department for the Year 1867*, by Harry Rivett-Carnac, pp. 57-8.

Visible and verbal instructions were rendered to peasants on proper methods of growing and preparing cotton for export. The various processes from which cotton passed from seed to its final export was depicted in different sheds created specially for this purpose. All articles of cotton packing such as ropes, gunny cloth, iron bands, clips, stencil plates, etc., were openly displayed for demonstration. The colonial government which always shirked from spending on public health, education, irrigation, and sanitation, spent enormous amounts of public money on these wasteful and useless expenditure of promoting experimental farms and exhibitions. However, it may not have been all that wasteful from the colonial point of view since it promoted the production and export of cotton. Except for some large landholders loyal to the state, the kunbi peasantry in general showed little or no interest in colonial experimental farms or exhibitions. With the result at the end of Akola Cotton Exhibition of 1867, all the prizes given out for cotton ginning and pressing went to European firms and their agents.[69]

The final feather in the colonial cap was the establishment of Cotton Market Committees in all major towns of Berar. These Committees comprised of agents from European firms and Indian merchants engaged in cotton business in Berar. These committees were all powerful bodies controlling cotton trade. The colonial government protected these Committees through Acts. The most notorious of these statutes was the 'Cotton Frauds Act' of 1863. By this Act any person doing business in cotton outside the officially designated markets was liable to be arrested and punished. All cotton was ordered to be sold only in the markets designated by the government and approved by the Cotton Market Committee. Any cotton sold outside the boundaries of these colonial markets was declared illegal transaction and subject to seizure as contraband under the provision of Act IX of 1863 of the Government of Bombay.[70] So even though outwardly the rhetoric of 'free trade' was used, in reality the state was heavily imposing its monopoly and restrictions on the marketplace all over Berar.

In order to coordinate the activities of all the Cotton Market Committees in Berar and throughout British India, a 'Fibre and Silk

[69] *Report on the Operations of the Cotton Department for the Year 1867*, by Harry Rivett-Carnac, p. 60.

[70] Ibid., p. 56. Also see Note on Indian Cotton, in the *Proceedings of the Department of Revenue and Agriculture*, Fibre and Silk Branch (May 1889), No. 25/27 (NAI).

Branch' was created (1873) within the Department of Agriculture, Revenue, and Commerce. Its job was to collect accurate cotton information from all parts of India for the use of mercantile community.[71] The development of cotton economy under colonial aegis gave a tremendous boost to cotton marketing and trade. The systematic bleeding of Berar was now begun.

The State and The Market

Patterns of Cotton Marketing and Trade

The journey of a bale of cotton from Berar to Liverpool is a fascinating story of adventure. Unfortunately the story does not begin with the primary producer. The primary producer had very little to do with cotton trade. In fact the cultivating peasants lost all rights to the produce even before the seed was sown in the ground.

The starting point of colonial trade was the colonial government. The government which was so instrumental in creating such a highly modernized cotton infrastructure could never have stood back and watched the operation of a free market economy. Even if the government would not have wanted to get involved, the external pressure was too enormous for it to stay neutral. The pressure came from the same channel through which cotton went on its adventurous journey. This was the beginning of the cotton trade in Berar:

When in consequence of the American War the United States had temporarily ceased to supply the raw material for the English cotton industry, and it came to be considered in England that it would be well if the attention of merchants and spinners were directed to other quarters, an association was formed in Manchester with the object of fostering and encouraging the production of cotton in various parts of the world, and especially in British colonies and dependencies. India was considered by the Cotton Supply Association to offer a great field for the development of cotton cultivation, and the Association entered into correspondence with the Secretary of State

[71] 'Cotton Cultivation in the Central Provinces, the Berars, and the North West Provinces', in *Proceedings of the Department of Agriculture, Revenue and Commerce*, No. 49, February 1873 (IOLR), Mr. A. J. Dunlop, Assistant Cotton Commissioner, West Berar, in *Annual Reports of the Cotton Department for 1869-70 and 1870-71*, in *Proceedings of the Department of Agriculture, Revenue and Commerce*, No. 8/4, dated February 1873, para 54.

for India on the subject of the most feasible means of improving the quality and increasing the quantity of the produce. After some desultory and tentative efforts have been made, a cotton commissioner was appointed in Bombay, and in 1866. . . .[72]

From his appointment to dismissal (1864-74), the Cotton Commissioner served as a loyal servant of the Manchester Chamber of Commerce which was the parent body of Cotton Supply Association. The primary object of this association was to search and develop alternative markets to guarantee the continued supply of raw cotton to England. It was an important instrument created to monitor the cultivation and trade of cotton throughout the British empire. It is no surprise therefore that Berar became the object of attention of the Association during the American Civil War. Instructions were issued to all the provincial governments (through the Government of India) to gear up the local economy for trade and exports. 'The Government of India having had under their consideration the possibility of a greatly and suddenly increased demand for Indian cotton in England, have directed the attention of each local government within the territories of which cotton producing and cotton exporting districts lie to certain measures, whereby the power of India to meet such increased demand for cotton may be augmented by the help of Government,'[73] wrote a colonial official in 1863.

The Government of India organized tours for the Manchester merchants to witness the cotton tracts of Berar. These tours were conducted by the agents of the colonial government specially trained and deputed for this purpose. While the agents conducted tours, the cotton merchants looked for ways to establish direct intercourse with the producers and avenues to take out cotton by cheapest possible route. This was essential for the stability of cotton trade and every effort was made to achieve this goal. In 1867 the Chief Commissioner wrote thus to the Cotton Commissioner: 'You have rightly seen that in order to promote the interest of an important branch of the national industry, it was essential to maintain intimate relations with

[72] 'Note on Indian Cotton', in the *Proceedings of the Department of Revenue and Agriculture,* Fibre and Silk Branch (May 1889), No. 25/27 (NAI).

[73] From: M. J. Shaw Stewart, Under Secretary to Government, To: W. C. Anderson, Superintendent Revenue Survey and Assessment, Southern Mahratta Country and Berar, No. 1977 of 1861, Revenue Department, in *The British Parliamentary Papers,* Vol. 44, 1863, p. 392.

all concerned in it. Not the least important part of your task has consisted in the smoothing of difficulties, and in the facilitation of direct intercourse between the producers and the purchasers of cotton, which could not have been attained without gaining the confidence of both classes.'[74]

The Manchester system of grading the cotton grown in different parts of the world was really a very superficial categorization of quality. Effort was made throughout the British empire to encourage the growth of a uniform variety which would suit the needs of British industries. Since British textile mills were designed to process American long-staple cotton, all other cotton was branded inferior to the American staple. The value of cotton was thus fixed by grading them on a scale of superiority and inferiority similar to the colonial categorization of people. However Dr. August Voelcker, a colonial cotton expert, has argued in the late nineteenth century that, 'after all, the remedy appears to me to lie rather with the trade than with agriculture. If the trade really complains of the inferiority of the short-stapled cotton, why does it continue to use up readily every bit of cotton the ryot can produce? If the cry for long-stapled cotton is so urgent, why will the trade not give more for it and refuse to take the short-stapled?'[75]

Manchester constantly exerted pressure on the colonial officials in India by reminding them of their duty to serve the interest of home country. The officials were only too glad to comply to this pressure. 'It cannot be denied that, to most of us out in India, whether we be officers ruling over Districts, or connected with the cotton Department, it is indeed a gladsome duty to assist in the improvement of the cultivation of cotton, and to feel that, by so doing, we are helping to supply a great want of many starving countrymen at home [Great Britain],'[76] wrote the Cotton Commissioner Harry Rivett-Carnac in 1869. But not all colonial officials were the loyal servants of Manchester. Some of them were aware that India was being exploited and robbed of its resources. Such men believed that the 'many starving countrymen

[74] *Report on the Operations of the Cotton Department for the Year 1867,* by Harry Rivett-Carnac, p. 6.

[75] 'Improvement of the Cotton Industry in Berar', by Dr. Augustus Voelcker, in the *Foreign Department Proceedings,* January 1891, Nos. 244-5.

[76] *Report on the Cotton Department for the Year 1868-69,* by Harry Rivett-Carnac, Cotton Commissioner for the Central Provinces and the Berars, Bombay, 1869, p. 145.

at home' were not really the operatives of the cotton textiles mills but the covetous cotton merchants and mill owners. Such officials grumbled that 'the pressure is being put on [us] to meet the cry of Manchester, and Manchester will be only too glad to seize the first opportunity of leaving India in the lurch.'[77] But the number of such 'enlightened colonizers' was really very small and they did not count for much. The enlightened colonizers were critical of the demands of Manchester but overlooked the fact that the colonial state was servicing the interest of Manchester and not India. Despite the grumbling of the enlightened colonizers, the colonial government went ahead with its plans of making police arrangements for the security of cotton merchants who came to Berar in large numbers.

During the Civil War years the merchants had complained about the weight of *candy*.[78] The government took immediate measures and standardized the weight of the *candy* of *kapas* (raw cotton) by 'Regulation'. 'In former day a khandy varied from 800 lbs. to 900 lbs., and each merchant had a standard of his own, the confusion was very great, and gave encouragement to cheating. The khandy has now, however, been fixed at 924 lbs. . . .'[79] By the start of 1870 the *candy* was completely standardized to 784 lbs, to suit the requirements of shipping and freight. The Cotton Supply Association was sending commendable letters to the Cotton Commissioner on the great job being done in the export of cotton while at the same time issuing instructions on the use of saw-gin for the processing of cotton. 'We think rather that all your efforts should be devoted to the improvement of the good cotton which is already grown; and in connection with this point we would suggest the use of the Macarthy gin, which does not damage the staple, and which cleans the cotton quite as efficiently as the saw-gin. It is now much used in Broach, and the cotton cleansed by it comes to market in a beautiful state. We enclose a letter from one Mr. Christian on the subject of Egyptian cotton, and wishing you every success in your good work.'[80] The development of export trade

[77] Ibid.

[78] *Candy* is the standard measured weight of packed cotton for shipping purposes.

[79] *Report on the Cotton Experiments in West Berar during the Season 1869-70*, by Mr. A. J. Dunlop, Assistant Cotton Commissioner, West Berar, in Annual Reports of the Cotton Department for 1869-70 and 1870-71, by Harry Rivett-Carnac, Cotton Commissioner, in *Proceedings of the Department of Agriculture Revenue and Commerce*, No. 8/4, dated February 1873, p. 51.

[80] *Report on the Operations of the Cotton Department for the Year 1867*, by Harry Rivett-Carnac, p. 40.

was the result of many years of combined efforts and labour of Manchester and the colonial government.

As already mentioned, almost all cotton was sold in market towns which developed along the railway line. The primary producer had very little to do with these large cotton emporiums at Amraoti, Shegaon, Akola, Khamgaon, Murtizapur and Chandur. Most of the articles of daily consumption of rural Berar were sold and exchanged at fairs and bazaars which occurred at regular intervals in the countryside. The villages were linked to each other not so much by the colonial railway or the metalled roads but through the means of these 'spontaneous fairs and bazaars' which moved from village to village and town to town. The articles of retail sales and daily consumption were transacted in these spontaneous fairs. The Cotton Department noted in 1867:

> In every circle of ten miles there is a weekly bazar for each day in the week. The principal towns have the larger bazars, in the smaller villages the gatherings are comparatively insignificant. Petty traders go round to these markets with foreign groceries and cheap manufactures, of much of the same quality as those now sold in England at the booths in a fair. Cattle, corn, vegetables, cloth, and fruit are brought by the peasants and bought by the dealers. The annual fairs *(jatras)*, as they intervene, attract all the traders within wide circles, and are visited by crowds from long distances.[81]

The wholesale trade as a rule was carried on in large emporiums or by means of private transactions at the farmgate. Often times the yield was mortgaged even before 'the cotton is actually picked, or even before almost the nature of the yield can be properly estimated'.[82] Under colonial condition, the cotton from being a subsistence crop became a high-value cash crop and was almost invariably grown on advances. Cotton was also a tool for the primary producer to raise credit and with it enter into a perpetual debt cycle. Most of the Berari cotton passed out into the control of the moneylender who provided operating cost for its cultivation. The village moneylender was also the local dealer of cotton and grain. In the Purna valley, the village moneylenders generally brought the cotton to large emporiums. Some valley cotton was also bought from the moneylenders by agents of European and Bombay firms who fanned over Berar during cotton season from November to May each year.

[81] A. C. Lyall, *Gazetteer of the Haidarabad Assigned Districts, Commonly called Berar*, p. 234.

[82] *Jalgaum Taluka Settlement Report*, No. 261 of 1865, para 33.

The course of trade of *ghat* cotton above and below the valley was somewhat different. The *ghat* villages were sometimes at great distances from the markets and metalled roads. Here most of the cotton was sold by moneylenders to cotton agents of European and Bombay firms who swarmed the *ghats* like summer locust. Some cotton was also sold to *dalals* or independent agents who then resold it to the foreign merchants in emporium towns.[83] The valley cotton was usually brought to the emporium towns unginned. The European firms in cotton towns owned most of the steam gins and presses. The valley cotton was ginned in these steam gins and then pressed in bales for export. The *ghat* cotton on the other hand was ginned by the primary producer on *charka* or hand gins supplied by moneylenders. Even in Purna valley some cotton was ginned by *charka.* The seed extracted from *charka* cotton was better for sowing compared to the seed from steam gins.

Bullock carts were the chief mode of transportation in the rural interior of Berar. Irrespective of cotton season, the carts were used for moving goods and services. Every bazar and fair swarmed with these carts. The carts also provided shelter to the carriers at night. During the season, long rows of cotton carts were seen all over Berar. But with the commencement of monsoon they disappeared as country roads became useless for traffic. In the pre-colonial period, many different types of carts were in use in Berar.[84] With the rise of colonial cotton trade the cart technology underwent drastic transformation. The old Berar cart capable of carrying only 10 maunds was gradually replaced by the Madras *bandy* which could carry 15 maunds.[85] Furthermore the old carts were 'execrated by Europeans, because they

[83] A. C. Lyall, *Gazetteer of the Haidarabad Assigned Districts, Commonly called Berar*, p. 225.

[84] The following were the types of carts most commonly used:

Burki—two-wheeled axle cart covered with curtains
Rath—four-wheeled cart for four persons
Miana—two-wheeled for six persons
Rein—drawn by one bullock
Khachar—two-wheeled large cart to hold several persons
Machi—small cart for two persons
Rekla—small cart for one person
Bandi and Gara—large carts used for fetching crops from the fields

See *Gazetteers of the Haidarabad Assigned Districts,* by A. C. Lyall, p. 241.

[85] *Report of the Famine Commission,* Appendix V: Irrigation as a Protection against Famine, 1881, p. 470.

will not contain boxes, packages, or other civilized domestic commodities'.[86] The new *bandy* was lighter in weight and faster in speed and much to the taste of European firms who hired them. They were '. . . made in the usual manner with two long poles meeting in front and joined by a cross beam behind, the floor being made of bamboos or strips of wood nailed on to the side pieces. It has no regular sides but curved uprights to which a load can be secured. The axle is of iron, and is secured outside the wheel by an iron nail. The wheel is made up of six pieces of wood composing its periphery, 12 spokes and a heavy nave usually of *babul* wood with an iron tyre'.[87] These carts were known as *ladha or bandy* and travelled at the rate of 6 miles an hour which was a marked improvement from the old Berar cart which did only 4 miles. The technology was imported from neighbouring Khandesh and Madras around 1870. Soon after the introduction of the *bandy*, several different types of carts which existed in Berar for centuries slowly disappeared.

Traditionally the Berar carts were locally made in the villages. But with the commercialization of agriculture the cart technology underwent a remarkable transformation in terms of speed and carrying capacity. The *bandy* and *ladha* revolutionized the movement of cotton inside Berar and triggered a drastic rise in its exports. After 1870 lighter carts were imported and sold in every market fairs and bazaars. Between 1870 and 1891, almost every taluka registered a marked increase in the total number of carts indicating that the cotton export trade was booming. Table 21 shows a per centage increase in the total number of carts in various talukas of Berar.

TABLE 21

Taluka	*Year*	*No. of Carts*		*% Increase*
		From	*To*	
Malkapur	1879 to 1891	7635	9376	22.8
Jalgaon	1870 to 1891	2723	4287	57.4
Chikli	1867 to 1894	1831	6366	247.6
Mehkar	1867 to 1896	1773	5581	14.7
TOTAL		13962	25610	83.4

[86] A. C. Lyall, *Gazetteer of the Haidarabad Assigned Districts*, 1870, p. 244.

[87] *Buldana District Gazetteer*, 1910, pp. 285-6 (NMML).

The owners of these new and faster carts were mostly the moneylenders and European firms. The cost of each cart ranged from 40 to 60 rupees and were too expensive for the ordinary indebted peasant.[88]

So far as the cotton trade was concerned the moneylenders and the European firms were operating in a collaborative market rather than a competitive market. Just as the primary producer was indebted to the moneylender and cultivated cotton on advances, so was the moneylender bound to European firms for the supply of cotton.[89] The gradual rise of indebtedness among the peasantry was due to the increasing obligation of the moneylender to supply cotton to European firms.

In addition to being the local dealer of cotton, the moneylender was also the local grain merchant. The cotton was not the only source of income of the moneylender. He dealt in opium, English piece-goods, hardware, precious metals, salt, ghi, oil, and such other sundry items.[90] The European firms concentrated solely on cotton trade and this was the main difference between the trading practices of European firms and the cotton merchants. Otherwise both of them were collaborators in cotton trade. The *sowcars* (moneylenders) borrowed capital on credit from the European firms for the delivery of cotton on already fixed prices. The *sowcars* and the European firms entered into legal contractual bonds known as *suttas*. The *sutta* obligated the *sowcar* to supply a certain weight of cotton at a certain price and by a certain time. A similar *sutta* was contracted between the *sowcar* and the primary producer which was basically a debt contract. It read in the following manner:

I [cultivator] agree by this cotton *sutta* at my own wish, and pleasure, to deliver cotton (Laonee) one *dokrah* [bale] at the rate of rupees 40 per bojah. At this rate, Government coin Company's Rupees 20 in ready cash. I have received and then given you [moneylender] this *sutta*. Time of delivery *Bassant Panchee* (February). The cotton to be new, grown this year, and without stain, and to be delivered and weighed in Khamgaon according to the custom, with sample and allowances at the scale. I agree to deliver the dokrah to the person you choose and bring his receipt to you.

[88] *Buldana District Gazetteer*, 1910, pp. 285-6 (NMML).

[89] From: A. J. Dunlop, Assistant Commissioner, Akolah District, To: Secretary, Chief Commissioner, Khamgaon, 13 February 1874, *Administrative Report of the Cotton Department (Bombay) for 1872-73*, in the *Proceedings of the Department of Agriculture, Revenue, and Commerce*, Fibre and Silk Branch (February 1874), No. 37/38 (NAI).

[90] A. C. Lyall, *Gazetteer of the Haidarabad Assigned Districts*, 1870, p. 230.

> My heirs and property are liable for this *sutta.* If I do not deliver the *dokrah* on the date appointed, I agree to settle the rate and pay the difference in price.[91]

By such *suttas* the cultivators entered into debt bondage and mortgaged their heirs, property, and future generation. Within two decades after the colonial takeover the moneylenders had occupied each and every village of Berar. Their main occupation in addition to wheeling and dealing was moneylending, pawn-brokerage and petty trading. They also owned and operated small village stores of sundries and other goods. In 1881 there were 11,949 moneylenders, petty traders, and pawn-brokers in Berar.[92] By 1891 their number increased to 19,282.[93] At the turn of the century there were 29,905 moneylenders in Berar.[94]

The iron hold of the moneylender on the primary producer was unshaken despite the continual effort of the colonial state and European firms to dislodge him. The British Resident at Hyderabad wrote as early as 1861: 'The only way in which it appears to me that real benefit could be derived from [sic] European capitalists, would be by encouraging them to establish agencies in the districts for the purpose of purchasing produce direct from the cultivating classes instead of through middlemen. Every facility should be afforded them of erecting cotton screws, gins, spinning machines, oil mills, and similar factories.'[95] It was physically impossible to root out the moneylender who had established strong roots in the countryside by extending credit on oral contracts and sometimes on threats of court proceedings. The moneylender also built his strength by effectively using the court system of the colonial state. He was closer to the primary producer than any European firm or even native merchant could get. He lived in the village and communicated in the language of the cultivators.

In a way the moneylenders and the European firms competed for

[91] Resolution on the question whether *Suttas* or Contracts entered into by the cultivators in Berar to deliver their cotton produce are liable to stamp duty when transferred by the endorsement, Foreign Department, Government of India, Nos. 5-7, dated April 1873.

[92] *Report on the Census of Berar, 1881,* Bombay, 1882, p. 172.

[93] *Census of India, 1891,* Vol. IV, *Berar or the Hyderabad Assigned Districts,* 1892, p. cxlv.

[94] *Census of India, 1901,* Vol. VIII, *Berar,* Allahabad, 1902, p. 228.

[95] From: Lieutenant Colonel Cuthbert Davidson, Resident at Hyderabad, To: G. R. Haywood, Esq., Secretary to the Cotton Supply Association, Manchester, 8 March 1861, enclosure 4, No. 12, in *The British Parliamentary Papers,* Vol. 44, 1863, p. 396.

control over the primary producer. The moneylender controlled the primary producer through debt contract, but he had little contro. over the market. The market was regulated by the laws of state which favoured European firms. The ginning and pressing was also controlled by European firms and protected by law. 'Amongst the foreign firms that conduct the trade in cotton, oilseeds and grains may be mentioned Messrs. Ralli Brothers and Volkart Brothers who have agencies at several important stations in the District such as Khamgaon, Shegaon, Nandura, Jalgaon, Malkapur, Buldana and Chikhli. The Mofussil Company have agencies only at Shegaon and Khamgaon. Bruel & Company and Gadam & Company carry on trade at Khamgaon.'[96] Among all the European firms, the Volkarts and Ralli Brothers were the two leading houses who did business in six cotton markets and carried on a considerable trade in grain and oilseeds as well.[97] They also owned several cotton gins and presses. Since the European firms were the largest purchasers of cotton, it was quite natural for them to monopolize ginning and pressing.

Cotton Ginning and Pressing

Until 1866 there were no European gins and presses in Berar. Prior to colonial control, cotton was never a big export crop. It was then mostly hand-ginned by women at home. Most of the cotton grown was consumed locally. Berar had a good handloom manufacturing home industry. Most of its clothing needs were supplied by castes specializing in weaving. The ginning was done by a native instrument known as the *churka*. Almost every agricultural household had a *churka*. The *churka* was a manually operated hand-gin with two rollers moving in the opposite direction and attached to a frame. This simple instrument was operated by two women, i.e. one rotated the roller with an attached wooden handle and the other fed the *kapas* (seed cotton) into the rollers. The lint and seed fell on either side of the rollers separating the two and thus clean cotton was obtained. Although the colonizers looked at *churka* as a 'primitive instrument'[98] yet it was the most effective means of obtaining cotton. Sometimes

[96] *Buldana District Gazetteer*, 1910, p. 276.

[97] *Amraoti District Gazetteer*, 1911, p. 253.

[98] *Report on the Trade of the Hyderabad Assigned Districts for the Year 1880-81*, Hyderabad, 1882, p. 13.

this double-roller manual gin was also known as *retsa*. A woman working on it cleaned about 2 to 3 seers or 6 lbs of cotton per day.[99] The cotton seed obtained from the *churka* was extensively used for the new year's sowing.[100] Therefore there was never a shortage of the supply of cotton seed in pre-colonial Berar.

In the colonial period, Berar continuously experienced shortage of cotton seeds. This was due to the introduction of steam gins in Berar. No doubt the steam cotton gin was more efficient than the *charka*, but the seed obtained from these gins was mostly damaged and could not be used for sowing purposes. Normally an acre of cotton field required only 10 lbs of hand-ginned seed for sowing, while 15 to 20 lbs of steam ginned seed was required to sow 1 acre.

In 1867 four large Platt's Macarthy gin manufacturing factories were set up in Berar. These machines were worked with bullock power[101] and could process larger quantity of cotton compared to the hand ginned *churka*. Macarthy gins gradually replaced human power with bullock power. Moreover the *churka* was incapable of catering to the needs of the export trade which demanded a large volume of cotton to be processed in a short period of time. Even the labour which was hitherto engaged in ginning and weaving was not available due to the demands of cotton cultivation.

As mentioned earlier, in Purna valley the cotton was sold unginned. Here the European firms purchased seed cotton from the moneylenders and dealers and ginned it in their own gins. The impact of the introduction of European gin was irreversible. Hand gins were relegated to minimal use. The moneylenders hired *churkas* to obtain seed for sowing. The control of *churkas* gave them control over the primary producer. The *churka* seed was given on credit to the cultivators. In fact the seed was also an important instrument of moneylender's control over the primary producer. The introduction of cotton gins

[99] *Note on Cotton in Berar*, by E. A. Hobson, Survey and Settlement Officer, Berar, Hyderabad, 1887, in the *Proceedings of the Department of Revenue and Agriculture*, Fibre and Silk Branch (November 1887), Nos. 22-3 (IOLR).

[100] Proposals for the Revision Settlement of the Darwa Taluq of Wun District, in the *Proceedings of the Hyderabad Administration on Matters of Routine for the Month of June 1901*, submitted to the Department of Revenue and Agriculture, No. 201, 22 June 1901, (IOLR).

[101] *Report on the Operation of the Cotton Department for the Year 1867*, by Harry Rivett-Carnac, 1869, p. 58.

made this control even stronger. The moneylender now not only owned the *churka* but also indulged in seed loaning. The indebted cultivators grew cotton for the moneylender and at the same time ginned seed cotton for sowing. The moneylender was obligated to supply seed cotton to the European firm. The European firm bought seed cotton from the moneylender and ginned and pressed it in bales for export. The ginning technology made the *churka* obsolete and strengthened the commercial bond between moneylender and the European firm. It also tightened moneylender's control over the primary producer. Modern technology thus helped in strengthening colonial domination over state and society.

If it can be said that ginning technology brought about a drastic change in the processing of cotton, the pressing technology revolutionized the export trade. As gins were introduced by European firms, so were the presses. Pressing was in fact more important for export than ginning. The first press was introduced in Berar in 1867. The year 1867-8 was an important landmark in the history of colonial cotton trade in Berar. It was during this season that Berar exploded with cotton presses and gins. Table 22 shows the number of cotton presses at work in 1867 and 1868.[102]

TABLE 22

Towns	*Full-Press*			*Half-Press*		
	1867	*1868*	*1869*	*1867*	*1868*	*1869*
Oomraotee	0	4	6	12	21	35
Budnaira	0	2	1	4	NA	2
Akola	0	0	0	0	3	6
Sheagaon	0	2	2	6	16	18
Khamgaon	2	6	8	10	25	38
Akote	0	2	2	0	8	8
Karinja	0	0	0	0	2	2
Julgaon	0	0	0	0	2	2
Moortizapur	0	0	0	0	4	9
Chandur	NA	NA	0	NA	NA	1
Nandoorah	NA	NA	0	NA	NA	2
Telara	NA	NA	0	NA	NA	2
TOTAL	2	16	19	32	81	125

[102] The data for this table is taken from the following sources: *Report on the Operations of the Cotton Department for the Year 1867,* by Harry Rivett-Carnac, 1869, p. 13; *Report on the Cotton Department for the Year 1868-69,* by Harry Rivett-Carnac, 1869, p. 186.

The table clearly shows that the cotton pressing business was significant all over Berar. Most of these presses were run by steam power. The total number of half-presses and full-presses increased at a remarkable rate in the course of just three years. The cotton press was the most commonly adopted machine by every European firm operating in Berar. Each half-press turned out fifty bales a day. During the cotton season these presses worked day and night turning as many as 100 bales (3.5 cwt each) a day. The pressing capacity of a full-press was almost double that of the half-press. Since most of these presses were run by steam power, the precious forest timber was used to ignite its belching chimnies. Never before were such huge smoke spitting chimnies ever seen in Berar. It must have been quite a sight although no description of it is left behind. Even the sanitary commissioner did not notice the impact of air pollution on general health of the population. An unusually large number of deaths recorded in the sanitary commissioner's report and designated under the column 'other causes' can be speculatively attributed to environmental degradation brought about by colonial technology like railways and steam gins.[103]

The gins and presses introduced in Berar were the best tested technology designed to perform in the particularly dry climate of the region. The aim was to compress as much cotton into a bale in order to secure as low a freight as possible. This was achieved in the following manner:

> Now, the climate of the Berars during the cotton season is so dry, and cotton so elastic, that the great difficulty is experienced in getting into the bale the quantity of cotton which can be packed without effort in the moist atmosphere of Bombay. In the first place, the 'box' which received the supply of cotton for the bale, can in most presses with difficulty be made to hold the requisite quantity of cotton, and then the pressing power is often insufficient to condense the cotton to the required size. With the help of improved machinery all these objections have now been met, and the disadvantages under which our up-country full-pressed bales at one time laboured have now been removed, and our bales are now made of such a size as to secure a low freight.[104]

Most of these presses were high density compressors and best in the

[103] See *Reports of the Sanitary Commissioner, Hyderabad Assigned Districts* [printed annually 1889-1902 in multi-volume series], Hyderabad.

[104] *Report on the Cotton Department for the Year 1868-69*, by Harry Rivett-Carnac, 1869, p. 111.

world at the time. Such an advanced technology in an economically backward society became an instrument of total exploitation—much more destructive than the colonial wars of the eighteenth and nineteenth century. It was the colonial legacy and the curse of cotton which the unfortunate cultivators of Berar carried with them like slaves of the American south. The peculiarity of the situation is that in spite of receiving the most advanced technology, Berar remained the most backward society of the nineteenth century. Why was it that Berar remained primarily agricultural and did not develop manufacturing or an industrial base? This was due to Berar's subservient position as a colony servicing the economic interest of Great Britain. There is no doubt that if local cotton was prevented from leaving the region, Berar would have seen the growth of cotton textile industries. It was the subservience of Berar's economy to London-based world economy that prevented the growth of manufacturing industries in the region. With the result Berar constantly languished in economic backwardness and want.

It is important here to note the difference between a full-pressed bale and a half-pressed bale. This was crucial to the colonial cotton trade. The quantity of cotton per bale and the shape of the bale was an important aspect of cotton export. The Berar cotton needed great preparation for its six-week adventurous journey to Liverpool. '*Oomra*' (name of Berar cotton) had a great name and reputation in the markets of London, Liverpool, and Manchester. Its name was heard as far as Natchez, Savannah, and New Orleans. '*Oomra*' was famous throughout the world and therefore great care was taken in its cleaning, ginning, pressing, packing, screwing, stamping, loading, etc. Most of the '*Oomra*' after 1870 went in full-pressed bales. The advantage of full-press over half-press was that the former could compress 25 lbs more cotton per bale than the half-press.[105] Normally in a half-pressed bale the lint was condensed to 12 lbs to a cubic foot or 3 to 3.25 cwt per bale. But in a full-press the lint compression was more than doubled to 28-32 lbs per cubic foot. The full-press also enhanced the lint capacity per bale to 3.5 cwt.[106]

Prior to the introduction of full-presses, the half-pressed bale was

[105] *Report on the Operations of the Cotton Department for the Year 1867,* by Harry Rivett-Carnac, 1869, p. 51.

[106] *Report on the Cotton Department for the Year 1868-69,* by Harry Rivett-Carnac, 1869, p. 107.

sent to Bombay where it was re-examined and passed through full-presses in order to obtain favourable shipping freight to Europe. This double pressing was expensive and caused enormous delays. Therefore the European firms introduced full-presses in Berar. This was necessary to compress as much cotton as possible at the source of its production. This was also important because the railway freight to Bombay and shipping freight to Europe was charged by the measurement of bale rather than by its weight. The only way to make profit was to press as much cotton into a bale as possible. As more cotton was pressed the more profits were made per bale. Therefore it was only feasible to introduce full-presses in Berar. Since most of the export trade was dealt by European firms, it was but natural for them to own and operate these presses to full capacity.

In order to force the manufacture of full-pressed bale, the railway company raised the carriage rate on half-pressed bale during the cotton season of 1869-70. This was done to encourage full-pressing as it was more advantageous for export trade. Half-pressed bales occupied more space in the railway wagon and steamships. In fact the steamships to England refused to carry half-pressed bales altogether. In order to discourage the half-pressed bales, the shipping companies re-opened and re-packed them into full-pressed bales at Bombay before loading. Full-pressing was encouraged so that the bale could be sent directly from Berar to Liverpool without unnecessarily rebaling at Bombay. This was very effective in putting most of the cotton into the hands of European merchants who owned presses in Berar and bought cotton for direct export to England. The following figures show a remarkable increase in the total number of full-pressed bales to constitute 60 per cent of the total exports from Berar (1868):[107]

Cotton Packing	*Bales*
Dokra (loose bags)	16,930
Half-pressed	69,585
Full-pressed	122,932
TOTAL	209,447

Until 1866 all cotton in Berar was packed in loose bags known as the *dokras* or *jinghas*. A *dokra* was a huge pile of cotton packed in a loose bag similar in appearance to a hot air balloon. These *dokras* were

[107] A. C. Lyall, *Gazetteer of the Haidarabad Assigned Districts,* 1870, p. 228.

usually carried on the creaking wheels of a slow moving Berari cart. In pre-colonial times the cart driver went from village to village selling cotton from his *dokra* to families and individuals. But with the introduction of steam gins in 1867, the *dokra* business was hit and by 1870 completely disappeared. 'In 1866, the whole of cotton went to Bombay in loose bags. In 1867, the system of pressing up-country was commenced, and during that year 15 per cent of the cotton crop was sent down in pressed bale while the remaining 85 per cent was still going in *dokras*. In 1868, the number of full-pressed bales alone represented 17 per cent exported crop, the full-pressed and half-pressed taken together, representing nearly three-quarters of the whole crop, and the loose cotton sinking to a quarter of the exports',[108] wrote the Cotton Commissioner in 1869. Table 23 shows the demise of *dokra* as a consequence of the rise in cotton pressing technology (in per centages.[109]

TABLE 23

Cotton Packing	*1867*	*1868*	*1869*
Dokra	85%	27.5%	8%
Half-pressed	30%	55.5%	66%
Full-pressed	2%	17.0%	26%
Total pressed	32%	72.5%	92%

The demise of *dokra* from 85 per cent to 8 per cent and its eventual disappearance in 1870 as a result of rise in pressed cotton per centage from 32 to 92 per cent is yet another example of the destruction of native skills under colonial subjection.

The establishment of European gins and presses was important to ensure the quality of cotton pressed and the bales exported. Manchester had always set the standards of the quality of cotton from India and the rest of the world. By establishing factories in Berar the European firms made sure that this demand is adequately met. In 1869 the Cotton Commissioner wrote: 'The large factories at the cotton markets are indeed one of the most interesting features of the Berars, . . . At the markets of Hingunghat, Deolee, Arvee, Oomraotee, Akotee, Sheogaon, and Khamgaon, we now have European firms established for the purchase of cotton.' The Commissioner further states that 'I have

[108] *Report on the Operations of the Cotton Department for the Year 1867*, by Harry Rivett-Carnac, 1869, p. 51.

[109] *Report on the Operations of the Cotton Department for the Year 1867*, by Harry Rivett-Carnac, 1869, p. 51.

always tried, so far as I legitimately could, to consult and protect their [European] interests. If I have succeeded in any degree in this object, I am confident that Government will consider that I have performed no unimportant part of my duty.'[110]

Portrait of a Market Town

Indeed the purpose of Cotton Commissioner's existence was to develop and supervise cotton markets which by 1870 had become a haven for European firms. One such emporium, which was the pet market of the Cotton Commissioner, was Khamgaon. It was the biggest cotton market in the whole of Asia and the British empire. Khamgaon had only 9000 inhabitants and was opened only during the cotton season from November to May each year. Here the European firms established two large cleaning factories and three equally large full-presses in addition to a large number of half-presses. All these establishments were run by steam power which was obtained by burning forest timber. It is difficult to estimate the impact of the smoke emitted by these colonial gins and presses but it would be more than enough to blacken the sky during cotton season. Khamgaon was just one of the many such cotton emporiums with many large steam gins and presses. For a small town like Khamgaon the total annual export of 100,000 bales worth over 1 million pound-sterling was overwhelming. Khamgaon alone accounted for nearly 40 per cent of the total annual exports from Berar. It drew cotton from a radius of 50 to 100 miles around and buried itself with cotton during the season.

The European factories had an enormous appetite for consuming and churning out cotton bales. At the peak of the season each of the three full-presses turned out more than 400 bales of cotton per day. The scale and the rapidity with which Khamgaon grew from an insignificant village to the largest cotton outpost of the British empire can be explained only by the ruination and devastation suffered by the inhabited villages for miles around it. Khamgaon was a colonial creation. Between 1867 and 1869 it transformed into an enormous cotton gobbling monster. This is how Khamgaon looked after its transformation as described by the Cotton Commissioner in 1869:

> These large factories and the steam cotton presses employ very large establishments, consisting of European Managers, Assistants, and Engineers.

[110] *Report on the Operations of the Cotton Department for the Year 1867*, by Harry Rivett-Carnac, 1869, p. 67.

The staff required by the European cotton agent for purchasing cotton is also considerable. And the European official population is now beginning to increase. Besides the Cotton Commissioner, who is obliged to spend much of his time at Khamgaon, an officer of the Commissioner has lately been appointed to the Small Cause Court and to the general charge of the town. An Assistant Engineer, an officer of police, and Apothecary of the Medical Staff, and some employer of the Telegraph Department, have been added during the year, and the appointment of so many new officers may be accepted as indicating the growing importance of the place. The wants of Khamgaon, in respect to public buildings, have been very liberally and promptly supplied, and a new cotton-market, a House and Court for the resident officer of the Commissioner, a market-place for the general market, a serai, traveller's bungalow, post office, dispensary, and new school-house have been built, or are in course of construction. The postal communication have been improved, and mail-carts now run between Khamgaon, Nandoorah, and Sheagaon, and a branch of the Government Telegraph, by which Khamgaon has been placed in communication with all the cotton market in India and Europe, has been opened.[111]

During the cotton season, Khamgaon was taken over by covetous merchants and agents, wheelers and dealers who came to Berar from far and near. Many village moneylenders were also seen in Khamgaon during this time. The indebted cultivators often times followed the moneylender with cotton carts. 'Khamgaon is undoubtedly the centre of trade. Here are the many merchants and the many traders, and the marwarees who advance money on cotton, and who, with their agencies spread over the country, have many of the koonbies in their books.'[112]

While European gins and presses operated on steam power, the presses owned by Indians were mostly manual. Compared to the mechanical European gins, the Indian gins were primitive and the Indians seldom owned presses. A British traveller in Berar described indigenous pressing in the following manner: 'The cotton is carried from a huge stack to the gin by coolies, and when ginned it is swept out of the gin on to a platform where sacks are hung up and filled with cotton by men who press it down with their feet. Instead of automatic transporters for cotton seed which are seen at many gins in India, women carry it in buckets on their heads to the yard, a distance of

[111] *Report on the Cotton Department for the Year 1868-69,* by Harry Rivett-Carnac, 1869, p. 125.

[112] *Report on the Cotton Department for the Year 1868-69,* by Harry Rivett-Carnac, 1869, p. 125.

about 100 yards from the factory.'[113] The volume of cotton handled by native gins was small compared to European firms.

But the cotton had first to pass through the market before it could be subjected to the process of ginning and pressing. Most of the gins and presses were located in the vicinity of the market. The role of the market in Berar cotton trade was only ceremonial. Most of the cotton was already on *suttas* (contracts) and delivered at pre-fixed prices. Therefore the cotton markets were heavily regulated by 'Cotton Market Committees' composed of representatives from European firms and their native agents.[114] The committee constituted of five members elected every year in the month of January. In 1870 there were six such Committees controlling the six large cotton emporiums of Khamgaon, Shegaon, Akola, Murtizapur, Badnera, and Amraoti. The members of non-merchant community were excluded from this Committee.

In 1928 a 'Royal Commission on Agriculture in India' was appointed to enquire into the marketing of agricultural products in India. This Commission highlighted some very interesting facts about cotton markets in Berar although the situation in the twentieth century had changed from what it was in the nineteenth century. It pointed out that the Cotton Market Committees excluded members of the non-merchant community from participating in the market regulation: '. . . no person is eligible for appointment to the Committee who has not resided within the limits or within five miles from the limits of the town in which the market is situated for at least three months prior to the date on which the list of persons eligible for appointment to the Committee is prepared'.[115] This meant that in practice the members of the cultivating classes and even the moneylenders in the area were ineligible from serving in the Committee. Backing the position of colonial government, the Royal Commission approved

[113] *A Report on Cotton Growing in India*, by Arno Schmidt, Secretary, International Federation of Master Cotton Spinners and Manufacturers' Association. This is a report of secretary's visit to India from December 1911-January 1912, p. 29 (NAI).

[114] From: Colonel E. J. Gunthorpe, Officiating Deputy Commissioner, Amraoti District, To: The Commissioner, Hyderabad Assigned Districts, Amraoti, dated 30 September 1891, in the *Proceedings of the Hyderabad Administration on Matters of Routine for the Month of April 1892*, submitted to the Revenue and Agricultural Department, No. 86, 16 March 1892 (NAI).

[115] *Royal Commission on Agriculture in India: Reports from Commissioners, Inspectors, and others*, in six volumes, *British Parliamentary Papers*, Session 7 (February 1928-August 1928), Vol. VIII, 1928, p. 390.

the system of regulated markets for Berar. This system was to be extended not only to cotton but to all other agricultural products.

The idea behind regulated markets was to control and safeguard the export trade in raw materials. Unauthorized markets within a certain radius of the wholesale markets were prohibited by statute. By the 1890s each agricultural commodity was controlled by a separate market committee indicating a high degree of external control over agricultural products in Berar. Laws were enacted to control the trade of cotton, jowari, and other grains.[116]

The Deputy Commissioner of Akola, Mr. A. J. Dunlop, writing about Khamgaon in 1891 clearly stated his aims thus: 'My aim has been to make the Cotton Market Committee an association for the complete control of cotton trade of Khamgaon.' He further unabashedly proclaimed that 'the system was not only thus deliberately established, but further has been in existence, at least in some towns, for a very long period . . .'.[117] Mr. Dunlop was absolutely right. From the time of its inception (1870) the Cotton Market Committees had established absolute control over the export trade of Berar. Its authority was unquestionable. Strongly backed by the colonial government, the Committees had imposed themselves by devising laws and regulations. They were the lynch-pin of cotton exports from Berar. All unwanted brokers were kept out of the market.

It was necessary to curb the smuggling of cotton which would otherwise cut into exports. The market was preserved exclusively for European interest. The only way to keep the 'native snoopers' away was by increasing the license fee. Commenting on Indian brokers, the Assistant Cotton Commissioner, West Berar, writes: 'In the early part of the season [1869-70] the *dulals* or brokers, who gave so much trouble last year, were licensed, and the fee raised from the former rate of Rs.16 to Rs.100. This prevented the smaller men from taking out licenses, and, as the number was reduced to thirteen men of substance, matters worked better.'[118] The license requirement naturally

[116] See 'The Berar Cotton and Grain Markets Law, 1897', in *British Enactments in Force in Berar,* compiled by C. S. Findlay, Office of the Superintendent, Nagpur, 1916, p. 167.

[117] From: A. J. Crawford, Secretary for the Berar to the Resident, To: The Commissioner, Hyderabad Assigned Districts, Hyderabad, dated 1 July 1891, in the *Proceedings of the Hyderabad Administration on Matters of Routine for the Month of July 1891,* submitted to the Foreign Department, No. 2457, 1 July 1891 (IOLR).

[118] *Report on the Cotton Experiments in West Berar during the Season 1869-70,* by Mr. A. J. Dunlop, Assistant Cotton Commissioner, West Berar, in *Annual Reports of the*

coerced all the buyers and sellers to register their names at the cotton market office. Since it was a buyer's market, all buyers were required by law to show proof of purchase of not less than 500 bales during the past year to be eligible for buying in the market. Since only European firms had the wealth and capacity to buy in such large quantity, all others were legally debarred from participating in the market. The market was protected for bonafide buyers who were mostly European firms and their agents. 'The Cotton Market Committee may strike out of the register the names of persons who are not bonafide buyers, and whose object in registering themselves as buyers is to evade the rule excluding public brokers,'[119] wrote one municipal official.

The cotton market was usually located in the womb of cotton towns and surrounded by high compound walls. The mode of conducting business inside these walls was also regulated by rules. The Committee employed its own standards of weights and measures to suit the whims and fancies of the European firms. The severity of these rules can be easily detected from the observations of Mr. J. A. Crawford, the Secretary for Berar:

> Mode of conducting business in the market between buyers and sellers is strictly regulated by the rules. All cotton must be weighed with certain scales and weights and by man called a weigher, who is apparently a public officer to be remunerated by parties at a certain rate, and these are the rules, . . . regulating certain 'trade allowances' and allowances for samples which are to be made between each parties on each sale. Any person who does not confirm to these rules may be debarred from using the market and is also liable to be punished by the magistrate.[120]

The cotton market rules prohibited the sale or trade of cotton outside government designated markets. And everyone was in danger of either being arrested or incarcerated under Cotton Frauds Act for dealing in cotton outside the designated markets. The cotton which

---

Cotton Department for 1869-70 and 1870-71, by Harry Rivett-Carnac, Cotton Commissioner, in *Proceedings of the Department of Agriculture, Revenue and Commerce*, No. 8/4, dated February 1873, para 50 (IOLR).

[119] Imposition of Cotton and Grain Market Cesses by certain Municipalities in the Hyderabad Assigned Districts, *Foreign Department Proceedings*, June 1889, Nos. 275-8 (IOLR).

[120] From: J. A. Crawford, Secretary for the Berar to the Resident, To: the Commissioner, Hyderabad Assigned Districts, 1 July 1891, in the *Proceedings of the Hyderabad Administration on Matters of Routine for the Month of July 1891*, submitted to Foreign Department, No. 2457, 1 July 1891 (IOLR).

entered the town had to follow the packing specifications of the Cotton Market Committee. By the order of the Committee, 'no cotton packed in any other kind of wrapper or in nets or "jalias" is to be allowed in the cotton market, but shall remain in the place appointed outside the market wall . . .'.[121]

Due to market controls, the cotton business in Berar was a very profitable venture for European firms. The total number of wholesale merchants dealing in raw cotton was very small. At the height of the cotton export trade (1866-7) there were only 22 wholesale merchants all over Berar.[122] The fabulous wealth of these wholesale merchants and the visible export trade caused some discontentment among the general populace. This generally manifested itself in crime. A marked increase in trade coincided with a marked increase in crime in the province. Murders, dacoities, robberies, and arson increased at a tremendous rate during the period of the American Civil War. In 1863 there were 77 cases of dacoities in Berar and in 1864-5 it rose to 197. Similarly the cases of robberies rose from 96 to 224 during this period. These robberies and dacoities often occurred against the booty sent out by the chief merchants at large cotton emporiums. Sometimes grain riots and attacks on government treasury also occurred.[123]

Despite the profits made by European firms and their collaborators, most of the cotton duties imposed by Cotton Market Committees was quietly passed on to indebted cultivators. One such irksome tax was the stamp duty. As all the cotton market business was conducted on *suttahs* (contracts), a stamp duty of 8 *annas* per *sutta* was levied on all such agreements and contracts. 'Financial Resolution No. 843 dated 3rd January 1872, affirmed that the documents called "*suttahs*" which are executed by cultivators in Berar and are of the nature of contracts binding them to deliver their cotton produce, are not exempt from stamp duty, and that they are not transferable by endorsement without the payment of further stamp duty.'[124] This stamp duty was collected by the European firms from the moneylender who in turn

[121] Imposition of Cotton and Grain Market Cesses by certain Municipalities in the Hyderabad Assigned Districts, in the *Foreign Department Proceedings*, June 1889, Nos.1, 275-8 (IOLR).

[122] From: Messrs W. Nicol & Co., To: The Executive Engineer, Akola, dated 11 June 1867, *Hyderabad Affairs*, Vol. IV (1883-86), pp. 261-75 (APSA).

[123] *The Hyderabad Assigned Districts*, 27 January 1866, in *Hyderabad Affairs*, Vol. 5, 1883, pp. 256-64 (APSA).

[124] Exemption of cotton '*suttahs*' from Stamp Duty [letters], in *Foreign Department Proceedings*, Government of India, Nos. 1-3, dated May 1872 (IOLR).

charged it on cultivators credit on a passing-the-buck system.[125] A system of 'debt peonage'[126] similar to *postbellum* American south existed in the cotton trade of Berar. The only difference was that unlike the American sharecropper, the Berari ryot owned the piece of land he cultivated but forfeited his right over the crop.

A strange phenomenon was taking place in Berar with the extension of export trade of cotton. As all cotton gravitated towards the railway line, large cotton emporiums developed around them. This gave a death-blow to several pre-colonial trading towns outside the line. Many important interior towns to the north and south of the line which had traditionally provided links between villages gradually lost their importance. The gravitational power of the railway line and the colonial cotton trade wiped out the fine urban-rural balance of pre-colonial Berar. In 1866 the colonial survey and settlement officers noted the existence of several towns and local markets in Berar. But by the turn of the century most of these towns had disappeared. The revision settlement (1890s) sadly observed this phenomenon in the following manner: 'Markets are apparently not more numerous than they were at the time of the original settlement.'[127] The loss of local markets meant loss of choices for the cultivators. It also meant further enhancement of moneylender's control over the cultivator.

The land survey and settlement operation was a great stream-lining force in directing cotton and all other ,trade to big marts on the railway line. The cotton trade nevertheless spelled doom on colourful small towns and villages like Jalgaon, Teelara, Argaon, Anjangaon, Rithupur, Warur, Devalghat, Chikli, Fatehkelda, Malegaon, Digras, Darwa, Kehlapur, etc., which were centres of innumerable fairs and bazars. The cotton carts during the season avoided these towns as they slowly wend their way to the nearest railway station.[128]

[125] Rules for the Collection of the *Sutta* tax framed by Municipal Committee under Section 7 of Act IV of 1873, under *Khamgaon Municipal Code*, in *Proceedings of the Hyderabad Administration for the Month of April 1884*, submitted to the Home Department, No. 1028, 22 April 1884 (IOLR).

[126] Robert Higgs. *Competition and Coercion: Blacks in the American Economy, 1865-1914*, Cambridge, 1977, p. 58.

[127] Proposals for the Revision Settlement of the Darwa Taluq of Wun District, in the *Proceedings of the Hyderabad Administration on Matters of Routine for the Month of June, 1901*, submitted to the Department of Revenue and Agriculture, No. 201, 22 June 1901 (IOLR).

[128] *Note on Cotton in Berar*, by E. A. Hobson, Survey and Settlement Officer, Berar, Hyderabad, 1887, in the *Proceedings of the Department of Revenue and Agriculture*, Fibre and Silk Branch (November 1887), Nos. 22-3 (NAI).

The European firms never operated outside the periphery of the railway line. The Cotton Market Committees controlled the large cotton emporiums located on the railway line. It was the colonial government's job to ensure the flow of cotton by eliminating all the obstacles in its way. Small towns were the biggest obstacles and therefore the survey and settlement operations were projected to neutralize these small towns and clear the way to facilitate free flow of cotton. Mr. A. J. Dunlop, the Assistant Cotton Commissioner, writes in an almost triumphant tone on the demise of the small markets: 'I have also given some attention to the smaller markets of Julgaon, Teelara, and Sheagaon. The two former are entirely in the hands of natives, and it would be better for the cultivators to bring their cotton to the large marts. I think they are gradually coming to see this, and I have observed of late a feeling against the way in which, at Teelara especially, they have been treated, and I trust it will gradually lead to the entire desertion of these small markets.'[129]

The Expansion of Cotton Exports and Regulation of the Cotton Market

The cotton export trade was booming on the ruins of small towns and markets. The demands of world market ruthlessly crushed the local economy and redesigned it to suit its own needs and interest. Berar alone supplied nearly a quarter of the total annual exports of cotton from British India. Of the total annual supplies of 1.7 million bales, Berar supplied on average 250,000 bales. This was equivalent to the entire production of Egypt. Table 24 shows the total consumption of Europe and its principal suppliers (1866-7).[130]

Some quarter of a million bales were condensed in the short season from December to May. Every railway station was activated during this period, '. . . precautions were taken for the safety of the cotton detained [and] the importance of reducing the accumulations by carrying off the traffic as fast as possible was not lost sight of. To

[129] *Report on the Cotton Experiments in West Berar during the Season 1869-70,* by Mr. A. J. Dunlop, Assistant Cotton Commissioner, West Berar, p. 63, in *Annual Reports of the Cotton Department for 1869-70 and 1870-71,* by Harry Rivett-Carnac, Cotton Commissioner, in *Proceedings of the Department of Agriculture, Revenue and Commerce,* No. 8/4, dated February 1873.

[130] *Report on the Operations of the Cotton Department for the Year 1867,* by Harry Rivett-Carnac, 1869, pp. 21-2.

TABLE 24

Countries	*Bales*
America	1,500,000
India	1,700,000
Egypt	250,000
Brazil	500,000
Other countries	350,000
TOTAL	4,300,000

return to the old sum of the cistern it is obvious that the quickest and best plan of emptying the reservoir is to enlarge the drain-pipe . . .'.[131]

The pace of emptying Berar of its cotton was accelerated by the construction of sidings at every railway station. These sidings were launching pads of the bale's journey to Europe. 'By it waggons were brought home to the piles of cotton stacked in the yards; and the porters, having to carry the cotton a much shorter distance than before, were able to load up the waggons with much greater rapidity.'[132] The sidings revolutionized the speed of export trade. The cotton sent away from Khamgaon in the evening was loaded and dispatched from Nandora the next day, and delivered in Bombay three days later or within four days of the bale leaving the market.[133] A merchant sitting in Liverpool sent orders to his agents in Khamgaon by electric telegraph and had full-pressed bales delivered to him within six weeks of despatching the order.[134] These orders were based on prices fixed by the Manchester Chamber of Commerce. The Chamber fixed the price at the rate most favourable to European firms doing business in Berar. 'There is practically no such thing as a local price for cotton. The price in Berar is what the price in Liverpool and Bombay makes it'[135] was the common maxim of trade. The colonial government welcomed these prices and assisted in enforcing it.

[131] *Report on the Operations of the Cotton Department for the Year 1867,* by Harry Rivett-Carnac, 1869, p. 49.

[132] *Report on the Operations of the Cotton Department for the Year 1867,* by Harry Rivett-Carnac, 1869, p. 52.

[133] From: Cotton Commissioner, Central Provinces and Berars, Harry Rivett-Carnac, Camp Sheogaon, 11 April 1868, No. 810. To: Secretary to Chief Commissioner, Bombay, in *Foreign Department Proceedings,* June 1868, Nos. 11-12.

[134] *Report on the Operations of the Cotton Department for the Year 1867,* by Harry Rivett-Carnac, 1869, pp. 53-4.

[135] *Cotton Report of the Hyderabad Assigned Districts for 1878-79,* Hyderabad, 1879, in *Proceedings of the Department of Revenue, Agriculture and Commerce,* Fibre and Silk Branch (August 1882), pp. 12-18. Also see: *Report of the Famine Commission,* Appendix V: Irrigation as a Protection against famine, London, 1881, p. 481.

The value of Berar cotton was determined not by supply and demand in world market but by price-fixing.[136] The colonial claim of Berar's progressive link to the world market was also very dubious. Berar cotton did not really compete in the world market. In fact Berar was linked specifically to the interest of the Manchester Chamber of Commerce. The Chamber's agent wrote in 1869 thus: 'For, speaking generally, the cultivator who produces and sells the cotton . . . cannot in any way regulate the market price. For this he is dependent on the home market [Manchester] and the many causes which combine to raise and lower the price in Liverpool. The ryot brings his cotton to market, and on the telegraphic notices from Europe the price which he receives for his crop almost entirely depends.'[137]

The price-fixing was a highly manipulative affair. The price at Liverpool say 10 pence a pound, orders were sent out to India for so many thousand bales, at about that rate landed in Liverpool. The purchasers in Berar (agents of Liverpool firms) took into consideration all charges which cotton incurred between Berar and Liverpool, i.e. pressing, railway freight, insurance, ship freight, home commission, etc.[138] Deducting the total of these items from the 'lod' which was technically called the 'limit', they calculated the price to be paid to the ryot. Ordinarily the Liverpool price minus the charges formed the Berar market price. At 10 cents an lb in Liverpool fixed-price, the Berar sellers were given only 2 to 3 cents a pound. Although the demand for Berar cotton was unlimited and it could be sold anywhere in the world yet *Oomra* could not fetch more than 2 to 3 cents a pound in Berar. This was due to India's colonial position vis-a-vis Great Britain.[139] The hypocrisy of the *laissez-faire* gave free reign to Manchester's monopoly and enormous profits were made just on the marketing of raw cotton. In fact 'Oomra' was selling a little higher at 12 to 13 cents per lb in London and Manchester and there was a price differential of 10 cents between Berar and Manchester.[140]

[136] *Report on the Trade of the Hyderabad Assigned Districts for the Year 1878-79*, Hyderabad, 1880, p. 26.

[137] *Report on the Cotton Department for the Year 1868-69*, by Harry Rivett-Carnac, 1869, para 142.

[138] For the cost of transportation from Bombay to Liverpool, see *A Report on Cotton Growing in India*, by Arno Schmidt, Secretary, International Federation of Masters Cotton Spinners' and Manufacturers' Association, 1912, p. 77 (NAI).

[139] Extract from the *Proceedings of the Resident at Hyderabad*, No. 961, Hyderabad, Residency, 20 April 1883.

[140] See *The Manchester Guardian*, 1860-1900, microfilm (HUL).

Price-fixing and the demands of the export market pronounced wanton destruction of handlooms all over Berar. The disappearance of handlooms naturally led to the decrease in local demand for cotton. In 1877-8 only 7.8 per cent of the total cotton crop was retained for home consumption.[141] Throughout the colonial period the domestic consumption of raw cotton stayed under 10 per cent indicating a high degree of European cloth import into the region. 'The Berars grow cotton almost exclusively for export. There is no large local demand for cotton, to be made up into fine and coarse cloth; the supplies of cloth for the Berars being drawn from Bombay, or the Nagpur country, in the shape of English piece goods . . .'.[142] From being self-sufficient in cotton and cloth production, Berar was relegated to the subservient position of the exporter of raw cotton and importer of finished goods.[143] Some contemporary Western educated Indian nationalists branded this process as the 'drain of wealth' and colonial exploitation of India.[144]

Once an export market was created for Berar cotton in London in the wake of American Civil War, the acreage under cotton consolidated itself over total cultivated acreage. In the decades after the Civil War, cotton on average constituted over 30 per cent of the total cultivated acreage. Table 25 gives the acreage figures for Berar.

The table demonstrates a steady rise in cotton cultivation with some fluctuation. The cotton acreage nearly doubled itself between 1867-8 and 1900 from 1.25 million acres to 2.44 million acres. The per centage of cotton acreage to total cultivated area also increased from 21.1 per cent in 1860-1 to 35.8 per cent in 1900, showing more than 65 per cent increase during the period under study. Similarly the cotton acreage from the beginning of Civil War (1860-1) to its end in 1865-6

[141] *Cotton Report of the Hyderabad Assigned Districts for 1878-79,* Hyderabad, 1879, in *Proceedings of the Department of Revenue, Agriculture, and Commerce,* Fibre and Silk Branch (August 1882), pp. 12-18 (NAI).

[142] *Annual Reports of the Cotton Department for 1869-70 and 1870-71,* by Harry Rivett-Carnac, Cotton Commissioner, in *Proceedings of the Department of Agriculture, Revenue, and Commerce,* No. 8/4, dated February 1873, para 33 (IOLR).

[143] This also became the theme of economic nationalism of the Indian National Congress in the late nineteenth century. For more on this subject, see R.C. Dutt, *The Economic History of India,* 2 Vols., London, 1906.

[144] See Dadabhai Naoroji, *Poverty and Un-British Rule in India,* Sonnenschein, London, 1901; R.C. Dutt (1848-1909), *The Economic History of India,* New York, 1968.

TABLE 25

Year	*Total Cultivated Acreage*	*Acreage under Cotton*	*Index No. Cotton Acreage*	*% of Cotton to Total Acreage*
1860-1	2,969,413	629,000	NA	21.1
1861-2	3,061,249	650,000	NA	21.2
1862-3	3,222,357	753,571	NA	23.3
1863-4	3,670,430	1,137,833	NA	30.9
1864-5	4,036,900	1,196,300	NA	29.6
1865-6	4,376,110	910,310	NA	20.8
1866-7	4,432,837	1,238,966	NA	27.9
1867-8	NA	1,254,552	NA	NA
1868-9	NA	1,286,742	NA	NA
1869-70	NA	1,415,786	NA	NA
1870-1	NA	1,547,427	100	NA
1871-2	NA	1,487,648	96	NA
1872-3	NA	1,603,913	103	NA
1873-4	NA	1,807,404	117	NA
1874-5	NA	1,944,971	126	NA
1875-6	NA	2,099,934	136	NA
1876-7	NA	2,024,806	131	NA
1877-8	NA	2,078,273	134	NA
1878-9	NA	2,207,889	143	NA
1879-80	NA	2,101,273	136	NA
1880-1	6,675,820	1,755,946	113	26.3
1881-2	6,641,022	2,189,688	141	32.9
1882-3	6,567,323	2,390,188	154	36.3
1883-4	6,537,802	2,026,923	140	31.0
1884-5	6,472,956	1,959,402	127	30.2
1885-6	6,558,379	186,470	12	2.8
1886-7	6,379,488	2,061,266	133	32.8
1887-8	6,436,628	1,919,894	124	29.8
1888-9	6,469,504	1,994,767	129	30.8
1889-90	6,610,027	2,303,378	149	34.8
1890-1	6,697,281	2,461,608	159	36.7
1891-2	16,675,963	2,238,935	144	33.5
1892-3	6,818,348	2,164,042	140	31.7
1893-4	6,791,129	2,184,770	141	32.1
1894-5	6,758,786	2,102,956	136	31.1
1895-6	6,731,629	2,071,856	134	30.7
1896-7	6,257,276	2,304,237	149	36.8
1897-8	6,653,884	2,150,709	139	32.3
1898-9	6,787,318	2,471,123	160	36.4
1899-1900	5,405,253	2,061,082	133	38.1
1900-1	6,820,124	2,444,439	158	35.8
		Average Percentage		31.5

Source: Cotton Report of the Hyderabad Assigned Districts for the Year 1880-81, Hyderabad (n.d.), in *Proceedings of the Department of Revenue, Agriculture and Commerce,*

Fibre and Silk Branch (August 1882), No. 12-18, Appendix A; Peter Harnetty, 'Cotton Exports and Indian Agriculture, 1861-70', *Economic History Review*, Vol. 24, No. 3 (1971), pp. 414-29; *Report on the Census of Berar, 1881*, Bombay, 1882; *Report of the Indian Famine Commission, 1880*, London, 1881; *Report on the Past Cotton Season in the Central Provinces and Berar*, in *Foreign Department Proceedings of the Government of India*, Nos. 6-10, September 1874; *Report on the Revenue Administration in the Hyderabad Assigned Districts*, Hyderabad, Printed annually 1877-8 to 1901-2; *Report on the Administration of the Hyderabad Assigned Districts for the Year 1875-76*, Hyderabad, 1876, printed annually 1855-6 to 1901-2; 'Forecasts of the Cotton Crops in Bombay, the Punjab, Berar and Central Provinces of India for 1898-99', in the *Proceedings of the Department of Revenue and Agriculture*, Agriculture Branch (February 1899), Nos. 12-15; 'Cotton Prospects in Central Provinces and Berar', in the *Proceedings of the Department of Revenue, Agriculture and Commerce*, Fibre and Silk Branch (November 1874), No. 5.

almost doubled itself from 629,000 acres to 1,238,966 acres showing a marked 49.2 per cent increase.[145]

The total per centage of cultivated land devoted to cotton in Berar was the highest in India. Table 26 gives the per centage of cultivable land devoted to cotton culture in various provinces of British India.[146]

TABLE 26

Provinces	*1884-5*	*1886-7*
Madras Presidency	6.2%	6.4%
Bombay Presidency	8.3%	10.0%
North-West Provinces	7.2%	7.0%
Oudh	1.0%	1.0%
Punjab	3.5%	5.9%
Central Provinces	4.3%	4.9%
Berar	30.2%	32.3%

Berar was then the largest producer of cotton leading every other province in cultivated acreage.

Corresponding to the acreage, raw cotton formed nearly half the total exports from Berar. Although the actual export figures from Berar during the Civil War years are lacking, the price of 'Oomra' in Manchester cotton exchange rose dramatically during the War years

[145] Peter Harnetty, Cotton Exports and Indian Agriculture, 1861-70, *Economic History Review*, Vol. 24, No. 3 (1971), pp. 414-29; *General Administration Report on the Hyderabad Assigned Districts, 1855-56 to 1900-01*, published annually, Calcutta; *Report on the Revenue Administration of the Hyderabad Assigned Districts, 1877-78 to 1901-02*, published annually, Hyderabad.

[146] 'Note on Indian Cotton', in the *Proceedings of the Department of Revenue and Agriculture*, Fibre and Silk Branch (May 1889), No. 25/27, para 6.

(1862-5) and thereafter.[147] Exports from Berar did not collapse until five years after the end of Civil War. It temporarily plummeted in 1869-70; 1871-2; and 1872-3 but thereafter maintained itself steady with minor fluctuations. After the Civil War, American cotton could not re-establish its monopoly over London market. The 'Oomra' had come to stay and secured for itself a permanent share in Manchester and London. Table 27 gives the cotton export figures for Berar.

On average then 42.2 per cent of the total exports from Berar constituted just one item—cotton. This overwhelming dependency on a single crop had its consequences on the society and economy of the region. It subjected the region to credit and debt and subsequently pushed it into scarcity and famines.

Modernization and Poverty

The Economic Impact of Colonial Cotton Economy

To any visitor travelling in the late nineteenth century, Berar looked an epitome of a most advanced society in the contemporary world. A traveller would see long and endless iron lines of railway with steam engines passing by at regular intervals. Along the railway line he would see an endless line of overhead cables buzzing with telegraphic messages. He would see post offices and neatly painted red and black postal mail dak carriages going from town to town. He would not fail to notice long lines of cotton carts obediently moving towards the railway line. He would also notice experimental stations and weather monitoring instruments every so often with amazement. He would see large cotton ginning factories in every important town along the railway line. He will also see large steam pressing factories belching smoke into the sky. He would notice large monolithic government buildings everywhere. Finally he would see the Union Jack (British flag) fluttering in every taluka headquarters and wonder at the progress made by Berar under the British rule. But he would only be naive and

[147] 'Oomra' was the nickname given to Berar cotton in London market. It was the best cotton from the empire. It competed well with 'New Orleans' from America and sold for as high as 23.5 d. per lb at the height of the Civil War (1864). Thereafter it maintained a steady price of 10.5 d. until 1870 and made a permanent niche for itself in Manchester and London. For cotton prices refer to *The Manchester Guardian* (1860-1900), available in microfilm at Widener Library, Harvard University.

TABLE 27

Year	*Total Berar Exports Mnds*	*Berar Cotton Exports Mnds*	*Index No. to Berar Cotton Exports*	*% of Berar Cotton Exports to Total Exports*
1869-70	NA	825,888	NA	NA
1870-1	NA	1,410,268	100	NA
1871-2	NA	890,520	63	NA
1872-3	NA	862,190	58	NA
1873-4	NA	1,241,400	88	NA
1874-5	NA	1,431,781	101	NA
1875-6	NA	1,054,438	75	NA
1876-7	NA	1,626,686	115	NA
1877-8	NA	1,699,737	120	NA
1878-9	2,527,415	1,200,662	85	47.5
1879-80	1,540,793	1,004,398	71	65.1
1880-1	2,037,754	1,020,059	72	50.0
1881-2	4,421,710	1,572,052	111	35.5
1882-3	4,402,510	1,430,931	101	32.5
1883-4	2,990,857	1,027,785	73	34.3
1884-5	3,294,844	807,598	57	24.5
1885-6	4,289,640	1,278,108	91	29.7
1886-7	5,251,732	1,726,364	122	32.8
1887-8	3,463,158	921,100	65	26.5
1888-9	4,276,377	1,866,461	132	43.6
1889-90	3,635,968	1,902,429	135	52.3
1890-1	3,926,000	NA	NA	NA
1891-2	5,355,000	1,714,330	121	32.0
1892-3	3,701,000	1,355,420	96	36.6
1893-4	3,760,000	1,651,022	117	43.9
1894-5	2,691,000	1,211,933	86	45.0
1895-6	3,809,000	1,954,056	138	51.3
1896-7	3,522,000	1,827,708	129	51.8
1897-8	3,128,000	1,686,115	119	53.9
1898-9	5,747,000	3,208,228	227	55.8
1899-1900	2,609,000	915,157	65	35.0
1900-1	4,233,000	2,183,142	155	51.5
1901-2	7,842,000	3,830,744	272	48.8
1902-3	6,324,000	3,218,399	228	50.8
			Average	42.2

Source: Report on the Rail and Road Borne Trade of the Hyderabad Assigned Districts, printed annually 1878-9 to 1902-3, Hyderabad.

foolish to make his judgement of progress by external appearance. The colonial reality was entirely divorced from the external appearance. In reality Berar under colonialism experienced deindustrialization;

encroachment; disappearance of waste lands; ecological degradation; disease; demise of bazars and fairs; indebtedness and poverty of the general mass of population. Colonialism and cotton relegated Berar into the depths of economic deprivation and backwardness.

Under colonialism Berar was systematically deindustrialized. By deindustrialization is meant the destruction of pre-colonial handloom industry as a result of export of raw cotton and import of British manufactured cloth.[148] By deindustrialization is also meant a continued subjection of the economy and deliberate legal measures to prevent the growth of manufacture. Traditionally Berar had been a great manufacturer of *chintz* cotton.[149] The salts from the pits of lake Lonar were used for washing and dyeing *chintz*. The imposition of salt tax gave a death blow to *chintz* manufacturing in the region. Similarly Berar was traditionally famous for its excellent *dhotis* (waist cloth). The locally manufactured *dhoti* was worn with great passion in Berar and all over south India. Mehkur in Buldana district was a famous cloth manufacturing centre in pre-colonial times. But its manufacture was discouraged by pumping cheap European cloth into the region. The heavy exports of raw cotton drastically reduced the amount of cotton available for local consumption. The high price of cotton in the retail market prevented the *mahars* from acquiring weaving material necessary for the manufacture of *dhoti*.[150] The railway traversing in and out taking raw cotton and driving in manufactured cloth destroyed all stimuli for local manufacturing and rapidly reduced the province to commercial agriculture.[151] The American Civil War was perhaps the most important event leading to the destruction of cloth manufacturing in Berar. All manufacture was checked during the Civil War as raw cotton disappeared from the local market.[152] The

[148] See Amiya Bagchi, *Private Investment in India, 1900-1939,* Cambridge, 1972; also see Marika Vicziany, 'The Deindustrialization of India in the 19th Century', A Methodological Critique of Amiya Kumar Bagchi, in *Indian Economic and Social History Review,* Vol. XVI, No. 2 (April-June 1979) p. 105.

[149] A. C. Lyall, *Gazetteers of the Haidarabad Assigned Districts, Commonly called Berar,* 1870, p. 25.

[150] Ibid., p. 171.

[151] *Report on the Trade of the Hyderabad Assigned Districts for the Year 1880-81,* Hyderabad, 1882, para 13.

[152] *Note on Cotton in Berar,* by E. A. Hobson, Survey and Settlement Officer, Berar. Hyderabad 1887, in the *Proceedings of the Department of Revenue and Agriculture,* Fibre and Silk Branch (November 1887), Nos. 22-3.

looms, which had been at work for centuries, suddenly came to a halt. And within a few years they rusted and were gone.

Weaving in India had always been the profession of lower castes and untouchables. Weavers have historically been the subject of folk songs, tales, poems, and protest. From times immemorial the weaving caste had produced a whole array of saints and singers who openly protested against the authority and oppression of the rulers. In the fifteenth and sixteenth century, weavers, poets, and singers like Kabir, Nanak, Ravidas, and Mira provided inspiration for the rise of 'bhakti'—the idea of devotion and service.[153] Their impact was felt in Berar also. The colonial gazetteers and census report a large number of wandering mendicants and singers all over the region, i.e. bairagis, fakirs, jogis, manbhaos, naths, guraos, bhats, prabhus, gondhalis, perkis, gosais, sanyasis, etc. The numerous shrines and pilgrim centres dotting the landscape of Berar provided relief to the oppressed. The sufi saints and singers like Khaki Shah Wala, and Mastan Shah at Malegaon inspired the message of communal harmony.[154] Weavers, sadhus, mendicants, and the victims of social and colonial oppression congregrated in these shrines and received inspiration. These shrines also provided relief during famines.

The local loom which had acquired a ceremonial position in every village came under attack from the railway and the British manufactured cloth. It was impossible for the handloom to compete successfully against the skill and energy of Manchester.[155] The traditional handloom manufacture in Berar was very similar to the putting-out system of pre-industrial Europe.[156] Left to itself and under due protection it would have developed into mechanized production as it did in Europe. The skilled artisans like the dhers, koshtis, and mahars were wiped out of their traditional occupation during the American Civil War and forced to become agricultural labourers.[157] These artisans were hitherto seen all over Berar moving from place to place and selling

[153] See John Stratton Hawley, *Songs of the Saints of India*, Oxford, 1988.

[154] A. C. Lyall, *Gazetteers of the Haidarabad Assigned Districts, Commonly called Berar*, Bombay, 1870, p. 191.

[155] *Jalgaum Taluka Settlement Report*, No. 261 of 1865, para 36.

[156] See Robert Brenner, *Merchants and Revolution: Commercial Change and Political Conflict in the London Merchant Community: 1550-1653*, New Jersey, 1991.

[157] *Report on the Operations of the Cotton Department for the Year 1867*, by Harry Rivett-Carnac, 1869, p. 18.

several different varieties of cloth. But with the colonial onslaught, they gave up their looms and seldom went beyond the confines of their villages.[158] The cotton cultivation and trade polarized the population of Berar.

The deindustrialization of Berar was a systematic process. Immediately after the outbreak of American Civil War a heavy tax was imposed on all spinning and weaving activity in Berar. In 1861-2 a tax of Rs. 30 was levied on all cotton *churkas* and a tax of Rs. 157-10-3 on all handlooms.[159] This left spinners and weavers with no other choice but to give up their looms and *churkas* and become agricultural labourers. Following upon the 'loom and churka' tax, a series of Cotton Duty Acts were passed.[160] These measures were so successful that for half a century of colonial rule not a single cotton textile mill developed in Berar. But despite these repressive measures the first and the only cotton mill for the production of low grade yarn was established in 1896 at Badnera in (Amraoti district). This rang alarm bells throughout colonial Berar. Immediate legal measures were taken by the state through a series of laws to control the growth of this mill. The colonial state was constantly haunted by the fear that such a mill would grow to challenge Manchester cloth imports in the region. The Cotton Duties Act, No. II of 1896 slapped a surcharge of 5 per cent on all yarn of count 20 and above produced in Berar.[161] This mill, known as the Berar Manufacturing Company Ltd., produced yarn of the lowest counts ranging from No.10 to No. 33 counts (the best in the world came from Liverpool counted at No. 130). A special Inspectorate of Steam Boilers and Factories was sent from Bombay to monitor this mill and report on each and every minute detail of its activity.[162] This kind of supervision on the only cotton mill was in response to measures ordered by the Governor General in Council to keep track of cloth manufacturing in British India. All provinces with cotton mills were ordered to submit annual reports.[163]

[158] *Amraoti District Gazetteer*, 1911, p. 249.

[159] *General Administration Report on the Hyderabad Assigned Districts for the Year 1861-62*, Calcutta, 1863, Appendix II.

[160] Submission of monthly statements of excise duty collected and refunds allowed on exports of duty-paid yarns under the Cotton Duties Act, 1894, in *Foreign Department Proceedings*, No. 346/49, dated July 1895 (IOLR).

[161] J. H. Sadler, Deputy Secretary Finance Department, To: Government of India, 22 July 1895, in *Foreign Department Proceedings*, No. 163, dated June 1896.

[162] *Report on the Working of the Cotton Duties Acts in the Hyderabad Assigned Districts*, 27 December 1894 to 31 March 1896.

[163] Resolution, Government of India, Finance and Commerce Department, Calcutta, 3 December 1895, in *Foreign Department Proceedings*, No. 187, dated June 1896.

The duty of 5 per cent was strictly levied and collected from every mill in British India producing count 20 and above.[164] All District Commissioners and Deputy Commissioners in whose districts cotton mills producing yarn of count higher than 20 were ordered by the Government of India to furnish monthly returns showing the production of yarn.[165] In addition to the above tax, a 3.5 per cent ad valorem surcharge was slapped on all cloth and woven goods manufactured in Berar.[166] This new duty was supposed to curb uneconomic competition between mills producing yarn and cloth in Native States with their counterpart in British India. But this hyperbolic colonial logic was in reality a dubious cover to prevent the growth of Indian cloth manufacturing industry and preserve India as a market for British manufactured cloth.

The indigenous weaving was directly hit by deindustrialization. The cheap machine made English cloth not only undersell the indigenous Berari cloth, but also caused deskilling of the population. Although the people preferred the strong long lasting indigenous cloth to the softer perishable machine cloth, they had no choice but to buy the latter.[167] The process of deskilling was necessary for establishing a market for European piece goods. As the Cotton Commissioner clearly states the aim of the railway and government policy thus: 'Now it is not too much to hope, that, with a branch railway to this tract, European piece goods might be imported so as to undersell the native cloth. And the effect would be, that, not only would a larger supply of the raw material be obtained . . . but the large population now employed in spinning and weaving would be made available for agricultural labour, and thus the jungle land might be broken up and the cultivation extended.'[168] With the introduction of cheap machine made cloth, the local spinners and weavers were driven out of the market altogether. As already mentioned

[164] Extracts from the Proceedings of the Government of Madras in Political Department, in *Foreign Department Proceedings,* dated June 1896, No. 169.

[165] Notice of Government of India's Finance and Commerce Department, Simla, October 1895, in *Foreign Department Proceedings,* No. 187, dated June 1896.

[166] Adoption by Native States of the form of taxation introduced in British India with respect of cotton goods, in *Foreign Department Proceedings,* December 1896, Nos. 143-60 (IOLR).

[167] *Dariapur and Mortizapur Taluka Settlement Report,* No. 368 of 1869, p. 20, para 50, (NMML).

[168] *Report of the Cotton Department for the Year 1868-69,* by Harry Rivett-Carnac, 1869, para 115.

all of them were from skilled artisan weaving castes of koshtis, salis, momins, dhangars, naths, and mahars. Some of them ended up as cheap labour working on roads and railways. But majority of them ended up as agricultural labourers and deteriorated into poverty. The Cotton Commissioner wrote in 1869:

> . . . European piece goods are fast driving the trade out of the market. Where ever the railway line passes this is invariably the case . . . European piece goods have become thoroughly established . . . since cotton became so expensive a commodity; and the poor native, who had been obliged to forgo his annual suit of clothes, has also had to think twice of purchasing a new pillow, or restuffing his resai, or counterpane, with cotton.[169]

The irony was that the people were unable even to buy Manchester cloth. They usually wore their clothes to rags and when it was utterly worn out the shreds were worn by their children. These were the same weavers who had never experienced stark nakedness before. The cotton was grown entirely for export. What was so ironical was that in spite of being such a large producer of cotton, half its population went naked. The annual cloth availability was reduced to only 3 lbs per capita.[170] It was little wonder that the people had to wear their clothes to rags. Once famous for its cloth, the Berar weaving population by 1896-7 shrank to 1.5 per cent of the total before disappearing completely.[171]

In the normal course of events the weaving population should expand and flourish with the increase in cotton cultivation. But in Berar exactly an opposite trend can be noticed. Before the American Civil War cotton was just one of the many staple products of Berar agriculture. But the war changed all this. It transformed cotton and made it 'the prevailing, absorbing, predominating product. Much of other sorts of culture was displaced to make room for it'.[172] The process

[169] Ibid., para 172.

[170] From: A. J. Dunlop, Assistant Commissioner in Charge of Cotton Statistics for Central Provinces and Berar, To: Secretary, Chamber of Commerce (Bombay), Camp Oomraoti District, 6 November 1874, in 'Cotton Prospects in Central Provinces and Berar', in the *Proceedings of the Department of Revenue, Agriculture and Commerce,* Fibre and Silk Branch (November 1874), No. 5 (NAI).

[171] *Monograph on Cotton Fabrics in the Hyderabad Assigned Districts, 1896-97,* published by F. W. Francis, Director of Land Records and Agriculture, Hyderabad Assigned Districts, pp. 1-4 (NAI).

[172] *Report on the Administration of the Hyderabad Assigned Districts for the Year 1866-67,* Hyderabad, 1867, p. 1.

of encroachment was proceeding simultaneous to the process of deindustrialization. Berar for the first time began importing large quantities of foodgrains from the neighbouring country. The Oomrawuttee Settlement Report in 1870 observed the problem of encroachment in the following manner:

> . . . although jowaree, the principal food of the people, stands in the reasonable proportion of 2 to 5 to the remaining crops, wheat occupied only 3 per cent of the entire area, whereas cotton covered actually 40 per cent, or nearly one half of the cultivated land. If the ryots continue to grow cotton to this extent, they must also continue . . . to grow it every alternate year in the same land, simply because they have not sufficient land available for a better rotation. . . .[173]

Yes, there was simply not much land available for practising rotation. Year after year cotton was grown in the same land leading to declining crop yields and soil exhaustion. Due to the absence of proper irrigation facilities this economy concentrating on cotton had nothing but a gloomy future. The rain-fed agriculture when disproportionately distributed inevitably spells disaster in foodgrain production in the event of failure of rains. But this has very little impact on cash crop like cotton which requires minimal rain and arid weather condition for growth. Berar presented ideal conditions for such a development. The fortnightly cotton reports of the mid-1870s showed some concern for the existence of this problem. It correctly suggests that 'the more the area of food stocks is diminished in favor of fibers, the greater the danger from any failure of the monsoon becomes, and the greater appears to be the necessity of providing some security against the consequences of such failure'. It further states the danger that, 'all the best ground has gone for cotton and a lot of new inferior land has been broken up for grain, because, the people absolutely required it'.[174]

As a case in point let us look at cotton acreage movement in Buldana district. This is the south-west border district of Berar. Northern half of this district was a part of the rich Poorna valley plain and the southern half is comprised of hills and forest. Cotton was the principal crop of this district. In 1894-5 it occupied 29.5 per cent of the gross cropped area and fourteen years later it rose to 42.2 per cent.[175]

[173] *Oomrawuttee and Ellichpur Settlement Report*, No. 444 of 1870, para 45 (NMML).

[174] *Report on the Past Cotton Season in the Central Provinces and Berar*, in *Foreign Department Proceedings of the Government of India*, Nos. 6-10, September 1874.

[175] *Buldana District Gazetteer*, 1910, p. 183.

This was in fact the worst famine decade of the century and such a rapid increase goes to show that cotton was immune to famine while jowari was devastated. This scenario was repeated in every district and became serious in Amraoti district. Amraoti was one of the champaign districts in north-eastern Berar. Here in 1876 cotton occupied 35.9 per cent of the gross cropped area; in 1882 it increased to 36.7 per cent; in 1891 it climbed to 38.2 per cent; in 1901 it stood at 47.7 per cent and peaked a record high of 52 per cent in 1905.[176] The cotton acreage all over Berar also increased considerably in the decades of 1880s and 1890s when the region experienced successive cycles of scarcity and famines. For example, between 1880-1 and 1882-3 cotton acreage gained 10 per cent over the total cultivated acreage in Berar. Similarly, between 1887-8 and 1890-1 it again gained 7 per cent. During the worst famine decade of 1890s the cotton acreage increased by a record high of 13 per cent suggesting that cotton gained in acreage whenever the region was hit by famine.[177]

The Colonial Cotton Economy and Environmental Degradation

The colonial government's obsession with land revenue, the development of cotton trade, and the coming of railways accelerated the pace of waste land occupation.[178] The decrease in waste lands as a result of the encroachment of cotton gradually altered the climate of the region. The gradual increase in the reclamation of land brought about ecological changes of a dangerous proportion. The problem was identified for the first time by Sir A. C. Lyall in 1870 when he stated:

> With the clearing of the land the influences which help to conserve moisture have been removed. Not only is it that the rainfall drains off more rapidly, but the face of the soil is exposed to evaporate influences to a far greater extent than formerly.
>
> The great depth to which the water has subsided, and the change in the culturable capacity of the black soil, seem to support the theory that the increase of cultivation by removing the protecting shade and the retentive influences of the roots of the old jungle has gradually dissipated the cold season of the climate of this district.[179]

[176] *Amraoti District Gazetteer,* 1911, p. 191.

[177] These percentage figures have been computed from data in Table 25.

[178] *Chiklee Taluka Settlement Report,* No. 51 of 1866, p. 19.

[179] *Gazetteer of the Haidarabad Assigned Districts, Commonly called Berar,* by A. C. Lyall, 1870, p. 45.

Manchester relentlessly pursued its demand for cotton. The colonial government systematically collected the land revenue. The European firms aggressively conducted their business. An absolute increase in cotton acreage did occur yet, '. . . no signs of any improvement in the mode of cultivation can be noticed anywhere', was how the Ellichpur settlement officer observed in his Report of 1870.[180] The Oomrawuttee Settlement Report also recorded the anguish of people in the following manner: 'The ryots are crying out that their soils are becoming exhausted, as they do not now yield as plentifully, or produce crops of as good a quality, as they did formerly.'[181] This painful cry was escalated by an insufficient cultivated land for a better rotation of crops. Cotton took nearly half the best cultivated land and left little for rotation or other agricultural experiments. Unfortunately people could not eat cotton.

Furthermore, the people were constantly complaining about the general decrease in rainfall. Such complaints were not unfounded. The average annual rainfall between the decades of 1880-90 and 1890-1900 declined from 38.65 inches to 33.82 inches.[182] Complaints were also made on the drying up of fresh water springs. It is a matter of no surprise that within a decade of the colonial rule, Berar began to experience successive cycles of scarcity and famine. A great number of cattle and people began to suffer for want of water, fodder, food and basic necessities of life. The Secretary to the Government of India penning his opinion in 1874 wrote: 'Even now a great number of cattle die in Berar yearly from want of water and fodder, and what the result would be, where man and beast are concerned, in the event of a serious and widely extended failure of the rains in that province, it is difficult to say.'[183] Cotton became the curse of Berar.

Sir Allan Octavian Hume was one of the most radical and enlightened colonial bureaucrats of British India. He was one of the founding members of the Indian National Congress (1885) and a great patron of Indian agriculture. In 1874 he wrote a detailed report on the state of

[180] *Oomrawuttee and Ellichpur Settlement Report*, No. 444 of 1870, p. 5.

[181] Ibid., p. 5, para 15.

[182] *Report on the Census of Berar, 1881*, Bombay, Education Society's Press, 1882, p. 225.

Census of India, 1901, Vol. VIII, *Berar*, Allahabad, 1902, p. 3.

[183] From: Secretary to Government of India, Foreign Department, Calcutta, dated 24 June 1874, in *Report on the Past Cotton Season in the Central Provinces and Berar*, in *Foreign Department Proceedings of the Government of India*, Nos. 6-10, September 1874 (IOLR).

agriculture in Berar. The colonial government naturally suppressed this report for the fear that his insurgent ideas would spread to other colonial officials and embarrass the government. It is therefore necessary to dwell at some length on A. O. Hume's study of Berar.

Hume became concerned with Berar after noticing that between 1867 and 1874, Berar registered an enormous increase in cotton acreage from 1.25 million to 1.8 million and exports from 38,150 to 45,597 tons. 'The abstraction of more than half a million acres of best land in a small province', like Berar led him to the understanding that 'the more the area of food stocks is diminished in favor of fibres, the greater the danger from any failure of the monsoon becomes. . . .'[184] This line of thinking which appears to us now so simple was in fact a very sharp observation of Berar's material condition in the late nineteenth century. With enormous foresight, Hume visualized a rise in temperature as a result of the encroachment of cotton cultivation on forest lands.[185] The chronic and recurring failure of monsoon rains he attributed to the extension of cotton cultivation. Therefore quite correctly he brought the village tank question to the forefront of the colonial debate on irrigation. He wisely recommended the 'construction of innumerable small works, tanks and reservoirs . . . , as a reserve against drought and its necessary consequences . . .'.[186] He was critical of the grand and costly irrigation schemes even though they existed only on paper. He openly expressed his discontent at the colonial schemes and ways of doing things:

> I entirely deprecated any grand or costly schemes of general irrigation—they may give a name and fame to the talented officers who design and execute them, and they may convince themselves to the profession, as looks worthy of their heads and hands, but they will be found very generally (I believe) to do more

[184] Note of A. O. Hume on 19 June 1874, in the *Report of the Cotton Trading Season of Central Provinces and Berar*, in the *Proceedings of the Department of Revenue, Agriculture, and Commerce,* Fibre and Silk Branch (June 1874), Nos. 41-2 (NAI).

[185] The temperature did show a marked increase of 10 degrees between 1870 and 1910. In 1870 A.C. Lyall first recorded the temperature to be 80.9 degrees. Forty years later the Buldana and Amraoti Gazetteers recorded an average mean temperature of 90.9 degrees. See A. C. Lyall, *Gazetteer for the Haidarabad Assigned Districts, Commonly called Berar*, Bombay, 1870, p. 40; *Central Provinces District Gazetteers: Amraoti District*, Bombay, 1911, p. 29; *Central Provinces District Gazetteers: Buldana District,* Calcutta, 1910, p. 22.

[186] Note by Hume on 19 June 1874, in the *Report of the Cotton Trading Season of Central Provinces and Berar*, in the *Proceedings of the Department of Revenue, Agriculture and Commerce,* Fibre and Silk Branch (June 1874), Nos. 41-42.

harm than good in the long run, in the present state of agriculture in India, and therefore not to such as these that I look as an insurance against famine in Berar.[187]

According to Hume, the professional engineers were totally incapable of grasping the problem of steadily decreasing area under food stock cultivation. Therefore he recommended inexpensive and simple irrigation works as a deterrence against failure of rains and famines.

However radical or critical Hume and other enlightened colonizers like him may have been, yet they were unable to grasp the nature of relationship between Great Britain and Berar. They were unable to understand the simple fact that Berar was linked to Great Britain not in a symbiotic relationship but in a parasitic relationship. They were incapable of perceiving that colonialism meant economic subservience of Berar. The solution to the problem of Berar therefore did not really lay in the construction of inexpensive, simple and innumerable small irrigation works, tanks, and reservoirs as Hume suggests. The problem of Berar's economic backwardness really lay in the systematic material exploitation of Berar's labour and resources under colonial subjection. The ideas of Hume like the ideas of the Indian National Congress were a 'safety-valve'[188] but not a solution to the problem of Berar. In any case, his ideas failed to make even a dent in the colonial public opinion either in India or in Britain. In fact Hume was unceremoniously booted out of the colonial bureaucracy after faithfully serving in it for thirty years of his life.

The Poverty of Colonial Capitalist Development

The relationship of the cotton economy to local society was parasitic in nature. As the cotton economy grew, the local society was drained. The majority of the people lived in want. The benefits of the cotton economy was reaped by the Manchester merchants, European firms, the colonial state and a slender crust of upper class Indians most of whom were from outside Berar, i.e. merchant-moneylenders and large landholding *khatedars*. The cotton was grown under twin pressure of poverty and indebtedness. The sellers were mostly native merchants and

[187] Note of A. O. Hume on 19 June 1874.

[188] See Britton Martin Jr., *New India 1885: British Official Policy and the Emergence of the Indian National Congress*, Berkeley, 1969.

moneylenders. The buyers were mostly European firms.[189] The cultivators were thus divorced from direct interaction with the market. In fact very little cotton was brought to the market by cultivators themselves. The village moneylender usually managed to secure greater portion of the crop.[190] When the cultivator was in debt to the moneylender, it was not difficult for the latter to manipulate the books and devalue the crop. Cotton was used as an instrument of bondage and social control. The cultivator was bound to the land and cotton was cultivated for the moneylender. The moneylender paid the government land revenue and sold cotton to European firms at prices fixed by Manchester. In 1880 the Famine Commission noted:

> It is an almost universal institution that shopkeepers should take the whole of the Government share of the crop, and pay the cash revenue for the agriculturist. The crops have generally been forestalled. When they are harvested the creditors carry off the whole, and the agriculturist has to begin again borrowing for his daily wants.[191]

Gyan Prakash in his work on bonded labour in eastern India has observed that bondage occurred when the *kamia* (labourer) and *malik* (landowner) were locked in a debt relationship of ceremonial social obligation reinforced by the expediency of political economy.[192] Prakash argued that similar pattern can also be noticed in pre-colonial Bihar. In the case of Berar however, large-scale indebtedness did not exist in pre-colonial period. With the rise in demand for cotton in the world market in the 1860s, the *khatedar* and *mahar* labour began to be contracted to the moneylender for the production of cotton on credit capital. The village marwari (moneylender) was in turn contracted to supply raw cotton to the European firms on advances. This chain of credit and debt relationship did not exist in pre-colonial Berar when cotton was a subsistence crop like any other crop grown in the region.

[189] 'Cotton Seed Adulteration in Berar', in the *Proceedings of the Department of Revenue and Agriculture.* Fibre and Silk Branch (November 1884), Nos. 1 and 2.

[190] *Cotton Report on the Hyderabad Assigned Districts for the Year 1882-83,* Hyderabad, 1883, in the *Proceedings of the Department of Revenue, and Agriculture,* Agriculture Branch (December 1883), p. 7.

[191] *Report of the Famine Commission,* Appendix V: Irrigation as a Protection against famine, London, 1881, p. 164.

[192] See Gyan Prakash, *Bonded Histories: Geneologies of Labour Servitude in Colonial India*, Cambridge, 1990; *Contesting Power: Resistance in Everyday Social Relations in South Asia*, Berkeley, 1991; *The World of Rural Labour in Colonial India,* New York, 1992.

The story of moneylender will be developed in a subsequent chapter.

So if indebtedness was the inevitable outcome of colonial cotton economy, then poverty was the inherent characteristic of debt bondage. Throughout the colonial period the majority of cultivators in Berar were in debt bondage. The cotton economy had created conditions for the perpetuation of this bondage. As more land was being brought under cotton cultivation, indebtedness was deepening. It is ironical that the rise in cotton acreage and exports led to a marked decline in the average per capita consumption of cotton in Berar. As mentioned earlier, the average consumption in Berar was only 3 lbs per capita per annum.[193] This meant that most Berari children went naked, most Berari men were half clad, and majority of the Berari women clothed themselves in rags. It was ironical that in spite of devoting more than 40 per cent of its cultivated acreage to cotton (probably the highest in the world at the time) and exporting enormous amount of cotton, the people of Berar went without proper clothing to cover their bare bodies. But when we look at the poverty of the masses and its relationship to colonial cotton trade, the irony may not be that obvious. As a product of colonial exploitation, cotton became the curse of Berar.

The General Administration Report of 1863-4 very carefully documented the general feeling of the people about the economy in the following manner: 'Half a Rupee, a few years ago, was worth as much as a Rupee is worth now. The rise in prices is not confined to grain and cotton, but extends to everything.'[194] These sentences very aptly explain the economic situation under colonialism. Life was becoming harder and harder. Eking out a living was becoming more and more difficult.

If the cotton economy was exploiting the general mass of people, the dominant groups in state and society were manipulating the cotton economy to the detriment of peasants. The intensification of colonial exploitation acted as a leverage for the intensification of caste oppression. It was in the interest of the colonial state to strengthen 'traditional' customs, prejudices, and hierarchical caste domination and use them to perpetuate their authority. The local support for the

[193] *Report on the Operations of the Cotton Department for the Year 1867*, by Harry Rivett-Carnac, 1869, p. 19.

[194] *General Administration Report on the Hyderabad Assigned Districts for the Year 1863-64*, Calcutta, 1865, para 52.

colonial state came from the upper caste who were the 'willing collaborators of the colonizers'. So long as the colonial state received its revenue it did not interfere between the cultivators and the moneylenders. Once the moneylender paid the revenue, he was free to deal with the cultivators in any manner he pleased. So it was in the interest of the moneylenders to acquire this revenue paying right. This right was easily acquired through colonial courts and laws. In the same manner the upper caste loyalty to the colonial state left them free to deal with the lower caste in any manner they pleased. So it was very much in the interest of the upper caste to acquire the loyalty of the colonial state in the same manner as it was in the interest of moneylenders to win support of colonial law courts. The intensity of caste oppression increased with the increasing intensity of colonial demand for cotton. It is therefore fair to argue that caste oppression increased under colonialism.

The majority of the cultivators in Berar belonged to lower caste. Most owned or leased land for cultivation. The problem of liquid capital to cover the operating cost forced them to enter into credit relationship with the upper castes. Since a majority of the lower caste were illiterate, the upper caste manipulated the books and accounts to hold the lower caste in bondage. Once a debt contract was entered there was no escape for the lower caste cultivators. The demands of the cotton economy further strengthened this bondage. Even though the kunbis and other lower caste cultivators were unwilling to devote half their cultivable lands to cotton, they had no choice. The decision of crop-mix was made by the upper caste who advanced capital on this precise condition. This was very similar to the system of sharecropping in the American south after the Civil War.[195] There the sharecroppers entered into a legal agreement with the planters to devote a certain amount of leased land to cotton. The planter provided the capital and assets in return for half the share of the crop. But unlike in Berar the sharecroppers did not own land. They merely cultivated it for the planter. In Berar the cultivators borrowed credit capital in exchange for cotton crop. In both cases the decision of crop-mix was heavily influenced by the creditors, i.e. the Indian moneylenders and American planters.

[195] For a detailed exposure of American sharecropping system see Roger L. Ransom and Richard Sutch, *One Kind of Freedom: The Economic Consequences of Emancipation*, Cambridge, 1977.

The primary producer thus lost the decision-making power on his own land. This was also the reason for such a vast increase in cotton acreage in Berar. The cultivator was left with no other choice but to bow to the dictates of local capital. It should be noted here that the local capital itself was responding to the demands of external market. From the cultivators' point of view it was easy to raise credit capital on cotton securities than on foodgrains. The nature of *suttah* contracts insisted on the growth of cotton. The pressure of debt coerced the cultivators to grow cotton.

The lower castes had diversified their economic activity between agriculture and handicraft in the pre-colonial times. But now the new colonial order coerced them into full-time agriculture. The ownership of land did not mean much in substance. The lower castes laboured on their own land as agricultural labourers. In addition to the lower castes, there was a large group of untouchables in Berar. As a rule the untouchables did not own land. They mostly worked as agricultural labourers and provided services to the upper caste. With the worsening economic situation the upper caste oppression also worsened. The position of untouchables was similar to the slaves of the ante-bellum south.[196] Their labour capacity was attached by the upper castes. The only difference between the American slaves and the untouchables was that the upper caste did not have much control over the leisure of the untouchables. The slaves were chattel property of the planter and the planter controlled both their labour and leisure.[197]

Not unlike the American slaves, the untouchables also lived in segregated villages and their freedom of movement was restricted. Their quarters were relegated outside the mud-walls of the village. Restrictions were imposed on their entry in and out of the city. They were forced to bow their heads, bend down and touch their forehead against the ground at the sight of the upper caste. The Cotton Commissioner writes: 'So low were the *dhers* in the social scale, that, when a marriage took place among them, the bride and bridegroom were not permitted to indulge in any more dignified mode of conveyance than bullocks, seated on the backs of which they appeared

[196] See Eugene D. Genovese, *Roll, Jordon, Roll: The World the Slaves Made*, New York, 1974.

[197] See Robert William Fogel and Stanley L. Engerman, *Time on the Cross*, Vol. I: *The economics of Negro Slavery;* Vol. 2: *Evidence and Methods*, Boston, 1974.

in the procession. They were not allowed to ride ponies instead of bullocks.'[198]

Several restrictions were placed on the untouchables. They were not permitted to wear red clothes during festivals. They were not allowed entry into the temples nor permitted to draw water from the village wells as their presence polluted the upper caste. They were not permitted to look at the upper caste in the eye nor speak in a high voice. They had to maintain certain physical distance from the upper caste in public places. The lower caste women were always in danger of being mistreated by upper castes. They were constantly ostracized and threatened with physical violence. Education was denied to them and so were better living conditions. They had to work for the upper caste often without wages.[199] The upper caste oppression of the lower caste was in a way no different but inextricably linked to the colonial oppression of Berar. In fact the intensification of the colonial oppression led to the intensification of upper caste oppression. The social aspect of colonialism will be dealt at some length in the next chapter.

Conclusion

In conclusion then it is argued that despite receiving the most advanced technology of the time, the economic condition of the people of Berar deteriorated. Berar's link to the world market and colonial capital investment led to the exploitation of labour and resources in the countryside. Far from enhancing the quality of life, it left the Berar peasantry in a state of impoverishment and want.

This chapter has established three important points related to Berar in the nineteenth century. Firstly, as modern technology altered the physical landscape, the colonial state and European firms manipulated the political economy to their own advantage by depriving the people of their due share. The metropolitan capitalists based in London, and Manchester, Indian merchant-moneylenders and landed *khatedars* cornered all the benefits of the cotton boom while the primary producer was left with low stagnating wages utterly insufficient for subsistence. Secondly, despite the rhetoric of 'free trade' the

[198] *Report on the Cotton Department for the Year 1868-69,* by Harry Rivett-Carnac, 1869, p. 145.

[199] For an anthropological study of untouchability see Bernard S. Cohn, *The Camars of Senapur: A Study of the Changing Status of a Depressed Caste,* Michigan, 1954.

colonial state imposed regulations and restrictions on the operation of market forces to cater to the interest of the world market and European firms. It prevented the development of the capitalist competitive wage system by pinning the peasantry into a state of labour servitude. Thirdly, cash crop driven colonial modernization inflicted heavy environmental damage which left in its trail disease, famine, and despair.

Much of the immediate despair was caused by the demands of world market and the state of indebtedness of the peasantry. Although the moneylender was a minor player in the game of colonial political economy, yet his role in extending local credit and working capital was very crucial to the production of cotton. The next chapter is therefore a study of the banias (moneylenders) of Berar.

CHAPTER 5

Economy-Sociey Nexus: Moneylenders and Peasant Debtors in Berar

THE SURVEY AND settlement operations introduced private property rights in land but did not develop a regular market in land. Similarly the colonial state succeeded in developing a cotton economy but no regular banking system. This had two implications for Berar: firstly, it depleted agrarian surplus by catering to the demands of an external market, and secondly it prevented the accumulation of savings. Consequently, capital at the disposal of Berar cultivators was frequently in short supply. Most of the local creditors in Berar were therefore outsiders. They settled not in the large cotton emporiums but in the villages of Berar. Attracted by cotton trade and property rights in land, the moneylenders came in considerable number during the early days of the British raj in Berar. 'The enlarged rights of property in agricultural holdings, the consequent expansion of credit, and the fluctuations in the value of land and produce under the influence of foreign trade having drawn the poorer occupants into difficulties, which attracted an inferior class of alien money-lenders',[1] was how a colonial officer remarked in 1881.

Who were the Moneylenders

Contrary to the colonial designation of occupation by caste, moneylending in Berar was practised by anybody with a little capital and organizational skills. The Berar moneylenders came from a variety of social and economic backgrounds. Moneylending only required a very basic education in counting and account

[1] Note by Mr. J. B. Peile, in the *Report of Famine Commission, 1881,* p. 163.

keeping.[2] Although a majority of the professional moneylenders were marwaris, nevertheless the business of moneylending cut across caste. The district gazetteers report that moneylenders came from diverse castes such as, i.e. komtis, brahmans, khatris, kunbis, telis, sonars, muhamadans, agarwals, bhatias, chhatrapuris, bhoras, and even pathans, afghans, and rohillas.[3]

The destruction of fortifications, immediately after colonial takeover, demobilized the rohillas, afghans, and pathans. Too proud to take up cultivation, these remnants of the Mughal times indulged in petty moneylending. They originally hailed from either the North-West Frontier Province or Afghanistan. In addition to being moneylenders, they were often itinerant hawkers of sundry goods and dry fruits. Their customers were generally the lower caste people such as mahars, mangs, kolis, kunbis, bhils, sweepers, etc., who enjoyed no credit with the regular marwari or the bania. Lower level and lowly paid colonial government employees and subordinate staff at large railway centres borrowed fast cash at high interest from the pathan. But once the date set for repayment had passed the pathan gave them no respite: 'He is at his [debtors] door before day dawns to demand his dues usually with a big stick which he displays in a threatening manner while making his demand in a persuasive tone',[4] wrote the *Buldana Gazetteer* about the habit of pathan.

However in general the professional moneylenders of Berar were known to people as *sahukars*. The *sahukars* often employed services of pathans and rohillas to recover their debts. The gazetteer note that:

> Many of them are employed by the sahukars to recover debts or collect rent from backward tenants. The pathan is generally successful in this line owing to his imposing appearance, uncouth manners, reputation for truculence, tyrannical methods and the tenacity with which he persecutes the recalcitrant debtor.[5]

[2] *Buldana District Gazetteer*, Calcutta, 1910, p. 126.

[3] *Yeotmal District Gazetteer*, Calcutta, 1908, p. 123; also see: A. C. Lyall, *The Gazetteers for the Haidarabad Assigned Districts, Commonly called Berar*, 1870, p. 230.

[4] *Buldana District Gazetteer*, 1910, pp. 151-2.

[5] *Buldana District Gazetteer*, 1910, p. 151.

The statistics of colonial census reports indicate that although the practice of moneylending was widely prevalent among different castes and classes, the majority of professional moneylenders were marwaris and banias. In fact they were identified by the common name *sahukar*. It was common for the marwari to move into a village with bare minimum of *dhoti, lota, and chaupai* (loin cloth, a metal-pot, and a portable mat). He also carried a small amount of cash as initial starting capital. The period from the outbreak of American Civil War (1861) to the end of first survey and settlement operation (1877) saw the formation of officially designated villages. The purpose was to establish a regular system of revenue collection and proprietary rights in land. This created a field for the inflow of capital. Realizing Berar's tremendous potential to grow cotton, the colonial state made every effort to put a cotton economy in place. It was assumed that once such an economy was established, then production and trade could be controlled by state power. It was precisely during this period that the villages of Berar attracted moneylenders. Since the volume of capital at moneylenders' disposal was just petty cash, it was only natural for them to move towards villages rather than large cotton towns. It was also during this period that gradually every village in Berar was settled by moneylenders. On average there was one moneylender per village. In 1874 there were 6,795 villages in the province[6] and by the close of the century it averaged between 7000 to 8000 villages.

According to the census of 1891 there were 6134 moneylenders in 1881 and 8360 in 1891.[7] A 26.6 per cent rise in their number indicates a rise in marwari immigration into Berar. This trend is also noticed in the figures for the number of people returned as speaking marwari language. In 1881 there were 21,687 people returned as speaking marwari while the number rose to 36,602 in 1891, a 40.7 per cent rise. In 1891 out of the total of 36,608 persons of marwari origin, 23,174 were males and 13,434 were females.[8]

The above data suggests that the majority of early moneylenders who came to Berar were either single or had left their families

[6] *Report on Survey and Settlement Operation in the Hyderabad Assigned Districts for the Year ending 31st October 1873,* Hyderabad, 1874, p. 1.

[7] *Census of India, 1891,* Vol. VI: *Berar or the Hyderabad Assigned Districts,* Calcutta, 1892, p. cxlv.

[8] *Census of India, 1891,* pp. lxxviii-lxxxii.

behind. They had ventured to establish a foothold on business before inviting their relatives. When a moneylender transformed from being a marwari to a *sahukar*, it was time for him to invite his family over to Berar. This transformation was marked by the success of his *kirana* shop which was the starting point of most marwari venture.

Usually a bania or marwari by habit led a frugal life. He started the business not as a moneylender but by opening a *kirana* shop of sundry goods either in a modest hut or under a tree by the village chowrie. It was a small operation compared to the countrystore of American south.[9] He initially sold basic necessities of consumption, i.e. salt, sugar, chilies, turmeric, dry lentils, oil, soap, brooms, copra, ropes, staples, lamps and wicks, matches, kites, etc. Without sparing himself and running the shop from the break of dawn till late in the dusk, the bania toiled day and night to build up his savings enough to start lending initially to his most trusted customers.

His customers were invariably the inhabitants of the village, i.e. the *khatedars* and *bhagindars*. He maintained only a credit (rather than personal or social) relationship with his customers and operated his business as a venture. He never exhibited a show of external prosperity and never related himself closely to any geographical locale except his native country of Rajasthan. Hailing mostly from Marwar, some of them also had connections with Ajmer, Jodhpur, and Jaipur.[10] But every one of them spoke and maintained accounts in marwari. Mr. W. N. Baput, the Tehsildar of Chandur, in 1872 mentioned that the bania lived in a world of his own defined by profits and fortune:

> Being a stranger in the Deccan, and looking to his native place as the repose of his latter days, he cares little what people think and speak about his actions, so long as he is allowed to make his fortune.[11]

The indifferent attitude of marwari towards the locale is also indicated by his attitude towards land. The moneylenders in Berar

[9] For a classic study of country stores in the American south see: Harold Woodman, *King Cotton and his Retainers*, Lexington, 1968.

[10] *Census of India, 1891*, Vol. VI: *Berar*, p. lxxviii.

[11] From: W. N. Baput, Tehsildar, Chandur, To: Deputy Commissioner, Oomraottee District, dated 28 April 1872, in *Proceedings of the Hyderabad Administration for the month of October 1874*, submitted to the Home Department, No. 99, 26 October 1874.

were not interested in acquiring land so much as acquiring control over produce of the soil. This produce included both cotton and jawari, the two principal staples of Berar. In 1873 out of a total number of 184,177 registered tenants only 196 or 0.1 per cent were marwaris.[12]

Some historians have suggested that the agricultural loans and acts of the nineteenth century was a government response to curb landownership from passing into the hands of non-agricultural classes.[13] Such a conclusion does not apply to Berar. In Berar the moneylenders were not so much interested in possessing land as much as acquiring control over the produce. The marwari generally acted as an intermediary between the primary producer and European firms. This intermediate position was his principal means of material survival. Such a position kept the moneylender always vulnerable to the pressure of colonial state from above and *khatedar* cultivators from below.

There is evidence of *khatedari* resistance to the moneylender in Berar countryside. This aspect will be dealt with in greater detail in the latter part of this chapter. It must however be noted that the typical moneylender of Berar was a miserable creature whose survival depended on the whims and fancies of the colonial state and European firms. The pressure of state and the market coerced moneylenders to adopt exploitative methods of controlling and extracting the produce of land. A state of general capital shortage and the colonial government's inhibition to finance agriculture no doubt left the field open for moneylenders but the moneylender himself had very little working capital and often times borrowed from European firms in return for a guaranteed supply of cotton. In a situation of limited price fluctuations, the moneylender could never accumulate enough capital to expand his activity. He was in

[12] Letter No. 1915, From: W. Nembhard, Commissioner, Hyderabad Assigned Districts, To: First Assistant Resident, Hyderabad, Oomraottee, 14 July 1874, in *Proceedings of the Hyderabad Administration for the Month of October 1874*, submitted to the Home Department, No. 99, 26 October 1874.

[13] The Punjab Alienation of Land Bill of 1900 and the Deccan Agricultural Relief Act of 1879 restricted the non-agricultural classes including the moneylenders from acquiring land because indebtedness and poverty was caused when non-cultivating classes acquired land and exploited the labour of cultivating classes. This view is held by N. G. Barrier, *The Punjab Alienation of Land Bill of 1900*, Durham, 1966, and Ravinder Kumar, *Western India in the Nineteenth Century: A Study in the Social History of Maharashtra*, London, 1968.

a way trapped in the village as a hostage of the market. His crucial role as a link between the primary producer and the market is undeniable. The high rates of interest charged was no doubt exploitative and was used as a lever to keep the *khatedars* under his control. He also used the threat of courts and laws to exercise control over cultivators. The moneylender was no doubt better off economically than the *khatedar* or the subtenant but vis-a-vis the market, he was a slave.

It will not be inaccurate to state that if the *khatedar* cultivator was indebted to the moneylender, the moneylender himself was tied to the market controlled by the colonial state and European firms. It is apt to state that the moneylender then was only a 'fly hovering around the twin wheels' of exploitation represented by the colonial state and European firms.[14] The reduction of Berar to this pathetic state of indebtedness cannot be understood without looking at the cause of debt.

The Causes of Indebtedness in Berar

Ten years after the American Civil War, Mr. A. Farrer, the Assistant Commissioner of Amraoti district, wrote to his boss the Commissioner that principal gainers of the war were the moneylenders, the grog-sellers and the government.[15] According to him the war triggered rash speculations in land as a response to the survey and settlement operations under way. Capital was borrowed at enormous interest rates for clearing wastelands and for the purchase of seeds and agricultural implements. Before the Civil War and before privatization, the landless had freely moved in search of agricultural work. But after the war this free mobility of the agrarian population was curbed consequent to the establishment of private property rights in land and with it bonds of indebtedness.

In Berar the Civil War failed to trigger a market in land as it did in cotton. One of the reasons for the absence of land-market was

[14] This metaphor 'fly in the wheel' was first used by the late Professor Eric Stokes in his book, *The Peasant and the Raj: Studies in Agrarian Society and Peasant Rebellion in Colonial India*, Cambridge, 1978.

[15] From: Mr. A. Farrer, Assistant Commissioner Amraoti District, To: Deputy Commissioner Amraoti District, dated 15 August 1872, in *Proceedings of the Hyderabad Administration for the Month of October, 1874*, submitted to the Home Department, No. 99, 26 October 1874.

the mortgage system. Being as foreign to Berar as the British, the moneylenders showed no interest in acquiring land. The motives of the moneylender and the British in fact complemented each other. 'It is a control of the cotton trade rather than the actual ownership of land that the money-lenders look to acquiring . . .'[16] declared the *Amraoti Gazetteer.* And even when the mortgage was foreclosed it served the creditor better to resell rather than cultivate the land himself. The moneylender and the British were not really interested in Berar except for its cotton and labour. They were partners in the exploitation of Berar although ultimately the moneylenders themselves were exploited by the latter.

The problem of indebtedness in Berar was very intricately connected with the timing of government land revenue demand. The Cotton Commissioner Harry Rivett-Carnac in 1869 stated:

> He [cultivator] was deeply in debt; and as if to remove all hope of his ever extricating himself, the instalments of the land revenue were so arranged that, the rents falling due at a season when the cultivator had no produce on hand to meet the demand, a recourse to the money-lender was a matter of certainty and necessity.[17]

The pressure of government land revenue demand forced *khatedars* to run to the moneylenders. Consequently, it became the regular practice for moneylenders to pay the government land revenue demand on behalf of *khatedars.* The tehsildars and government agents worked closely with moneylenders in collecting revenue. The revenue report of 1878-9 clearly reveals this:

> And it may almost be said that in Berar land revenue is paid in one kist some time in the two months from 15th January and 15th March. That Tahsildars find it convenient to themselves to realize in one kist, and as early as possible, is no doubt true.[18]

Although land revenue could be paid in two instalments yet most of it was cleared in the month of January. Punctuality in government revenue collection, brought the village banker to the forefront of rural economy. 'Without doubt the village banker has much to do

[16] *Amraoti Gazetteer,* Bombay, 1911, p. 228.

[17] *Report on the Operations of the Cotton Department for the Year 1867,* by Harry Rivett-Carnac, 1869.

[18] *Report of the Revenue Administration of the Hyderabad Assigned Districts for the Year 1878-79,* Hyderabad, 1879, p. 16.

with the punctuality of our revenue collection,'[19] wrote captain R. Hudleston in 1872. As mentioned earlier, the Famine Commission Report of 1880 states that the rights of property in agricultural holdings and the influence of foreign trade resulted in the expansion of credit and '. . . having drawn the poorer occupants into difficulties . . . attracted an inferior class of alien money-lenders'.[20] Although this observation was made for Bombay Deccan yet its relevance to Berar cannot be disregarded. In fact the rise of proprietary rights in land coincided with indebtedness. Therefore, the rise of *khatedari* system is directly related to the problem of debt bondage in Berar.

In 1872 on the eve of an enquiry into the state of indebtedness, a debate ensued among colonial officials of the Berar Commission. One group represented by Colonel W. Nembhard, Judge F. W. Grant, and Major W. Tweedie arguing in favour of the *khatedari* system threw the blame entirely on the marwari moneylender. While another group represented by Judge H. C. Menzies, Commissioner J. Allardyce, Mr. J. H. Burns, and Mr. R. Bullock held the *ryotwari* and *khatedari* system responsible for the prevailing indebtedness in Berar. Although the issue itself was superficial, nevertheless the debate was illuminating since it revealed the connection between moneylending and the government sponsored *ryotwari* and *khatedari* system.

The *khatedari* system, based on colonial ryotwari model of landholding, created an excellent opportunity for the moneylender to operate in Berar. Colonel Nembhard in his memorandum clearly states the connection between the two:

> . . . I consider the mischievous lending propensities of sahukars dependent on the raiatwari settlement. The raiatwari settlement invests the raiat with valuable property in land to a greater extent than any other. If they did not possess this property, their credit would be curtailed; and the sahukars would lend them small sums instead of large . . . they will borrow as much as they can; and their powers of borrowing being increased by the

[19] Letter No. 3521, From: R. Hudleston, Officiating Commissioner, West Berar, To: First Assistant Resident, Hyderabad dated 22 October 1872, Akola, in *Proceedings of the Hyderabad Administration for the Month of October 1874*, submitted to the Home Department, No. 99, 26 October 1874.

[20] *Report of the Famine Commission, 1880*, London, 1881, p. 163.

raiatwari settlement, the mischievous influence of the lending sahukars is enhanced by the same cause.[21]

However Colonel Nembhard failed to notice that in a state of debt the property in land ceased to conserve its value and instead became an instrument of control. Similarly, another colonial official Judge F. W. Grant observed in 1872 that *khatedari* holdings were extremely small and largely subdivided. He contended that 'even if money-lending was absolutely prohibited, the same result would be reached'.[22] According to this line of thinking, borrowing was necessary for the peasantry of Berar.

The total absence of revenue remission was yet another cause of indebtedness in Berar. It made the role of *sahukar* vital in the payment of revenue. The land revenue never remained uncollected. It is a moot point whether *khatedari* system depended upon the *khatedars* or moneylenders. In fact by paying revenue on behalf of cultivators, the moneylenders made the job of revenue collection easy for the colonial state. The state therefore accepted moneylenders as necessary for Berar countryside. The state believed that:

It by no means follows . . . that the money lender has always [sic] an influence for evil. He has often no doubt done much good in a certain way, and his presence helps us in a revenue point of view to an enormous extent, but the raiat pays for it all.[23]

The colonial government contended that the creation of private property rights in land was a blessing in disguise for the cultivators. This position was very articulately stated by the Judge of Amraoti Small Cause Court:

[21] Memorandum by Commissioner, Hyderabad Assigned Districts, on the Correspondence relative to the indebtedness of landowners in the Assigned Districts, by Lieutenant Colonel W. Nembhard, in *Proceedings of the Hyderabad Administration for the Month of November 1874,* submitted to the Home Department, No. 111, 18 November 1874, pp. 1-5.

[22] Letter No. 139, From: F. W. Grant, Judge, Small Cause Court, Khamgaon, To: Commissioner, West Berar, Khamgaon, dated 10 September 1872, in *Proceedings of the Hyderabad Administration for the Month of October 1874,* submitted to the Home Department, No. 99, 26 October 1874.

[23] Letter No. 2127, From: J. Allardyce, Officiating Commissioner, East Berar, To: First Assistant Resident, Hyderabad. Oomraottee, 1 August 1872, in *Proceedings of the Hyderabad Administration for the Month of October 1874,* submitted to the Home Department, No. 99, 26 October 1874.

This very position gives him increased borrowing powers [to cultivators]: he can mortgage or sell his right of occupancy at will, and, until he has so done, holds a most valuable security to offer as cover for a loan.[24]

The state in fact condoned indebtedness as the suitable way of letting the agriculture finance itself. The 'auction-like' manner in which surveyed plots were sold by government also indirectly caused debt to occur. One colonial official, Mr. J. H. Burns, calls this 'the distempered'[25] condition of the *khatedars* by which when a survey number is opened and a *khatedari* right created, the government registered tenant borrows capital to pay off the government and enters into debt even before the first scrap of the soil is turned. Some colonial officials were more sharp in their observation of a close connection between the colonial institutions and debt. One such observer Major J. Allardyce stated:

Our legislation in the way of Small Cause Courts, Registration Acts, etc, etc, has all tended to assist the moneylender against his usually obtuse and at all times unforeseeing victim. The facilities afforded on all sides to the money-lender for securing his loan, for obtaining his decree, and for recovery of the sum decreed, must be considered, amongst other reasons, as one which has induced the class to settle so readily in Berar.[26]

The colonial state created conditions in which the moneylender thrived. The same document goes on to suggest that in nine cases out of ten, the cultivator took money from the lender to pay his rent.

The introduction of the system of courts and decrees provided protection to the moneylending business in Berar. The colonial system facilitated the accumulation of debt loads by permitting the moneylenders to accumulate decrees which could be used in the

[24] Letter No. 106, From: H. C. Menzies, Judge Oomraottee Small Cause Court, To: Commissioner, East Berar Division. Oomraottee, dated 18 June 1874, in *Proceedings of the Hyderabad Administration for the month of October 1874*, submitted to the Home Department, No. 99, 26 October 1874.

[25] From: Mr. J. H. Burns, Extra Assistant Commissioner, To: Deputy Commissioner, Oomraottee District, dated 26 June 1872, in *Proceedings of the Hyderabad Administration for the Month of October 1874*, submitted to the Home Department, No. 99, 26 October 1874.

[26] Letter No. 2127, From: J. Allardyce, Officiating Commissioner, East Berar, To: First Assistant Resident, Hyderabad, Oomraottee, dated 1 August 1872, in *Proceedings of the Hyderabad Administration for the Month of October 1874*, submitted to the Home Department, No. 99, 26 October 1874.

court of law as evidence. The moneylenders also charged fees for executing these decrees in addition to the interest. Hiding behind these decrees, the moneylender usually enhanced his rate of interest enormously. This was achieved in the following manner according to Mr. R. Bullock:

> Another way in which our system assists in accumulating a load of debt is by accumulative decrees; that is, a sahukar obtains a decree for Rupees 100 and 10 costs. When he takes out a warrant, the debtor appeases him by giving him a fresh bond, adding costs and various items of interest, etc, which perhaps bring the bond up to Rupees 150. This bond has to be stamped and registered, all the expense of which the debtor has to pay, and then, a year hence, a fresh suit will be brought on this fresh bond, and the unfortunate debtor will have to pay for a year 50 to 60 per cent on the original debt.[27]

The colonial government's indifference in providing relief to indebted cultivators only enhanced indebtedness in Berar. From the time of Sultan Mohammad Bin Tuglaq (1325-51), the state had provided cultivators with agricultural loans known as *taccavi* for cultivation and irrigation purposes.[28] This practice was continued through the Mughal period. It was not until the colonial period that the cultivators were for the first time faced with the problem of obtaining state support for the maintenance of dams, anicuts, wells, and such other common village property. After the colonial takeover, the system of *taccavi* loans was done away with in many talukas. The only recourse left for cultivators was to seek the moneylenders for capital. *The Yeotmal District Gazetteer* mentions:

> A considerable fraction of the total number of cultivators borrow money at one time or another . . . they almost always prefer to borrow from a moneylender. . . . The chief reason seems to be that there is still great delay in getting money from Government.[29]

In some talukas a meager sum was available under Land

[27] Letter No. 1577, From: R. Bullock, Officiating Deputy Commissioner, Buldana, To: Commissioner, West Berar. Buldana, dated 5 July 1872, in *Proceedings of the Hyderabad Administration for the Month of October 1874*, submitted to the Home Department, No. 99, 26 October 1874.

[28] See Ziya al-Din Barani (1284-1356), *Tarikh-i-Firuzshahi* (English trl.), John Dowson, ed., Lahore, 1974; Shyama Prasad Basu, *The Tughluqs: Years of Experiments*, Calcutta, 1970.

[29] *Yeotmal District Gazetteer*, Calcutta, 1908, p. 119.

Improvement Act (1871) and Agricultural Loans Act (1891). During the period between 1877 and 1907 only 2 lakhs was given out in government loans. This amounted to only Rs.2631 per annum. The average land revenue demand during this period was Rs.66 lakhs per annum and the amount of government loans as agricultural relief was a mere 0.03 per cent of the annual land revenue.[30] This indicates that neither the colonial state nor the government officials were interested in this matter. Moreover, the government loans were also very unpopular as these were given mainly for clearing wastelands and maintenance of boundary marks rather than for actual agricultural purposes.

Applying for government loans involved a lot of delays and bureaucratic paper work. When a cultivator applied for a government loan, a detailed scrutiny was immediately launched on the character, reputation and capacity of the borrower to repay the loan. Any cultivator who had defaulted in the past was declared undesirable and unworthy of government sponsored agricultural loans. Furthermore, the loans were advanced only on the display of adequate security. And the government loans were given only to groups of people rather than to individuals. As a part of enquiry anyone who applied for it was visited by a government official. The dread of such a visit encouraged reluctance in availing a government loan even though the need was acute. A systematic enquiry was conducted into the purpose for which all the authorized loans were sought. In most cases inspection of the work was also conducted. Any misapplication was immediately reported to the government by tehsildars, patels, and patwaris. The Act clearly stated:

> It is one of the duties of patwaris and revenue inspectors to verify that taccavi loans have been utilized for the purpose for which they were granted and to report immediately any case of misapplication of a loan.[31]

All cases of misapplication were penalized by immediate recovery.

The *Amraoti Gazetteer* stated that the government insistence on

[30] *Amraoti Gazetteer*, Bombay, 1911, p. 225. The average land revenue figure is calculated from the following sources: *Report on the Revenue Administration of the Hyderabad Assigned Districts*, Hyderabad, printed Annually from 1877-8 to 1901-2; *Report on the Administration of the Hyderabad Assigned Districts for the Year 1889-90*, Hyderabad, printed Annually from 1860-1901.

[31] *The Berar Revenue Manual Containing Revenue Book Circulars*, Vol. 2, corrected up to 31 December 1951, Nagpur, 1968, p. 199.

prompt repayment in addition to refusal of non-agricultural loans left no choice for the cultivators but to turn to the moneylender. The volume of loan available from the moneylender was much larger than what the government offered to the cultivators. Furthermore, the cultivator who tried to seek government *taccavi* was in danger of jeopardizing his chances of obtaining a loan from the moneylender. The moneylenders were hesitant to advance loans to cultivators who were involved too much with the government.[32]

The prevalence of mass illiteracy among the population was yet another significant cause of indebtedness in Berar. The moneylender could terrorize borrowers by manipulating accounts and books. In any case receipts were almost invariably denied. As already noted the low literacy rate was a landmark of Berar's social backwardness. The skimming of agricultural surplus and the government indifference to investing in schools and training of teachers kept the populace vulnerable to debt and exploitation. 'The true remedy and prevention of indebtedness will be found in the promotion of education, in the development of proper and popular institutions for organized credit and thrift at the very doors of the cultivator and in the advancement of agricultural efficiency in all its branches,'[33] observed the *Buldana District Gazetteer*. What Berar needed was an overall economic development with heavy investment in social overheads. This was precisely what the colonial government was incapable of undertaking. In a state of general impoverishment, it was impossible for the people to take the initiative themselves. There was no other recourse left but to turn to the moneylender.

One of the colonial ideas behind the introduction of *khatedari* system was to create a class of capitalist cultivators who would develop Berar's agriculture on capitalist lines. But the *Buldana Gazetteer* laments that 'instead of the capitalist cultivator that the system is expected to create, in too many cases the sahukar serf has been the result'.[34] Inquiry into the state of indebtedness were conducted twice in Berar in 1874 and 1896. In both instances the conclusion was that:

> . . . the condition of the ryots was not such as to call for any interference on the part of Government with respect to their transactions with moneylenders.[35]

[32] *Amraoti Gazetteer*, Bombay, 1911, p. 226.
[33] *Buldana District Gazetteer*, Calcutta, 1910, p. 238.
[34] *Buldana District Gazetteer*, Calcutta, 1910, p. 234.

But no such *laissez-faire* was practised in cotton trade which witnessed stringent colonial control and monopoly over the market.

As early as 1869 when the survey and settlement operations were still in progress the fragmentation of holdings became noticeable. The scarcity of cultivable land was yet another cause of indebtedness in Berar. The inability of *khatedars* to forego land despite the expansion of population forced them to remain on it. The state of indebtedness forced the cultivation of cotton. In addition to preventing proper rotation it also led to encroachment over fallow lands. Quite appropriately then the Dariapur settlement officer noted:

> Owing to the denseness of the population, however, there is so little land available for either fallow or a varied rotation of crops that it will not be easy to persuade the people to let their land lie fallow or increase the intervals of rotation. . . .[36]

The reason why the colonial state tolerated the moneylenders was to perpetuate the agricultural base of the economy in Berar. It can be noticed that all land revenue acts and codes were directed towards this purpose. Even though land was not passing into the hands of non-cultivating classes as it was in Punjab and Gujerat, a Land Revenue Act was passed to restrict such transfers in Berar.[37] This prevented the diversification of the economy.

The Famine Commission Report of 1880 has very sharply captured the poverty of Berar in the following manner:

> The domestic expenditure appears to be often unduly swollen by the excessive number of persons subsisting on small holdings, and this is no doubt a cause of indebtedness . . . excessive sub-division, leading to the multiplication of minute holdings, is another cause of poverty.[38]

The general state of depression in the material condition left the cultivators with no capital to defray charges attendant on cultivation,

[35] *Buldana District Gazetteer*, Calcutta, 1910, p. 235.

[36] *Dariapur Taluka Settlement Report*, No. 368 of 1869, para 19.

[37] *Buldana District Gazetteer*, 1910, p. 236; also see N.G. Barrier, *The Punjab Alienation of Land Bill of 1900*, Durham, 1966; Ravinder Kumar, *Western India in the Nineteenth Century: A Study in the Social History of Maharashtra*, London, 1968; Neeladri Bhattacharya, 'Lenders and Debtors, Punjab Countryside, 1880-1940', *Studies in History*, Vol. 1, No. 2 (1985), 'The Logic of Tenancy Cultivation, Central and South-East Punjab, 1870-1935,' *Indian Economic and Social History Review*, Vol. 20, No. 2 (1983), pp. 121-70.

[38] *Report of the Famine Commission, 1880*, London, 1881, p. 164.

i.e. cleaning, ploughing, weeding, etc., for which they borrowed money but utilized it for domestic consumption as well.[39]

Creditor-Debtor Relations

Typically two types of cultivators borrowed capital from the moneylender: (a) Those who borrowed to start their own fields either for buying land rights or for registering as government tenants, and (b) those who already had fields but needed operating capital to work it.[40]

It was in the nature of colonial officials to hold one individual or a group responsible for the ills of the agrarian order. Almost every colonial document which refers to moneylenders point the finger at marwari. This puts a blanket over the diverse forms of moneylending activity in the region. The marwari was one of the several players in the business of moneylending in Berar. Although the colonial documents do not reveal the diversity of lending and borrowing practices, they mention other vaishya castes like the komtis (Telugu-speaking moneylenders). Similarly the colonial documents also do not distinguish between a marwari and a bania. Many wealthy *khatedars* also indulged in lending agricultural goods and commodities to *bhagindars* and *asamis*.[41] Agricultural implements, bullocks, seeds, manure, and such other non-cash items were often advanced as credit and recoverable at the harvest time in grains.

Then there were the rohilla lenders who carried business alongside the marwari. As mentioned earlier, the rohillas sometimes assisted the marwaris in recovering debts but often times did business independently by advancing short term high interest petty cash

[39] From: Mr. Dinshaji Sorabji, Extra Assistant, To: Deputy Commissioner, Ellichpur District, Ellichpur, dated 15 July 1872, in *Proceedings of the Hyderabad Administration for the Month of October 1874,* submitted to the Home Department No. 99, 26 October 1874.

[40] From: D. E. P. Rennick, Assistant Commissioner, Badnera District, To: Deputy Commissioner, Oomraottee, dated 19 June 1872, in *Proceedings of the Hyderabad Administration for the Month of October 1874* submitted to the Home Department, No. 99, 26 October 1874.

[41] The diverse forms of land tenure was in fact based on the credit system. The *ang* (body) unit and the *bail* (bullock) unit were calculated when the annual interest rates were computed. For various forms of tenure see: B. D. Baden-Powell, *The Land-Systems of British India,* Vol. III, New York, 1972; A. C. Lyall, *Gazetteers for the Haidarabad Assigned Districts, Commonly called Berar,* Bombay, 1870.

loans. The rohilla did not compete with the marwari. The volume of his lending capital was small compared to the marwari. While the marwari lent by the hundreds, the rohilla advanced only petty cash ranging from Rs. 5 to Rs. 50. But his rate of interest was almost double than what the marwari charged. The usual marwari rate was about 24 per cent per annum or 2 per cent per mensem and the marwari was hesitant to lend any amount below Rs.100. The rohilla on the other hand provided short term credit and charged 2 annas per rupee per month[42] (75-150 per cent per annum). While the marwari rate ran from year to year, the rohilla rate ran from month to month and sometimes week to week.

Frequently when the persons developed bad credit with the marwari or did not possess landed security then they were forced to seek the rohilla. The *Amraoti Gazetteer* reports:

> Persons who can neither show well known credit in the money market nor produce landed security must pawn valuables to the amount of their loan and will then receive the money on terms similar to those in force for mortgages. If they cannot do this, they will have no choice but to resort to the village Shylock or the Rohilla who deals in petty loans at high risk and shows but little compassion either in the rates he charges or in his method of collecting debt.[43]

In spite of so much diversity in moneylending practices, the majority of professional moneylenders in Berar were marwaris. Therefore it is now necessary to turn our analysis to the marwari activity.

In the local language of people, the village marwari was referred to as either a 'sahukar' or 'seth'. The *sahukar* usually lent money only to those cultivators who were *khatedars* or government registered tenants. Mr. J. Allardyce has left for us an almost textbook definition of this situation: 'The state and condition of a large body of the cultivating class; the absolute necessity that impels the needy cultivator, who takes up land without capital, to apply to the moneylender. . . .'[44]

[42] *Buldana District Gazetteer*, Calcutta, 1910, p. 228.

[43] *Amraoti Gazetteer*, Bombay, 1911, pp. 226-7.

[44] Letter No. 2127, From: J. Allardyce, Officiating Commissioner, East Berar, To: First Assistant Resident, Hyderabad, Oomraottee dated 1 August 1872, in *Proceedings of the Hyderabad Administration for the Month of October 1874*, submitted to the Home Department, No. 99, 26 October 1874.

Typically the cultivators of Berar needed to borrow money three times a year. Firstly, just before the start of cultivating season in the beginning of June. At this time money was required to purchase seeds, bullocks and agricultural implements. Secondly, in late August, September and October when the kharif crop was a couple of months away and money was essential for purchasing the necessaries of life. Thirdly, in the month of January and March when the government revenue fell due.[45] Most commonly the *sahukar* paid the government assessment direct to the patel and patwari and recovered it from the cultivator. Generally the *sahukars* took payments in grain. However, there were several different ways in which the *sahukar* lent his capital. The following were the principal terms of credit between the *sahukar* and cultivators:[46]

(1) The prosperous and thrifty cultivators borrowed a lumpsum at low rate of 1 per cent per month. These cultivators were also speculators and traders. They could hold their crop during the harvest when the prices were low and sell it later to obtain better prices. They were wealthy enough to ask the *sahukar* to allow the loan to stand over till the stocks of grain reserves were disposed.

(2) When the cultivator's credit did not stand high, a bond was passed by the *sahukar*, by which the latter took his payment in grain which was sold to him at the market rate. The only difference being that in weighing about 4 to 5 seers (8 or 10 lbs) was added to every 240 lbs as 'kussur' (grain bonus).

(3) The *sahukar* pays the government assessment direct to the patel and patwari and recovers it from the cultivator. The period of such loans never exceeded more than 3 months.

(4) The cultivator often raised loans on standing crops. The

[45] Letter No. 131, From: Abdul Hakk Kurnalkar, Extra Assistant Commissioner, Basim District, To: Assistant Commissioner-in-charge, Basim District, Basim, July 1872, in *Proceedings of the Hyderabad Administration for the Month of October 1874*, submitted to the Home Department, No. 99, 26 October 1874.

[46] The following result was the outcome of the survey of 5 villages done in the 1880s in Aurangabad District adjacent to Berar. Except for the random colonial demarcation, the social and economic conditions in Aurangabad were similar to Berar. See *Notes on the Agriculturists of the District of Aurangabad, H. H. The Nizam's Dominions*, by Furdoonji Jamshedji, Superintendent Revenue Survey and Assessment, N. W. Division, in *Hyderabad Affairs*, Vol. I, compiled by Moulvie Syed Mahdi Ali, Bombay (n.d.), p. 821.

sahukar forms an estimate of what would be the probable ruling prices at harvest time. He then leaves a margin of 10 to 15 per cent profit, agrees to purchase the crops at a certain fixed price. The contract is written out 4 to 5 months before the harvest.

(5) Besides cash loan, the cultivator also took seed-grains from the *sahukar*. The agreement being to return at harvest at 50 per cent over and above the quantity borrowed. The quantity was usually doubled if the prices at the time of signing the loan contract were high.

(6) Cultivators usually raised a loan in grain for home consumption. Since such loans were made during the lean months of the year, there was no limit to the interest charged. They ran from 25 to 100 per cent over and above the quantity lent. This loan was usually signed on a bond.

(7) When a cultivator breaks down and is unable to repay his debt for 5 years, he binds himself to the *sahukar* and tills the land for a certain number of years for the *sahukar*. The *sahukar* pays the operating cost and the cultivator makes over the field to him. The *sahukar* basically owns the labour and the crop and reaps it when it is ready.

The majority of the cultivators in Berar were indebted to the *sahukar*. 'The state of indebtedness, of course, varied in degree. In some instances, the cultivators are hopelessly sunk in debt; in others the proportion of their debts may amount to their income for three or four years, while in many cases their indebtedness certainly amounts to their income for one year.'[47]

Despite all types of debts incurred by peasants, the most common was one in which the rate of interest charged was 24 per cent per annum. The standard rate paid by majority of small peasants in Berar was 2 per cent per mensem. Usually, there were two types of interests charged by the *sahukars*: (a) cash interest and, (b) grain interest. Both these interests were commutable and compatible to each other. But for a better understanding of the interplay of cash and grain interest, they need to be separated for the purpose of analysis.

[47] *Notes on the Agriculturists of the District of Aurangabad*, by Furdoonji Jamshedji, p. 822, op. cit.

Cash Interest

Cash interest was the numerical percentage of the actual capital which was given out in credit as the principal. It was invariably a written document in the form of a bond. Typically in this kind of transaction the *sahukar* executed a promissory note called *purza* for payment of a certain sum of money, say Rs. 100 at an interest of 24 per cent per annum.[48] However, the full amount was never transacted. The *sahukar* secured a deed and deducted the 24 per cent interest on the spot. This deduction was called *batta*. In addition to *batta* or advance interest deduction, a premium fee of 7 per cent was levied on the principal. This fee was charged by the *sahukar* for accepting the cultivator as his debtor. Popularly known as *manwuttee*, this 7 per cent was added on to the 24 per cent interest and deducted from the principal.[49] *Batta* and *manwuttee* together constituted more than 30 per cent of the deductions. This happened even before the actual cash changed hands. In fact very little of the actual borrowed amount reached the borrower.[50] After deducting the premium, brokerage and all other paltry items, a bond drawn for Rs.100 left less than Rs.70 for the borrower to begin with.[51] Here also the *sahukar* did not pay the total amount in lumpsum but let the cultivator have it from time to time to pay government assessment, or buy cattle or similar other expenditure involved with the operating cost of cultivation.[52] It was estimated that at 24 per cent

[48] Letter No. 106, From: H. C. Menzies, Judge, Oomraottee, Small Cause Court, To: Commissioner, East Berar Division, Oomraottee, 18 June 1874, in *Proceedings of the Hyderabad Administration for the Month of October 1874,* submitted to the Home Department, No. 99, 26 October 1874.

[49] From: H. D. Rennick, Assistant Commissioner, Badnera District, To: Deputy Commissioner, Oomraottee, 19 June 1872, in *Proceedings of the Hyderabad Administration for the Month of October 1874,* submitted to the Home Department, No. 99, 26 October 1874.

[50] From: J. H. Burns, Extra Assistant Commissioner, To: Deputy Commissioner, Oomraottee District, Omraottee, 26 June 1872, in *Proceedings of the Hyderabad Administration for the Month of June 1874,* submitted to the Home Department, No. 99, dated 26 October 1874.

[51] From: Atmaram Bhicaji, Extra Assistant Commissioner, Oomraottee District, To: Deputy Commissioner, Oomraottee District, Oomraottee, 5 July 1872, in *Proceedings of the Hyderabad Administration for the Month of October 1874,* submitted to the Home Department, No. 99, 26 October 1874.

[52] Op. cit., *Notes on the Agriculturists of Districts of Aurangabad,* by Furdoonji Jamshedji, in *Hyderabad Affairs,* Vol. 1 by Moulvie Syed Mahdi Ali, p. 821, op. cit.

interest the moneylender doubled his capital in 3.5 years by just collecting interest.[53]

The most crucial aspect of the moneylending activity was the date and time on the bond. Generally the dates agreed upon by the *sahukar* and the cultivator coincided with the time when government revenue fell due. In Berar the government collected revenue in two instalments. The first fell due on January 15 when the kharif (autumn) crop came to the market. The second instalment fell due on 1 March at the time of rabi (spring) harvest.[54]

It was customary among Berar moneylenders to calculate the interest from the date on which the government revenue demand fell due. The dates on loan deeds coincided with the dates of the government revenue demand. The *sahukar* made interest calculation on the basis of the date on which the deed was entered and the date on which the loan fell due. In case of default, the loan lapsed into compound interest.[55] There were a large number of cases of default in Berar. The *sahukar* did not dun his cultivators until after the due date.[56] Even when the debtor paid, say one month after the due date, the loan interest charged was double the regular rate (24 per cent). In case of inability to pay the 48 per cent demand (which was invariably the case) the cultivator was bound by the deed to mortgage not only the produce of his field but also his cattle, his house and often times himself and his family by means of a *sutta* (contract).[57]

The *sahukar* volunteered to pay the government revenue demand only after taking complete control of cultivators property. Therefore

[53] From: D. E. P. Rennick, Assistant Commissioner, Badnera District, To: Deputy Commissioner, Oomraottee, dated 19 June 1872, in *Proceedings of the Hyderabad Administration for the Month of October 1874,* submitted to the Home Department, No. 99, 26 October 1874.

[54] 'Peasantry of Aurangabad: Review of Furdoonji Jamshedji's Notes on the Agriculturists of Aurangabad', *Bombay Review,* 13 September 1879, pp. 461-6.

[55] *Notes on the Agriculturists of the District of Aurangabad, H. H. The Nizam's Dominion*, by Furdoonji Jamshedji, Superintendent, Revenue Survey and Assessment, N.W. Division, in *Hyderabad Affairs,* Vol. 1, compiled by Moulvie Syed Mahdi Ali, Bombay (n.d.) 821.

[56] Letter No. 106, From: H. C. Menzies, Judge, Oomraottee Small Cause Court, To: Commissioner, East Berar Division, Oomraottee, 18 June 1874, in *Proceedings of the Hyderabad Administration for the Month of October 1874,* submitted to the Home Department, No. 99, 26 October 1874.

[57] *Notes on the Agriculturists of the District of Aurangabad*, by Furdoonji Jamshedji, in *Hyderabad Affairs,* Vol. 1, by Moulvie Syed Mahdi Ali, p. 821.

despite such a high rate of indebtedness, the government land revenue was always paid on schedule and remission was unnecessary. This was also the method by which *sahukar* perpetuated his control over the cultivator's land and its produce. It was a common practice among *sahukars* to pay the government assessment (in cash) direct to the patel and patwaris and recover it from the indebted cultivators in the form of grain interest. In other words the *sahukar* after paying government revenue on behalf of the cultivator, recovered the loan and interest in agricultural produce, i.e. cotton and grain.

The Produce Interest

The interest payment in produce began when the *sahukar* made 'advances to the cultivators before the season for growing cotton arrives, stipulating to receive so much cotton at a certain rate . . . '.[58] The rate was stipulated by the marwari, and the cultivator bound his crop by giving a *laonee* or contract to supply a certain quantity of *kupas* or seed cotton by a fixed date. 'The crop thus virtually passed out of the cultivator's hands, and his interest in it ceased before the plant was in blossom.'[59] It is not difficult to guess that the terms of the *laonee* (contract) rate was fixed extremely low so as to favour the marwari. Thus even before the crops were gathered and the market price was known, the *sahukar* laid claim to cotton and often this extended to grain and garden crops as well.[60]

Often times the *laonee* was also known as a *sutta* contract. It was by means of the *sutta* that cultivators bonded their future crops. The *sutta* also provided marwari with an alternative to take the cultivator to court if necessary. Since the marwari was really not interested in land, he seldom took the *khatedar* to court. Nevertheless the *sutta* became a tremendous lever of control comparable almost to the chains of slavery in American south during the antebellum period. It was important for marwari to hold the cultivator on land. It was only through this method that the cultivation of cotton could be guaranteed. In addition to binding him to land, the marwari also took advantage of the economic necessity of Berar cultivators for subsistence. This need for subsistence was a colonial phenomenon which developed as a result of the creation

[58] *British Parliamentary Papers, 1863,* Vol. 44, p. 397.

[59] *Report on the Operations of the Cotton Department for the Year 1867*, by Harry Rivett-Carnac, 1869, p. 64.

[60] *Morsi Taluka Settlement Report,* No. 563 of 1861, para 22, p. 8.

of property rights in land. The moneylender took advantage of this colonial settlement and held the cultivators and their labour. The cultivators barely kept their body and soul together. They produced for the moneylender and worked on their own lands as agricultural labourer.[61]

The debt situation was much more complicated than the description given in colonial documents. There was a serious reason behind moneylender's effort to hold the cultivator's labour and produce in debt. Although the marwaris charged exorbitant interest rates (24 per cent p.a.) yet they constantly needed capital to run their own trade. This operating capital was provided to the Berar moneylenders by European firms doing business in cotton. The moneylenders generally committed themselves by *sutta* contracts to the European firms to supply a stipulated amount of cotton by a stipulated date at pre-fixed prices. This type of *sutta* was in fact an exact replica of the *sutta* which bound the cultivators to marwari. Therefore it is worth reproducing both the *suttas* as a comparison to highlight the subservient status of (a) cultivators to the moneylenders, and (b) moneylenders to European firms.

Here is the *sahukars* bonafide *sutta* to European firms and merchants:

> To buyer of cotton A.D., from the seller of cotton C.D., Salaam. I agree to deliver on Khamgaon Tak, 25 bojahs new, pure Bunee (or Jarry) cotton, grown in this year, at rupees 63 per bojah of 10 maunds, including scale allowance, sample, and gunnies, etc., without any other allowance. The weights to be used in weighing are those which are current and tested by Government. The cotton to be delivered from Mah or Fagan Sood 5th to 15th February and March. Hamalage or weighing to be paid by me. I have received a hundee for rupees 1,575 the full amount of this sutta at rupees 63 per bojah. A hundee of the balance cost of the cotton to be given to me on Mah or Fagan Sood 5th and the cotton to be delivered up to Mah or Fagan Sood 15th as the case may be.

As a comparison here is the cultivator's bonafide *sutta* to the *sahukar* :

> I agree by this cotton sutta at my own wish, and pleasure, to deliver cotton (Laonee) one dokrah at the rate of rupees 40 per bojah. At this rate, Government coin Company's Rupees 20 in ready cash. I have received and

[61] From: D. E. P. Rennick, Assistant Commissioner, Badnera District, To: Deputy Commissioner, Oomraottee, dated 19 June 1872, in *Proceedings of the Hyderabad Administration for the Month of October 1874,* submitted to the Home Department, No. 99, 26 October 1874.

then given you this sutta. Time of delivery Bassant Panchee (February). The cotton to be new, grown this year, and without stain, and to be delivered and weighed in Khamgaon according to the custom, with sample and allowances at the scale. I agree to deliver the dokrah to the person you choose and bring his receipt to you.

My heirs and property are liable for this sutta. If I do not deliver the dokrah on the date appointed, I agree to settle the rate and pay the difference in price.[62]

The *suttas* then bound the cultivators to the marwaris on the one hand and the marwaris to European firms on the other. Thus the entire cotton economy operated on the hinges of *sutta* bondage.

It is estimated that in Berar more than 80 per cent of the *kupas* was cultivated on advances and was claimed by the moneylenders early in the season (November and December). The cotton report of 1878-9 had stated:

The great bulk of the cotton crop passes out of the cultivator's hands as kupas (seed cotton), and it is subsequently cleaned and brought to market by the purchaser. Comparatively few of the cultivators gin their own cotton.[63]

If the moneylenders were the principal purchasers then the above statement may not be accurate. True that the native *churka* disappeared when European gins were first introduced in the early 1860s. But some of the *churkas* came into the possession of moneylenders. The *churkas* were in use on a limited scale for extracting cotton seeds for sowing purposes because it was found that the European gins damaged the seed. But the moneylenders of Berar did not gin cotton except retaining a small quantity of seed cotton for next years crop. The great bulk of cotton which traded hands between the moneylenders and European firms was seed cotton. Almost all the big gins in the large cotton emporiums of Berar were owned by European firms.[64]

[62] Copies of Suttas in use in West Berar, in *Resolution on the question whether Suttahs or Contracts entered into by the cultivators in Berar to deliver their cotton produce, are liable to stamp duty when transferred by endorsement,* Foreign Department, Government of India, Nos. 5-7, dated April 1873.

[63] *Cotton Report of the Hyderabad Assigned Districts for 1878-79,* Hyderabad, 1879, para 23.

[64] For a list of all European ginning and pressing firms operating in Berar see the following: *Report on the Administration of the Hyderabad Assigned Districts for the Year 1896-97,* Hyderabad, 1897, p. 118.

The moneylenders of Berar also operated the village provision store of sundry goods, seeds, and foodgrains. Survival on the margin of subsistence meant that the cultivators had pledged even staple crops to moneylenders. This obligated them to purchase seeds and foodgrains from the moneylender's provision store on credit. The *sahukar* supplied cultivators with grains and other necessary articles for four months before each harvest. The rate of interest charged was usually double the amount of grain after harvest. This left hardly enough for the cultivators to survive and soon they had to go back to the provision store to borrow more. This state of perpetual debt was observed by the famine commission in 1880:

> . . . and when the produce of the field is ready he takes nearly the whole away in satisfaction of these advances and interest. . . . A great portion of small cultivators borrow their seed. The rate of interest is 25 per cent, or when the security is bad 50 per cent.

The same report continues to tell the story that once the cultivator is indebted, the lender takes control of the produce and compels the cultivator to sell only to the lender.

> He [lender] ultimately demands liquidation of his debts, and compels the debtor to sell to him the produce of his land before it is raised at a low rate, to be delivered at the harvest; and if he fails to fulfil the contract debits him with the prices at the rates, which are always high, prevalent in the market.[65]

Due to the general shortage of operating capital, a large number of cultivators in Berar were indebted to the moneylender. The number in some districts was as high as three-quarters. Due to the shortage of storage space, almost every cultivator borrowed seed in loans. The interest rate charged on such loans was either *sawai* (quarter) or *adha* (half) during the harvest. In some taluqs a *lawani* was demanded which meant loan in seed had to be repaid in cash.[66]

The Berar cultivators usually needed provisions to survive from harvest to harvest. Their need was particularly acute between sowing and harvest. Since cotton and jawari were both kharif crops sown in June and reaped in November-December, the moneylenders were busy signing *suttas* during this season. After the kharif harvest moneylenders were busy claiming crop credit. The winter months from December to

[65] *Report of the Famine Commission, 1880*, London, 1881, pp. 165 and 298.

[66] *Yeotmal District Gazetteer*, Calcutta, 1908, p. 121.

March were the toughest for cultivator's survival. With all the crops gone and no credit coming until the commencement of next season (June), most of Berar cultivators languished on the margin of subsistence in poverty and hunger. It was also during this period that the famines struck Berar causing starvation and death.

It was the moneylenders grain interest demand that caused havoc in Berar. While the cash interest was mostly on paper, the grain interest was determined on the threshing floor. This was generally done immediately after the harvest or sometimes on standing crops. The interest was then determined by *sahukar* on the basis of prevailing prices in the market. Since the cultivator had already mortgaged his crop, the *sahukar* set the grain interest rate at 50 per cent less than the bazar rate. If suppose the proper price of grain is 10 rupees per *candy*, the sahukar took 12 *candies* of grain at 5 rupees per *candy*. If the price remained unaltered he was a large gainer. If the price rose, his gains were much larger. In both cases he gained.[67] If the price fell then the *sahukar* demanded cash. In case of default he forced another bond on the cultivator. Mr. Dinshaji Sorabji, Extra Assistant Comm-issioner of Ellichpur district, wrote thus in July 1872:

> If at the harvest time the bazar rates are below or equal to the rate stipulated, they [sahukars] raise frivolous objections as to the quality of the produce, and demand ready cash with interest; but, on the other hand, if the prices are higher, they demand the grain and cotton, or in default they ask for value of the stipulated quantity of grain at the ruling bazar rates; if he is unable to do it, they ask for a fresh bond for that amount, interest running on it, or bind him to give the produce at 25 per cent more at the next harvest time. If the debt is not liquidated in time agreed upon, a new bond is taken for the amount, inclusive of interest, and thus in the course of a few years the debt increases several times over the principal.[68]

The *sutta* dealing which was recognized as legal tender by the colonial judicial system was in fact designed by the colonial laws and courts. It was an effective instrument of European firms and moneylenders to

[67] Letter No. 1577, From: R. Bullock, Officiating Deputy Commissioner, Buldana District, To: Commissioner, West Berar, Buldana, 5 July 1872, in the *Proceedings of the Hyderabad Administration for the Month of October 1874,* submitted to the Home Department, No. 99, 26 October 1874.

[68] From: Dinshaji Sorabji, Extra Assistant Commissioner, To: Deputy Commissioner, Ellichpur District, Ellichpur, 15 July 1872, in the *Proceedings of the Hyderabad Administration for the Month of October 1874,* submitted to the Home Department, No. 99, 26 October 1874.

extract raw cotton and grains from the debtor cultivators at as low a price as possible. For instance, in 1871 in a village in Argaon (West Berar) district the cultivator sold his cotton beforehand at Rs. 15 per bale while on the day of delivery the price of cotton was Rs. 45 per bale.[69] Under the pretext of non-fulfillment of the contract, the cultivator was obliged to sell his cotton at one-third the prevailing price. The colonial state and the moneylender collaborated with each other in the extraction of agrarian surplus from cultivators.

An Indian collaborator of the colonial state, Mr. Atmaram Bhikaji, noted that the scarcity of capital and short stock of grain were the principal reasons for mounting interest and debt. But Mr. Bhikaji failed to notice a causal connection between cash-grain interest extraction and general capital-grain shortage in Berar. How could the borrowers ever liquidate their debts when transactions ran from year to year?[70]

The collaboration which existed between the colonial state and moneylenders reduced Berar peasantry to subsistence. Although colonial documents throw the entire blame on moneylenders, it was in fact the partnership between them that kept Berar peasantry in such dire straits. Mr. W. N. Baput, another Indian collaborator, failed to notice this partnership. However, his observation about the moneylender can also be applied to the colonial state. He states thus:

> He [moneylender] has the sagacity to foresee that unless he supplied his victims with means of subsistence, death, a far more relenting creditor, would set them free for ever from his close grasp: such exceptional terms yield the Bania an exceptionally plentiful harvest. He binds his victims closer, compels them to pass formal documents which would not fail him in Law-courts for money ten times the sum originally borrowed, to pledge their fields, cattle etc., as securities for due discharge, and thus makes them live only for him.[71]

[69] Letter No. 857, From: Shrikrishna Nurhur, Extra Assistant Commissioner, Argaon, To: Commissioner, West Berar, Argaon, 17 September 1872, in the *Proceedings of the Hyderabad Administration for the Month of October 1874,* submitted to the Home Department, No. 99, 26 October 1874.

[70] From: Atmaram Bhikaji, Extra Assistant Commissioner, To: Deputy Commissioner, Oomraottee District, Oomraottee, 5 July 1872, in the *Proceedings of the Hyderabad Administration for the Month of October 1874,* submitted to the Home Department, No. 99, 26 October 1874.

[71] From: W. N. Baput, Tehsildar Chandur, To: Deputy Commissioner, Oomraottee District, 28 April 1872, in the *Proceedings of the Hyderabad Administration for the Month of October 1874,* submitted to the Home Department, No. 99, 26 October 1874.

Therefore it became customary in Berar to pay the government revenue demand by means of a single payment much to the relief and support of the government.[72] The court of law maintained a strong bond between the moneylender and the colonial state. The Small Cause Courts and the speedy manner of civil justice benefited both the state and the marwari.[73] 'The influence of the lender over borrower is so great . . . that the latter is unavoidably obliged to yield to all the conditions extorted from him, which ultimately tend to his utmost ruin,' wrote Atmaram Bhikaji to his boss the Deputy Commissioner in 1874. He further elaborated the condition of the peasantry by stating that the Courts of Justice and the existing rules and regulations deprived the borrower 'of his every pittance' and thus utterly ruined him.[74]

The crucial difference between a rohilla and a marwari was that the former seldom resorted to the colonial courts while the latter used the threat of colonial courts as a lever for extraction. While the rohilla seldom demanded documentary evidence, the marwari never effected a loan without papers. 'The usual custom is for the lender to promise an advance, provided the act of registration is completed, and to make a portion of such advance subsequent to the title deed having been registered.'[75] Therefore the marwaris extended loans only to government registered tenants.

On moveable property, the borrower had to first purchase a stamp paper of the value of his loan. He then had to get the bond properly written. It was then registered with the court and eventually the borrower received the balance after an 18 to 25 per cent interest

[72] From: A. Williams, Secretary for Berar to the Resident, To: The Secretary to the Government of India, Department of Revenue and Agriculture, Hyderabad, 11 January 1896, in the *Proceedings of the Hyderabad Administration on Matters of Routine for the Month of January 1896,* submitted to the Revenue and Agriculture Department, No.13, 11 January 1896.

[73] Letter No. 409, From: J. T. Bushby, Deputy Commissioner, Oomraottee, dated 27 July 1872, in the *Proceedings of the Hyderabad Administration for the Month of October 1874,* submitted to the Home Department, No. 99, 26 October 1874.

[74] From: Atmaram Bhikaji, Extra Assistant Commissioner, To: Deputy Commissioner, Oomraottee District, Oomraottee, dated 5 July 1872, in the *Proceedings of the Hyderabad Administration for the Month of October 1874,* submitted to the Home Department, No. 99, 26 October 1874.

[75] Letter No. 409, From J. T. Bushby, Deputy Commissioner, Oomraottee, dated 27 July 1872, submitted to the Home Department, No. 99, 26 October 1874, in the *Proceedings of the Hyderabad Administration for the Month of October 1874.*

deduction as advance. Typically the Berar cultivators borrowed Rs.100 minimum at the commencement of the agricultural season. Suppose a *khatedar* needed to borrow Rs.100, he had to first buy a stamp paper and register his property with the court. The moneylender who was engaged in the dealing deducted Rs.18 to Rs.25 on account of interest even before the actual money changed hands. On expiry of the terms of the deed, repayment was demanded with interest accruing from the date of the deed. In case of default the Court of Small Causes summarily issued a decree against the debtor in honour of the bond signed by him as a proof of his default. The law facilitated the lender to recover his loan. The borrower never went to court as a defendant in a civil suit against the marwari plaintiff. He did not have the resources nor the capital to fight a case against the lender. He just gave up and settled down on his land as a day labourer.[76]

Although the moneylenders charged 24 to 50 per cent interest from the general mass of cultivators yet when one marwari borrowed from the other, the rate charged was only 6 per cent or less.[77] We do not have much data on the volume of such lending and borrowing among the moneylenders of Berar. Nevertheless such borrowings were an important medium of mutual assistance among moneylenders. Similarly the marwaris also advanced low interest loans to the local level revenue officials who were mostly Indians. Since every Indian revenue official had to provide a cash security deposit at the time of appointment, everyone of them turned to the moneylender for loans.[78] This gave the moneylender some influence in government at the local level. And also since the village moneylender was a crucial link between the primary producer and European firms, the colonial government felt the need of moneylenders as much as the moneylenders dependency on the colonial state for legal protection.

[76] Letter No. 409, From J. T. Bushby, Deputy Commissioner, Oomraottee, dated 27 July 1872, submitted to the Home Department, No. 99, 26 October 1874, in *Proceedings of the Hyderabad Administration for the Month of October 1874.* Also see From: W. N. Baput, Tehsildar, Chandur, To: Deputy Commissioner, Oomraottee District, dated 28 April 1872, in the *Proceedings of the Hyderabad Administration for the Month of October 1874,* submitted to the Home Department, No. 99, 26 October 1874.

[77] *Yeotmal District Gazetteer*, Calcutta, 1908, p. 119.

[78] *The Berar Land Revenue Code, 1896*, in British Enactments in Force in Berar, 1916 (n.d.), p. 108.

The Material Condition of the Peasantry under Debt

The peasantry and the moneylenders of Berar were caught in the grip of colonial cotton trade. Although the moneylenders were definitely better off than the exploited peasantry, yet the lender was subservient to the cotton economy. The severity of lender's exploitation was only a reflection of the economic exploitation of the cotton trade.

The attitude of Lancashire merchants towards Indian cotton generally kept the price of Berar cotton low. The colonial status of India in the world market acted against Indian agricultural products as well. Even though the *jari* and *bani* of Berar were the two best quality cotton exported from Bombay, the British merchants never offered good prices for them. Indian cotton was prejudicially branded as inferior in quality vis-a-vis American strain. The hypocrisy of *laissez-faire* was also clearly visible in Berar. While the colonial government followed a strict non-interference policy with regard to public spending, the market and trade was freely manipulated to favour European firms. Even before the colonization of Berar, Mr. J. Forbes Royle in 1851 pronounced the curse on Berar's cotton to deprive the moneylenders of an equal share in the cotton business:

> The middleman, with ingenuity, seeks to change the nature of his purchase, and thinks to add to its value by making additions to its weight, but he succeeds in deceiving himself. The European manufacturers, taught by long experience, have ceased to expect a pure article, and therefore never gives the price which he otherwise would for cotton of the same quality; and all the expenses of carriages, freight and insurance have to be deducted from this lower price.[79]

Even though the moneylender extracted cotton from the primary producer at lowest possible price yet he was unable to secure a fair price for the product from European merchants.

As early as 1866 the Chicklee Taluka Settlement Report noted that 'the agricultural classes...were becoming more and more deeply involved, and scarcely able to keep their heads above water.'[80] This was in fact the situation while all the standard colonial documents portray Berar as being prosperous under British rule. Capital depletion and general scarcity is a hallmark of an indebted peasantry and

[79] J. Forbes Royle, *On the Culture and Commerce of Cotton in India and Elsewhere*, London, 1851, p. 60.

[80] *Chicklee Taluk Settlement Report*, No. 51 of 1866.

Berar was no exception to this rule. The cotton trade in addition to causing capital scarcity among working peasants also caused the scarcity of water, wood and grass for man and beast.[81]

The colonial state and the moneylenders prevented the accumulation of capital in Berar. They both possessed the power to fleece the cultivators.[82] This prompted Mr. K. J. L. Mackenzie to observe that there was practically no one in Berar who was not indebted and that Berar had an indebted hand-to-mouth tenantry.[83] The average indebtedness was four times the average yearly income of the cultivators.[84] A still more stark picture was presented by the Assistant Commissioner of Wun, Mr. R. Thompson, who clearly elucidated the close connection between moneylender exploitation and colonial exploitation:

> . . . a case occurred 6 months ago in my court (Krishnaji versus Channamian and 2 others), where the interest sued on a Bond was Rupees 150 per cent. per annum! and very much against my will, I was obliged to give the plaintiff a decree according to the terms of the bonds, the interest being 4.5 times the amount of the principal, and the defendants protesting to me and the merciless plaintiff that they were utterly ruined.[85]

The condition of the cultivator was made more precarious with the loss of his claims over the product of his own labour. Normally his field, his house, his bullocks, and his agricultural implements were under mortgage. The constant threat of civil courts discouraged him from laying claims over the produce of his labour. It also kept him in a state of constant poverty from which he could not escape. The 'distempered condition' which several of the Indian officials refer to was a state in which 'the cultivator had to borrow at the stern

[81] *Report on the Administration of the Hyderabad Assigned Districts for the Year 1872-73*, Calcutta, 1874, para 81.

[82] *Darwa Taluka Settlement Report*, No. 420 of 1872, para 10.

[83] Letter No. 1540, From: K. J. L. Mackenzie, To: Commissioner, East Berar Division, Ellichpur, dated 18 July 1872, in *Proceedings of the Hyderabad Administration for the Month of October 1874*, submitted to the Home Department, No. 99, 26 October 1874. Also see Letter No. 353, From: H. Sczepanski, Deputy Commissioner, Woon District, To: Commissioner, East Berar, Yeotmal, dated 1 July 1872, in the *Proceedings of the Hyderabad Administration for the Month of October 1874*, submitted to the Home Department, No. 99, 26 October 1874.

[84] *Report of the Famine Commission, 1880*, London, 1881.

[85] Letter No. 18, From: R. Thompson, Assistant Commissioner, Wun District, To: Deputy Commissioner, Wun District, Yeotmal, dated 11 July 1872, in the *Proceedings of the Hyderabad Administration for the Month of October 1874*, submitted to the Home Department, No. 99, 26 October 1874.

bidding of his necessities. He cannot go on with his field work unless he borrows money, and the necessity obliges him to . . . '.[86]

Except for the bungalows of the British colonial bureaucrats and officials, Berar gave an appearance of utter destitution. Dilapidated huts and *bay chiragh* (lampless) villages presented a picture of intense poverty. Dogs, pigs, animals, and human beings defecated everywhere due to the absence of proper sanitary facilities. Often times human beings and cattle lived in the same house as depicted by Mr. J. T. Bushby in the following manner:

> He [cultivator] rarely had a habitation suited to his position. In fact, he and his family, in a great number of instances, occupy the same house with his bullocks; and these animals are better cared for and fed than himself, his wife and children.[87]

Often times the colonizers have compared the Indian marwari with the jew in Europe. One colonial official writes, 'he [cultivator] borrows from the Indian Jew, the marwari, money at an unreasonable and preposterous interest. To effect this loan he executes a note on hand, generally a satta, for delivery of next year's crop or mortgages his property.'[88] Although this type of analogy is pejorative and stems out of the colonizers' anti-semitic attitude, yet a comparison will not be out of place here. Marwaris like the Jews of Europe were a migratory caste and deprived of land ownership by all kinds of colonial laws and acts. While historically the Jews were debarred from owning land in most parts of Europe, the colonial state became hostile to the moneylenders and non-agriculturist classes owning agricultural land in British India.

To blame the victim was one of the characteristic features of colonialism in Berar as elsewhere. The colonial officials and the

[86] Letter No. 857, From: Shrikrishna Nurhur, Extra Assistant Commissioner, Argaon, To: Commissioner, West Berar, Argaon, dated 17 September 1872, in the *Proceedings of the Hyderabad Administration for the Month of October 1874,* submitted to the Home Department, No. 99, 26 October 1874.

[87] Letter No. 409, From: J. T. Bushby, Deputy Commissioner, Oomraottee District, To: Commissioner, East Berar Division, Oomraottee, dated 17 July 1872, submitted to the Home Department, No. 99, 26 October 1874.

[88] From: D. E. P. Rennick, Assistant Commissioner, Badnera District, To: Deputy Commissioner, Oomraottee, Badnera, dated 19 June 1872, in the *Proceedings of the Hyderabad Administration for the Month of October 1874,* submitted to the Home Department, No. 99, 26 October 1874.

moneylenders naturally assumed the cultivators to be foolish, stupid, ignorant and incapable of saving or bettering their lives. Colonial racism pitted the marwari against cultivators by stating that the general mass of people lacked characteristics which the moneylender possessed. Even though the colonizers treated the moneylender as an inferior creature yet they believed he possessed superior characteristics vis-a-vis the cultivators. According to colonial attitude, the cultivators could never acquire the quality of courage to stand up against the marwari:

> In the present abnormal state of things 'raiat versus the marwari', the former invariably goes to the wall, unless he has sufficient strength of mind to abide by his time and meet his demands. There is palpable proof that he has not got that courage, and he will never become possessed of that quality.[89]

This kind of attitude in fact favoured moneylenders against cultivators and naturally put the latter in a subservient position.

The colonial documents generally categorize the moneylender as a capitalist. The poverty of Berar was thus logically attributed to the surplus extracted by moneylenders. Since the moneylender provided investment capital to finance agriculture, he was held responsible for the depressed condition of ryots in the countryside. An Indian official, Mr. Nago Rao Jeyakrishna states, thus:

> The Berar raiat is generally very poor, and they are not at present in a position to cultivate the farms without the assistance of the capitalist, . . . The bania, or village Sahukar, is the person to whom they look for assistance, . . . and most of the proceeds of the year's produce is taken off by the lender, leaving scarcely sufficient for the next year's maintenance.[90]

This kind of categorization of the bania as a capitalist is rather misleading. In the context of colonial cotton trade, Berar was a peculiar case. At one level the most advanced technological instruments devised in the west were introduced to exploit and extract cotton. Yet at another level

[89] From: D. E. P. Rennick, To: Deputy Commissioner, Oomraottee, 19 June 1872, in the *Proceedings of the Hyderabad Administration for the Month of October 1874,* submitted to the Home Department, No. 99, 26 October 1874.

[90] Letter No. 979, From: Nago Rao Jeyakrishna, Assistant Cotton Commissioner, East Berar, To: Deputy Commissioner, Oomraottee District, Oomraottee, dated 24 June 1872, in the *Proceedings of the Hyderabad Administration for the Month of October 1874,* submitted to the Home Department, No. 99, 26 October 1874.

the agricultural technology remained unchanged and stagnant. At one level Berar was linked to the world market while at another level vast majority of its cultivators crawled in debt. At the level of colonial state and cotton trade there was order, discipline, centralized authority, and an enormous sense of 'time' reminiscent of the situation in contemporary Europe. But yet all this led neither to the development of manufactory nor industry. Even after fifty years of colonial rule, Berar did not have a single cloth or yarn manufacturing factory or industry. The economy primarily remained agrarian and produced cotton for the world market. Berar did have a wage labour system but its scale and volume was limited to very short periods of agricultural cycle every year. The mode of exchange primarily remained produce-oriented rather than cash oriented. In other words, capitalist relations of production in agriculture developed only partially. At the lowest level of primary production, the relations remained primarily feudal. Indebted peasantry laboured for *khatedars* and moneylenders as serfs although limited wage labour system did develop. Capitalist agriculture remained restricted to cotton processing (ginning and pressing) rather than production. Berar was neither totally capitalist nor totally feudal. It had elements of both. Its society throughout the nineteenth century remained semi-feudal and semi-capitalist in nature.

Normally the cultivator needed capital to pay rent to the *khatedar* and revenue to the government, to buy food and seeds, to hire labour and replace implements, to purchase clothes and livestock, etc. To cover for the above expenses, the entire produce of harvest was usually made over to the lender who then provided kind or cash loans when necessary. The famine commission report of 1880 states that 'the crops have generally been forestalled. When they are harvested the creditors carry off the whole, and the agriculturists has to begin again borrowing for his daily want.'[91] The commission also reports of the moneylender manipulation of books and accounts and open cheating of the illiterate cultivators. The ignorance of *khatedars* and agricultural labourers often rendered them the dupes of the artful brahmans and moneylenders.[92] The state of indebtedness made the accumulation of savings difficult. It also made it impossible for cultivators to extricate themselves from the stranglehold of the *sahukar*.[93]

[91] *Report of the Famine Commission, 1880,* London, 1881, p. 164.

[92] *Buldana District Gazetteer,* Pune, 1901, p. 163.

[93] *Report of the Famine Commission, 1880,* London, 1881, p. 296.

TABLE 28

1 year's debt	23.4%
2 year's debt	34.1%
3 year's debt	10.6%
4 year's debt	6.4%
5 year's debt	4.3%
10 year's debt	10.6%
15 year's debt	2.1%
20 year's debt	6.4%
Always in debt	2.1%
Total in debt	63.4%

Source: Notes on the Agriculturists of the District of Aurangabad, H. H. The Nizam's Dominions, by Furdoonji Jamshedji, Superintendent, Revenue Survey and Assessment, N. W. Division, in *Hyderabad Affairs,* Vol. 1, Bombay (n.d.), pp. 801-33.

In the 1880s Mr. Furdoonji Jamshedji, the superintendent of revenue survey, conducted a survey of five agricultural villages in the adjacent Aurangabad district of the Nizam's dominion. He found the prevalence of indebtedness in several instances amounting 'to their income for three or four years, while in many cases their indebtedness certainly amounts to their income for one year'.[94] In Aurangabad districts more than half (63.4 per cent) of the agrarian population was in debt ranging from 1 to 20 years. Table 28 shows the extent of indebtedness in five villages of Aurangabad in the last quarter of nineteenth century.

The total number of moneylender-landholders in Berar was less than 3 per cent , and majority of them came to acquire land during times of famine and scarcity. During such times the state of the cultivators became so worthless that there was no other course left for the marwari but to reluctantly take possession of the land. And by the decade of 1890s, with the maturing of colonial institutions, 'the moneylender can now sell up a cultivator living on his field, and give a lease for it . . .'[95] commented Baden-Powell in 1891. As the famine progressed in Berar, the transfer of title deeds to moneylenders became more frequent and increased in number.

[94] *Notes on the Agriculturists of the District of Aurangabad, H. H. The Nizam's Dominions,* by Furdoonji Jamshedji, Superintendent, Revenue Survey and Assessment, N. W. Division, in *Hyderabad Affairs,* Vol. 1 (n.d.), Bombay, pp. 801-33.

[95] B. H. Baden-Powell, *The Land-systems of British India,* 1891, p. 372.

The colonial documents do not record any large-scale land transfers prior to the 1899 famine. Such transfers however became a common occurrence after 1900. Sumit Guha in his study of Bombay Presidency has observed the existence of a land market in mid-nineteenth century Bombay Deccan. He has also argued that a regular market in land altered the creditors mode of operation in the countryside. By the late nineteenth century the merchant-moneylender of Bombay Presidency had transformed into merchant-moneylender-cum-landowner-creditor.[96] The case of Berar suggests a different development. As mentioned, the marwari moneylender of Berar was not really interested in acquiring land. As an intermediary between land and the market, it was more practical for him to hold the labour and produce of the cultivator rather than land. It should be noted that a regular market in land did not develop in Berar until the end of the nineteenth century. Although chronologically different, the moneylending system in Berar differed in many respects from Sumit Guha's observation of Bombay Deccan. While no figures exist for earlier period, the colonial registration of regular title deed (from 1899) show a fluctuating trend. The following figures reveal the extent of such title deeds at the turn of the twentieth century:

Year	*No. of Deeds Registered*
1899-1900	40,186
1900-1	34,662
1901-2	37,371
TOTAL	112,219

Source: From: Lieutenant Colonel Warren Hastings, IG of Registration, Hyderabad Assigned Districts, To: The Commissioner, Hyderabad Assigned Districts, Chikalda, dated 29 May 1908, in *Report on the Administration of the Registration Department of the Hyderabad Assigned Districts for the Year 1901-1902*, Hyderabad, 1902.

For the first time the colonial documents also begin registering land prices. Table 29 gives land prices in the three selected talukas (Rs. per acre).

The degree of intensity of debt differed from district to district according to the density of population and fertility of soil. The intensity

[96] See Sumit Guha, *The Agrarian Economy of Bombay Deccan, 1818-1941*, Delhi, 1985.

[97] F. S. Bullock, *Narrative of the Famine in the Hyderabad Assigned Districts during the Year 1896-97*, Hyderabad, 1898, p. 13.

TABLE 29

Taluka	*Sale by Court*	*Ordinary sale*	*Simple mortgage*	*Mortgage with Possession*	*Leases*
Darwa	24	23	14	15	3.5 yrs
Mangrul	10	16	15	17	3.5 yrs
Murtizapur	6	15	10	10	3 yrs

Source: Proposals for the Revision settlement of the Darwa Taluq of the Wun District, From: F. W. Francis, Director of Land Records and Agriculture, Hyderabad Assigned Districts, To: The Commissioner, Hyderabad Assigned Districts, Akola, dated 11 February 1901, in the *Proceedings of the Hyderabad Administration on Matters of routine for the Month of June 1901,* submitted to the Department of Revenue and Agriculture, No. 201, 22 June 1901.

was more pronounced in the thickly populated districts of Akola, Amraoti, southern Ellichpur, and northern Buldana compared to the forest and hill districts of Basim, Wun, southern Buldana, and northern Ellichpur.[97] The situation intensified during periods of scarcity and famine. The colonial state adhering to principles of non-interference (*laissez-faire*) allowed the grain market to take its course. The belief was that competition would bring grain into the market and push prices down. The state therefore encouraged the bania to expand his operation during famines by withdrawing all governmental responsibility.[98] Consequently during famine cycles (of the 1890s) the moneylenders increasingly took charge of grain shops and rationshops in the districts. These shops operated with the permission of government and were racked with rampant corruption.[99] It also strengthened the moneylender's hold over agricultural produce even though he did not have much influence in setting the prices. The Tahsildar of Amraoti taluk, Mr. Narayan Singh Babhut Singh, in his testimony before the famine commission categorically asserted that '. . . from my experience I can state that a large part of the annual yield of crops goes to the sowcars towards payment of their debts'.[100] The famines in fact further intensified debt and made the cultivators vulnerable to accept more stringent conditions. In addition this also resulted in the breakup of land into minute holdings. Simply put the Berar cultivator was 'in debt because he is poor, and his poverty prevents him obtaining the means of escape from debt',[101] noted the Buldana District Gazetteer. It was also noted

[98] *Report of the Indian Famine Commission, 1898,* London, 1899, p. 324.
[99] *Report of the Indian Famine Commission, 1898,* London, 1899, p. 49.
[100] *Report of the Indian Famine Commission, 1898,* London, 1899, p. 54.
[101] *Buldana District Gazetteer*, Calcutta, 1910, p. 227.

that the demands of colonial cotton trade on the marwari intensified the exploitation of Berar peasantry.

Debt and Discontentment

Alan Kulikoff while writing about the late seventeenth and eighteenth century tobacco and slaves in the mid-Atlantic colonies of Virginia and Maryland has alluded to the fact that Chesapeake Bay's debt to British and Scottish bankers was one of the several reasons for the development of slave trade and slavery in the American south.[102] Similarly, Peter Coclanis has also alluded to the pressure of credit as a reason for the employment of slaves in low country South Carolina rice production in the eighteenth century. The demands of European merchants on invested capital in seventeenth, eighteenth, and nineteenth centuries consolidated the institution of slavery in the American south.[103] Both the authors have argued that the New World's debt bondage to Great Britain was the cause of the development of Atlantic slave trade and slavery in southern American colonies.

The pressure of world cotton trade on Berar led to the intensification of pressure on the primary producer. What kind of response did the cultivators exercise in this state of social and economic subjection? The answer to this question leads us to recreate and analyse the mode of everyday forms of resistance employed by the cultivators to alleviate themselves from the misery of debt servitude.

Gyan Prakash in his study of kamia-malik relationship in Bihar has traced an entire genealogy of bondage to show the transformation of bonded labour class from precolonial to colonial system. He has argued that the colonial state while attacking the traditional and precolonial institution of bonded labour (kamia) only ended in juridically redefining the institution of bondage with the aim of strengthening the support of the pre-colonial zamindar (malik) class in Bihar countryside.[104] The case of Berar suggests some parallels although here debt servitude was much

[102] See Alan Kulikoff, *Tobacco and Slaves: The Development of Southern Cultures in the Chesapeake, 1680-1800,* Chapel Hill, 1986.

[103] See Peter A. Coclanis, *The Shadow of a Dream: Economic Life and Death in the South Carolina Low Country, 1670-1920,* New York, 1989.

[104] See Gyan Prakash, *Bonded Histories: Genealogies of Labour Servitude in Colonial India,* Cambridge, 1990; *The World of Rural Labourer in Colonial India,* New York, 1992; *Contesting Power: Resistance and Everyday Social Relations in South Asia,* Gyan Prakash and Douglas Haynes' eds., Berkeley, 1991; *Production and Reproduction of Bondage: Kamias and Maliks in South Bihar, circa 1300-1930,* Ph.D Thesis, Pennsylvania, 1984.

more widely prevalent. The region's strong links to the world market subjected every class to the *sutta* (contractual bondage). Every class from the marwari moneylender down to the mahar agricultural labourer was webbed in the large net of the world market. The mahar was indebted to the *khatedar* and *khatedar* to the marwari and marwari in turn was bonded to supply a contractual amount of cotton to European firms. This chain of servitude was much more complicated and embraced a much larger section of the population than what Gyan Prakash has pointed out in Bihar.

In the early colonial period of the 1860s when cotton economy was still developing, the moneylenders did not have much control over grain crops. The cultivators had pledged their cotton fields but grain fields were still their own and therefore they naturally gave more attention to the grain crop rather than cotton crop. The Cotton Commissioner in league with moneylenders noticed this problem but was unable to cope with it. The Commissioner's concern about the quality of cotton prompted him to note:

> The jowaree being his own, and not pledged to the village banker, the ryot would have a direct interest in paying to it the first attention, and in getting it cut and stored without delay, and the whole family would, therefore, busy themselves with the harvest which was to provide the food for themselves and the cattle during the year.[105]

Neither the marwari nor European firms gave a better price for cotton so that it was left unpicked for days much to the regret and complaints of the marwari and European firms.[106] In only very rare instances the colonial officials have registered the feelings of people. In one such instance Deputy Commissioner R. H. Hudleston of Akola district has noted the prevalence of general hostility among cultivators towards growing cotton although their credit line depended on it. The cultivators always felt that they were working for someone else rather than for themselves and thus lost all incentive to grow cotton.[107] Although Mr. Hudleston does not notice but it certainly appears that

[105] *Report on the Operations of the Cotton Department for the Year 1867*, by Harry Rivett-Carnac, 1869, p. 64.

[106] *Report on the Operations of the Cotton Department for the Year 1867*, by Harry Rivett-Carnac, 1869, p. 15.

[107] Letter No. 5391, From: R. H. Hudleston, Officiating Deputy Commissioner, Akola District, To: Commissioner, West Berar Division, Akola, dated 24 August 1872, in the *Proceedings of the Hyderabad Administration for the Month of October 1874*, submitted to the Home Department, No. 99, 26 October 1874.

cultivators of Berar were coerced to grow cotton by the pressure of their economic condition.

The European firms often regretted and complained about their inability to directly deal with the primary producer. The presence of moneylender as an intermediary was an irritant which was not liked by European firms. The marwaris devised their own elaborate system of account keeping to control local trade. It was a system quite unintelligible to anyone outside the marwari caste. This also created problems for the colonial government and European firms in estimating the extent of marwari wealth for tax purposes. Furthermore, the marwaris followed the traditional Hindu *vikrama** calendar instead of the standard christian timetable on which the entire operation of cotton economy was based.[108]

Although marwaris considered Europeans as outsiders, the fact was that marwaris themselves were outsiders to Berar. The European firms with the aid of colonial government did try to remove moneylenders from the cotton scene of Berar. But the venture failed. The moneylenders used colonial institutions, specially the law courts, to preserve their position as intermediaries. They also competed with European firms for the control of countryside. Their persistence was stronger and their control better because they lived in villages. Although marwari was a stranger to Berar he was no stranger to the villagers. The colonial institutions in addition to aiding his persistence also assisted him in exercising control over cultivators. And whenever the European firms tried to reach the cultivators directly, the moneylenders resorted to passive resistance and non-cooperation against them. This passive resistance took the form of stoppage of work and constant holidays.[109] The European firms countered this by fixing the price of cotton and thus reducing the margin of moneylender's profit.

Once the moneylender succeeded in keeping European firms out of the countryside he concentrated his attention on the cultivators activities. But the moneylender's authority in villages could never become absolute. The indebted cultivators found ways to resist his

*The *vikrama* samvat (era) is supposed to have started in 57 BC and is obtained by deducting 57 years from the christian era.

[108] *Buldana District Gazetteer*, Calcutta, 1910, p. 259.

[109] *Report of the Operations of the Cotton Department for the Year 1867*, by Harry Rivett-Carnac, p. 65.

authority. Usually the cultivator never came to marwari after the expiry of due date. It was the marwari who went looking for him thus:

On the expiry of the time given in the bond, the marwadi sends for or waits upon, his client; who at such a crisis is usually seen in a somewhat depressed mood thinking as to the best course he could adopt by which he could possibly make arrangements with his sahukar to extricate himself from the impending evil.[110]

The cultivators looked at the moneylender as an 'impending evil' and devised ways and means to avoid him. The most common means adopted was absenteeism. The *khatedar* would just absent himself from his hut at the approach of marwari. Under such circumstances the marwaris usually sought the services of a pathan or rohilla to hunt absconding debtors. As mentioned earlier the Court of Small Causes was created at the request of merchants and moneylenders. The primary function of these courts was to bring the revenue and debt defaulters to trial.[111]

Some cultivators in Wun district resisted the *sahukars* by resorting to land transfer after the execution of loan. The Assistant Commissioner of Wun wrote:

'Numerous complaints have been made to me', regarding transfers of fields. A cultivator takes a loan from the soucar and mortgages his fields as security, and then gives a razinama [agreement to transfer] of his field and some relative or friend gives a kabooliat [acceptance]. The transfer is really fictitious, but the soucar loses his security and complains that he has no means of knowing the transfer until at the jamabandi [annual rent-roll] time, when the register of holding is altered.[112]

Under such a transaction the *sahukar* was kept ignorant of the transfer and the new occupant declined responsibility for the loan.

In the early days of settlement when land was in abundance and population was mobile, the cultivators often defied the *sahukar* by

[110] From: Atmaram Bhicaji, Extra Assistant Commissioner, Oomraottee District, To: Deputy Commissioner, Oomraottee District, Oomraottee, dated 5 July 1872, in the *Proceedings of the Hyderabad Administration for the Month of October 1874*, submitted to the Home Department, No. 99, 26 October 1874.

[111] *The Berar Small Cause Courts Law, 1905*, in *The Berar Code*, Nagpur, 1931, p. 81.

[112] *Report on the Revenue Administration of the Hyderabad Assigned Districts for the Year 1877-78*, Hyderabad, 1878, p. 32.

threatening to move to a different village. Cases of such movements were reported to the famine commission (1880) by Mr. W. B. Jones, the Deputy Commissioner of Basim district.[113] And when the marwaris sent rohillas and pathans after them, the kunbis beat up these marwari agents and drove them out of the villages. Sometimes the moneylenders also got beaten up and thrown out of the village.[114] This was often followed by looting of marwari grain shops and burning of account books.

The cotton lands in Berar in some districts of Buldana, Basim, Wun, and Ellichpur were scattered and not lumped at one place. This difficulty of not having large holdings in one block created the problem of management for the moneylender. The cultivators took advantage of this weakness by using their extended kinship network to evade the moneylender and his agents.

The colonial state believed that marwari was not interested in land because he looked to his native country of Rajasthan as a repose for his latter days. It was also suggested that moneylender's interest in claiming the produce of the soil was the reason for his lack of interest in acquiring land. This may be one plausible explanation but not the entire story. It should be noted that landownership was a very sensitive issue in Berar as in the rest of British India. The marwaris were certainly aware of this feeling. In places where they grabbed land or tried to acquire ownership rights, it caused great displeasure and reaction against them. For instance in 1890 the *Buldana District Gazetteer* noted that the marwaris in Jalgaon taluk were boycotted and any man working for them was put out of caste.[115] In several instances picketing was also resorted to as a response to marwari exploitation. This happened when a large body of cultivators of a village became indebted and lost claims over the produce. The *Buldana District Gazetteer* mention the seriousness of this resistance in the following manner:

> Any man working for a marwari was put out of caste, and where that was not sufficient often threats were used and a kind of picketing resorted to . . . . Their crops were left ungathered, and one man had a large garden ruined for want of water. He could get no one to work the wells.[116]

[113] *Report of the Famine Commission, 1880,* London, 1881.
[114] *Yeotmal District Gazetteer*, Calcutta, 1908, p. 123.
[115] *Buldana District Gazetteer*, Calcutta, 1910, p. 236.
[116] *Buldana District Gazetteer,* Pune, 1910, pp. 234-6.

Conclusion

In conclusion then, the Berar *sahukar* in addition to being a moneylender was also a merchant-trader. He generally ran a small village *kirana* shop similar to the country stores of American south. He traded in cotton and grains and kept track of market prices. He was the middleman between the primary producer and cotton agents from the big market towns of Amraoti, Akola, Khamgaon, and Bombay. These agents often represented European firms and Bombay merchants. The agents procured cotton from the *sahukar* who in turn appropriated it from the indebted ryots at half the market price. Much of the cotton in Berar passed through *sahukar's* books, as it was under advances and changed hands early in the season in November and December of each year. The *sahukar* naturally got the crop from the cultivators as debt payment and sold it to the dealer of European firms who then ginned it for export.[117] The cotton report of 1878-9 stated that 'there is practically no such thing as a local price for cotton. The price in Berar is what the price in Liverpool and Bombay makes it'.[118]

In a demand driven economy, the *sahukar* operated very much within the framework of already fixed prices. He may have charged exorbitant interest rates and fleeced the indebted peasants but he himself was a puppet of the colonial state. The state controlled the economy and the *sahukar* thrived under it. No doubt the *sahukar* fixed the price of mortgaged crop at less than half the bazar rate and fleeced the cultivators. But the bazar rate itself was fixed in Liverpool. In an economy driven by the forces of external demand and supply, neither the *sahukar* nor the cultivator had much influence over the price of cotton. The total volume of capital extended and interest charged by the *sahukar* was also small compared to the value of Berar cotton in the international market. The principal reason for the indebtedness of Berar's peasantry was the pressure of the colonial state, European firms and the world market. The moneylender was a minor player in the big game of cotton trade.

[117] *Cotton Report of the Hyderabad Assigned Districts for the Year ending June 1879,* From: W. B. Jones, Commissioner, Hyderabad Assigned Districts, To: The Secretary for Berar to the Resident, Amraoti, dated 24 October 1879, in the *Proceedings of the Hyderabad Administration for the Month of November 1879,* submitted to the Home, Revenue and Agricultural Department, No. 2661, dated 25 November 1879.

[118] *Cotton Report of the Hyderabad Assigned Districts for 1878-79,* Hyderabad, 1879, para 17.

He was only a 'fly in the wheel' of the colonial machine. The bigger sharks were European firms, Bombay merchants and Manchester traders who set the rhythm of the world cotton economy. No doubt the *sahukar's* role was crucial in providing the final link of Berar to the world market. But it would be an over simplification to lay the entire responsibility of indebtedness on *sahukar* alone.

Before analyzing the material condition of the peasantry and their victimization by famine and disease (the subject of the final chapter), it is necessary to recreate the colourful but grim episode of the Banjaras of Berar.

CHAPTER 6

Colonial Sedenterization and Subjugation: The Case of Banjaras of Berar

THE BANJARAS WERE the carriers of goods and services in the Deccan plateau. They were also the keepers of bullock carts. In addition to being traders, they hired carts to other traders and merchants. Their lifestyle was mostly migratory although they usually took quarters in villages during the monsoon months (June to August). It was very much in the context of this migratory nature of their existence that their social life was organized. The Banjaras and their carts were a common sight in pre-colonial Berar. The long winding country roads jingling to the bells of swaying and swinging Banjara bullock-carts had attracted the gaze of Beraris who often must have wondered whence the carts were coming and where they were going. Often the people must have heard the banjara songs and tales and idealized their life. However the Banjara life was not as romantic as it is generally made out to be.

The Banjaras were cart carriers who took cotton from Berar to all parts of India and in return brought kirana, groceries, salt, and spices for local consumption.[1] Their shrewd sense of geography, time, and direction and their ability to communicate with the people of the forest and the plains with equal ease made them a flexible and mobile community. They were trustfully employed for the transportation of goods even by ever suspicious Indian merchants, traders, and moneylenders. Historically the Banjara carts moved along the Mughal highways stretching from Arcot to the northern reaches of the Hindu

[1] J. Forbes Royle, *On the Culture and Commerce of Cotton in India and Elsewhere*, London, 1851, p. 59.

Kush mountain ranges and from Burhanpur-Murshidabad to the ports of western India. They fanned across the country and were familiar with the ecology, geography, climate, and people. So were the people familiar with Banjaras and Berar was one of the main transit points in the heart of Deccan plateau. Here their bullocks could relax under the cool shade of the *tiwas* and prepare for the journey in one of the four directions.

In the pre-colonial period Berar had provided free and abundant grazing lands for the Banjara bullocks. Often the Banjaras and *balutedars* collaborated in fertilizing the fields by manure from the Banjara cattle. In exchange for food, drink, and hospitality, the Banjaras herded their cattle for a night or two in the open fields. The overnight cattle dropping thus provided fresh manure to the soil. J. Forbes Royle wrote in 1851 that:

> . . . by the bringing in a piece of ground used as an encampment by the passing Brinjarras (carriers) or by the villagers as a herding-place for their cattle; when this does happen, the superiority of the cotton is very remarkable.[2]

This type of activity was resorted to usually in the months from February to May when the cotton lands lay fallow in preparation for next sowing. Water from the monsoon rain when mixed with the dropping of Banjara bullocks provided an excellent source of nourishment to cotton and jawari crops. The soil of Berar thus nourished by the Banjaras was famous throughout Indian history. No wonder the planter-slaveholder Mr. Mercer from the American south on his journey through Berar in 1843 saw droves of rich white 'Oomra' cotton being carried on the backs of Banjara bullocks on its way to Mirzapur.[3] However the bullocks were not the only animals the Banjaras owned. In the region above the ghats where carts did not ply, the cotton *bhojahs* were slung pannier-fashion on the backs of camels and donkeys.[4] The Banjaras were also familiar with horses and mules although there was never a dearth of these animals. Different types of animals were used in different types of terrain and topography. For instance in the wetlands, the bullocks and buffaloes moved well, while camels, horses, and mules were well adapted to the dry lands.

In addition to transporting cotton and salt, the Banjaras also indulged in cattle trade. They often bought cattle in Nagpur, Gujerat, central

[2] J. Forbes Royle, p. 325.

[3] J. Forbes Royle, p. 54.

[4] Harry Rivett-Carnac, *Report of the Cotton Department for the Year 1868-69,* p. 116.

India, and the south and sold them in the country fairs and markets of Berar. Every village fair and weekly bazar in pre-colonial Berar was flooded with a diverse variety of animals from all across India brought in by the Banjaras. The Banjara caravans came from all directions heavily laden with the needs of the populace. This extraordinary mix and diversity of cattle was a unique feature of pre-colonial times which assisted agriculture by maintaining a regular supply of good breed of cattle in Berar.[5]

The diversity of the Banjara activity was reflected in a wide variety of articles and commodities which they carried in their carts. One of the most unique article of daily consumption which developed a close amity between the people and the Banjaras was the *supari nut*. The pieces of *supari* when rolled in *pan* leaves with aromatic herbs and spices provided a sweet chewing sensation after every meal. The settlement officer at Mortizapur recorded in 1869:

> The supari nut, which is quite a necessary of life to the Indian, is very largely imported. . . . In April and May long strings of Brinjari bullocks, numbering from 200 to 300 head, laden with these nuts alone, frequently pass along the main roads.[6]

Greatly venerated in temples and shrines, the supari nut, the coconut, and flowers provided a unique opportunity to the Banjaras to freely mingle with people all across the sub-continent and more specially in Berar. In addition they also carried commodities like oilseeds, wheat, spices, dry coconuts, pan creeper, plantain, sugarcane, opium, mangoes, custard apple, etc. They also traded in forest produce, i.e. gum, lac, chironji (for confectionery), mhowa (for liquor and food), berries, bel, behera (a dye), honey, san or hemp, etc.[7] In addition the common necessities like tobacco, grass and hay, fruits and vegetables were brought down from the hills to the plain.[8] The needs of plains were brought from the forest and the Banjaras became the communicating link between the plains folks and the forest dwellers. While perishable articles were carried over short distances, the dry goods were shipped over long distance. Whenever a Banjara cart passed by the village, the small children would leap at it and the kind Banjara cart driver would

[5] *Mortizapur Taluka Settlement Report,* No. 368 of 1869, para 55.

[6] *Mortizapur Taluka Settlement Report,* No. 368 of 1869, para 60.

[7] A. C. Lyall, *Gazetteer for the Haidarabad Assigned Districts, Commonly called Berar,* Bombay, 1870, p. 55.

[8] *Morsi Taluka Settlement Report,* No. 562 of 1871, para 17.

throw pieces of dry coconut, sugarcane, supari, etc., and they would stand there and watch the Banjara carts slowly disappear beyond the horizon leaving behind a large cloud of dust gently drifting in the sunset.

Baden-Powell mentioned in 1891 that the Banjaras were traditionally the keepers of the passes especially from the north through the Satpura ranges.[9] The Melghat korku tribes also performed this function. So a rapport must have existed between the korkus and Banjaras. The dhangars and hatgars were the traditional herdsman of the region.[10] It is possible that the Banjaras must have utilized the services of dhangars and hatgars for tending their cattle and animals. This may well be true considering the fact that the Banjara tandas (camps) and naiks (camp leaders) sometimes possessed as many as 100,000 carts in a single unit. For instance, the legendary bhangi and jhangi naiks possessed 190,000 bullocks and supplied cart trains to both the Mughal armies and their rivals in the Deccan. They monopolized the transportation business and knew the trade routes well. Since the armies also moved via trade and caravan routes it was but natural for them to seek the assistance of the Banjaras. When the Duke of Wellington campaigned against the Marathas in the Deccan he regularly employed the services of Banjaras as a part of the commissariat staff of his army. The colonial mentality of the Duke is clearly noticed in his address to the Banjaras thus: 'The Banjaras I look upon in the light of servants of the public, the price of whose grain I have a right to regulate.'[11]

Banjara Social Organization

In pre-colonial period the Banjaras mostly lived in make-shift mobile villages in addition to permanent villages where their older folks lived. Far from being homogeneous the Banjaras lived in highly diverse communities. Their status as Banjaras was circumscribed by the colonial state disregarding the rich diversity which existed among various groups of Banjaras. Most of the permanent Banjara villages in Berar were located in Wun and Basim districts. In Wun there were four distinct tribes of Banjaras, i.e. charans, mathurias, dharis, and labanas. The Banjaras in general were tolerant and syncretic in their

[9] B. H. Baden-Powell, *The Land Systems of British India*, 1891, p. 380.

[10] *Amraoti Gazetteer*, Bombay, 1911, p. 132.

[11] *Buldana District Gazetteer*, Calcutta, 1910, pp. 109-10.

religion although some of them like dharis considered themselves Muslims and practised circumcision. Similarly the labhanas considered themselves Hindus and specialized in salt trade as their name indicates.[12] A sect closely associated with the Banjaras were the manbhaus. The brahmans and the Hindu orthodoxy hated the manbhau sect for their belief in lord Krishna and casual attitude towards sex and cohabitation.[13] Furthermore, the Banjaras had their own priests and never employed the services of brahmans.[14] This must have been aggravating to the brahmans.

In Hyderabad state and Madras Presidency, the Banjaras were known as Lambadis. If their religion was ambiguous so was their declaration of caste. When census takers began the inquisition, the Banjaras responded in many different ways. Mathuria Banjaras like kanyakubja brahmans adopted upper-caste surnames, dube, chaube, tiwari, pande, etc., and even wore the sacred thread.[15] While some like the dhalias declared themselves as mangs (sweepers and undertakers). Since the Banjara tandas (groups) spread throughout the sub-continent it was a common tendency to adopt local caste and religious names. For instance, the charans were one banjara community who were found in the North-West Province, Rajputana, Central Provinces, and the Deccan. So were the kolhati pastoralists who reared dogs and practised hunting with spears. Mukheris or multani Banjaras appeared like Muslims in dress and hairstyle but had Hindu surnames. Kainjar Banjaras traded in firewood and were feared for cattle lifting and dacoity.[16] Different groups of Banjaras followed different social customs and norms. Charans claimed rajput ancestry and freely feasted on flesh and strong liquor. Labhans on the other hand claimed brahmanical origins and the men wore *janwah* the sacred thread across their chest. Some labhans also indulged in meat and alcohol but in moderation. The mathurias were strict vegetarians and wore *janwah* like brahmans. It is possible that when a Banjara tanda acquired some degree of material prosperity it preferred to settle down by adopting uppercaste customs, habits and names.

[12] *Yeotmal District Gazetteer,* Calcutta, 1908, p. 68.

[13] A. C. Lyall, *Gazetteer for the Haidarabad Assigned Districts, Commonly called Berar,* 1870, pp. 184-5, 193 and 221.

[14] *Yeotmal District Gazetteer,* Calcutta, 1908, p. 68.

[15] *Buldana District Gazetteer,* Calcutta, 1910, p. 108.

[16] *Report on the Census of Berar, 1881,* Bombay, 1882, pp. 150-1.

The Banjaras spoke diverse languages coinciding with the diversity of their customs and habits. Although majority of them spoke banjari and labhani, nevertheless there were fourteen different languages spoken in the various Banjara tandas. The census of 1891 recorded the names of languages spoken by the Banjaras along with their numbers and these are given in Table 30.

TABLE 30

Name	*Number*
Banjari	35,905
Labhani	33,256
Beldari	1,473
Kaikadi	1,033
Pardhi	763
Wadari	536
Kolhati	488
Ladsi	420
Takankari	326
Tirguli	270
Ghisadi	174
Charani	91
Waghri	48
Kangedi	34
Ladi	13
Kangari	1
TOTAL	74,831

Source: *Census of India, 1891,* Vol. VI: *Berar or the Hyderabad Assigned Districts*, Calcutta, 1902, p. lxxxii. Out of the total number of 74,831, 92.4 per cent or 69,161 spoke distinct banjari or labhani dialects.

After their settlement the density of their population declined in the plain districts of the Purna valley but increased in the hill districts of Wun and Basim. Table 31 shows the proportion of the two most popular Banjara languages spoken per 1000 population.

Although we do not have adequate figures to map the behaviour of Banjara population over time but we do have two fragmentary figures covering a period of two decades for Buldana district. By the 1890s the Banjara population had quite drastically declined throughout Berar. In 1891 there were 9842 Banjaras in Buldana district. But by 1910 their number had dropped to 4000.[17] This 40.6 per cent drop was in fact an indicator of the prevalence of such a trend in earlier decades of

[17] *Buldana District Gazetteer*, Calcutta, 1910, p. 108.

TABLE 31

Taluka	*Labhani*	*Banjari*	*Total*
Chandur	4	3	7
Amraoti	0	2	2
Murtizapur	8	2	10
Akola	7	3	10
Akot	0	2	2
Balapur	2	2	4
Ellichpur	0	1	1
Mehkar	31	8	39
Yeotmal	19	17	36
Darwa	54	86	140
Kelapur	27	32	59
Wun	5	1	6
Basim	33	8	41
Mangrul	37	37	74
Pusad	36	69	105
Average	17	18	35

Source: Census of India, 1891, Vol. VI: *Berar or the Hyderabad Assigned Districts,* Calcutta, 1902, p. lxxxv.

the colonial period. After their demobilization as a result of the introduction of railways they preferred to settle in their permanent villages where their older folks and disabled had hitherto resided. Their heavy concentration in Wun and Basim is suggestive of this pattern of settlement. Some settled in agriculture while some took to dacoity and highway robbery. The colonial state then branded them as criminal tribes and began their systematic persecution. From the census of 1881 onwards the Banjaras were included in the list of criminal castes and tribes.

Major K. J. L. Mackenzie wrote a report on the Banjaras for the Berar census of 1881. In this report he observed that the Banjaras:

> . . . live quite by themselves in such numbers as convenience dictates, away from settled villages in the jungles, chiefly for the sake of grazing, and such separate body thus settled calls itself a 'tanda' or camp, electing for its own regulation and government the ablest and most influential of its body, who is called 'Naik'. [18]

The Banjara communities usually moved in groups known as tandas. Far from 'living quite by themselves' as Mackenzie suggests these tandas communicated with the local society where ever they moved.

[18] Major K. J. L. Mackenzie's note on the Banjaras, in *Report on the Census of Berar, 1881,* Bombay, 1882, pp. 152-4.

Trading in goods and services from bazar to bazar kept the Banjaras in close touch with the local populace and trade.

The Banjara tandas were organized communities under the leadership of an elected head known as the 'naik'. The institution of the naik was in fact a carry over from pre-colonial times. During the heyday of Mughal empire the entire central India was a stronghold of Banjara tandas. In fact within Mughal empire the Banjaras had carved out a territory of their own in central India and the Deccan. Although Mackenzie does not give the source of his information yet he states that central India on the eve of takeover was divided into jurisdictional territory of three supreme naiks who were above the smaller naiks of various tandas. These territories were named after the legendary naiks of earlier times. The Jangi naik at Pune, the Bhangi naik in the heart of Deccan at Narsi and the Bartiah naik in Telingana had traditionally provided siege trains to the Mughal emperors from Akbar to Aurangazeb in their campaigns in central India and Deccan.

The naikship of all tandas including the jurisdictional head was an elected institution rather than hereditary. It was based upon the ability of the individuals in each tanda. Most able-bodied Banjaras competed for naikship of a tanda and it combined in their person the office of the lawgiver. The authority of the tanda naik was not absolute but was seldom questioned. However, all the tanda naiks were under the jurisdictional head of the supreme naik or territorial heads. In the event of dissatisfaction with the award of the law in a local tanda, a Banjara had the option to appeal to the territorial jurisdictional head or the supreme naik of the area in which the tanda happened to be located. Any conflict was always settled within the tanda itself. The Banjaras seldom took their conflict to the colonial courts much to the discomfort of British authorities. Since tandas constantly moved throughout the territory, no tanda belonged to any particular jurisdictional territory. Jurisdictional territory was demarcated not so much to set boundaries for the tanda movement but to provide support and protection to the moving tandas. This was important for the community as a whole for it made the fluidity, safety and rapid mobility of tandas possible.[19]

[19] Major K. J. L. Mackenzie's note on the Banjaras, in *Report on the Census of Berar, 1881*, 1882, pp. 152-4.

Banjara Attitude Towards Religion

The Banjara attitude towards religion makes a very interesting case study for the rest of India as well. Originally they were supposed to be closely associated with the bhakti tradition of Nanak, Kabir, Meera, Ravidas, and Sur.[20] This tradition pronounces the primacy of the teacher in leading the way to the supreme being. So there was an entire line of teachers or 'bhagats' within and outside the Banjara society who acted as powerful entities in keeping the entire community together. This was important for the cohesion of such a mobile community as the Banjaras. The naiks often venerated the bhagats but had little faith in organized religion. The bhakti tradition of meditation and concentration also assisted the Banjaras in developing a tremendous capacity to memorize complex transactions to the accuracy of a ledger. Even though the Banjaras were illiterate by the colonial standards yet their history, their songs, and their tales were learnt by heart and transmitted orally from generation to generation of the passing Banjaras. Although none of the songs of the nineteenth century are available to us yet Mr. Mackenzie has acknowledged the existence of a rich oral tradition among the Banjaras of Berar. He has reported that the songs represented their truthfulness and bravery.[21]

The Banjara attitude towards religion was to a great extent divorced from religious orthodoxy. Idolatry was unknown as the bhagats set the tone of spiritual contemplation rather than ritual practice. Almost every tanda had a spiritual head in addition to the naik. Often times the naik himself was the bhagat. The existence of female bhagats is not known but such a possibility cannot be ruled out. The bhagats were expected to lead a reserved, contemplative, sacred, and spiritual life of celibacy. But it is feasible to imagine them to be married and have a

[20] See Kenneth Bryant, *Poems to the Child God: Structure and Strategies in the Poetry of Surdas*, Berkeley, 1978; 'The Manuscript Tradition of the Sursagar: The Fatehpur Manuscript', in G. N. Bahura, ed., *Pad Surdasji Ka/ The Padas of Surdas*, pp. vii-xx, Jaipur, 1982; Jack Hawley, *Sur Das: Poet, Singer, and Saint*, Seattle, 1984; Charlottee Vaudeville, *Kabir-Vani*, Pondicherry, 1982; *Pastorales par Sour-Das*, Paris, 1971; Mark Juegensmeyer, *Religion as Social Vision: The Movement Against Untouchability in 20th Century Punjab*, Berkeley, 1982; N. Gerald Barrier, ed, *Sikh Studies: Comparative Perspectives on a Changing Tradition*, Berkeley, 1979.

[21] Major K. J. L. Mackenzie's note on the Banjaras, in *Report on the Census of Berar, 1881*, 1882, pp. 152-4.

family. Often times the bhagats lived in hamlets and provided spiritual and material relief to the moving Banjara communities.[22]

The Banjaras greatly participated in the fairs and festivals which occurred all over Berar in spite of colonial control over them. Many Banjara hamlets had shrines which attracted people of all castes and creeds. Generally fairs and festivals revolved around these shrines. The shrines also provided relief during times of famine and distress when the colonial state withdrew from the countryside. One such fair at Pahora in Mangrul Taluka was most attractive and revered by the people in general and Banjaras in particular.[23] These shrines in addition to providing an occasion for social gathering were syncretic in nature. While not being particular to any creed, the people of all creeds congregated at these shrines to worship and celebrate. The shrines also acted as trade centres for the exchange of goods and services. The diversity of products available at these fairs gave a tremendous degree of choice to the people in articles of daily consumption which became scarcer as the colonial state began the persecution of Banjaras.

Often times when cholera or disease hit the region the Banjaras worshipped *mariai* or the cholera goddess. Such an appeasement was meant for the general population rather than for just Banjara tandas. Sometimes they also worshipped legendary bandits and highway men. Mitu Bhukia, the famous bandit who had defied the authority of the state, became a symbol of Banjara independence and protest. Nearly every tanda of the charan Banjaras set apart a hut with a white flag over it.[24] This type of reverence disguisedly challenged the authority of the colonial state which felt threatened of the Banjara practices, customs and beliefs. Further the Banjaras sought spiritual guidance from the shrine of Guru Gobind Singh who perished on the banks of Godawari fighting the Mughal authority in the early eighteenth century.[25] The Sikhs were suppressed just a few years before the takeover of Berar (1853). The Sikh resistance was still fresh in the minds of the colonizers and any group or individual who sympathized with them was regarded with suspicion. The distrust of the banjaras

[22] See *Times of India*, 23 January 1873, in *Hyderabad Affairs*, Vol. IV, compiled by Moulvie Syed Mahdi Ali, Bombay (n.d.), pp. 331-2.

[23] *Mangrul Taluka Settlement Report*, No. 312 of 1900, para 12, p. 2.

[24] *Buldana District Gazetteer*, Calcutta, 1910, p. 110.

[25] See W. H. Mcleod, *Guru Nanak and the Sikh Religion*, Oxford, 1968; C. A. Bayly, *The New Cambridge History of India: Indian Society and the Making of the British Empire*, Cambridge, 1988.

was a response of the colonial state which felt threatened by the moving groups of people.[26] When the census inquisitors began questioning the Banjaras about their religious affiliation, various groups of tandas declared a wide variety of affiliation causing confusion among the ranks of colonial census takers.[27] Colonial segregation of people on the basis of religion was a means adopted to socially control groups by breaking the syncretic nature of popular approach to religion. The diversity of the Banjaras threatened the basis of the colonial state as much as their mobility.

Banjara Women

The reason for the aversion of the colonial state, and the Hindu-Muslim orthodoxy towards the Banjaras was the informal and unorthodox nature of Banjara social customs and practices. For instance, infant marriage was strictly prohibited among the Banjaras while the Hindu orthodoxy practised it. Similarly the Banjara tandas also prohibited marriages of girls before attaining the age of puberty. A. C. Lyall notes that the custom of courtship of young couples before marriage was also prevalent in the Banjara tandas.[28]

In 1873 there were 30,000 Banjaras in the Wun district. Half of them were women and children.[29] Although the Banjara men did not care much about dress and appearance, the women dressed with great taste and elegance. They wore both sarees and lahengas of varied colours but red was the favourite in Berar. The saree was a large piece of single cloth of 10 feet length and 5 feet width generally wrapped around the waist with one end hanging down the shoulder. The lahenga was a long skirt tied at the waist and hung down to the ankles. It was usually worn with a single piece blouse. Both these garments were made from Berari cotton *bani* and *jari*.[30] The Banjara women

[26] A. C. Lyall, *Gazetteers for the Haidarabad Assigned Districts, Commonly called Berar*, 1870, p. 193.

[27] *Census of India, 1891*, Vol. VI: *Berar, or the Hyderabad Assigned Districts*, Calcutta, 1892, p. xxxii.

[28] A. C. Lyall, *Gazetteers for the Haidarabad Assigned Districts, Commonly called Berar*, 1870, p. 221.

[29] From: Inspector General of Police, Hyderabad Assigned Districts, To: The First Assistant Resident, Oomraottee, dated 26 February 1874, in the *Proceedings of the Hyderabad Administration for the Month of April 1874*, submitted to the Home Department, No. 107, dated 16 April 1874, pp. 1-5.

[30] *Buldana District Gazetteer*, Calcutta, 1910, p. 108.

normally wore a string of little beads which hung loosely from the neck. She generally preferred to cut and tailor her own apparel. The skirts and blouses were beautifully embroidered and coloured with great care. The ornaments were mostly handcarved from fine scented wood and ivory.[31] The *Yeotmal District Gazetteer* has left an almost complete description of the appearance of the Banjara women in the following manner:

> The women wear two little sticks fixed upright in their hair, over which their cloth is drawn. Their front hair hangs down beside the face, and behind it is woven into a plait with silk thread and hangs down the back. They have large ornaments of silver tied over the head and hanging down beside the ears; and to these are attached little bells. Their arms are covered with bangles of ivory, and they have tinkling anklets on the feet. The women wear skirts and short cloths drawn over the shoulders, and along their skirts double lines of cowries are embroidered. Their breast-clothes are profusely ornamented with needlework embroidery, with small pieces of glass sewn into them, and are tied behind. . . .[32]

Like in matters of dress, the Banjara women exercised a great degree of independence and influence in the decision-making of the tanda. Almost all Banjara women drove bullock carts and some of them even rode horses and ponies.[33] In the absence of their men folks they also managed the business of trading and transportation of goods and services. The widow remarriage and divorce, which was prohibited by the Hindu and Muslim orthodoxy, was quite prevalent among the Banjaras.[34] It is even possible that in conjugal condition the Banjara men were younger than the women. The problem of widowhood was not that common as it was found in the orthodox Hindu and Muslim communities. The Banjara marriage system was exactly the opposite of the Hindu and Muslim system. In the latter system the marriage was usually preceded by a dowry which was paid by the bride's family to the groom's family. Then after the wedding the bride came to stay

[31] A. C. Lyall, *Gazetteers for the Haidarabad Assigned Districts*, 1870, p. 221. Also see From: Inspector General of Police, Hyderabad Assigned Districts, To: The First Assistant Resident, Oomraottee, dated 26 February 1874, in the the *Proceedings of the Hyderabad Administration for the Month of April 1874*, submitted to the Home Department, No. 107, dated 16 April 1874, pp. 1-5.

[32] *Yeotmal District Gazetteer*, Calcutta, 1908, pp. 69-70.

[33] *Report on the Census of Berar, 1881*, Bombay, 1882, p. 182.

[34] A. C. Lyall, *Gazetteers for the Haidarabad Assigned Districts*, 1870, pp. 184-5.

in groom's residence permanently. In the Banjara nuptial the groom paid the price of Rs.40 and four young bullocks with a cart. The groom then went to stay at the bride's parental home until such time as the nuclear family was established. Also unlike the Hindus and Muslims the marriage was less a religious affair than a social gathering. The services of the brahman was not sought. The ceremony was usually performed by the Banjara bhagat.[35] The Banjaras were hardy, frank and independent people. They never begged or starved as they lived in communities where children and older folks were taken care of. Sometimes they earned their living by cutting wood and grass. They were fearless travellers and had tremendous surviving capability like the pastoral Mongols of central Asia.[36] Continual residence in the wilds of nature had given them a sense of freedom and a right to travel anywhere in India irrespective of empires and governments.[37]

The manifestation of freedom and independence was perceived by the colonial state as a threat. In fact the colonial state was fearful of the moving people in general. It was petrified by the diversity which perhaps stemmed out of the colonizers' inability to understand the complex nature of Indian society. This ignorance enhanced their confusion and fear. Although the Banjaras never directly challenged the authority of the colonial state yet the mobile nature of their life posed a threat to the colonial political, commercial and economic interest. Right from its formation the colonial state looked at the banjaras with suspicion. This prompted them to devise legal and political measures to sedentarize the Banjaras. Gradually the colonial policy not only became hostile but threatened the very existence of the Banjaras. This policy was pronounced by Sir A. C. Lyall in the following manner:

> No other conduct or policy could in those times be expected of independent border tribes; their strategy has been the same all over the world. They are never tamed until their tribal union and autocracy have been broken up by a strong hand.[38]

[35] *Yeotmal District Gazetteer*, Calcutta, 1908, p. 68.

[36] See Michael Prawdin, *Dschingis-Khan*, Lubbe, 1979; Yuan Chao Pi Shih, *Index to the Secret History of the Mongols*, by Igor de Rachhewiltz, Bloomington, 1872.

[37] Major K. J. L. Mackenzie's note on the Banjaras, in *Report on the Census of Berar, 1881*, Bombay, 1882, pp. 152-4.

[38] A. C. Lyall, *Gazetteers for the Haidarabad Assigned Districts*, 1870, p. 221.

The 'strong hand' was what the colonial state finally adopted to suppress the Banjaras.

The Colonial Policing and Persecution of the Banjaras

Berar in the nineteenth century was a land of fairs and bazars. These were weekly, fortnightly, monthly and yearly events. It was in fact a reflection of the social life of the province. People from all castes, classes, and creeds came to these fairs. These gatherings were also centres of pre-colonial commodity exchange. It was here the rural producer brought his produce for sale or exchange. It was through these regular fairs and bazars that the demands of the rural countryside was catered. The region in the pre-colonial times exhibited the vibrancy of buyers and sellers traveling great distances to acquire goods and services. In this type of a mobile society the Banjaras were a very important factor. Their services were freely employed by traders, merchants, moneylenders, and hawkers for commodity transportation. By the time of colonial takeover the Banjaras had developed a complex network of fairs and bazars along which their carts moved. Since they formed the most visible group of people attending these fairs and easily identifiable by their trade, the colonial state became suspicious of the Banjara activity. This suspicion gave place to fear which led them to brand the Banjaras as 'criminal castes and tribes'. This fear emanated from the threat these mobile communities posed to the newly formed colonial state. The sedenterization of the Banjaras then became one of the principal goals of the colonial state.

The process of sedenterization began with legal recourse. Numerous fairs and bazars and their often spontaneous nature caused confusion among the ranks of colonizers. It also created difficulties for the state to tax and control them. The contemporary colonial world economy demanded a highly organized domestic market. The necessity to organise these numerous fairs and bazars to cater to external demand became the prime concern of the state. As the cotton economy developed new laws were enforced to control the trade of cotton. Such a control meant the control of fairs and bazars where most of the cotton traded hands. The only way to channelize cotton to the world market was by shaping the domestic demand. The legal course was the most feasible way of attaining this objective and the 'Berar Fairs Law' was devised and implemented. This law clearly proposed to 'provide for the regulation of fairs and other large public assemblies in Berar'.[39]

Since the time of the suppression of thugs and pindaris in the early nineteenth century, all moving people became the target of the colonial state.[40] A separate Thugee and Dacoity Department was created to supervise jails and punishment houses and deal with the moving people.[41] The relegation of such people as 'criminal and dangerous' followed immediately after the takeover. The fate of the Banjaras was sealed with the erection of colonial jails and confinement places. The census of 1881 noted an unusually large number of Banjaras languishing in jail for nothing more than just being Banjaras. Their only crime was that they were Banjaras and designated as a criminal class:

> 147 men . . . and one women of the caste were in gaol on the Census night [1881]. If the criminality of a caste be estimated by the number of its members who are convicted of offences against the penal laws, then the . . . Banjaras are less criminal than the Muhammadans, the Brahmans, the Wanis, the Koshtis, Kalals, Sonars, and Mangs. But the proportion in gaol is higher than for any of these castes, thus showing that the sentences have been more severe. . . .[42]

As the contradiction between Slave States and Free States sharpened in north America and the cotton supplies to Britain were at risk, the colonial state in India became desperate to settle people in agriculture. Such large number of Banjaras moving across Berar if successfully settled could be made to produce cotton for the world market. It became the political objective of the colonial state to coerce the Banjaras to give up their migratory habits and settle down on the land as agricultural labourers. This trend can be seen as early as 1858—within five years of the colonial takeover. The Court of Directors in

[39] Although recorded in 1923 its genesis can be traced to the early colonial period. *The Berar Fairs Law, 1923*, in *The Berar Code*, Nagpur, 1931, p. 109.

[40] See Francis Ivan Simms Tuker, *The Yellow Scarf: The Story of the Life of Thuggee Sleeman*, London, 1961; James Hutton, *Thugs and Dacoits of India*, Delhi, 1981; Mahendra Prakash Roy, *Origin, Growth and Suppression of the Pindaris*, New Delhi, 1973; Birendra Kumar Sinha, *The Pindaris, 1798-1818*, Calcutta, 1971.

[41] From: J. H. Bullock, Deputy Commissioner, North Berar, To: Major L. Davidson, Ist Assistant Resident at Hyderabad, 31 July 1854, Buldana, No. 303, in *Foreign Department Political Proceedings*, 28 March 1856.

[42] *Report on the Census of Berar, 1881*, Bombay, 1882, p. 151.

London wrote back praising the Government of India for doing such a marvelous job of achieving this object:

> We have learned with much satisfaction the beneficient effects of the operations of the Department which had resulted from bringing Berar and the Nagpore territory under British authority not only by rendering combined plans of operation possible . . . but also because the predatory classes in Berar had in a great degree renounced their predatory habits, and taken to tillage and other honest occupation. This happy change . . . has been induced by the Deputy Commissioner incharge of districts in Berar. . . . [43]

Since the Mughal times the Banjaras had provided carts and pack bullocks for the movement of cavalry and infantry siege trains. It is interesting to note that similar services were also rendered to their rivals—the Sikhs, the Marathas, and the Shia kings of the Deccan.[44] While the rival armies laid waste the countryside, the Banjaras amassed carts and cattle and enhanced their position as carriers and transporters. During times of warfare most of their burden was military hardware and artillery pieces. Their expertise in handling military equipment seasoned their knowledge of gunpowder technology. Little is known about the militaristic nature of Banjara tandas. But the settlement reports mention that the Banjaras had a monopoly over the trade of saltpetre which was the principal ingredient in the manufacture of gunpowder. The report elaborates in the following manner:

> It is a valuable product and manufactured in the country, I think it advisable to draw attention to it, in case Government should require supplies of saltpetre for the manufacture of gunpowder. . . . The nitre appears to be present in more or less quantity throughout the valley. . . . It is estimated that about 8,000 lbs of saltpetre could be produced yearly in the villages. . . .[45]

Although the militaristic nature of the Banjara tandas is unknown, it is possible that they must have acquired some militaristic character to defend the tandas since the nature of their profession demanded the adoption of such measures.

As mentioned earlier Sir Arthur Wellesley freely employed the services of Banjaras to move his siege trains to achieve his imperialistic ambition in India. The non-political strain of the Banjara activity

[43] From: The Court of Directors in London to the Government of India, *India and Bengal Despatches,* Vol. 114, Political Department No. 39, 13 July 1858, pp. 827-9.

[44] See Christopher A. Bayly, *The New Cambridge History of India: Indian Society and the Making of the British Empire,* New York, 1988.

[45] *Chicklee Taluk Settlement Report,* No. 51 of 1866.

often made them into active collaborators of the British. Such a course was fraught with danger as it ultimately led to their destruction at the hands of the British. But it is beyond doubt that their handling of European arms and artillery while loading and unloading equipment from the carts had given them some knowledge of western military technology. The colonial state was aware of this and their suspicion was enhanced when they found that the Banjaras were a well organized society which settled their disputes among themselves without recourse to colonial courts. The colonial state was also shocked to know that the loyalty of the tandas was to the authority of their naiks and supreme naiks rather than to the colonial state.[46] So the state felt the need to settle and contain the Banjaras in the southern part of Berar where they had permanent villages and where their activities could be closely monitored. One way to drive the Banjaras in enclosures was by establishing cattle pounds in villages frequented by the Banjaras.

When a Banjara tanda alighted in a village with their cattle and carts, they generally camped in the outskirts in order not to disturb the rhythm of village life. In fact they formed their own temporary villages and communicated with the village at the social, cultural, and commercial level. They frequently participated in festivities and fairs of the village and often let their cattle in the culturable fields for manuring. With the coming of the colonial state this type of interaction between the Banjaras and local society was labelled incendiary. It was again this haunting fear of the colonial state of the moving people that generated a paranoia among the colonial officials. It was the fear of Banjaras inciting local people against the state. As a measure to counter this unfounded threat, the colonial state raised cattle pounds in every village of Berar which were known to be frequented by the Banjaras. These pounds were left under the charge of the local village officials, i.e. patel (headman) and patwari (accountant). These officials were urged to impound any stray cattle illegally grazing on government land.[47] This was in fact a strategy adopted to break the bond of commensality between the Banjaras and the people of Berar.

Sir Richard Temple in 1867 declared that 'it should be a great object [of the state] to induce these people to settle down on the land as cultivators'.[48] The process of sedentarization which had commenced

[46] A. C. Lyall, *Gazetteers for the Haidarabad Assigned Districts*, 1870, p. 184.

[47] *Yeotmal District Gazetteer*, Calcutta, 1908, p. 186.

[48] Sir Richard Temple, *Observation on the State and Administration of Hyderabad Assigned Districts*, dated 14 December 1867, p. 15.

immediately after the takeover (1853) received a boost after the introduction of railways in 1862. Sir Harry Rivett-Carnac in a sarcastic tone penned the passing away of the Banjaras in the following manner:

> Like the old stage-coachman, they, too, have been thrown out of employment by the Railway and improved communication, and both they and their bullocks now afford valuable co-operation in the cause of the extension of cotton cultivation.[49]

The process of sedentarization as a result of the introduction of railways had a devastating impact on the importation of superior breeds of bullocks. The settlement officer of Amraoti the richest district of Berar lamented in 1870, '. . . such importations are now only occasional, in consequence of the change which the railway had brought about in the carrying trade . . . '.[50] This type of an impact could have done more harm than good for the agriculture of Berar.

The railway in Berar primarily transported cotton but the Banjara bullock carts carried both cotton and grains. After the demise of Banjaras the cotton was transported by European firms and moneylenders in their own carts. The grain supply became more localized as the 'old grain-carriers of former years before the days of the railway' disappeared from the roads and became cultivators.[51] With this disappearance many small articles of daily consumption which were hitherto available to the village population were no longer available.[52] The Banjara carts had hitherto travelled easily through ruts and reached every village of Berar with goods and services. But the census of 1901 reports that 'as their trade has been much affected by made roads and railways many of them have taken to agriculture'.[53] This transformation also reduced their numbers drastically. The 1891 census returned 73,762 as speaking banjari and labhani tongues while 1901 census reported their number to be 56,254 which marked a decline of 23.7 per cent.[54] This decrease in their

[49] *Report of the Cotton Department for the Year 1868-69,* by Harry Rivett-Carnac. 1869, p. 17.

[50] *Oomrawuttee and Ellichpur Taluka Settlement Report,* No. 444 of 1870, para 21.

[51] *Note on the Cotton in Berar,* by E. A. Hobson, Survey and Settlement Officer, Berar, Hyderabad, 1887, in the *Proceedings of the Department of Revenue and Agriculture,* Fibre and Silk Branch (November 1887), Nos. 22-3.

[52] *Buldana District Gazetteer,* Calcutta, 1910, p. 110.

[53] *Census of India, 1901,* Vol. VIII: *Berar,* Allahabad, 1902, p. 182.

[54] *Census of India, 1901,* Vol. VIII: *Berar,* Allahabad, 1902, pp. 140 and 182.

numbers could either be attributed to their natural demise or to their hiding under changed identities to escape colonial persecution. Under Banjaras the trade originated from Berar and spread outward while under the railway system everything converged inward towards the railway line.[55]

In addition to settling the Banjaras the sedentarization process also settled the mobile tribes such as bhils, korkus, kolis, andhs, kolams and lower castes such a mahars, dhers, mangs, bhangis etc. With this process in place the migratory labour gradually seized as cotton cultivation demanded a settled labour force.[56] The mobile people were familiar with settled agriculture and their older folks in permanent villages did practice agriculture. But agriculture was not their principal occupation. During monsoon times when the Banjara tandas quartered in permanent villages they did engage in cultivation of agricultural produce. But they were more comfortable with animal husbandry and herdsmanship which was their traditional profession. Some of their tribes like the dhangars and hatkars were traditional herdsman. Generally the colonial state treated the moving people as refractory.[57]

The colonial state perceived all non-agricultural activity with suspicion. The stringent measures were in a way motivated to eliminate the political threat which the mobile people posed to the state. It also took a hardline towards cattle tenders and herdsman communities of the Banjaras. The naiks of such communities often defied colonial authority. Therefore the state adopted harsh measures towards them. A. C. Lyall mentions an instance which can be cited as an example of the fate meted out to the Banjaras:

> The power of naiks [chiefs] was broken by Brigadier Sutherland. He hanged so many that the naiks pronounce his name to this day [1870] with awe. To some of the naiks he gave money, and told them to settle down in certain villages. Others who also came expecting money, were at once hanged.[58]

The Banjaras were in fact settled in villages which were closer to the police stations so that a much tighter supervision could be maintained over their activity. Since the Banjaras never referred their problems either to police or colonial law courts, they became perspective targets of state investigation. Some tribes like the manbhaus, before being

[55] *Morsi Taluka Settlement Report*, No. 563 of 1871, para 17.

[56] A. C. Lyall, *Gazetteer for the Haidarabad Assigned Districts*, 1870, pp. 184-5.

[57] *Amraoti Gazetteer*, Bombay, 1911, p. 132.

[58] A. C. Lyall, *Gazetteer for the Haidarabad Assigned Districts*, 1870, p. 195.

destroyed, were disgraced as being involved in human sacrifices and other secret activities against the state.[59] The Banjara defiance by refusing to refer their affairs to the colonial institutions led the state to introduce the 'pass-system' to curb their activities. Under this new system every tanda had to obtain a pass from the colonial authorities which had to be produced at every police station on their route of march. The pass-system applied to all parties of Banjaras moving from one police station range to another. This meant that any party, which included 5 or more adult males, had to obtain a pass in order to move about in Berar. The party of 5 or more males was considered a moving tanda and any group of Banjaras which failed to obtain a pass was declared illegal and unauthorized. A rather thorough and careful inspection was conducted on a tanda when it took monsoon quarters or *kooree*. The headman of a moving tanda entering Berar from outside had to report to station-house as a mandatory obligation.[60] The system of surveillance of the moving tandas and the system of supervision of the *koorees*, became the standard instruments adopted by the colonial state to sedentarize the Banjaras.[61]

Often times the police stations were located miles off the route of Banjara tanda. Often the entire tanda had to alight and the naik had to report the journey route to the nearest station-house. At the station house the naik had to state the number of cattle and persons going in the tanda, its destination and purpose, the articles of carriage, the number of carts, and such other minute and uncomfortable details. This had to be done on every police station in the tanda route.[62] The

[59] 'Memorandum on the Habits and Tenets of the Manbhaus', by Captain Lane, District Superintendent of Police, Oomraottee, in *the Proceedings of the Hyderabad Administration for the Month of May 1874*, submitted to the Home Department, No. 270, 16, 30 April and 19 May 1874, pp. 1-9.

[60] From: Inspector General of Police, Hyderabad Assigned Districts, To: The First Assistant Resident, Hyderabad, Oomraotee, dated 26 February 1874, in the *Proceedings of the Hyderabad Administration for the Month of April 1874*, submitted to the Home Department, No. 107, 16 April 1874, pp. 1-5.

[61] From: Inspector General of Police, Hyderabad Assigned Districts, To: The First Assistant Resident, Hyderabad, Oomraotee, 26 February 1874, in the *Proceedings of the Hyderabad Administration for the Month of April 1874*, submitted to the Home Department, No. 107, 16 April 1874, pp. 1-5.

[62] From: Officiating Inspector General of Police, Hyderabad Assigned Districts, To: First Assistant Resident, Hyderabad, Oomraottee, dated 26 December 1873, in the *Proceedings of the Hyderabad Administration for the Month of January 1874*, submitted to the Home Department, No. 1865, 16 January 1874, pp. 1-2.

difficulties which the pass-system caused to the moving Banjaras is graphically portrayed by the Commissioner of West Berar Division in the following manner:

> Take a Tanda located ten miles west of the station-house range, which has to carry grain westwards say 50 miles. Before starting, the Naik has under rule 2 to take all his bullocks, his men, their wives and children ten miles east to the station-house before he can start on his westward journey, that is to say he has to trudge with all his belonging an extra 20 miles. If the station-house officer happens to be absent, the tanda is detained until he returns to the station, and this is not at all an unfrequent occurrence. Having got his pass the Naik cannot even then go his journey unmolested, or by the most direct route, but under rule 7 must present himself at every station house through the range of which his journey may lie, whether the road passes the station house or not. He must also then take his cattle and belongings. . . .[63]

A tanda which generally had about a dozen families on the march faced enormous difficulties with such interference. 'The constant interference of the police, indiscriminately, with all tandas must have a pernicious effect, harassing people often to no purpose . . . ', wrote the Commissioner of West Berar in 1873.[64] The Banjaras were also harassed by the police and station-house officers for no purpose.

Often times the Banjaras had to move only on routes designated by the police. The people who had hitherto moved freely all over Berar were now designated limited zones on which they could move. These zones were in constant inspection of the police and every Banjara move was reported. Any movement or wandering outside the designated zone was hazardous for the tanda. As one colonial official writes that every tanda '. . . is open to inspection of the police, through whose jurisdiction the tanda travels. When a tanda starts intimation is sent direct to the superintendent of police of the district into which the tanda is about to enter. Any discrepancy noticed is entered in the pass . . . '.[65]

[63] From: The Officiating Commissioner, West Berar, To: The First Assistant Resident, Hyderabad, Akola, dated 17 November 1873, in the *Proceedings of the Hyderabad Administration for the Month of December 1873,* submitted to the Home Department, Nos. 1601, 1602 and 1603, 10 December 1873, pp. 1-8.

[64] From: Officiating Commissioner, West Berar, To: Inspector General of Police, Berar, Akolah, 11 August 1873, in the *Proceedings of the Hyderabad Administration for the Month of December 1873,* submitted to the Home Department, Nos. 1601, 1602 and 1603, 10 December 1873, p. 3.

[65] From: Officiating Inspector General of Police, Hyderabad Assigned Districts,

It was a common practice among Banjara families and individuals to frequently leave one tanda and join another. Since most of the tandas were related by extended kinship and family network, these ties provided strength and stability to the entire community. One tanda often helped another on the march and during times of crisis. The exchange of goods and services was frequent and the meeting of the tandas was an occasion for social gathering and commensality. Sometimes several tandas met to participate in fairs, bazars, marriages, and shrines. Hundreds of carts gathered to celebrate such occasions. The colonial state was suspicious of such gatherings and on the pretext of pursuing criminals they often disturbed and interfered with the internal organization of the tanda. The fear of such large gatherings and the general fear of the moving people drove the Inspector General of Police to declare:

> . . . the Banjaras are the most dangerous class in Berar; and I fear that any relaxation of the measures in force against them would be followed by consequences which could not but be regretted.[66]

Thereafter the colonial state adopted more rigorous measures to sedentarize the Banjaras. The tandas were 'chullanned' (fined) and detained if found travelling without a proper pass. After 1873 the passes had to be obtained even when an individual or a tanda wished to visit a weekly bazar or fair in the neighbourhood. The pass was also necessary when the Banjara family or an individual moved from one tanda to another. Harsh punishments were meted out to naiks and men who left monsoon quarters without intimation. It is possible that the Banjara youth moved clandestinely between tandas without passes. But there is no evidence to document such a movement. However the pass-system did not apply when the Banjaras were stationed at one place for long periods of time. But even under such circumstances the supervision continued.[67]

To: Officiating Commissioner, West Berar (Camp Manigaon), 30 October 1873, in the *Proceedings of the Hyderabad Administration for the Month of December 1873,* submitted to the Home Department, Nos. 1601, 1602 and 1603, 10 December 1873, p. 5.

[66] From: The Officiating IG of Police, Hyderabad Assigned Districts, To: Officiating Commissioner, West Berar (Camp Manigaon). 30 October 1873, in the *Proceedings of the Hyderabad Administration for the Month of December 1873*, submitted to the Home Department, Nos. 1601, 1602 and 1603, 10 December 1873.

[67] From: The District Superintendent of Police, Buldana District, To: The Inspector-General of Police, Hyderabad Assigned Districts (Camp Chicklee), 14 February 1873, in the *Proceedings of the Hyderabad Administration for the Month of December 1873,* submitted to the Home Department, Nos. 1601,1602 and 1603, 10 December 1873, p. 6.

In many cases constables were attached to the tandas. The constant presence of police kept the Banjara communities in a state of fear and awe. 'There is no doubt that the system is to a greater or less extent irksome to the Brinjaras. They are brought into contact with the police—an effect which they particularly dislike, and in some cases I have little doubt they are detained on one pretext or other,' wrote the Deputy Commissioner of Akola district carelessly in 1873.[68]

Within a few years of the introduction of pass system (1872), the process of sedentarization began to bear fruits. 'Many Brinjaras are gradually settling down as tillers of the soil and doing a little carrying business between some of the Cusba towns in the district in which they may happen to be located',[69] wrote a colonial official in 1873. The pass-system also put drastic restriction on their carrying trade. It restricted the mobility and relegated the Banjaras to small towns and villages. The restrictions did not cease even after the Banjaras settled on the land. The Deputy Commissioner of Amraoti in fact found it necessary to continue the enforcement of restrictions since Banjaras moved about even after their sedentarization. He made a strong recommendation that he would:

> . . . certainly not withdraw the [pass] system merely because it is not much needed in the Amraoti district. This I think is the proper light to look at the matter in four-fifths of the Bunjaras' line [sic] in the Wun & Basim districts, but the system could not work unless it was extended to all districts, because although the other districts have not many Bunjaras living in them, still many thousands pass through them. . . .[70]

The colonial suspicion in fact strongly prevailed throughout the period. Once the entire community or a tanda was branded criminal the persecution became indiscriminate. Mr. R. J. Meade writes:

[68] From: Deputy Commissioner, Akolah District, To: The Commissioner, West Berar Division. Akolah, June 26, 1873, in the *Proceedings of the Hyderabad Administration for the Month of December 1873,* submitted to the Home Department, Nos. 1601, 1602 and 1603, 10 December 1873, pp. 1-8.

[69] From: The Officiating Commissioner, West Berar, To: The First Assistant Resident, Hyderabad, Akolah, 17 November 1873, in the *Proceedings of the Hyderabad Administration for the Month of December 1873,* submitted to the Home Department, Nos. 1601, 1602 and 1603, 10 December 1873, pp. 1-8.

[70] See Report by Inspector General of Police on Working of Pass System of Surveillance of Banjaras suspected of Criminal Proclivities, in the *Proceedings of the Hyderabad Administration for the Month of February 1875*, submitted to the Home Department, No. 1637, 11 February 1875, pp. 1-2.

There can be no doubt that the restriction and surveillance under which the Bunjaras were placed by the tentative rules initiated in 1872 interfered very considerably with their freedom, and must have pressed heavily upon those members who conducted themselves honestly and respectively, as well as upon the criminal portion of the tribe; but such a result was not only unavoidable, but the restriction upon the whole class were at the commencement intentional and necessary.[71]

In order to escape the surveillance and persecution many Banjaras adopted the habits of kunbees and upper-castes as a disguise.[72] But it also resulted in the loss of Banjara culture and its disappearance from Berar. Mr. Cumberlege, the British Superintendent of Police in Wun has passed the following colonial judgement on the fate of Banjaras in 1870: 'Neither their trade nor their tribal system can survive another generation of English predominance where some account of their more striking peculiarities has at least the interest that attaches to a picture of things which we shall never see again.'[73] Similarly Major K.J.L. Mackenzie notes the gradual disappearance of Banjara tradition and culture in the following manner:

And now not having foreseen their own fate, or at least not timely having read the warnings given by a yearly diminishing occupation which slowly has taken their bread away, it is a bitter pill for them to sink into the ryot class, or oftener still under stern necessity become the ryots servant. But they are settling to their fate and the time must come when all their peculiar distinctive marks and tradition will be forgotten.[74]

After demobilization a majority of the Banjaras worked as daily field labourers. A small number of them ended up as grain chandlers, masons, sugar-refiners, timber and bamboo workers, carpenters, daily labourers, road labourers, firewood and grass cutters. Banjara women worked as grass and firewood sellers, grain-pounders, road labourers,

[71] From: R. J. Meade, Officiating Resident, Hyderabad, To: The Government of India, Foreign Department, No. 12, Hyderabad Residency, 10 April 1879.

[72] From: The Assistant Commissioner in Charge, Basim District, To The Commissioner, West Berar, Basim, 28 May 1873, in the *Proceedings of the Hyderabad Administration for the Month of December 1873,* submitted to the Home Department, Nos. 1601-3, 10 December 1873, pp. 1-8. Also see *Yeotmal District Gazetteer,* Calcutta, 1908, p. 59.

[73] *Gazetteer for the Haidarabad Assigned Districts, Commonly called Berar,* ed. A. C. Lyall, Bombay, 1870, p. 195.

[74] Major K. J. L. Mackenzie's note on the Banjaras; *Report on the Census of Berar, 1881,* Bombay, 1882, pp. 152-4.

etc.[75] But such occupations were not natural to them and only provided temporary relief. Loss of their traditional occupation forced some of them to resort to highway robbery for survival. Some Banjaras also resorted to stealing cotton from the fields at night. Since they knew the routes well, initially it was easy for them to escape. Because of the extended kinship network and group solidarity an escaped Banjara could move from village to village in hiding. But when this type of subversive activity became frequent, the colonial government imposed a 'roll-call system' on the Banjara villages. By this system a head-count was conducted in every Banjara village late at night and sometimes twice to make sure that every adult member of the village was accounted for. Any absentee had to be fully explained and accounted for or else he/she came under immediate suspicion of crime. In 1875 the Inspector-General of Police noted that in order to avoid this type of nightly police harassment, the Banjaras usually never lighted their huts at night.[76]

Conclusion

In this chapter it is argued that the colonial state was hostile to any type of mobility among the people of Berar. It felt especially threatened by occupationally mobile community like the Banjaras. The Banajara society was a 'state within a state'. It seldom referred its problems to the colonial courts or bureaucracy. It almost functioned parallel to the colonial government. However, the Banjaras never directly challenged the state. It was their lifestyle and the nature of their daily existence that was threatening to the colonial state. The state was in general suspicious of the moving people. Therefore it felt necessary to eliminate the Banjara threat by sedentarizing them.

The free and independent spirit of the Banjara society in general caused some concern to the Hindu-Muslim orthodoxy as well. The Banjara belief in the Bhakti tradition and non-conformity to institutional religion drove the Hindu-Muslim orthodoxy to

[75] *Report on the Census of Berar, 1881*, Bombay, 1882, p. 152.

[76] *Yeotmal District Gazetteer*, Calcutta, 1908, pp. 69-70 and 77. Also see Report by Inspector General of Police on Working of Pass System of Surveillance of Banjaras Suspected of Criminal Proclivities, in the *Proceedings of the Hyderabad Administration for the Month of February 1875*, submitted to the Home Department, No. 1637, 11 February 1875, pp. 1-2.

collaborate with the British in the suppression of the Banjaras. The Banjara practices of courtship and premarital sex, divorce and widow re-marriage, more freedom of women in socio-economic life, rejection of dowry in marriage, absence of idolatry and infant marriage, etc., were some of the customs which threatened the basis of institutional religion in the same manner as it threatened the existence of the colonial state. Therefore the combined wrath of the colonial state and religious orthodoxy fell on the Banjaras of Berar.

In addition to suffering continuous persecution, the famines of the 1890s gave a tremendous blow to the Banjara culture and society. However, the Banjaras were one of the several groups of people to suffer the onslaught of famine. Therefore it is only fitting to turn the analysis to the impact of colonial political economy on the people of Berar.

CHAPTER 7

Famine in Berar: 1850-1900

WITHIN A DECADE of the takeover of Berar, reports of food crisis began to be registered in the colonial documents. It is unknown whether these calamities were a carry-over from pre-colonial times or a later development. But its connection to the growth of cotton economy is undeniable. More than 60 per cent of the years for which data is available were periods of high mortality of over 30 per thousand (see Table 32). C. A. Bayly in his work on north India has suggested that eighteenth century was relatively free for famines despite the wars of the regional successor states of the post-Mughal India.[1] But nineteenth century opened with famines which repeated in cycles every thirty years. Berar did not come under British rule until 1853 but census reports of the colonial period record two pre-colonial famines, i.e. 1803 and 1832-3,[2] suggesting that the region was a part of the rhythm of all-India famine cycle.

BACKGROUND OF THE FAMINES

Sanitary Condition

A gradual rise in population corresponding with the growth of cotton cultivation led to the rise of several cotton towns along railroad tracks. The rise of cotton towns naturally attracted population from the surrounding countryside. The rapid rise of railway stations in cotton towns along Nagpur-Bombay line created problems of

[1] See C. A. Bayly, *Rulers, Townsmen and Bazaars: North Indian Society in the Age of British Expansion, 1770-1870*, Cambridge, 1983; *The New Cambridge History of India: Indian Society and the Making of the British Empire*, Cambridge, 1988.

[2] *Report on the Census of Berar, 1891*, Bombay, 1892, p. 225.

management. The market towns of Malkapur, Chandpur, Nandura, Jalam, Khamgaon, Paras, Akola, Borgaon, Murtizapur, Badnera, Amraoti, Chandur, and Dongargaon in the heart of cotton belt were simply not equipped to handle the rising population pressure. The rise of cotton cultivation and colonialism triggered the growth of peculiar types of urban centres and market towns which performed no other function other than serve as transit points for loading cotton into railway wagons. A few big emporiums like Akola and Amraoti did develop a semblance of urban culture because of the presence of colonial army, police, European and Indian merchants, and moneylenders.[3]

The colonial state organized municipality and sanitary department in large market towns of Khamgaon, Akola, and Amraoti. But in numerous smaller towns and transit points, the services of sanitary department and municipality were not extended. Even in large centres the facilities did not extend beyond the immediate vicinity of towns. The severity of famine very much depended on the sanitary condition of towns and villages. The large towns were able to weather the severity of droughts and famines better than small towns. The sanitary commissioner's jurisdiction was primarily restricted to limited number of larger towns. The responsibility of maintaining sanitation in smaller towns and villages was left to the individual initiative. Even in large towns the sanitary commissioners often aired complaints about lack of adequate funding for the department.

The sanitary condition in a way was a precursor to famine in Berar. Since responsibility was left to the individual initiative of every town and village, the problem grew along with the population. The scarcity of private and public privies made defecation on open grounds a matter of necessity than choice. It was reported that the outskirts of every village and town was surrounded with overgrown prickly-pears and poisonous weeds. In addition, no village was free from the problem of the scarcity of drinking water. 'Good water is scarce in this district, in some places shallow "jhieries" alone can be depended upon for a supply, the wells being brackish, and even the river gravel furnishing brackish water if pierced to any considerable depth,' wrote the Geological Survey of India as early as 1869.[4]

[3] See *Central Provinces District Gazetteer: Amraoti District*, Bombay, 1911. Also see A. C. Lyall, *Gazetteer for the Haidarabad Assigned Districts, Commonly called Berar*, Bombay, 1870.

[4] *Records of the Geological Survey of India*, Vol. II, Part I, 1869 (February); *The Valley*

The mortality in Berar was principally due to the problem of sanitation, water, and disease. Groundwater wells were the main source of supply of drinking water. The general state of sanitary condition made the availability of clean drinking water difficult. The wells were exposed to wind-borne refuge. The domestic sullage accumulated in pits near the houses sank into the ground and freely mixed with well water. The dripping wells provided a breeding ground for guinea worms. Albuminoic Ammonia (a water-based chemical) was produced in the tanks of Berar by decaying vegetable matter. This contamination was caused by the inadequacy of waste disposal facilities. Dust-bin garbage was usually disposed to bricklayers who smoked it to fire bricks. The smoke from the brick mounds mixed freely with fresh air in the atmosphere. The cremation grounds were usually located at the outskirts of the villages adding further to the problem of clean air. The Sanitary Commissioner reported (1891) a fetid odour of night-soil at the approach of every town or village in Berar.[5] The Commissioner also saw heaps of garbage and manure piled up alongside open cesspools which emitted foul odour in the neighbourhoods.

Berar is dotted with shrines in every district of the province. The fairs and festivals held all year round attracted large numbers of people to these shrines. Bahiram (Ellichpur) alone attracted 60 to 100,000 people annually. The absence of an organized sanitary system left these shrines in a state of great health hazard. Writing about Bahiram the Sanitary Commissioner reported (1889): 'The shrine is situated some 500 feet high; on the side of the hill and all around were deposits of fickle matter in various stages of decomposition.'[6] Even though the Sanitary Commissioner had a genuine desire to improve the conditions, lack of funding made the implementation of any planned programme impossible. The Commissioner's bitterness towards government indifference was justified. Reacting to the government famine relief operation of 1897-8 the Commissioner C. L. Fecal wrote:

---

of the Poorna River, West Berar; by A. B. Wynne, esq., in *Hyderabad Affairs*, Vol. 1, Bombay, 1883, pp. 407-12.

[5] *Report of the Sanitary Commissioner, Hyderabad Assigned Districts for the Year 1891*, Hyderabad, 1892.

[6] *Report of the Sanitary Commissioner, Hyderabad Assigned Districts for the Year 1889*, Hyderabad, 1890.

> Your town may be a couple of centuries old with a filth sodden site and an atmosphere surcharged with impurity, harmful to good health; and your once sweet wells may be salt, the result of percolation of ruin of both man and beast during the two centuries. What do you do to prevent the growing evil? Is what you do sufficient? Go to, and see how many of your private privies are in a filthy state for want of sufficient or proper cleaning, and how many compounds contain filthy sinks, the dung of cattle, filthy rags, and other household rubbish. On your way count the number of adults urinating in the public bye-lanes, and say whether all that you do is sufficient to keep the earth you live on, the air you breathe, and the water you drink clean and pure. Is not the subject worthy of your first consideration, and considering that it is a question of life and death effecting the man, should you not direct your best efforts to remove the evils and to educate the people, the children in schools, and the adults by the enforcement of rules calculated to attain the object in view?[7]

After penning such a dramatic note, the Commissioner went on to propose a long-term plan for investment in sanitary improvement with the aim of preventing diseases and thus reducing mortality.

Mortality

Disease related mortality was the natural outcome of the neglected state of sanitation. The data on disease borne mortality for pre-colonial Berar is lacking but they are available for the colonial period (1850-1900). So it is now possible to assess the impact of insanitary condition on the health of people. Table 32 gives a breakdown of mortality by disease per 1000 as compiled by the Sanitary Commissioner of Berar.

The period is also marked by the prevalence of several diseases in the region. Although mortality was generally caused by bowel complaint, dysentery, diarrhea, and cholera but malaria fever (sun-fever, sun-stroke, heat apoplexy), anaemia, scurvy, ulcer of the cornea, ulcer of extremities also took the toll. It is interesting that small-pox was generally associated with cotton and dreaded locally as 'kapsi matha.'[8] The precise origins of the popular perception of associating

[7] *Report of the Sanitary Commissioner, Hyderabad Assigned Districts for the Year 1898*, Hyderabad, 1899.

[8] *Report of the Sanitary Commissioner, Hyderabad Assigned Districts for the Year 1896*, Hyderabad, 1897, para 33.

TABLE 32

Year	*Cholera*	*Small-pox*	*Fevers*	*Dysentery*	*Injuries Diarrhea*	*All Other Causes*	*Total Death Rate 1000*	*Total Birth Rate 1000*
1868	2.9	1.9	5.8	2.9	0.5	5.2	19.1	18.6
1869	5.2	3.6	6.2	2.9	0.4	4.8	22.8	16.2
1870	0.2	0.6	10.5	6.4	0.4	6.2	24.6	24.1
1871	0.2	0.2	8.3	4.2	0.4	4.2	17.7	27.4
1872	0.7	3.8	14.5	10.0	0.4	7.5	37.1	26.4
1873	NA	3.8	8.8	5.0	0.4	4.7	22.8	28.1
1874	0.1	0.5	12.2	8.5	0.4	6.1	27.9	36.1
1875	10.2	0.4	11.9	9.5	0.4	7.7	40.3	36.8
1876	1.2	0.2	18.2	7.5	0.4	4.3	31.9	39.1
1877	0.4	2.9	15.8	4.8	0.5	3.7	28.1	39.5
1878	15.6	2.7	38.9	12.6	0.5	11.1	81.5	34.6
1879	0.1	0.1	14.8	3.8	0.5	4.4	23.7	37.8
1880	0.1	0.1	14.2	3.6	0.5	5.3	23.6	41.7
1881	1.3	0.1	15.8	4.5	0.4	7.0	29.1	39.9
1882	1.4	0.1	15.0	5.1	0.4	7.4	29.4	42.0
1883	10.6	1.5	20.3	7.2	0.4	11.3	51.3	40.3
1884	0.1	0.2	11.6	3.5	0.4	8.9	24.6	41.3
1885	1.4	0.1	14.1	6.0	0.4	12.0	34.0	42.9
1886	0.4	0.1	17.3	6.4	0.4	12.2	36.7	37.3
1887	5.5	0.1	18.3	8.2	0.4	12.8	45.3	40.5
1888	0.1	0.3	11.4	3.8	0.4	8.6	24.7	41.3
1889	4.2	0.7	17.9	6.6	0.4	12.7	42.5	39.6
1890	0.3	0.1	18.2	5.1	0.4	11.3	35.4	42.5
1891	2.8	0.1	17.5	7.7	0.4	12.2	28.8	42.8
1892	0.7	0.1	14.6	3.9	NA	9.1	32.6	39.9
1893	0.4	0.1	16.0	5.2	0.4	10.6	42.0	39.3
1894	1.2	0.3	23.6	5.2	0.4	11.3	49.9	33.3
1895	4.2	0.2	23.2	8.6	0.4	13.3	43.3	37.2
1896	4.3	0.3	21.8	6.2	0.3	10.9	52.6	38.8
1897	3.5	0.2	23.0	10.3	0.5	15.1	23.4	39.7
1898	NA	0.2	11.5	3.5	0.3	7.9	39.9	31.3
1899	0.2	0.1	17.5	7.1	0.3	14.7	82.7	50.5
1900	6.4	0.3	29.5	22.4	0.5	23.6	NA	31.3
1901	0.1	0.1	13.9	4.4	0.4	8.8	27.6	38.2
1902	0.1	0.1	13.7	4.2	0.4	11.8	32.8	56.9

Sources: Report of the Sanitary Commissioner, Hyderabad Assigned Districts for the Year 1890, Hyderabad, 1891, Table 14; *Report of the Sanitary Commissioner, Hyderabad Assigned Districts for the Year 1889,* Hyderabad, 1890, Table Nos. 1 and 9.

disease and mortality with the growth of cotton culture is not easy to locate. But abundance of cotton crop throughout the famine decade of the 1890s and the appearance of small-pox in the summer of 1896 was enough for the people to associate colonialism with disease and death.[9] As mentioned in an earlier chapter, cholera as a disease was introduced when large masses of labourers were mobilized to build railway tracks.

Reporting of diseases was also very chaotic and often inaccurate. Perhaps it was not easy to distinguish one disease from the other considering the state of medical knowledge in the late nineteenth-century Berar. Often time many more deaths occurred due to a particular disease and went either unreported or reported incorrectly. Writing in 1898 the Sanitary Commissioner reported the seriousness of the error in reporting deaths due to various diseases in Berar:

> From personal enquiry made at several villages, I am of the opinion that there were many more deaths from cholera then were actually registered under that head. I should say that, roughly speaking, there were over 10,000 deaths from cholera, which were erroneously registered.[10]

Absence of proper disease identification made preventive measures difficult. Often the disease was recognized after the death of patient. In several instances the patient contacted the disease and died within 24 hours. Cholera was one such fatal disease which uniformly rampaged the region. The cholera inquiry reported a dramatic case in village Meljanooree in Buldana district on 12 September 1890:

> Gummi, murd Marotee [Gummi wife of Marotee] female, aged 16 years, was the person first attacked. She was in perfect health previously, worked all day in the field, prepared the usual meal the night before (consisting of dhall and jowari cakes) in which her husband joined her. She took ill at 12 noon (1st August, 1890) and died the next day at 3 p.m., and was buried on the bank of the stream running along-side the village.[11]

The report mentions in detail the symptoms of Gummi's death—'vomited five times, purged six times, attacked by severe cramps in

[9] See *Reports of the Sanitary Commissioner, Hyderabad Assigned Districts*, printed annually, 1889-1902, Hyderabad.

[10] *Report of the Sanitary Commissioner, Hyderabad Assigned Districts for the Year 1898*, Hyderabad, 1899, para 14.

[11] *Report of the Sanitary Commissioner, Hyderabad Assigned Districts for the Year 1890*, Hyderabad, 1891.

limbs and stomach, urine almost immediately suppressed, voice became husky leading to deafness'.

Sanitary conditions to a great extent determined the surviving capability of the disease victim. People often resorted to traditional methods of fighting diseases. One such method to cure illness was cauterization with hot iron or a piece of gold. So largely was cauterization resorted to, that Mr. Furdoonji Jamshedji an Indian district official, reported in 1883 that more than half the population showed marks of having been scarred on either stomach, back, neck, or temples.[12] The absence of proper sanitary condition coupled with exports of cotton and foodgrains became the primary cause of scarcity and famine in Berar.

The Causes of Famine

Colonial officials from the time of Captain Meadows Taylor (1858) strongly believed that the deep black soil of Berar was naturally rich and therefore did not need much irrigation.[13] This became the standard line of reasoning in the official opposition to investment on public irrigation projects. The state interest in agriculture basically lapsed outside cotton cultivation. And since cotton did not need too much water, the need for any general irrigation scheme seemed unnecessary and the colonial anti-irrigation attitude seemed to be justified.[14] In the absence of public support, the traditional rural practice of building temporary dams and anicuts through communal labour was discontinued. It is not surprising that throughout the colonial period only a very small percentage of total cultivated acreage (on average 1.65 per cent) was under irrigation.[15] The anti-irrigation stance took such strong roots among colonial bureaucrats that Berar was declared

[12] *Notes on the Agriculturists of the District of Aurangabad, H. H. The Nizam's Dominions*, by Furdoonji Jamshedji, in *Hyderabad Affairs*, Vol. 1, by Moulvie Syed Mahdi Ali, Bombay, 1883, pp. 801-33.

[13] In fact Meadows Taylor even put forth the belief that '. . . irrigation of the plant on deep black soil would prove injurious, both to fibre and produce'. From: Captain Meadows Taylor, Deputy Commissioner, North Berar, To: F. N. Maltby, Commissioner, Hyderabad Assigned Districts, dated 25 January 1858, Camp Hamerkher, in *Foreign Department Proceedings*, No. 147/8, 9 April 1858 (IOLR).

[14] *Report of Famine Commission, 1880*, London, 1881, p. 52.

[15] Source: *Report of Famine Commission, 1880*, London, 1881.

to be immune from famine. Therefore it was concluded that a regular programme of relief was not necessary for Berar.[16]

The colonial state and the administration then was completely surprised at the severity of famine cycles of the 1890s which struck again and again and caught the officials unaware. Mr. R. A. W. Swinnerton, the Executive Engineer of West Berar when called in for an interview by the Famine Commission (1898), very appropriately remarked that, 'no plans and estimates were ready prepared when the distress appeared, as it was the opinion of the Commissioner that Berar would never suffer from famine'.[17] Lack of infrastructural facilities in the face of crisis intensified the impact of famine. Colonial Berar was unprepared to deal with such a crisis.

Almost every colonial document in the nineteenth century has attributed the failure of rains to be the principle cause of famine. In the case of Berar then how can famine occur due to failure of rains if the soil is naturally rich and needs very little water to grow crops? There is a basic contradiction in the colonial reasoning of the cause of famines.

Amartya Kumar Sen in his work on colonial and post-colonial societies has very forcefully argued that the famines are caused not so much by the actual shortage of foodgrains as by a 'decline of exchange entitlement.'[18] By this he meant that there was more than sufficient foodgrains available but the general masses could not have access to it because of: (a) an inflationary situation of high prices caused by foreign export; and (b) low wages coupled with the government inability to respond to the material condition of people.

A villager in 1864 when asked about the general tenor of life commented: '. . . half a rupee, a few years ago, was worth as much as a rupee is worth now. The rise in prices is not confined to grain and

[16] According to one of the colonial officials Mr. F. S. Bullock, '. . . a program of relief works was not required for Berar because it was not subject to famine, and might be considered exempt from the ordinary rules to meet such a contingency', F. S. Bullock, *Narrative of the Famine in the Hyderabad Assigned Districts During the Year 1896-97*, Hyderabad, 1898, para 8.

[17] Mr. R. A. W. Swinnerton, Executive Engineer, West Berar Division, called in and examined, 8 March 1898, in *Report of the Indian Famine Commission, 1898*, London, 1898, p. 41.

[18] Amartya Kumar Sen, *Poverty and Famine*, Delhi, 1982. 'Famine Mortality: A Study of the Bengal Famine of 1943', in Hobsbawm *et al.*, eds.; *Peasants in History*, Oxford, 1980.

cotton, but extends to everything'.[19] Almost every colonial document confirms that prices had the tendency to appreciate while wages showed very little mobility.[20] While there was never an actual scarcity of foodgrains, the wage price exchange of jawari did show a declining tendency[21] (see Table 34). A steep rise in mortality occurred whenever the wage-price exchange rate of foodgrains declined. A seasoned colonial official of Berar, Mr. F. S. Bullock, confirmed this fact in his report of 1896-7 famine by boldly narrating that:

> It [is] evident that the famine of 1896-7 in Berar has not been so much a period of actual scarcity of food so much as a famine caused by high prices, and this is the central fact that must be borne in mind in dealing with the subject.[22]

Even if caution is employed in the universal application of Bullock's observation, yet the famine was caused not so much by nature or failure of rains but by the colonial political economy of control and indifference, i.e. control of market and indifference to public works.

In an interview to the Famine Commission of 1880, Major Sczepanski of Wun observed that the payment a casual labourer 'receives for field work are not sufficient to keep himself and family throughout the whole year . . .'.[23] So the labourer always had to find some other work for subsistence. Such miscellaneous work in times of famine was not only scarce but difficult to find.

The inability of wages to keep up with prices kept a large number of agricultural labourers on the brink of subsistence. The famine years

[19] *General Administration Report on the Hyderabad Assigned Districts for the Year 1863-64*, Calcutta, 1865, para 52.

[20] According to the census reports the wages of unskilled labourers of Berar remained between 2 annas and 5 annas per diem on average between 1869-70 and 1900-1. while the jawari prices rose from being as low as 51.76 seers per rupee to as high as 22.44 seers in two non-famine years of 1875-6 and 1903-4 respectively. Note: The wage data taken from: *Report on the Census of Berar, 1881*, Bombay, 1882, p. 233; *Report on the Revenue Administration in the Hyderabad Assigned Districts*, Hyderabad, published annually from 1877-8 to 1901-2; *General Administration Report on the Hyderabad Assigned Districts*, Calcutta, published annually from 1855-6 to 1900-1; The data on wages taken from: *Prices and Wages in India*, 22nd issue, compiled in the Office of the Director General of Commercial Intelligence, Calcutta, 1905, pp. 34-7.

[21] *Prices and Wages in India*, 22nd issue, compiled in the Office of the Director-General of Commercial Intelligence, Calcutta, 1905, pp. 34-7.

[22] F. S. Bullock, *Narrative of the Famine in the Hyderabad Assigned Districts During the Year 1896-97*, Hyderabad, 1898, para 14.

[23] *Report of the Indian Famine Commission, 1880*, London, 1881, p. 427.

were a fallout. 'The wages of labour were scarcely half the normal average; the prices of food were double the average, and the produce of the fields half the usual amount',[24] was how the revenue administration report looked at the whole situation. There is some validity to this statement especially considering the decline in per acre yield of jawari from 178 seers per acre in 1886-7 to 145 seers in 1897-8.[25]

The Reports of the Famine Commission and the Sanitary Commissioner found that the average per capita consumption of 22 oz per diem was inadequate to maintain nourishment of the body. Female diet was taken to be 2 to 4 oz. less than the male diet.[26] Insufficient calorie intake always kept the general mass vulnerable to disease.

The agricultural labourers received cash wages only for certain field operation such as ploughing and weeding. Of the two types of field labourers, it was more common to pay the daily casual labourer in cash and the regular permanent labourer in kind and cash. The permanent labourer when hired by the year usually received food, leather slippers, blanket, lungi, shirt, and *pugri* (headgear). The typical Berari saying went: 'Khaun piun pach pangrun ane thevila', which meant 'food, drink and five articles of dress'.[27] Generally the wages of permanent labour were approximately Rs. 30 with food and Rs. 45 to

[24] *Report of the Revenue Administration in the Hyderabad Assigned Districts for the Year 1896-97*, Hyderabad, 1897, para 38.

[25] *Report on the Trade of the Hyderabad Assigned Districts, 1878-79 to 1902-3*, Hyderabad, published annually. Also known as *Rail and Road Borne Trade Report: Berar, 1878-79 to 1902-3.*

[26] The Reports of the Famine Commission and the Sanitary Commissioners found that the average per capita consumption per diem of 22 oz. was found to be inadequate to maintain the nourishment of the body. Female diet was taken to be 2 to 4 oz. less than the male diet. Source: *Report on the Trade of the Hyderabad Assigned Districts for the Year 1881-82*, Hyderabad, 1882; *Report on the Trade of the Hyderabad Assigned Districts for the Year 1878-79*, Hyderabad, 1880 (also known as the *Rail and Road-Borne Trade Reports of Berar, 1878-79 to 1885-86*, published annually (New Delhi); Memorandum submitted by A. J. Dunlop, Assistant Commissioner, Hyderabad Assigned Districts with reference to the information asked, in the *Proceedings of the Hyderabad Administration for July 1878*, No. 1043; *Home, Revenue and Agriculture Department*; *Report on the Census of Berar, 1881*, Bombay, 1882; Memorandum on the subject of Dietary in Jails of the Hyderabad Assigned Districts for 1880, in the *Proceedings of the Hyderabad Assigned Districts for the Month of September 1881*, submitted to the Home Department, No. 363, 19 September 1881; *Report of the Sanitary Commissioner, Hyderabad Assigned Districts for the Year 1897*, Hyderabad, 1898; *Report of the Indian Famine Commission, 1898*, London, 1898.

[27] *Central Provinces Gazetteers: Buldana District*, Pune, 1910, p. 246

55 without food. This approximated to only 1.9 annas per diem (while the average daily wage was 3.0 annas) although it did not entail the insecurity of the casual labourer.[28] Most of the agricultural labour contracts were oral.[29] The *khatedars* basically gave up their responsibility in times of famine and left their labourers to fend for themselves. The absence of any kind of social and economic insurance caused the burden of famine to fall much more severely on labourers than on *khatedars.*

A small class of *khatedar*-landowners and merchant-moneylenders did reap the benefits from high prices of foodgrains. A rise in the prices of foodgrains generated by export trade coupled with no comparative rise in wages of labour created cash surpluses.[30] When the grain was cheap the wages were paid in kind and when the grain was expensive it was paid in cash.[31] The permanent labour on oral contract for twelve months was generally held for thirteen months.[32] All this led to the enrichment of landholding *khatedar* merchants under the aegis of colonial political economy.

A considerable amount of grain was held by Berar landowners in anticipation of high prices. These grains preserved in 'peos' (underground pits) were brought out when the prices were dear. Table 33 indicates the volume of foodgrain and raw cotton exports from Berar.

It is ironical that despite famine conditions, the region continued to export foodgrains and raw cotton. On average 23.9 per cent of Berar's total annual exports constituted foodgrains (Table 33). In a

[28] In the 1880s, one rupee contained 16 annas, each anna had 12 paise and 15 rupees constituted 1 pound-sterling. Source: K. L. Datta, *Report on the Enquiry into the Rise of Prices in India*, 4 Vols., Calcutta, 1914; *Index Numbers of Indian Prices, 1861-1926*, Department of Commercial Intelligence and Statistics, India, Calcutta, 1928; also see: G. A. Watt, *Dictionary of the Economic Products in India*, 6 Vols., in 9 pts., Calcutta, 1889-93; H. H. A., *Glossary of Judicial and Revenue Terms of British India*, Calcutta, 1855, revised edition, with case notes by A. C. Ganguli and N. D. Basu, eds., Calcutta, 1940; H. Yule and A. C. Burnell, *Hobson-Jobson: A Glossary of Colloquial Anglo-Indian Words and Phrases*, London, 1886, reprinted, 1968; *Encyclopedia Britannica.*

[29] *Notes on the Agriculturist of the District of Aurangabad, H. H. The Nizam's Dominion*, by Furdoonji Jamshedji, in *Hyderabad Affairs*, Vol. 1, pp. 801-33.

[30] *Report of the Indian Famine Commission, 1898*, London, 1898, p. 363.

[31] *Report of the Census of Berar, 1881*, Bombay, 1882, pp. 233-4.

[32] *Notes on the Agriculturist of the District of Aurangabad, H. H. Nizam's Dominion*, by Furdoonji Jamshedji, in *Hyderabad Affairs*, Vol. 1, pp. 801-3.

TABLE 33

Year	Foodgrain Exports in Mds.	% Foodgrain Exports to Total Exports	Raw Cotton Exports in Mds.	% Cotton Exports to Total Exports	Total Exports in Mds.
1879-80	250,130	16.1	1,004,398	64.8	1,549,793
1880-1	411,223	20.1	1,020,059	50.0	2,037,754
1881-2	2,011,062	45.0	1,572,052	35.5	4,421,710
1882-3	1,488,429	33.8	1,430,931	32.5	4,402,510
1883-4	847,408	28.3	1,027,785	34.3	2,990,857
1884-5	721,764	21.9	807,598	24.5	3,294,844
1885-6	1,320,721	30.7	1,278,108	29.7	4,289,640
1886-7	2,356,618	44.8	1,726,364	32.8	5,251,732
1887-8	1,519,458	43.8	921,100	26.5	3,463,158
1888-9	1,023,801	23.9	1,866,461	43.6	4,276,377
1889-90	580,521	15.9	1,902,429	52.3	3,635,968
1890-1	NA	NA	NA	NA	3,926,000
1891-2	1,943,000	36.2	1,714,338	32.0	5,355,000
1892-3	1,067,000	28.8	1,355,420	36.6	3,701,000
1893-4	2,020,372	53.7	1,651,022	43.9	3,760,000
1894-5	235,000	8.7	1,211,933	45.0	2,691,000
1895-6	475,000	12.4	1,954,056	51.3	3,809,000
1896-7	655,000	18.5	1,827,708	51.8	3,522,000
1897-8	257,000	8.2	1,686,115	53.9	3,128,000
1898-9	500,000	8.7	3,208,228	55.8	5,747,000
1899-1900	747,000	28.6	915,157	35.0	2,609,000
1900-1	198,000	4.6	2,183,142	51.5	4,233,000
1901-2	835,000	10.6	3,830,744	48.8	7,842,000
1902-3	483,000	7.6	3,218,399	50.8	6,324,000
Average	954,195	23.9%	1,709,284	42.7%	4,010,889

1 Md. = 80 lbs

Source: Report on the Rail and Road Borne Trade of the Hyderabad Assigned Districts, 1878-79 to 1902-3, published annually, Hyderabad.

situation of competitive prices, the export trade created bottlenecks in the free distribution of essential commodities. It encouraged hoarding and speculative trading and did little to abate the plight of the people. Table 34 presents a statistical picture of Berar in the late nineteenth century.

The data in Table 34 suggests there were several years of steep decline in wage/price exchange of jawari, i.e. 1876-80, 1887-9, 1896-7, and 1899-1900. During most of these years the region was exporting foodgrains. The death rate remained above 30 per 1000 for more than 60 per cent of the time while the region continued to export foodgrains.

TABLE 34

Year	Wage Annas per Day	Wage Index	Price of Jawari Rs. per seer	Jawari Price Index	Wage/ Price Exchange Jawari in seers	Wage Price Index	Mortality per 1000 in Berar	Mortality per 1000 Bombay Deccan
1870-1	4.33	100	.054	100	5.01	100	24.6	NA
1871-2	4.75	110	.044	82	6.70	134	17.7	NA
1872-3	3.75	87	.038	70	6.14	123	37.1	NA
1873-4	3.66	85	.024	46	9.29	186	22.8	NA
1874-5	3.5	81	.019	36	11.32	226	27.9	NA
1875-6	3.25	75	.026	48	7.80	156	40.3	NA
1876-7	3.33	77	.052	97	3.96	79	31.9	NA
1877-8	3.0	69	.061	113	3.04	61	28.1	NA
1878-9	3.5	89	.072	133	3.03	60	81.5	NA
1879-80	3.5	89	.056	105	3.85	77	23.7	NA
1880-1	3.0	69	.026	50	6.98	139	23.6	NA
1881-2	3.0	69	.031	58	5.99	120	29.1	NA
1882-3	3.0	69	.035	66	5.24	105	29.4	NA
1883-4	3.5	89	.039	72	5.59	112	51.3	NA
1884-5	3.0	69	.035	66	5.25	105	24.6	NA
1885-6	3.0	69	.040	75	4.60	92	34.0	NA
1886-7	3.0	69	.040	75	4.60	92	36.7	NA
1887-8	3.0	69	.058	108	3.22	64	45.3	NA
1888-9	3.0	69	.050	93	3.72	74	24.7	NA
1889-90	3.5	89	.044	81	4.96	99	42.5	NA
1890-1	3.75	87	.039	73	5.92	118	35.4	31
1891-2	3.91	90	.050	93	4.84	97	28.8	31
1892-3	3.91	90	.060	112	4.02	80	32.6	31
1893-4	3.91	90	.053	98	4.61	92	42.0	38
1894-5	3.91	90	.045	85	5.34	107	49.9	37
1895-6	3.91	90	.051	94	4.79	96	43.3	36
1896-7	3.16	73	.096	179	2.04	41	52.6	51
1897-8	3.33	77	.040	76	5.08	101	23.4	26
1898-9	3.33	77	.042	78	4.92	98	39.9	40
1899-1900	2.58	60	.102	189	1.58	32	82.7	66

* 1 Seer = 2.057 lbs
1 Rs = 16 Annas
1 Anna = 12 Paise
1 Rupee = 192 Paise

Sources: *Report on the Census of Berar, 1881*, Bombay, 1882; *Report of the Sanitary Commissioner, Hyderabad Assigned Districts for the Year 1897*, Hyderabad, 1898; *Prices and Wages in India*, Calcutta, 1905; *Manchester Guardian, 1850-1900*; K. L. Datta, *Report on the Enquiry in the Rise of Prices in India*, Vol. II (*Statistics of Prices*), Calcutta, 1915; *Statistical Abstracts Relating to British India, 1874-1917* (in multi-volumes), London, printed annually; *Index Numbers of Indian Prices, 1861-1926*, Calcutta, 1928.

General Administration of the Hyderabad Assigned Districts, printed annually from 1855-6 to 1901-2, Calcutta; *Report on the Revenue Administration of the Hyderabad Assigned Districts*, printed annually 1877-8 to 1901-2, Hyderabad; Bombay Mortality rate taken from Michelle Burge McAlpin, *Subject to Famine: Food Crisis and Economic Change in Western India, 1860-1920*, New Jersey, 1983.

The death rate increased to staggering proportion of above 40 per 1000 for more than ten years of the thirty year period for which the data is available. After 1890 there is also evidence of aggregate food availability decline. During that decade famines decimated 5 per cent of Berar's population. More than 143,000 lives were lost directly from starvation (see Table 36).

According to the Famine Commission Report of 1880, the average per capita consumption for Berar was 5 maunds (400 lbs) per annum.[33] The Census Report of 1881 gave 480,000 tons as the average annual consumption requirement of foodgrains in Berar.[34] The annual requirement increased with the rise in population. Table 35 gives total foodgrain output for Berar.[35]

TABLE 35

Year	*Total Foodgrain Output in Tons*	*Total Foodgrain Export in Tons*
1886-7	576,496	94,264
1887-8	540,813	759
1888-9	581,938	511
1889-90	515,709	290
1890-1	458,399	NA
1891-2	386,361	971
1892-3	391,207	533
1893-4	361,659	1,010
1894-5	354,109	117
1895-6	381,185	237
1896-7	177,735	327
1897-8	447,549	128
1898-9	390,185	250
1899-1900	10,998	373
1900-1	410,192	99

[33] *Report of Famine Commission, 1880*, London, 1881, p. 81.

[34] *Report on the Census of Berar, 1881*, Bombay, 1882, p. 236.

[35] The data for Tables 35 and 36 have been taken from the following sources: *Report on the Census of Berar, 1881*, Bombay, 1882; Tim Dyson, 'The Population History of Berar

The annual requirement of 480,000 tons when applied to the decade of the 1890s indicates a period of food availability decline compounded by entitlement failure. The decade of the 1890s was a period of successive famine cycles and high mortality rate per 1000 (see Table 34). Table 36 gives the figures for population, total foodgrain output and consumption requirement.[36]

TABLE 36

Census Year	*Population*	*Total Foodgrain Output in Tons*	*Total Requirement in Tons*	*Surplus/ Shortage in Tons*
1867	2,227,654	NA	445,530	NA
1871	2,231,565	580,332	446,313	+134,019
1881	2,672,673	600,000	536,967	+ 63,033
1891	2,897,491	458,399	579,498	- 121,099
1901	2,754,016	410,192	550,803	- 140,611
	Average	512,230	528,395	- 16,165

It should however be noted that throughout the colonial period, Berar's foodgrain exports averaged at 48,000 tons per annum.[37] Import figures are not available except for the year 1878-9. In that year Berar imported only 8,320 tons of rice and wheat—two luxury grains consumed only by the society elites.[38]

---

since 1881 and its Potential Wider Significance', *The Indian Economic and Social History Review*, XXVI, No. 2 (April-June 1989), pp. 167-203; *Report on the Revenue Administration in the Hyderabad Assigned Districts*, printed annually, 1877-8 to 1901-2, Hyderabad; *Seasons and Crop Report of Berar for the Year 1902-03*, Hyderabad, 1903; *General Administration Report on the Hyderabad Assigned Districts*, printed annually, 1855-6 to 1901-2, Calcutta; *Report on the Trade of the Hyderabad Assigned Districts*, printed annually, 1878-9 to 1902-3, Hyderabad; Peter Harnetty, 'Cotton Exports and Indian Agriculture', *Economic History Review*, Vol. 24, No. 3 (1971), pp. 414-29; *Famine Commission Report, 1880*, London, 1881; Tim Dyson, 'The Population History of Berar since 1881 and its Potential Wider Significance', *Indian Economic and Social History Review*, XXVI, No. 2 (1989), pp. 167-202.

[36] The data in Tables 35 and 36 has been analysed in the following manner:
(a) The foodgrain output has been calculated by multiplying jawari and wheat acreage with yield per acre, (b) Total requirement is calculated by multiplying per head consumption of foodgrains with total population.

Note: The sources for this data is the same as for footnote number 35.

[37] *Report on the Rail and Road Borne Trade of the Hyderabad Assigned Districts*, published annually from 1878-9 to 1902-3, Hyderabad.

[38] *Report on the Trade of the Hyderabad Assigned Districts for the Year 1878-79*, Hyderabad, 1880, para 35.

Due to the region's link to world market, over 30 per cent of the cultivated acreage was tied to cash crop cotton. The colonial state structure and rural credit network prevented a shift from cotton to foodgrain in times of need. The rigidity of the political economy deprived people of their entitlement. While famine devastated the land, the groups least affected were precisely those who profited from the cotton economy, i.e. the colonial state, European merchants, large landholding *khatedars*, merchant-moneylenders, and the village bania.[39] The primary producer lost out to cotton and in turn was effected by its impact. As mentioned earlier, the population of Berar in fact declined from 2,897,491 in 1891 to 2,754,016 in 1901 showing a dramatic decimation of 5 per cent of the population in the famine decade of the 1890s (see Table 36).

The structural changes brought about by the colonial cotton economy exposed the region to diseases such as cholera, small-pox, dysentery, diarrhea, fevers, etc. Under-nourishment and absence of institutional (medical/sanitary) safeguards kept the population constantly vulnerable to disease. Hunger was omnipresent but the prime reasons for deaths were: (a) gradual deterioration of the body, (b) diseases, (c) absence of proper facilities (medical/sanitary), (d) hoarding and export of foodgrains, and (e) inability of the wages to buy foodgrains at the prevailing prices.

The impact of famine differed in different parts of Berar. In some arid and hilly areas of the north and south (Melghat, Mehkar, Pusad, and Wun talukas), there was an actual shortage of food supplies. But in the plain talukas of Amraoti, Akola, Khamgaon, and Malkapur, the scarcity and famine was caused by entitlement failure as a result of high prices. In general then some classes were unaffected by famine while others were its severe victims. Lack of proper medical facilities and poor sanitary condition made mortality a universal factor that victimized all classes who were unfortunate to be caught in the grasp of famine.

Famine Victimization

The colonial literature of the period is replete with racial categorization of people and classes. During famine years such categorization were further peppered with race theories. It was generally believed among the officials that the lower castes and classes were racially weaker and

[39] *Central Provinces District Gazetteers, Buldana District*, Calcutta, 1910, pp. 310-24.

lethargic and therefore victims of famine. This idea heavily influenced the attitude of the colonial officials towards famine relief. For instance, Mr. J. A. Crawford, an official directly involved in famine relief operations, openly maintained that:

> The Berari is lazy and naturally averse to continuous labour. The discomfort and discipline of a large relief camp, resort to works at a distance from their homes, and a working day of 8 hours were sufficient tests to show that most applicants were in need . . . . It is true that many preferred to remain on the lowest wage to earning more by doing a fair task; but this was due more to the characteristic idleness of the Berari than to his having other resources.[40]

It was rather cruel and inhuman to expect long hours of labour from the famine victims who came to the relief camps broken in body and spirit. The reasons for coming into prominence of colonial race theory during famines are many: (a) the colonial state's inability to see a connection between the political economy and material condition of the people; (b) to shirk responsibility from involvement and expenditure in relief work; and (c) to provide a viable justification for famine mortality. A very strong economic justification for mortality was accorded thus:

> Birth and Death ratio are influenced by prices, especially among poorer sections of the population. In years of plenty when the prices of food grains is low, the people are able to obtain more food and of better quality for the small wages they earn, here their vigour and reproductive powers are increased [then] when prices are high. . . .[41]

Most victims of the famines were women, children, landless agricultural labourers, and small landholders who depended on family labour. The substantial farmers, big landholders, and merchant-moneylenders acquired government loans and employed cheap famine labour to improve their lands and grow cotton.[42] The lower classes were also the worst victims of diseases.

However the classes most severely hit by famines were small peasants and agricultural labourers. This class formed the bulk of Berar's population and 35.2 per cent of them were landless labourers

[40] J. A. Crawford, *Report on the Famine in the Hyderabad Assigned Districts in the Years 1899 and 1900*, Nagpur, 1901, para 13.

[41] *Report on the Administration of the Hyderabad Assigned Districts for the Year 1901-2*, Hyderabad, 1903, p. 191.

[42] An interview with F. W. A. Prideaux, Officiating Deputy Commissioner, Akola District, *Report of the Indian Famine Commission, 1898*, Vol. IV: *Central Provinces and Berar*, London, 1899, p. 40.

who survived by cadging during slack season.[43] The landless were usually low caste mahars and kunbis who also performed menial work such as: conservation, assistance in revenue collection, escorting revenue to treasury, as night watchmen, carrying reports of government officials, working as servants of public officers, guarding village boundaries, handling dead animals, sweeping public buildings, carrying corpses, carrying official property, repairing boundary marks, assisting in survey operation, repairing roads and such other menial work. In return they usually received a 'huq' from the village landholders which was usually an irregular sum and which was also paid irregularly.[44]

The small kunbi peasants employed family labour, devoted their entire time in fields and seldom hired labour.[45] Such small family farms which survived from crop to crop fared no better than the landless in weathering famine. The mortality rate among this class was the highest. The pressure of government revenue demand and the responsibility of landownership kept them pinned to the land. Mortality in the countryside was primarily as a result of this factor. The landless were more mobile in availing whatever little the government provided as relief. But the government relief was conditional to stern labour service. And relief licenses were issued to curb the landless from wandering during famines.

The ease with which full land revenue was collected even during famine years suggest that the landholding *khatedars* and marwari merchant-moneylenders were not so much affected by the famine as the cultivators.[46] Since the entire revenue was collected as usual, the government felt no need of granting remission. This hit the small kunbi peasants more harshly than the speculative landlords or merchant moneylenders.

[43] *Report on the Census of Berar, 1881*, Bombay, 1882, p. 145.

[44] *Rules under the Berar Land Revenue Code*, Nagpur, 1907.

[45] 'Peasant Life in the North East Deccan: Aurangabad', A Review of Furdoonji Jamshedji's, *Note on the Agriculturists of the District of Aurangabad, H. H. The Nizam's Dominion*, *Times of India*, 19 September 1879, in *Hyderabad Affairs*, Vol. 4, Bombay, n.d., pp. 371-7.

[46] *Central Provinces District Gazetteers, Yeotmal District*, Calcutta, 1908, pp. 149-62; *Report on the Revenue Administration in the Hyderabad Assigned Districts*, Hyderabad, printed annually from 1877-8 to 1901-2; *Report on the Administration of the Hyderabad Assigned Districts for the Year 1889-90*, Hyderabad, printed annually, 1860-1901.

The government did provide agricultural loans during famine years. But a meager sum of Rs. 15,000 per district was hardly sufficient to counter famine, considering that total revenue collected in a typical famine year (1896-7) was Rs. 71,81,170.[47] Such loans however were granted only to large landholding *khatedars*. Since such loans were recoverable and spending on relief was an expenditure without return, it was feasible for the government to advance loans only to the landholding classes of Berar.[48] According to Narayan Singh Babhut Singh, the tahsildar of Amraoti taluk: 'state advances made under the above Acts [Agriculturist Loans Act] are made after due enquiry into the solvency of the borrowers, and there is very little chance of either the principal amounts or their interest turning out to be irrecoverable debts. Therefore Government money thus spent always comes back to Government with interest, while money spend on relief works does not always bring a commensurate return.'[49] It was ironical that those who did not need assistance were given help while those who needed it could not avail it.

Famine Relief

One of the biggest problems of relief operation was the lukewarm attitude of the colonial state towards famine relief. The parasitic relationship between the state and agrarian society is a point to note. The official definition of famine (on which the entire famine relief was based) was often criticized by the officials themselves as 'inadequate and indifferent'. In 1897 the Sanitary Commissioner maintained:

> The official definition of death from starvation signifies that so long as a person has food before him, or the means of procuring it, he cannot die of starvation. This is a mistake, for physiologically the human body may be starved of every essential to its vitality in spite of the most nutritious food if digestion has been so impaired by the effects of chronic starvation that nutrient cannot be assimilated, and this form of starvation caused directly or indirectly many deaths. . . .[50]

[47] F. J. Bullock, *Narrative of the Famine in the Hyderabad Assigned Districts During the Year 1896-97,* Hyderabad, 1898.

[48] According to the *Report of the Indian Famine Commission, 1898*, on average only Rs. 15,000 were spent as Government loans for agricultural improvements.

[49] Mr. Narayan Singh Babhut Singh, Tahsildar, Amraoti Taluk, called in for interview, in *Report of the Indian Famine Commission, 1898*, London, 1898.

[50] *Report of the Sanitary Commissioner, Hyderabad Assigned Districts for the Year, 1897,* Hyderabad, 1898, para 37.

The government famine relief was usually in the form of repairing roads, railways, tanks, bridges, digging wells, etc. The famine labour was either paid in cash on sight or fed in kitchens and poor houses. The relief labour was paid either by task rate in groups or to individual labourer on a daily wage basis.

The victims were categorized according to their caste and physical traits for the purpose of relief. This random categorization was based not so much on need but on the victims' social background. A caste-based social and occupational categorization was adopted for the purpose of relief. The Famine Commission of 1898 found the following categories prevailing in Berar on the eve of the famine of 1899-1900:

Class I 'Special Class'—'It will include all workers of special qualifications, of whom a certain number will be required on the works. . . . It will include generally only good caste men for supplying water to the workers. . . .'

Class II 'Digger Class'—'Will ordinarily comprise all able bodied male workers who are capable of performing a full digger's task, but more generally all able-bodied men who are required to perform tasks, whether in quantity or kind, which are beyond the capacity of those who will be relegated to class No. III.'

Class III 'Carrier Class'—'Will include majority of the workers, the weaker men and those unable to dig, and almost all women and big children.'

Clause (e) 'This classification of relief workers is obligatory on both large and small works when carried out by daily labour.'[51]

Such a 'process of natural selection' was employed which naturally gave preference to one caste over another and to males over females.[52]

Every official of the Famine Commission generally agreed that the wage rate paid on both categories of task (group) labour or individual labour was inadequate to support existence at the prevailing prices.[53] The famine wage was fixed in relation to the price of the lowest kind of jowari in the market—a grain of discarded quality and a cause of health hazard. Even this type of consumer grain was always in scarcity due to high demand and the inability of famine wage to buy any other

[51] *Report of the Indian Famine Commission, 1898*, Vol. IV: *Central Provinces and Berar*, London, 1899, p. 36.

[52] *Report of the Sanitary Commissioner, Hyderabad Assigned District for the Year 1894*, Hyderabad, 1895, para 18.

[53] *Report of the Indian Famine Commission, 1898*, London, 1898, p. 42.

type of grain.[54] The famine relief wage and market supply of affordable grain did not in anyway help relieve the misery of famine victims. The irregular famine meal of bread, vegetables and *khichri* proved inadequate in protecting the relief seekers from starvation. The Sanitary Commissioner captured a rather dramatic image of the starvation victims of the famine of 1897 in the following manner:

> Shrivelled and haggard in appearance, arms thin and flabby, legs spindly and wasted in flesh, elbows and knees knobby, flattening of the buttocks, and atrophy of the mammary glands. The skin had a dirty and scurfy appearance; the hair lustreless, and of the color of dried grass, and the sufferers had often a patient and sad expression of face, like a dumb animal in pain, which was pitiable to see.[55]

Generally two groups of people sought famine relief. The first group were the settled families in the villages and the second were wanderers. At the approach of famine, hundreds and thousands of peasants and labourers abandoned their villages and began wandering the countryside and moving towards the cities. But families with small patches of land preferred to remain in the village come what may.

The colonial state was generally suspicious of the moving people as a political threat. During famines the state quickly moved to curb the mobility of wandering population by prohibiting people from one village to seek relief in the camps of other villages. Famine tickets were issued to families and individuals and its use was prohibited outside village boundaries. Government attempt to control mobility made the people reluctant to accept public relief. It prevented them from seeking relief from their kinsmen in other villages. The migration of labour from hills to plains was also constrained because of the limited volume of governmental relief operations.[56]

The famine relief works were often marred with bureaucratic delays and technical bottlenecks. When a village was designated for relief, the families in that village often had to wait for weeks before the Circle Inspector came around to issue a relief ticket which would

[54] Mr. Narayan Singh Babhut Singh, Tahsildar of Amraoti Taluk, called in for interview, *in Report of the Indian Famine Commission, 1898*, London, 1898.

[55] *Report of the Sanitary Commissioner, Hyderabad Assigned Districts for the Year 1897*, Hyderabad, 1898.

[56] Mr. C. Bagshawe, Conservator of Forest, Hyderabad Assigned Districts called in and examined, 8 March 1898, in *Report of the Indian Famine Commission, 1898*, London, 1898.

qualify them for availing government aid. After this process the families had to wait for the opening of actual relief houses. During the famine of 1896-7 the actual relief works were not opened until March of 1897 even though famine-like conditions existed all over Berar from November 1896.[57] This victimized the wandering as well as settled families.

As mentioned earlier the famine relief work was organized either on an individual labour-wage basis or in gangs under the supervision of gangman. The official time-keepers supervised the wage disbursement of both the categories of famine labour. The labourers generally had to pay a weekly *dasturi* (commission) to the gangman and time-keepers to guarantee their continued employment. Since work was conditional to relief, hiring and firing became a profitable business.[58] The government paid relief work was thus ranked with misuse and corruption which added on to already victimized famine relief seekers of Berar.

Often the famine victimization was caused by conflict and friction between officers of Public Works Department and the Civil Service.[59] The differential rate between Bombay Famine Commission and the Berar wage caused confusion, conflict, and delays in the disbursement of finances. It was noted that Berar grain wage in both categories of diggers and carriers was 1 chattack less than the rate prescribed by the Famine Commission.[60] Often times the relief works provided uncooked food without water and people had to wander in search of water. The absence of any provision of drinking water was a common problem of the government relief works. Furthermore, the relief works were generally closed during Sundays and holidays while the daily wage was insufficient to procure a day's food supply.[61]

[57] F. J. Bullock. *Narrative of the Famine in the Hyderabad Assigned Districts During the Year 1896-97*, Hyderabad, 1898.

[58] From: Rustomji Faridonji, Deputy Commissioner, Buldana District, To: The Commissioner, Hyderabad Assigned Districts, dated 2 November 1901, in the *Proceedings of the Hyderabad Administration on Matters of Routine for the Month of December 1901*, submitted to the *Department of Revenue and Agriculture*, No. 416 (11 December 1901).

[59] *Report on the Famine in the Hyderabad Assigned Districts in the Years 1899 and 1900*, by A. J. Crawford, Nagpur, 1901, para 54.

[60] *Report on the Famine in the Hyderabad Assigned Districts in the Years 1899 and 1900*, by A. J. Crawford, Nagpur, 1901.

[61] Mr. Narayan Singh Babhut Singh, Tahsildar of Amraoti Taluk, called in and examined, in *Report of the Indian Famine Commission, 1898*, London, 1898.

Gender Bias and Famine

Traditionally women have played an active role in the society and economy of Berar. They performed a variety of work in the field, at home, and in the marketplace. But everywhere the gender roles were defined. At home she was engaged in cooking, cleaning, washing, taking care of the children, the elderly, the cattle and animals. Berari men spent relatively little time at home.

In fields the Berari women worked as agricultural labourers alongside men. The gender role in the field was defined by work differentiation.[62] Women seldom did ploughing or indulge in irrigation. Their labour was expended in preparing the ground for sowing, transplanting, weeding, picking (in the case of cotton), husking, winnowing, transporting, and storing grains in addition to ginning, spinning, grain-pounding, grass-cutting, selling cowdung fuel, wage-cotton and firewood in the market.[63] The life of toil of a typical Berari women is described by A. C. Lyall in the following manner:

> . . . with a heavy load on her head, an infant wrapped up and slung to her back, the kunbi women of the poorer classes will sturdily tramp some six or seven miles to market, sell the produce of her field there, and from the proceeds buy articles for household consumption, she will then trudge back home in time to prepare the evening meal for the family.[64]

The wages of agricultural labourers were also differentiated by gender. Jobs reserved exclusively for men were paid higher wages than jobs reserved exclusively for women. The Famine Code defined the gender roles in relief works by designating the work of 'digging' to males and the work of 'carrying' (earth or gravel) to females. The rationale of this wage differential was that the physical strength expended on

[62] *Report on the Census of Berar, 1881*, Bombay, 1882, p. 233.

[63] *Note on Cotton in Berar*, by E. A. Hobson, Survey and Settlement Officer, Berar, Hyderabad, 1887, in the *Proceedings of the Department of Revenue and Agriculture*, Fibre and Silk Branch (1887), Nos. 22-23; *Report on the Census of Berar, 1881*, Bombay, 1882, p. 233; *A Report on Cotton Growing in India*, by Arno Schmidt, Secretary, International Federation of Master Cotton Spinners and Manufacturers Association. This is a report of Secretary's visit to India, December 1911-January 1912. From: Captain Meadows Taylor, Deputy Commissioner, North Berar, To: F. N. Maltby, Commissioner of Hyderabad Assigned Districts, in the *Proceedings of the Home Department*, Revenue Branch, No. 4/11, dated 20 August 1858.

[64] As quoted in *Rules under the Berar Land Revenue Code*, Nagpur, 1907, pp. 126 and 146.

certain tasks like digging and ploughing were physically more demanding than carrying and weeding.[65] The authoritarian males at the level of the state and civil society basically determined the gender based wage differential in which women had no voice. Colonial officials noted that Berari men seriously objected to the equalization of wage rate on famine relief works. The colonial state basically accepted such an objection without question.[66]

The wage differential was also determined by gender based differential in the quantity of food intake. It was observed that since women consumed less ounces of food per meal compared to men, it was concluded that their labour performance was also less than that of men. So the ratio of difference was ordinarily set at the rate of 3:2.[67] This type of prejudice against women labour forced them to flock in large numbers at government relief works.[68] Children generally accompanied the mother and their plight was equally acute. Bias can also be noticed in the system of disbursing wages. Men were always paid in cash while women labour was paid both in kind and cash. The cash wage rate for female labour was fixed an anna lower than male wages. Similarly the grain wage rate for women was 2 to 4 oz lower than men.[69] Therefore the worst victims of Berar famines were women and children.

Resistance and Peasant Consciousness

In an atmosphere of general scarcity and hunger the grain-trains and carts plying in and out of Berar were targets of thefts, dacoities, robberies and general looting. Grain riots took place in Amraoti early

[65] Mr. Narayan Singh Babhut Singh, Tahsildar of Amraoti Taluk, called in for interview, in the *Report of the Indian Famine Commission, 1898*, London, 1898.

[66] *Report of the Indian Famine Commission, 1898*, London, 1898.

[67] Mr. Narayan Singh Babhut Singh, Tahsildar of Amraoti Taluk, called in for interview, in the *Report of the Indian Famine Commission, 1898*, London, 1898.

[68] Mr. Rustomji Faridonji, Deputy Commissioner, Basim District, called in and examined, 28 March 1898. *Report of the Indian Famine Commission, 1898*, London, 1899, p. 49.

[69] The data on cash and kind wages taken from the following sources: *Report on the Trade of the Hyderabad Assigned Districts for the Year 1881-82*, Hyderabad, 1882; *Report on the Trade of the Hyderabad Assigned Districts for the Year 1878-79*, Hyderabad, 1880 also titled *Rail and Road-Borne Trade Reports of Berar, 1878-79 to 1885-86*, published annually, New Delhi; Memorandum submitted by Mr. A. J. Dunlop, Assistant Commissioner, Hyderabad Assigned Districts with reference to the information asked, in the *Proceedings of the*

in the famine of 1899-1900. Peasants resorted to incendiarism to protest against high prices, export of grain, hoarding and speculation in expectation of higher profits.[70] There were petty riots in bazars, house trespass and general rise in offence against persons and property. In the cotton rich districts of Akola, Amraoti, Ellichpur, and Buldana, unemployed bands of people moved at night and attacked merchants and moneylenders. The government measures to curb 'crime' led to an increase in the number of persons in jails leading ultimately to overcrowding of prisons.[71] Table 37 gives total 'crime' figures for two comparative years of famine.

TABLE 37

District	*1898-9*	*1899-1900*	*% Increase*
Amraoti	1052	1907	81.2
Ellichpur	377	1260	234.2
Wun	428	1147	167.9
Akola	714	1542	115.9
Buldana	484	1369	182.8
Basim	464	1439	210.1
TOTAL	3519	8664	149.1

Source: Report on the Famine in the Hyderabad Assigned Districts in the Years 1899 and 1900, by J. A. Crawford, Nagpur, 1901, para 19.

In fact 1899-1900 saw the most severe famine ever to happen in Berar. Generally during famine the people from all parts of Deccan swamped into Berar with the expectation of obtaining relief from the cotton rich districts. These 'famine-wanderers' came in large numbers from

Hyderabad Administration for July 1878, No. 1043, Home, Revenue and Agriculture Department; *Report of the Famine Commission, 1880*, London, 1881; *Report on the Census of Berar, 1881*, Bombay, 1882; Memorandum on the subject of dietary in jails of Hyderabad Assigned Districts for 1880, in the *Proceedings of the Hyderabad Assigned Districts for the Month of September 1881*, submitted to the Home Department, No. 363, 19 September 1881; *Report of the Sanitary Commissioner, Hyderabad Assigned Districts for the Year 1897*, Hyderabad, 1898; *Report of the Indian Famine Commission, 1898*, London, 1898.

[70] *Report on the Famine in the Hyderabad Assigned Districts in the Years 1899 and 1900*, by J. A. Crawford, Nagpur, 1901, para 25.

[71] F. S. Bullock, *Narrative of the Famine in the Hyderabad Assigned Districts During the Year 1896-97*, Hyderabad, 1898, para 19.

Central Provinces in the north, Bombay Presidency in the west, and Hyderabad state in the south. For instance in the first three months (January-March) of 1899 more than 140,000 famine-stricken people swamped into Berar from the south but were marched back and handed over to Hyderabad authorities in April. Thefts and dacoities in the vicinity of relief works suggest the prevalence of general resistance to the transfer of population but force and violence was employed to drive the people back.[72]

The influx of starving people to the cities and towns remained a constant source of trouble and irritation to the colonial state.[73] The system of issuing licenses and relief tickets (mentioned earlier) was a scheme designed to curb the mobility of famine- stricken people.

In 1898 Mr. F. W. A. Prideaux, the officiating Deputy Commissioner of Akola, reported seeing people eating the flesh of dead animals.[74] It was also during this time Mr. F. S. Bullock recorded that the 'idea of dying in one's own village became stronger' so that the people were reluctant to go to government relief works.[75] Bullock also observed that the people were suspicious of the government relief works and kitchens. Hard work and low pay discouraged them from seeking relief. The works were generally located at a distance from the villages. Sickness and weakness prevented people from going to work and/or looking for work. In such a state of misery the people often lost their ability to protest.

Dipesh Chakrabarti in his study of British colonialism has observed the violent manner in which colonial medicine was introduced in Bengal and the dread which the hospitals and dispensaries caused in the countryside. He has also shown how people perceived colonial field hospitals and dispensaries as instruments of terror rather than relief.[76]

[72] *Rules under the Berar Land Revenue Code*, Nagpur, 1907, pp. 311-17.

[73] Written statement of evidence by the Reverend Father A. Sanchon, Roman Catholic Priest, Ellichpur, dated 26 February 1898, *Report of the Indian Famine Commission, 1898: Being Minutes of Evidence*, etc., Vol. IV: *Central Provinces and Berar*, London, 1899, p. 342.

[74] Interview of Mr. F. W. A. Prideaux, Officiating Deputy Commissioner, Akola District, in the *Report of the Indian Famine Commission, 1898*, London, 1899, p. 40.

[75] F. S. Bullock, *Narrative of the Famine in the Hyderabad Assigned Districts During the Year 1896-97*, Hyderabad, 1898, para 18.

[76] See Dipesh Chakrabarti, in *Subaltern Studies: Writings in South Asian History and Society*, Vols. 3 and 4, Ranajit Guha, ed., Delhi, 1984 and 1985.

Colonial medicine introduced in Berar added similar plight to the suffering of the people. The field hospitals, relief kitchens and poor houses became dreadful symbols of awe and fear which the people generally avoided. The government ordered village patels to distribute cholera pills and instruct the famine-stricken people to administer it.[77] The coercive violence of colonial approach to treatment, without prior education of the people, could only lead to further perpetration of oppression.

Conclusion

This chapter argued that the development of cotton economy under colonial patronage had a deleterious impact on the material condition of people. The rise of cotton towns along railroad tracks attracted population and created the problem of sanitation. Absence of institutional safeguards and preventive measures created conditions for the rise of water- and wind- borne diseases. The rich black soil of Berar was a justification for an anti-irrigation attitude of the colonial bureaucrats. A basic flaw in the colonial understanding of the cause of famine was exposed when the officials surmised that famines in Berar occurred due to the failure of rains. If the soil is naturally rich and needs very little water to grow crops, then how can famine occur due to failure of rains?

A close scrutiny of the data reveals that there was never a shortage of foodgrains in Berar except in the decade of the 1890s. Hoarding and export trade kept the prices high and wages relatively immobile. The wage-price exchange of jawari showed a slow declining tendency. The consequence of such a decline was a steep rise in mortality rate. More than 60 per cent of the time (18 of the 30 years) showed mortality rate exceeding 30 per thousand. This was higher than the neighbouring province of Bombay Deccan (Table 34). The decade of the 1890s and the years of high mortality, i.e. 1872-3, 1875-6, 1878-9, 1883-4, 1886-8, 1889-90 were clear cases of entitlement failure when mortality exceeded 35 per 1000 (see Table 34). The general tendency was also towards a gradual decline in entitlement leading to undernourishment, disease vulnerability, and mortality.

[77] *Report on the cholera outbreak in the Akola Districts for the Year 1890*, by Dr. Reilly, Civil Surgeon and Mr. Steinhoff, the Medical Officer, in the *Report of the Sanitary Commissioner, Hyderabad Assigned District for the Year 1890*, Hyderabad, 1891.

The worst victims of famine were the landless agricultural labourers and small landholders. Foodgrain and hoarding excited crime and protest as a reaction to famine victimization. The commercialization of agriculture instead of generating prosperity relegated Berar to a state of economic and social backwardness in which famine and death stalked the land.

Conclusion

MANY GENERAL arguments have been made about the relationship between colonialism, capitalism and cotton in India. The historical evidence from Berar adds nuances to and suggests qualifications to those general arguments. Berar's case is somewhat distinctive but at the same time relevant to the broader arguments about agrarian relations under colonial conditions and transition to capitalism. This book has attempted to place Berar within the framework of India's colonial experience. As a part of the colonial economy and linked to the world market, Berar's experience was not very different than the experience of India as a whole. But within the framework of a broader colonial experience, Berar's case was somewhat distinctive. The occupation, development and the ruin of Berar was a step by step process of change.

While other regions of Bombay, Bengal, and Madras presidencies developed some manufacturing industries by the close of the century, Berar did not develop a single industry even though 35 per cent of its cultivable land was engaged in cotton. As a major supplier of raw cotton to Great Britain, Berar remained connected to the world economy. The capital accumulation necessary for the material improvement of the economy and society did not happen. Despite a highly organized cotton economy, famines could not be prevented.

The transition from pre-colonial *balutedari* to *khatedari* was a process which required homogenization and standardization of the society. This was a transformation from crop share system under *balutedari* to land proprietary system under the colonial state. This basic change led to the decline of *balutedari* system and the creation of a new social class of government registered *khatedars*. The *khatedari* rights on land were guaranteed only so long as the revenues were remitted in due time. The *balutedars* had to be eliminated because they formed local power bases and threatened the position of the colonial state. Therefore all forms of alternative systems had be replaced with a single power—of the colonial state. *Balutedari* was also perceived as a political danger. Its class based structure and caste hierarchy was too strong for the colonial state to penetrate. Disarming and destroying the ghurries and citadels of the *balutedars* was necessary to neutralize their power in the countryside. This was shrewdly undertaken by transforming the patels and patwaris into local colonial officials. The assistance of patels and patwaris was also essential for conducting land survey and settlement operations to standardize the revenue system.

Although the main aim of the survey and settlement operation was to account for all the cultivable land in Berar, much more was achieved in the process. The standardization of land revenue rate and the creation of private property rights in land was the direct outcome of the survey and settlement operations. Private proprietorship guaranteed regular payment of land revenue. It also strengthened the colonial state control. The standardized measurement was undertaken to account for all the cultivable land in the region. The technical instruments needed for the achievement of uniformity were brought from Europe, i.e. the theodolite, the prismatic compasss, standard English acre, uniform weights and measures, soil classification and crop experimental stations.

The land settlement made the mineral resources of the province available to the colonial state. The colonial survey parties identified and located the wealth of Berar for future extraction. Its recommendation opened new avenues for the state to raise revenues through new taxes, i.e. salt tax, *abkari* (liquor and opium), transit duty, forest tax, town duty, custom duty, village tax and several other taxes. Survey operations gave the colonial state access to pastures and forests. The state takeover of the hitherto freely available natural resources occurred as a result of colonial survey. The gradual disappearance of forests and pastures under the impact of theodolite and prismatic compass had dramatic consequences on the environment of Berar. Nevertheless, the main purpose of the colonial state was achieved. A strong class of government registered tenants (*khatedars*) came into being. The loyalty of this class guaranteed the political support which the colonial state sought in Berar.

The *khatedars* were created by the survey and settlement opeartions. The creation of this class guaranteed land revenue to the state as the landholding rights were made conditional to revenue payments by law. Artificial boundaries were drawn to define property rights in land. This was a dramatic shift from the pre-colonial *balutedari* system under which, the right over the produce of the land was more important than land itself. But under the new dispensation, every individual *khatedar* was made responsible for revenue payment. This institutionalized form of private property in land was a major development in Berar agrarian society. The creation of this new class did not in any way obliterate the caste basis of the society. If anything the class nexus made caste more hierarchical than before. This manifested itself in the development of sub-tenancy in the region. A very large number of cultivators in Berar were *bhagindar* share-croppers. The colonial state officially did not recognize the existence of subtenancy in Berar. The fate of *bhagindars* was left in the hands of the *khatedars*. The *bhagindars* had no recourse to the courts even though *khatedars* charged them rental rates five times higher than the regular assessment rate. Eventually subletting, rack-renting and indebtedness became the characteristic feature under the state sponsored *khatedari* system.

Once the *khatedari* system was put in place, it became easy for the colonial state to redefine the social standing of various castes according to their loyalty and disloyalty towards the state, i.e. castes of good social standing and castes of bad social standing. The colonial law was applied to the group as defined in the Census Reports, Gazetteers, Settlement Reports and Government Proceedings. The groups of people met their fate according to the category in which they fell, i.e. loyal castes and tribes, criminal castes and tribes, etc. However, such categorization proved to be fallacious because generally a wide diversity of occupation existed within a caste. For instance, within the caste of kunbi there were mali kunbis (gardners), teli kunbis (oil pressers), nai kunbis (barbers), manbhav kunbis (brahmans), etc.

The *khatedari* system further gave rise to the *izaradari* system. Under the latter, the government gave large chunks of forests and pastures to be cleared and brought under the plough at a gradually increasing rate of revenue until such time when full *khatedari* rights could be established. This gave a fatal blow to the pastures and forest reserves of Berar.

Even though cotton cultivation was undertaken, the technology remained stagnant. The economy was caught in a situation of labour abundance and capital scarcity. The *khatedars* as colonial agents organized labour on the land. This relieved the colonial state of the responsibility of undertaking the production of raw cotton. The *khatedari* class and the colonial policies kept the region pinned to agriculture and prevented the growth of industries. The local skills of consumer goods manufacturing got severly hit, i.e. bricktile making, pottery, salt making, glass making, soap, ghur and sugar manufacturing, etc. Since the raw material was under the control of the colonial state, the local skills could not develop and gradually died out. During the days of famine, the people were left with no other alternative except to suffer in starvation. Over 97 per cent of the population in Berar was illiterate and neither the state nor the *khatedars* were interested in educating the masses. Nevertheless, the *khatedars* as a class collaborated with the state in catering to the demands of the London-based world market for cotton.

The tension between Slave States and Free States in North America in the mid-nineteenth century created a demand for cotton in the world market. The occupation of Berar in 1853 and the eventual development of a cotton economy was a direct result of this tension. The outbreak of the American Civil War and Lincoln's blockade of southern ports created a 'cotton gap' in the Atlantic trade. The cotton economy in Berar received an enormous boost during the civil war years (1861-5). It brought in a period of apparent boom and huge surpluses. As modern technology altered the physical landscape, the colonial state and European firms manipulated the political economy to their own advantage. Nothing percolated down to the masses. The metropolitan capitalists in London, the Indian merchant-moneylenders and landed *khatedars* cornered all the benefits of the cotton boom while the wages of peasant labourers remained below subsistence. Caught in the web of the colonial state and the world market, the primary producer lived in a constant state of desolation, devastation and famine. Despite the rhetoric of 'free trade', the state imposed restrictions on the operation of the market and prevented the development of a competitive wage system by pinning the peasants to land. The cash crop driven colonial economy inflicted heavy environmental damage resulting in hunger, famine, disease and death.

After the establishment of the cotton economy, Berar was never to be the same again. Despite its link to the world market, there was always a shortage of working capital in the countryside. The creation of a government registered tenant and *khatedari* rights on land attracted a new class of moneylender marwaris to the region. The lure of cotton and *khatedari* rights on land brought the marwari's to Berar villages. Settling down in rural areas in *kirana* shops, the marwaris extended small credit to cultivators in return for raw cotton and grains. The moneylenders were not so much interested in land but the produce of the soil. The standard practice was to extend credit and lay claims on the produce of the soil. They also acted as middlemen and suppliers of cotton to European firms and Bombay merchants.

Much of the cotton in Berar passed through the *sahukar's* books and was under advances. But the price of cotton was fixed in Liverpool and London. The moneylenders controlled the local supply of cotton but did not have much control over setting its price value. The value of Berar cotton was determined not by the moneylenders or cultivators but by the world market. The moneylender was only a small player in the big game of cotton. The exorbitant interest in Berar was due to the moneylender's inability to control the price of cotton. The colonial state controlled the economy and the only way the moneylender survived was through extortionate demands from the peasantry by controlling the produce of the soil. The moneylender was therefore not the sole reason for the existence of large-scale indebtedness in Berar. In an economy driven by the forces of external demand and supply, neither the *sahukar* nor the cultivator had much influence in setting the price of cotton. The European firms acquired cotton from the *sahukar's* at pre-fixed prices and the *sahukars* extracted cotton from indebted peasantry at a high interest rate. The ultimate looser was neither the *sahukar* nor the European firms. The primary producer besides being the ultimate looser was also heavily committed to produce cotton at the expense of foodgrains. The poverty and indebtedness of Berar were the twin results of the extortion of the colonial state and the moneylenders. Both were the agents of the capitalist world market.

As noted earlier, the survey and settlement operations of the early colonial period standardized and homogenized Berar by introducing uniformity on the ruins of the balutedari system. Such a step was necessary for the development of cotton economy. In fact this process was extended to sedenterize the entire population of Berar. The colonial state perceived mobility in the society as a threat to the state. Furthermore, the needs of raw cotton demanded a sedenterized population. The most mobile class of the Berarian society in the nineteenth century were the Banjaras. Traditionally they were the carriers of goods and services accross the land. Over the course of centuries, the Banjaras had developed a social organization of their own. The mobile villages of the Banjara tandas governed their affairs by their own laws and seldom referred their cases to the colonial courts. They also provided a communicating link between the people living in isolated pockets of the region. This was perceived by the state as a political threat. Similarly the Banjara attitude towards religion was outside the mainstream Hindu-Islamic tradition. The Bhagats of the Banjara society were more closely associated with the bhakti and sufi tradition which had historically questioned the beliefs and practices of the Hindu-Muslim orthodoxy. The Banjara social customs and practices were unorthodox and informal. Their attitude towards women was also very different. While the Hindu-Muslim society practised infant marriage and prohibited widow remarriage, the Banjara society permitted widow remarriage and prohibited the marriage of girls before the age of puberty. Similarly the Banjara custom even allowed courtship and sex among couples before marriage. Although distinct and different, the Banjara society and culture challenged neither the colonial state or the mainstream Hindu-Muslim culture. But the distinct, independent and fluid nature of the Banjara culture invited the combined wrath of the colonial state as well as the mainstream religious orthodoxy. The systematic persecution of the Banjaras was another grim tale of colonial legacy in Berar. The introduction of the 'pass system' to curb Banjara mobility was a colonial device not only to destroy the Banjara unity and culture but to sedenterize them as well.

Right from the beginning the state shied away from spending on the general economic development outside the framework of cotton economy. An official anti-irrigation argument was provided to justify the absence of government spending on irrigation and public works. Accordingly the state argued that since the soil of Berar was naturally rich, it needed very little water to grow crops. Therefore the colonial officials saw no need of public spending on building dams and irrigation projects. But ironically, whenever famines and scarcity occurred, the state pointed to the failure of rain as the cause of such calamity. If the soil was naturally rich and needed little water to grow crops then how can famine be caused by the 'failure of rain'. The colonial reasoning was self-contradictory. The devastating famines which took hundreds and thousands of lives was a consequence of such a defaulted colonial reasoning. The famines in Berar were caused not so much by failure of rains but by the colonial political economy of control and indifference—

control of the market and indifference to public works. The absence of any type of social or economic insurance caused the burden of famine to fall much more heavily on peasant labourers than on any other class.

The colonial logic of explaining famine fell short of explaining the declining wage-price exchange rate of jawari as the cause of mortality. The inability of wages to keep up with prices kept a large percentage of agrarian population on the brink of subsistence. Insufficient calorie intake kept the general mass undernourished and vulnerable to disease. The grim irony of the late nineteenth-century Berar was that the region was exporting foodgrains and cotton even though the 1890s was clearly a period of entitlement failure and resulting subsistence crisis. The available statistics show that there was no aggregate food availability decline but a decline in exchange entitlement. This decline was a consequence of inflationary prices caused by the rise in external demand for foodgrains and cotton from Berar.

The book has highlighted the conflict of interest between the colonial state and general mass of population. As the state began to attack and sedentarize the diverse, dynamic, and mobile society of pre-colonial Berar, the people reacted to it by resistance. The first thing the colonial state did after the takeover was to deal with the mobility of the society which posed an active threat to colonial political power. So naturally the colonial political and military machine was directed towards Gonds, Korkus and Banjaras. The Gonds and Korkus had from time immemorial lived in the forests and hills and had constantly communicated with the plains people of the Poorna valley. They had traditionally provided labour during the harvest season and exchanged forest products with those of the plains. Similarly the Banjaras were the keepers of bullock carts and carriers of goods and services from one part of the province to another. The colonial state ever suspicious of the moving people felt its authority challenged. But not without resistance was such mobility suppressed and even then not completely.

Resistance in Berar expressed itself in many different forms. It was primarily a challenge to colonial authority and its collaborators. It never let the colonial state to be at ease until such time as their will to resist was broken by the devastating famines of the 1890s. The resistance began immediately after the takeover when the state tried to implement survey and settlement operations in the region. Resistance in the form of strikes in the measuring and classing establishments against oppressive superintendents was prevalent from the early days of British raj in Berar. The colonial bureaucracy also had to grapple with the agrarian discontent of *khatedars* and *bhagindars* in the countryside. Such discontentment was usually expressed in the form of crop robbing and illegal sale of agricultural goods; raids on government controlled pastures and woodlands; illegal grazing; unauthorized contraband agriculture along hill slopes and river banks, etc. When the cotton economy came into existence and the state imposed market control laws, the sale and purchase of cotton outside the government designated markets continued despite the official ban. Similarly, the short staple *khandeshi* cotton was continued to be grown despite government warning against its cultivation due to the lack of its export value. In fact native *khandeshi* eventually succeeded in replacing the export variety of *jhari* and *bani* cotton. During periods of scarcity and famines when cotton and foodgrains continued to be exported on the face of hunger, the people reacted by resorting to dacoities, robberies, riots, and attacks on railways and state treasury offices.

Since moneylenders were the agents between the colonial state and cultivators, the latter's resentment was often directed towards the moneylenders. The moneylenders were frequently perceived as collaborators of the colonial state. Often times they were beaten and chased out of the village for dishonest practices. A similar fate awaited the pathan and afghan moneylenders who pestered people on pay days. Absenteeism from home and neglect of the cotton crop was also resorted to because in most instances the cotton crop was mortgaged to the moneylenders. There was a general antipathy towards the moneylender because of his activities and relationship to the colonial state.

Resistance to colonialism was also expressed by the people in the form of refusal to answer questions on race, caste, religion and language to the census takers. The Banjara resistance to the colonial state was much more social than political. The Banjara society had always been a self-sufficient community with its own laws and courts which provided a parallel alternative to the colonial system. The Banjaras seldom referred their disputes to colonial courts and preferred to settle their differences among themselves. Their lifestyle also challenged both the Hindu and Muslim orthodox beliefs and practices. The orthodox looked with disdain at Banjara practices of the prohibition of infant marriages, sanction for divorce and widow remarriages, courtship before marriage, pre-marital sex, parity between genders, etc. It was no surprise then that the colonial state and the Hindu-Muslim orthodoxy became instrumental in the suppression of the Banjara tradition and culture.

In conclusion then even though the period began with the boom of cotton economy and ended with devastation, desolation and famine, yet the human factor of resistance provided the people with sustenance from the tragedy of colonialism. The colonial documents do not record the sentiments of people. It was of no use to the colonial state. However, once in a while a proverb or two slipped out into the colonial documents. One such saying was about the change of weather during the cotton season which can also be applied to the people's feelings about colonialism in general:

> *Pade swatee-kapoos na mile wati* [1]
> (Should it rain during swati—October—you will
> not be able even to get cotton for wicks)

It is well known that when Berar came under British colonial rule, severe shortages of all resources were felt. Ironically this was also the case with cotton, despite Berar being the largest producer of cotton in colonial India. A. C. Lyall in his early Gazetteer reports many *be chiragh* (lampless) villages in Berar. The metaphor then can even be applied to the coming of colonialism in Berar, like the rain in October which took away all cotton and left nothing even for the wicks to light lamps in the homes.

[1] *Notes on Cotton in Berar, by* E. A. Hobson, Survey and Settlement Officer, Hyderabad, 1887, in the *Proceedings of the Department of Revenue and Agriculture,* Fibre and Silk Branch (November 1887), No.12.

Glossary

acre	43,000 sq. ft. or 14,333 sq. yds.
ainkali	deep black cotton soil
ang bail ki	share of body and bullock
asami	landless agricultural labourers
babul	a wild and thorny tree found commonly in the region
bahiram	a popular shrine in Ellichpur
bale	400 lb weight full-pressed
balutedar	distribution of village produce by caste or social rank
bandy	bullock cart
bani and jari	two popular raw cotton strains from Berar
banjaras	carriers of goods and services (gypsies)
bhagats	teachers in the Banjara community
bhagindar	share-cropper
bhakti	devotion and service
bhiga	1.75 English acres or 19,173 sq. yds.
bhoja	280 lbs weight
brahman	upper caste
candy	784 lbs weight in one Bombay candy
charka	indigenous manual cotton gin
cordery system	a colonial system of stacking cotton bales in the railway station
dangars and hatgars	Herdsman castes of Berar
deshmukh	district head in pre-colonial Berar
deshpandya	district accountant
dher	untouchable caste
dhura	landstrip demarcating the fields
dimmat	primary clan of the branch families
do amli	double government
dokra	a loose bag of cotton (130 lbs)

gaothan	common village sites for threshing and winnowing
ghurry	fortification around a village
gonds and korkus	forest and hill tribes of Melghat
gota pather	stone pillars to demarcate land
hoondakurs	pre-colonial tax farmers of cotton routes
inam	revenue free land grants
izara	waste lands and forests given out for clearance on leases ranging from 10-30 years on an increasing rental scale of assessment
jaglia	village watchman
jawari	millet – the main staple crop of Berar
kalaspati	lighter soil of the hill region
kapas	raw cotton
kati vilayati	foreign cotton strain from Khandesh
kharif	autumn crop
khatedar	government registered tenant
khel	lands held by an extended family of a primary clan
khichri	a broth of rice and vegetables
kirana	village sundry goods store
kunbi	a cultivating caste
mahars and mangs	lower caste menial labourers
malguzars	landowners of Narmada valley
mali	a caste of garden cultivators
mansabdar	a Mughal governor of a province
marwari or bania	moneylending caste
melghat and balaghat	forest and hill districts of Berar
metaire	subtenant or land sublet
miankalas	black soil mingled with lighter soil
monsoon	rain and winds
motasthal bagait	rain irrigated land
mound	a weight measure of 82 lbs
nagar and bukhur	light and heavy plough
naik	leader of a Banjara camp
nizam	head of the princely state of Hyderabad
oomra	name of Berar cotton in London market
palampat	land held on payment of a quit-rent but not necessarily hereditary
panchayat	local village government
pargana	an administrative district under Mughals
patasthal bagait	lands irrigated by channels, streams and wells
patel	village headman

patwa patrak	village rent rolls
patwari	village accountant
payanghat	dark alluvial land north and south of the Purna river
peos	grain pits used for storage
pluviometer	a rain gauging instrument
purna	main river in Berar
purza or poorza	paper or written contract used in cotton trade
rabi	spring crop
raj	British rule over India
sahukar	village moneylender
sanad	title deed for land ownership
subah	a province of Mughal empire
sutta	a written contract for transaction
taccavi	government loans for agriculture
taluka	subdivision of a district
tanda	a Banjara encampment
thuck	weighing yard for cotton
warli	earthen mound to demarcate field boundaries
watan	geographical area or territory of affinity
zamindar	landlord or holder of an estate on a fixed assessment

Bibliography

PRIMARY SOURCES

Archival/Manuscript Sources

Governement Reports (NAI, IOLR, BML and CSL)

An interview by Mr. C. Bagshawe, Conservator of Forest, Hyderabad Assigned Districts, called in and examined, 8 March 1898, in *Report of the Indian Famine Commission, 1898,* London, 1898.

Cotton Report of the Hyderabad Assigned Districts for 1878-79, Hyderabad, 1879.

Mr. Bahmanji Jamasji's Report, in the *Indian Famine Commission, 1881*, p. 299.

Note by Mr. J. B. Peile, in the *Report of Famine Commission, 1881*, p. 163.

'Irrigation as a protection against famine', a note by the General Secretary, Public Works Department, in the *Report of Famine Commission, 1881*, p. 52.

Report of the Indian Famine Commission, 1880, London, 1881.

Report of the Indian Famine Commission, 1898, Being Minutes of Evidence, etc., Vol. IV: *Central Provinces and Berar*, London, 1899.

Prices and Wages in India, 22nd Issue, compiled in the Office of the Director-General of Commercial Intelligence, Calcutta, 1905.

General Administration Report on the Hyderabad Assigned Districts for the Year, printed annually from 1855-6 to 1869-70 by John Gray, Calcutta. Thereafter as *Report on the Administration of the Hyderabad Assigned Districts*, from 1870-1 to 1904-5 by Residency Government Press, Hyderabad (IOLR and BML).

Index Numbers of Indian Prices, 1861-1926, Department of Commercial Intelligence and Statistics, Calcutta, 1928.

F. W. A. Prideaux, Officiating Deputy Commissioner, Akola District, *Report on the Administration of the Registration Department of the Hyderabad*

Assigned Districts for the Year, printed annually from 1872-3 to 1901-2, Hyderabad.

From: Lt. Col. Warren Hastings, IG of Registration, Hyderabad Assigned Districts, To: The Commissioner, Hyderabad Assigned Districts, Chikalda, dated 29 May 1908, in *Report on the Administration of the Registration Department of the Hyderabad Assigned Districts for the Year 1901-2*, Hyderabad, 1902.

Report of the Indian Famine Commission, 1898, Vol. IV: *Central Provinces and Berar*, London, 1899.

An interview by Mr. Narayan Singh Babhut Singh, Tahsildar, Amraoti Taluk, in *Report of the Indian Famine Commission, 1898*, London, 1898.

Interview of Mr. F. W. A. Prideaux, Officiating Deputy Commissioner, Akola District, in the *Report of the Indian Famine Commission, 1898*, London, 1899.

Dr. Reilly, Civil Surgeon and Mr. Steinhoff, the Medical Officer, *Report on the Cholera Outbreak in the Akola District for the Year 1890*, in the *Report of the Sanitary Commissioner, Hyderabad Assigned Districts for the Year 1890*, Hyderabad, 1891.

Rivett-Carnac, Harry, *Report on the Operations of the Cotton for the Year 1867*, Bombay, 1869; *Report on the Cotton Department for the Year 1868-69*, Bombay, 1869 (IOLR); *Annual Report of the Cotton Department for 1870-71*, in the *Proceedings of the Department of Agriculture, Revenue and Commerce*, No. 8/11, dated February 1873.

Report on the Revenue Administration of the Hyderabad Assigned Districts for the Year, printed annually from 1877-8 to 1901-2, Hyderabad.

An interview by Rustomji Faridonji, Deputy Commissioner, Basim District called in and examined, 8 March 1898, *Report of the Indian Famine Commission, 1898*, London, 1899.

Written Statement of evidence by the Reverend Father A. Sanchon, Roman Catholic Priest, Ellichpur (26 February 1898), in the *Report of the Indian Famine Commission, 1898, Being Minutes of Evidence*, etc., Vol. IV: *Central Provinces and Berar*, London, 1899.

Report of the Sanitary Commissioner, Hyderabad Assigned Districts for the Year, printed annually from 1870-1 to 1901-2, Hyderabad.

Seasons and Crop Report of Berar for the Year 1902-03, Hyderabad, 1903.

Report on Survey and Settlement Operations of the Hyderabad Assigned Districts for the Year, printed annually from 1872-7, Hyderabad.

R. A. W. Swinnerton, Executive Engineer, West Berar Division, called in and examined, 8 March 1898, in *Report of the Indian Famine Commission, 1898*, London, 1898.

Report on the Trade of the Hyderabad Assigned Districts for the Year. Sometimes also known as *Rail and Road-Borne Trade Report of Berar*, published annually 1878-9 to 1902-3, Hyderabad.

Temple, Richard, *Observations on the State and Administration of Hyderabad*

Assigned Districts, dated 14 December 1867 (IOLR).

Report on the Working of the Cotton Duties Acts in the Hyderabad Assigned Districts, 27 December 1894 to 31 March 1896.

From: Lt. Col. Warren Hastings, IG of Registration, Hyderabad Assigned Districts, To: The Commissioner, Hyderabad Assigned Districts, Chikalda, dated 29 May 1908, in *Report on the Administration of the Registration Department of the Hyderabad Assigned Districts for the Year 1901-2*, Hyderabad, 1902.

Hyderabad Affairs, 8 Vols., Moulvie Syed Mahdi Ali, ed., Bombay, 1883-6. The following references were located in these volumes (hereafter *HA*) (APSA).

Lord Dalhousie's Minute on his Indian Administration, Hyderabad, *Madras Spectator*, 2 August 1856, in *HA*, Vol. II, 1883.

Extract from Chapter XVIII of Edwin Arnold's, 'Marquis of Dalhousie's Administration of British India', in *HA*, Vol. 2, 1883, p. 401.

Extract from Dr. W. W. Hunter's *Imperial Gazetteers of India*, Vol. III, pp. 517-26, in *HA*, Vol. 1, pp. 359-65.

Furdoonji Jamshedji, *Note on the Agriculturists of the District of Aurangabad, H. H. The Nizam's Dominion*, Superintendent, Revenue Survey and Assessment, North West Division, in *HA*, Vol. 1, 1883, pp. 801-33.

Meadows Taylor, *The Story of My Life, 1857*, in *HA*, Vol. 2, 1883, p. 725.

'Peasant Life in North-Western Deccan: Aurangabad: A Review of Furdoonji Jamshedji's Note on the Agriculturists of the District of Aurangabad', in *Times of India*, 19 September 1879 and *Bombay Review*, 13 September 1879, in *HA*, Vol. 4, pp. 371-7 and 461-6.

Times of India, Bombay, 21 August 1867, in *HA*, Vol. I.

Times of India, Bombay, 21 June 1882, in *HA*, Vol. 4 (n.d.).

Records of the Geological Survey of India, Vol. II, pt. I, 1869 (February); *The Valley of the Poorna River, West Berar*, by A. B. Wynne, esq., in *Hyderabad Affairs*, Vol. 1, Bombay, 1883, pp. 407-12.

From: G. V. Yule, Est., C. B., Resident at Hyderabad to Secretary, To: The Government of Bombay in the Public Works Department, No. 185, dated 23 January 1865, in *Hyderabad Affairs*, Vol. IV, 1884.

India Political Consultations and Despatches (IOLR)

India and Bengal Despatches, Vol. 82, 17 August 1853, pp. 1140-2, from Board of Directors, EIC (London) to Financial/Railway Department, Government of India.

From: The Court of Directors in London, To: The Government of India, *India and Bengal Despatches*, Vol. 114, Political Department, No. 39, 13 July 1858.

From: S. H. Bullock, Deputy Commissioner in Charge of Commissioner's

Office, To: J. Allardyce, Office of Deputy Commissioner, East Berar, Ellichpur, 2 May 1859, in *India Political Consultations*, No. 109, *General Financial*, No. 147 of 1859, dated 8 July 1859.

From: S. H. Bullock, Deputy Commissioner in Charge of Commissioner's Office, Jaulnah, To: Thornhill, First Assistant Resident, Jaulnah, 7 May 1859, *General Financial*, No. 810 of 1859, Dept. No. 182, *India Political Consultations*, No. 109, 8 July 1859.

From: Messrs W. Nicol & Co., To: The Executive Engineer, Akola, dated 11 June 1867, *Hyderabad Affairs*, Vol. IV (1883-6).

The Hyderabad Assigned Districts, *India Daily News*, 27 January 1866, in *Hyderabad Affairs*, Vol. 5, 1883.

Newspapers

The Manchester Guardian, 1860-1900 (HUL).

'Peasantry of Aurangabad', Review of Furdoonji Jamshedji's *Note on the Agriculturists of Aurangabad*, *Bombay Review*, 13 September 1879, pp. 461-6.

PROCEEDINGS (NAI AND IOLR)

Foreign Department Proceedings

From: Meadows Taylor, Deputy Commissioner, Western Districts, To: Major Davidson, First Assistant Resident, Hyderabad, dated 13 May 1854, in the *Proceedings of the Foreign Department*, 1854.

From J. H. Bullock, Deputy Commissioner, North Berar, To: Major L. Davidson, Ist Assistant Resident at Hyderabad, 31 July 1854, Buldana, No. 303, in *Foreign Department Political Proceedings*, 28 March 1856.

From: Captain Taylor, Deputy Commissioner, North Berar, To: F. N. Maltby, Commissioner, Hyderabad Assigned Districts, dated 25 January 1858, Camp Hamerkher, in *Foreign Department Proceedings*, Nos. 147-8, 9 April 1858.

From: Harry Rivett-Carnac, Cotton Commissioner, Central Provinces and Berars, Camp Sheogaon, 11 April 1868, No. 810, To: Secretary to Chief Commissioner, Bombay, in *Foreign Department Proceedings*, June 1868, Nos. 11-12.

From: H. Rivett-Carnac, Cotton Commissioner, Central Provinces and Berar, To: Lt. G. H. Trevor, Officiating Ist Assistant Resident, Hyderabad, No. 50, dated 13 February 1869, in *Foreign Department Proceedings*, May 1869, Nos. 49-51.

Exemption of cotton 'suttahs' from Stamp Duty [letters], in *Foreign Department Proceedings*, Government of India, Nos. 1-3, dated May 1872.

Resolution on the question whether Suttahs or Contracts entered into by the cultivators in Berar to deliver their cotton produce are liable to stamp duty when transferred by the endorsement, Foreign Department, Government of India, Nos. 5-7, dated April 1873.

From: A. J. Dunlop, Assistant Commissioner, Akola District, To: Secretary, Chamber of Commerce, Bombay, dated 11 June 1874, in *Foreign Department Proceedings of the Government of India*, (January 1874), Nos. 6-10.

Report on the Past Cotton Season in the Central Provinces and Berar, in *Foreign Department Proceedings*, Government of India, Nos. 6-10, September 1874.

From: Secretary to Government of India, Foreign Department, Calcutta, dated 24 June 1874, in *Report on the Past Cotton Season in the Central Provinces and Berar*, in *Foreign Department Proceedings of the Government of India*, Nos. 6-10, September 1874.

Note of A. O. Hume on 19 June 1874, in the *Report of the Cotton Trading Season of Central Provinces and Berar*, in the *Proceedings of the Department of Revenue, Agriculture and Commerce*, Fibre and Silk Branch (June 1874), Nos. 41-2.

From: R. J. Meade, Officiating Resident, Hyderabad, To: The Government of India, Foreign Department, No. 12, Hyderabad Residency, 10 April 1879.

Cotton Report on the Hyderabad Assigned Districts for the Year 1882-83, Hyderabad, 1883, in the *Proceedings of the Department of Revenue and Agriculture*, Agriculture Branch (December 1883), No. 7.

Cotton Seed Adulteration in Berar, in the *Proceedings of the Department of Revenue and Agriculture*, Fibre and Silk Branch (November 1884), Nos. 1 and 2.

Memorandum on the Special Features of the Hyderabad Assigned Districts Bearing on their Administration, in the *Proceedings of the Hyderabad Administration for the Month of April 1887*, submitted to the Foreign Department, No. 1025-R, dated 25 April 1887.

Memorandum by Lieutenant Colonel J. Fitzgerald, Deputy Commissioner, Wun District, dated 13 March 1886, in the *Proceedings of the Hyderabad Administration for the Month of October 1887*, submitted to the Foreign Department, No. 445-G, 31 October 1887.

Proceedings of the Hyderabad Administration for the Month of April 1887, submitted to the Foreign Department, No. 1025-R, dated 25 April 1887.

Imposition of Cotton and Grain Market Cessess by certain Municipalities in the Hyderabad Assigned Districts, *Foreign Department Proceedings*, June 1889, Nos. 275-8.

From: T. Chichele Plowden, Commissioner, Hyderabad Assigned Districts, To: The Secretary for Berar to the Resident at Hyderabad, dated 31 January 1890, in the *Proceedings of the Hyderabad Administration on*

Matters of Routine for the Month of October 1890, submitted to the Foreign Department, No. 70-G, 4 March 1890.

'On the proposed measures in connection with cotton cultivation in Berar', a note by D. Fitzpatrick, Resident at Hyderabad, in *Foreign Department Proceedings* (July 1890), No. 328.

From: A. J. Crawford, Secretary for the Berar to the Resident, To: The Commissioner, Hyderabad Assigned Districts, Hyderabad, dated 1 July 1891, in the *Proceedings of the Hyderabad Administration on Matters of Routine for the Month of July 1891*, submitted to the Foreign Department, No. 2457, 1 July 1891.

'Improvement of the Cotton Industry in Berar', by Dr. Augustus Voelcker, in the *Foreign Department Proceedings*, January 1891, Nos. 244-5.

Submission of monthly statements of excise duty collected and refunds allowed on exports of duty-paid yarns under the Cotton Duties Act, 1894, in *Foreign Department Proceedings*, No. 346/49, dated July 1895.

J. H. Sadler, Deputy Secretary, Finance Department, To: Government of India, 22 July 1895, in *Foreign Department Proceedings*, No. 163, dated June 1896.

Resolution: Government of India, Finance and Commerce Department, Calcutta, 3 December 1895, in *Foreign Department Proceedings*, No. 187, dated June 1896.

Extracts from the Proceedings of the Government of Madras in Political Department, in *Foreign Department Proceedings*, No. 169, dated June 1896.

Notice of Government of India's Finance and Commerce Department, Simla, October 1895, in *Foreign Department Proceedings*, No. 187, dated June 1896.

Adoption by Native States of the form of taxation introduced in British India with respect to cotton goods, in *Foreign Department Proceedings*, December 1896, Nos. 143-60.

Home Department Proceedings

From: Captain Meadows Taylor, Deputy Commissioner, North Berar, To: F. N. Maltby, Commissioner, Hyderabad Assigned Districts, in the *Proceedings of the Home Department*, Revenue Branch, No. 4/11, dated 20 August 1858.

From: The Officiating Commissioner, West Berar, To: The First Assistant Resident, Hyderabad, Akola, dated 17 November 1873, in the *Proceedings of the Hyderabad Administration for the Month of December 1873*, submitted to the Home Department, Nos. 1601, 1602 and 1603, 10 December 1873.

From: The Officiating Inspector General of Police, Hyderabad Assigned Districts, To: Officiating Commissioner, West Berar (Camp Manigaon), 30

October 1873, in the *Proceedings of the Hyderabad Administration for the Month of December 1873*, submitted to the Home Department, Nos. 1601, 1602 and 1603, 10 December 1873.

From: The District Superintendent of Police, Buldana District, To: The Inspector-General of Police, Hyderabad Assigned Districts, Camp Chicklee, 14 February 1873, in the *Proceedings of the Hyderabad Administration for the Month of December 1873*, submitted to the Home Department, Nos. 1601, 1602 and 1603, 10 December 1873.

From: Deputy Commissioner, Akolah District, To: The Commissioner, West Berar Division, Akolah, 26 June 1873, in the *Proceedings of the Hyderabad Administration for the Month of December, 1873*, submitted to the Home Department, Nos. 1601, 1602 and 1603, 10 December 1873.

From: Assistant Commissioner in Charge, Basim District, To: The Commissioner, West Berar, Basim, 28 May 1873, in the *Proceedings of the Hyderabad Administration for the Month of December 1873*, submitted to the Home Department, Nos. 1601, 1602 and 1603, 10 December 1873.

Proceedings of the Hyderabad Administration for the Month of October 1874, submitted to the Home Department, No. 99, 26 October 1874.

From: W. N. Baput, Tehsildar of Chandur, To: Deputy Commissioner, Oomraottee District, dated 28 April 1872, in the *Proceedings of the Hyderabad Administration for the Month of October 1874*, submitted to the Home Department, No. 99, 26 October 1874.

From: Mr. A. Farrer, Assistant Commissioner, Amraoti District, To: Deputy Commissioner Amraoti District, dated 15 August 1872, in the *Proceedings of the Hyderabad Administration for the Month of October 1874*, submitted to the Home Department, No. 99, 26 October 1874.

Letter No. 5391, From: R. H. Hudleston, Officiating Deputy Commissioner, Akola District, To: Commissioner, West Berar Division, Akola, dated 24 August 1872, in the *Proceedings of the Hyderabad Administration for the Month of October 1874*, submitted to the Home Department, No. 99, 26 October 1874.

Letter No. 3521, From: R. Hudleston, Officiating Commissioner, West Berar, To: First Assistant Resident, Hyderabad, dated 22 October 1872, Akola, in the *Proceedings of the Hyderabad Administration for the Month of October 1874*, submitted to the Home Department, No. 99, 26 October 1874.

Letter No. 139, From: F. W. Grant, Judge, Small Cause Court, Khamgaon, To: Commissioner, West Berar, Khamgaon, dated 10 September 1872, in the *Proceedings of the Hyderabad Administration for the Month of October 1874*, submitted to the Home Department, No. 99, 26 October 1874.

Letter No. 2127, From: J. Allardyce, Officiating Commissioner, East Berar, To: First Assistant Resident, Hyderabad, Oomraottee, 1 August 1872, in the *Proceedings of the Hyderabad Administration for the Month of October*

1874, submitted to the Home Department, No. 99, 26 October 1874.

Letter No. 106, From: H. C. Menzies, Judge Oomraottee Small Cause Court, To: Commissioner, East Berar Division, Oomraottee, dated 18 June 1874, in the *Proceedings of the Hyderabad Administration for the Month of October 1874*, submitted to the Home Department, No. 99, 26 October 1874.

Letter No. 1577, From: R. Bullock, Officiating Deputy Commissioner, Buldana, To: Commissioner, West Berar, Buldana, dated 5 July 1872, in the *Proceedings of the Hyderabad Administration for the Month of October 1874*, submitted to the Home Department, No. 99, 26 October 1874.

Letter No. 131, From: Abdul Hakk Kurnalkar, Extra Assistant Commissioner, Basim District, To: Assistant Commissioner-in-charge, Basim District, Basim, July 1872, in the *Proceedings of the Hyderabad Administration for the Month of October 1874*, submitted to the Home Department, No. 99, 26 October 1874.

Letter No. 409, From: J. T. Bushby, Deputy Commissioner, Oomraottee, dated 27 July 1872, in the *Proceedings of the Hyderabad Administration for the Month of October 1874*, submitted to the Home Department, No. 99, 26 October 1874.

Letter No. 1540, From: K. J. L. Mackenzie, To: Commissioner, East Berar Division, Ellichpur, dated 18 July 1872, in the *Proceedings of the Hyderabad Administration for the Month of October 1874*, submitted to the Home Department, No. 99, 26 October 1874.

Letter No. 857, From: Shrikrishna Nurhur, Extra Assistant Commissioner, Argaon, To: Commissioner, West Berar, Argaon, 17 September 1872, in the *Proceedings of the Hyderabad Administration for the Month of October 1874*, submitted to the Home Department, No. 99, 26 October 1874.

Letter No. 353, From: H. Sczepanski, Deputy Commissioner, Woon District, To: Commissioner, East Berar, Yeotmal, dated 1 July 1872, in the *Proceedings of the Hyderabad Administration for the Month of October 1874*, submitted to the Home Department, No. 99, 26 October 1874.

Letter No. 18, From: R. Thompson, Assistant Commissioner, Wun District, To: Deputy Commissioner, Wun District, Yeotmal, dated 11 July 1872, in the *Proceedings of the Hyderabad Administration for the Month of October 1874*, submitted to the Home Department, No. 99, 26 October 1874.

Letter No. 979, From: Nago Rao Jeyakrishna, Assistant Cotton Commissioner, East Berar, To: Deputy Commissioner, Oomraottee District, Oomraottee, dated 24 June 1872, in the *Proceedings of the Hyderabad Administration for the Month of October 1874*, submitted to the Home Department, No. 99, 26 October 1874.

From: Mr. Dinshaji Sorabji, Extra Assistant, To: Deputy Commissioner, Ellichpur District, Ellichpur, dated 15 July 1872, in the *Proceedings of the Hyderabad Administration for the Month of October 1874*, submitted to the

Home Department, No. 99, 26 October 1874.

From: Inspector General of Police, Hyderabad Assigned Districts, To: The First Assistant Resident, Oomraottee, dated 26 February 1874, in the *Proceedings of the Hyderabad Administration for the Month of April 1874*, submitted to the Home Department, No. 107, dated 6 April 1874.

From: Officiating Inspector General of Police, Hyderabad Assigned Districts, To: First Assistant Resident, Hyderabad, Oomraottee, dated 26 December 1873, in the *Proceedings of the Hyderabad Administration for the Month of January 1874*, submitted to the Home Department, No. 1865, 16 January 1874.

From: D. E. P. Rennick, Assistant Commissioner, Badnera District, To: Deputy Commissioner, Oomraottee, dated 19 June 1872, in the *Proceedings of the Hyderabad Administration for the Month of October 1874*, submitted to the Home Department, No. 99, 26 October 1874.

From: Mr. J. H. Burns, Extra Assistant Commissioner, To: Deputy Commissioner, Oomraottee District, dated 26 June 1872, in the *Proceedings of the Hyderabad Administration for the Month of October 1874*, submitted to the Home Department, No. 99, 26 October 1874.

From: Atmaram Bhicaji, Extra Assistant Commissioner, Oomraottee District, To: Deputy Commissioner, Oomraottee District, Oomraottee, 5 July 1872, in the *Proceedings of the Hyderabad Administration for the Month of October 1874*, submitted to the Home Department, No. 99, 26 October 1874.

Memorandum on the Habits and Tenets of the Manbhaus, by Captain Lane, District Superintendent of Police, Oomraottee, in the *Proceedings of the Hyderabad Administration for the Month of May 1874*, submitted to the Home Department, No. 270, 16, 30 April and 19 May 1874.

Memorandum by Commissioner, Hyderabad Assigned Districts on the Correspondence relative to the indebtedness of land-owners in the Assigned Districts, by Lt. Col. W. Nembhard, in the *Proceedings of the Hyderabad Administration for the Month of November 1874*, submitted to the Home Department, No. 111, 18 November 1874.

Report by Inspector General of Police on Working of Pass System of Surveillance of Banjaras suspected of Criminal Proclivities, in the *Proceedings of the Hyderabad Administration for the Month of February 1875*, submitted to the Home Department, No. 1637, 11 February 1875.

Memorandum on the subject of Dietary in Jails of the Hyderabad Assigned Districts for 1880, in the *Proceedings of the Hyderabad Assigned Districts for the Month of September, 1881*, submitted to the Home Department, No. 363, 15 September 1881.

Rules for the collection of the *Sutta* tax framed by Municipal Committee under Section 7 of Act IV of 1873. Under *Khamgaon Municipal Code*, in the *Proceedings of the Hyderabad Administration for the Month of April 1884*, submitted to the Home Department, No. 1028, 22 April 1884.

Book Circular No. XXXV of 1889, in the *Proceedings of the Hyderabad Administration on Matters of Routine for the Month of December 1889*, submitted to the Home Department, No. XXXV, 23 December 1889.

Hyderabad Residency Proceedings (APSA)

Extract from the *Proceedings of the Resident at Hyderabad*, No. 961, Hyderabad Residency, 20 April 1883.

Revenue, Agriculture and Commerce Department Proceedings

From: Cotton Commissioner, Central Provinces and Berar, To: Secretary, Chamber of Commerce, Bombay, dated 12 February 1868, in *Foreign Department Proceedings*, March 1868, Nos. 124-5.

From: The Commissioner, West Berar, To: First Assistant Resident, Hyderabad, Akolah, dated 13 May 1871, in the *Proceedings of the Department of Agriculture, Revenue, and Commerce*, No. 8/11, dated February 1873.

Harry Rivett-Carnac, *Annual Report of the Cotton Department for 1869-70 and 1870-71*, in the *Proceedings of the Department of Agriculture, Revenue and Commerce*, No. 8/11, dated February 1873.

Report on the Cotton Experiments in West Berar during the Season 1869-70, by Mr. A. J. Dunlop, Assistant Cotton Commissioner, West Berar, in *Annual Reports of the Cotton Department for 1860-67 and 1870-71*, by Harry Rivett-Carnac, Cotton Commissioner, in the *Proceedings of the Department of Agriculture, Revenue and Commerce*, No. 8/4, dated February 1873.

'Cotton Cultivation in the Central Provinces, the Berar, and the North West Provinces', in the *Proceedings of the Department of Agriculture, Revenue and Commerce*, No. 49, February 1873.

Report on the Cotton Trading Season in Central Provinces and Berar, 19 June 1874, in the *Proceedings of the Department of Revenue, Agriculture, and Commerce*, Fibre and Silk Branch (June 1874), Nos. 41-2.

From: A. J. Dunlop, Assistant Commissioner, Akolah District, To: Secretary, Chief Commissioner, Khamgaon, 13 February 1874, *Administrative Report of the Cotton Department (Bombay) for 1872-3*, in the *Proceedings of the Department of Agriculture, Revenue and Commerce*, Fibre and Silk Branch (February 1874), No. 37/38.

From: A. J. Dunlop, Assistant Commissioner in Charge of Cotton Statistics for Central Provinces and Berar, To: Secretary, Chamber of Commerce (Bombay), Camp Oomraoti District, 6 November 1874, in 'Cotton Prospects in Central Provinces and Berar', in the *Proceedings of the Department of Revenue, Agriculture and Commerce*, Fibre and Silk Branch (November 1874), No. 5.

Memorandum submitted by A. J. Dunlop, Assistant Commissioner, Hyderabad Assigned Districts, with reference to the information asked, in the *Proceedings of the Hyderabad Administration for July 1878*, No. 1043, Home, Revenue and Agriculture Department.

Cotton Report of the Hyderabad Assigned Districts for the Year ending June 1879, From: W. B. Jones, Commissioner, Hyderabad Assigned Districts, To: The Secretary for Berar to the Resident, Amraoti, dated 24 October 1879, in the *Proceedings of the Hyderabad Administration for the Month of November 1879*, submitted to the Home, Revenue and Agricultural Department, No. 2661, dated 25 November 1879.

Cotton Report of the Hyderabad Assigned Districts for 1878-79, Hyderabad, 1879, in the *Proceedings of the Department of Revenue, Agriculture and Commerce*, Fibre and Silk Branch (August 1882), Nos. 12-18.

Cotton Report of the Hyderabad Assigned Districts for the Year 1879-80, Hyderabad, 1881, Report written by Lt. Col. J. B. Bell, Officiating Commissioner, Hyderabad Assigned Districts, To: The Secretary for Berar to the Resident at Hyderabad, Amraoti (23 December 1880), in the *Proceedings of the Department of Revenue, Agriculture and Commerce*, Fibre and Silk Branch (August 1882), Nos. 12-18.

Cotton Report of the Hyderabad Assigned Districts for the Year 1880-81, Hyderabad (n.d.), in the *Proceedings of the Department of Revenue, Agriculture and Commerce*, Fibre and Silk Branch (August 1882), Nos. 12-18.

Mr. A. J. Dunlop's Memorandum on 'Cotton Prospects in the Berar', in the *Proceedings of the Revenue and Agricultural Department*, Fibre and Silk Branch (October 1883), No. 122.

Cotton Report on the Hyderabad Assigned Districts, 1882-83, Hyderabad, 1883, in the *Proceedings of the Department of Revenue and Agriculture*, Agriculture Branch (December 1883), No. 7.

Cotton Prospects in the Berars: A Memorandum, by Surgeon T. Hume, in the *Proceedings of the Revenue and Agriculture Department*, Fibre and Silk Branch (October 1883), Nos. 1 and 2.

Cotton Seed Adulteration: A Report, in the *Proceedings of the Department of Revenue and Agriculture*, Fibre and Silk Branch (November 1884), Nos. 1 and 2.

Note on Cotton in Berar, by E. A. Hobson, Survey and Settlement Officer, Berar, Hyderabad, 1887, in the *Proceedings of the Department of Revenue and Agriculture*, Fibre and Silk Branch (November 1887), Nos. 22-3.

From: Lt. W. H. Cornish, Officiating Secretary for Berar to the Resident at Hyderabad, To: Secretary to Government of India Revenue Department, Bombay, No. 178-G, dated 9 May 1887, Hyderabad Residency, in the *Proceedings of the Hyderabad Administration for the Month of May 1887*, submitted to the *Revenue and Agriculture Department*, No. 178-G, dated 9 May 1887.

From: R. D. Hare, Assistant Commissioner on Special Duty, To: The Commissioner, Hyderabad Assigned Districts, Bulgaon, 14 April 1887, in the *Proceedings of the Hyderabad Administration for the Month of January 1888*, submitted to Revenue and Agriculture Department, No. 9-R, 3 January 1888.

'Note on Indian Cotton', in the *Proceedings of the Department of Revenue and Agriculture*, Fibre and Silk Branch (May 1889), No. 25/27.

Memorandum on the Improvement of the quality of cotton grown in Berar, by Mr. E. C. Ozanne, Director of Land Records and Agriculture, Bombay, in the *Proceedings of the Department of Revenue and Agriculture*, Fibre and Silk Branch (July 1890), No.11.

From: R. D. Hare, Survey and Settlement Officer, Hyderabad Assigned Districts, To: The Commissioner, Hyderabad Assigned Districts. Yeotmal, dated 12 June 1890, in the *Proceedings of the Hyderabad Administration on Matters of Routine for the Month of October 1890*, submitted to the *Revenue and Agriculture Department*, No. 351, 6 October, 1890.

Note by Mr. H. E. M. James, Bombay Civil Service, on Cotton Trade Frauds and Deterioration of Staples, in the *Proceedings of the Revenue and Agricultural Department*, Fibre and Silk Branch (November 1891), Nos. 1 to 13.

From: Col. E. J. Gunthorpe, Officiating Deputy Commissioner, Amraoti District, To: The Commissioner, Hyderabad Assigned Districts, Amraoti, dated 30 September 1891, in the *Proceedings of the Hyderabad Administration on Matters of Routine for the Month of April 1892*, submitted to the Revenue and Agricultural Department, No. 86, 16 March 1892.

Statement showing years of survey and settlement and the year in which the thirty year settlement will expire, by the Director of Land Records and Agriculture, Hyderabad Assigned Districts, Amraoti, dated 15 December 1894, in the *Proceedings of the Hyderabad Administration on Matters of Routine for the Month of December 1894*, submitted to the Revenue and Agriculture Department, Circular No. 5, 15 December 1894.

From: G. S. Khaparde, High Court Vakil, Amraoti, To: The Commissioner, Hyderabad Assigned Districts, dated 19 July 1895, Amraoti, in the *Proceedings of the Hyderabad Administration on Matters of Routine for the Month of September 1895*, submitted to the Revenue and Agriculture Department, No. 337, dated 28 September 1895.

From: R. D. Hare, Deputy Commissioner, Akola, To: The Commissioner, Hyderabad Assigned Districts, dated 27 July 1895, in the *Proceedings of the Hyderabad Administration on Matters of Routine for the Month of September 1895*, submitted to the Revenue and Agriculture Department, No. 337, 28 September 1895.

From: A. Williams, Secretary for Berar to the Resident, To: The Secretary to the Government of India, Department of Revenue and Agriculture, Hyderabad Residency, dated 11 January 1896, in the *Proceedings of the Hyderabad Administration on Matter of Routine for the Month of January 1896*, submitted to the Revenue and Agricultural Department, No. 13, 11 January 1896.

Note on the Proposals in Revenue Department, Nos. 1543/180-2, dated 9 July 1897, for revision of the *Berar Patels and Patwaris Law, 1886*, by Chichele-Plowden, Resident at Hyderabad, in the *Proceedings of the Hyderabad Administration on Matters of Routine for the Month of July 1898*, submitted to the Revenue and Agricultural Department, No. 206, 19 July 1898.

Agricultural Ledger Series, Hyderabad Assigned Districts, No. 2, *Cotton Cultivation in Berar or the Hyderabad Assigned Districts*, in the *Proceedings of the Department of Revenue and Agriculture*, Fibre and Silk Branch (Dec. 1898), No. 19.

Forecasts of the Cotton Crop in Bombay, the Punjab, Berar and Central Provinces of India for 1898-99, in the *Proceedings of the Department of Revenue and Agriculture*, Agriculture Branch (February 1899), No. 12/15.

Proposals for the Revision Settlement of the Darwa Taluq of Wun District, From: F. W. Francis, Director of Land Records and Agriculture, Hyderabad Assigned Districts, To: The Commissioner, Hyderabad Assigned Districts, Akola, dated 11 February 1901, in the *Proceedings of the Hyderabad Administration on Matters of Routine for the Month of June 1901*, submitted to the *Department of Revenue and Agriculture*, No. 201, 22 June 1901.

From: Rustomji Faridonji, Deputy Commissioner, Buldana District, To: The Commissioner, Hyderabad Assigned Districts, dated 2 November 1901, in the *Proceedings of the Hyderabad Administration on Matters of Routine for the Month of December 1901*, submitted to the Department of Revenue and Agriculture, No. 416 (11 December 1901).

Settlement Reports (NMML)

Akola Taluka Settlement Report, No. 268 of 1867.

Akote Taluka Settlement Report, No. 268 of 1867.

Basim Taluka Settlement Report. Camp No. 203, Chikalda, dated 25 April 1900.

Chandur Taluka Settlement Report, No. 470 of 1873.

Chicklee Taluka Settlement Report, No. 51 of 1866.

Dariapur and Mortizapur Taluka Settlement Report, No. 368 of 1869.

Darwa Taluka Settlement Report, No. 420 of 1872.

Jalgaon Taluka Settlement Report, No. 261 of 1865.

Mangrul Taluka Settlement Report, No. 312 of 1900.

Malkapur Taluka Settlement Report, No. 347 of 1866.
Mehkur Taluka Settlement Report, No. 1098 of 1868.
Morsi Taluka Settlement Report, No. 563 of 1871.
Oomrawuttee and Ellichpur Settlement Report, No. 444 of 1870.
Yeotmal Taluka Settlement Report, No. 382 of 1874.
Wun Taluka Settlement Report, No. 340 of 1875.
From: Major P. A. Elphinstone, Superintendent Revenue Survey and Assessment, Hyderabad Assigned Districts, To: The Second Assistant Resident, Hyderabad, from Superintendent's Office, Malligaum, 7 October 1871, in *Morsi Taluka Settlement Report, 1871*, No. 563 of 1871.
From: Major P. A. Elphinstone, Superintendent Revenue Survey and Assessment, Hyderabad Assigned Districts, To: Major C. J. Prescott, Acting Survey and Settlement Commissioner, Hyderabad Assigned Districts, dated 14 October 1869, in *Mehkar Taluka Settlement Report*. No. 426 of 1868, p. 6, para 6.

Printed Sources

Aitchison, C. U. A., *Collection of Treaties Engagements and Sanads Relating to Indian and Neighbouring Countries*, Vol. II, Delhi, 1930.
Baden-Powell, *Land Systems of British India: Being a Manual of Land Tenures and of the Systems of Land-revenue Administration Prevalent in Several Provinces*, Oxford, 1892.
Bullock, F. S., *Narrative of the Famine in the Hyderabad Assigned Districts During the Year, 1896-97*, Hyderabad, 1898; *The Berar Alienated Villages Tenancy Law, 1921*, in the *Berar Code*, Nagpur, 1931.
The Berar Cotton and Grain Markets Law, 1897, in *British Enactments in Force in Berar*, compiled by C. S. Findlay, Nagpur, 1916.
The Berar Fair's Law, 1923, in the *Berar Code*, Nagpur, 1931.
The Berar Inam Rules, 1859, in the *Berar Code*, Nagpur, 1931.
The Berar Land Revenue Code, 1896, in *British Enactments in Force in Berar*, 1916.
The Berar Patels and Patwaris Law, 1900, D. V. Shiddore, ed., Amraoti, 1935 (HUL).
The Berar Revenue Manual Containing Revenue Book Circulars, Vol. 2, corrected up to 31 December 1952, Nagpur, 1968.
The Berar Small Cause Courts Law, 1905, in *The Berar Code*, Nagpur, 1931.
Crawford, J. A., *Report on the Famine in the Hyderabad Assigned Districts in the Years 1899 and 1900*, Nagpur, 1901.
Cassells, Walter R., *Cotton: An Account of its Culture in the Bombay Presidency*, Prepared from Government Records and Other Authentic Sources, in Accordance with a Resolution of the Government of India, Bombay, 1862.
Central Provinces and Berar: A Review of the Administration of the Provinces,

Vol. II, Nagpur, 1923 (CUL).

Datta, K. L., *Report on the Enquiry into the Rise of Prices in India*, 4 Vols., Calcutta, 1914.

Encyclopedia Britannica, New York, 1911.

Index Numbers of Indian Prices, 1861-1929, Department of Commercial Intelligence and Statistics, Calcutta, 1928.

Monograph on Cotton Fabrics in the Hyderabad Assigned Districts, 1896-97, published by F. W. Francis, Director of and Records and Agriculture, Hyderabad Assigned Districts.

Royle, Forbes J., *Review of the Measures which have been adopted in India for the Improved Culture of Cotton*, London, 1857; *On the Culture and Commerce of Cotton in India, and Elsewhere*, London, 1851.

Rules under the Berar Land Revenue Code, 1896, Nagpur, 1907; 'The History of the Assignment of the Berar Provinces in Trust for the Maintenance of the Hyderabad Contingent', *The Statesman* of July 1881, p. 17.

Schmidt, Arno, *A Report on Cotton Growing in India*, Secretary, International Federation of Master Cotton Spinners and Manufacturers Association. This report is a report of Secretary's visit to India, December 1911-January 1912.

Statistical Abstracts of British India from 1882-83 to 1891-92, No. 27, London, 1893. Also titled *Statistical Abstracts Relating to British India, 1874-1917* (in multi-volumes), printed annually, London.

Temple, Sir Richard, *Observation on the State and Administration of Hyderabad Assigned Districts*, dated 14 December 1867 (IOLR).

British Parliamentary Papers

From: M. J. Shaw Stewart, Under Secretary to Government, To: W. C. Anderson, Superintendent, Revenue Survey and Assessment, Southern Mahratta Country and Berar, in the *Proceedings of the Revenue Department*, No. 1977 of 1861, in *British Parliamentary Papers*, Vol. 44, 1863, p. 392.

From: Lt. Colonel Cuthbert Davidson, Resident at Hyderabad, To: G. R. Haywood, Est., Secretary to the Cotton Supply Association, Manchester, 8 March 1861, Enclosure 4, No. 12, in the *British Parliamentary Papers*, Vol. 44, 1863.

From: Captain W. Cadell, Assistant Commissioner in Charge of Commissioner's Office, To: First Assistant Resident at Hyderabad, Nos. 2059-301, dated 19 September 1861, in the *British Parliamentary Papers*, Vol. 44, 1863. Correspondence from 1 January 1861 to the present time between the Secretary of State for India and the Governor General or other persons in India, on the subject of cotton cultivation in India, and the prospects of supplies of that article to this country during the present year 1864.

Royal Commission on Agriculture in India, Reports from Commissioners, Inspectors and others, in six Vols., *British Parliamentary Papers*, Session 7 (Feb. 1928-Aug. 1928), Vol. VIII, 1928.

Census Reports

Report of the Census of Berar, 1881, Eustace J. Kitts, ed., Bombay, 1882.
Census of India, 1891, Vol. VI: *Berar or the Hyderabad Assigned Districts*, Calcutta, 1892.
Census of India, 1901, Part II: *Imperial Tables*, Allahabad, 1902; Major K. J. L. Mackenzie's note on the Banjaras, in *Report on the Census of Berar, 1881* Bombay, 1882.

Dictionaries (IOLR)

H. H. Wilson, *A Glossary of Judicial and Revenue Terms of British India*, Calcutta, 1885, A revised edition with case notes by A. C. Ganguli and N. D. Basu, eds., Calcutta, 1940.
H. Yule and A. C. Burnell, *Hobson-Jobson: A Glossary of Colloquial Anglo-Indian Words and Phrases*, London, 1886.
G. A. Watts, *Dictionary of the Economic Products in India*, 6 Vols, in 9 pts, Calcutta, 1889-93.

Gazetteers

Amraoti Gazetteer, Bombay, 1911 (CUL).
Central Provinces and Berar District Gazetteers, Akola District, Calcutta, 1910.
Central Provinces District Gazetteers, Buldana District, Vol. A: Descriptive, A. E. Nelson, ed., Calcutta, 1910.
A. C. Lyall, *Gazetteer of the Haidarabad Assigned Districts, Commonly called Berar*, 1870 (IOLR).
Yeotmal District Gazetteer, Calcutta, 1908.

SECONDARY SOURCES

Alam, Muzaffar, *The Crisis of the Empire in Mughal North India: Awadh and the Punjab, 1707-1748*, New Delhi, 1986.
Ali, Athar M., *The Mughal Nobility Under Aurangzeb*, New York, 1966; *The Passing of Empire: The Mughal Case, Modern Asian Studies* 11, No. 3 (July 1975), pp. 385-96.
Asakawa, Kan'ichi, *The Documents of Iriki*, Tokyo, 1955.
Asani, Ali Sultan Ali, *The Bujh Niranjan: An Ismaili Mystical Poem*, Cambridge, 1991.

Bagchi, Amiya, *Private Investment in India, 1900-1939*, Cambridge, 1972.

Baker, David E. U., *Changing Political Leadership in an Indian Province: The Central Provinces and Berar, 1919-1939*, Delhi, 1979; *Colonialism in an Indian Hinterland: The Central Provinces, 1820-1920*, Delhi, 1993.

Barani, Ziya al-Din (1284-1356), *Tarikh-i-Firuzshahi* (Engl. tr.), John Dowson, ed., Lahore, 1974.

Barrier, N. G., *The Punjab Alienation of Land Bill of 1900*, Durham, 1966.

Basu, Syama Prasad, *Rise and Fall of Khilji Imperialism*, Calcutta, 1963; *The Tughluqs: Years of Experiments*, Calcutta, 1970.

Bates, Crispin, 'Class and Economic Change in Central India: The Narmada Valley 1820-1930', in Clive Dewey, ed., *Arrested Development in India: The Historical Dimension*, Maryland, 1988; 'Regional Dependence and Rural Development in Central India: The Pivotal Role of Migrant Labour', *Modern Asian Studies* 19, No. 3 (1985), pp. 573-92.

Bayly, Christopher A., *The Imperial Meridian: The British Empire and the World, 1780-1830*, London, 1989; *Rulers, Townsmen and Bazaars: North Indian Society in the Age of British Expansion, 1770-1870,* Cambridge, 1983; *The New Cambridge History of India: Indian Society and the Making of the British Empire*, Cambridge, 1988.

Beaglehole, T. H. *Thomas Munro and the Development of Administrative Policy in Madras, 1792-1818: The Origins of the Munro System*, Cambridge, 1966.

Bhattacharya, Neeladri, 'Lenders and Debtors: Punjab Countryside, 1880-1940', *Studies in History* 1, No. 2 (1985); 'The Logic of Tenancy Cultivation: Central and South-East Punjab, 1870-1935', *Indian Economic and Social History Review* 20, No. 2 (1983), pp. 121-70.

Bloch, Marc L'eopold Benjamin, *French Rural Society: An Essay on its Basic Characteristics*, Berkeley, 1966.

Bose, Sugata, 'Peasant Labor and Colonial Capital: Rural Bengal Since 1870', in the *New Cambridge History of India*, Cambridge, 1992.

Bosworth, Clifford Edmund, *The Later Ghaznavids: Splendour and Decay: The Dynasty in Afghanistan and Northern India, 1040-1186*, New York, 1977.

Brenner, Robert, 'Agrarian Class Structure and Economic Development in Pre-Industrial Europe', *Past and Present*, No. 70 (Feb 1976); *Merchants and Revolution: Commercial Change and Political Conflict in the London Merchant Community: 1550-1653*, New Jersey, 1991.

Bryant, Kenneth, *Poems to the Child God: Structure and Strategies in the Poetry of Surdas*, Berkeley, 1978; 'The Manuscript Tradition of the Sursagar: The Fatehpur Manuscript', in N. G. Bahura., ed., *Pad Surdasji Ka/The Padas of Surdas*, pp. vii-xx, Jaipur, 1982.

Chakrabarti, Dipesh, *Rethinking Working Class History: Bengal, 1890-1940,* Princeton, 1989.

Chaladar, Haran C., *Social Life in Ancient India*, 2nd rev. edn., Calcutta, 1954.

Chandel, L. S., *Early Medieval State: A Study of Delhi Sultanate*, New Delhi, 1989.

Chandra, Bipin, *The Rise and Growth of Economic Nationalism in India: Economic Policies of Indian Nationalist Leadership, 1885-1905*, New Delhi, 1966.

Chaudhuri, K. N., *Asia Before Europe: Economy and Civilization of the Indian Ocean from the Rise of Islam to 1750*, Cambridge, 1990.

Choksey, R. D., ed., *Twilight of the Marathas, 1818*, Queries from Mr. Mountstuart Elphinstone, Commissioner of the Deccan to the Collectors in the Deccan and Political Agent, Satara (Peshwa Daftar), Poona, 1976.

Coclanis, Peter A., *The Shadow of a Dream: Economic Life and Death in the South Carolina Low Country, 1670-1920*, New York, 1989.

Cohn, Bernard S., *The Camars of Senapur: A Study of the Changing Status of a Depressed Caste*, Michigan, 1954.

Cronon, William, *Nature's Metropolis: Chicago and the Great West*, New York, 1991.

Darval, Frank Ongley, *Popular Disturbances and Public Order in Regency England: Being an Account of the Luddite and other Disorders in England During the Years 1811-1817 and the Attitude and Activity of the Authorities*, New York, 1969.

Desai, A. R., *Social Background of Indian Nationalism*, Bombay, 1966.

Dobb, Maurice Herbert, *Studies in the Development of Capitalism*, New York, 1964.

Dunn, Porter, *The Fall and Rise of the Asiatic Mode of Production*, New York, 1982.

Dutt, R. C., *The Economic History of India Under the Early British Rule, from the Rise of the British Power in 1757 to the Accession of Queen Victoria in 1837*, London, 1956; *The Economic History of India in the Victorian Age, from the Accession of Queen Victoria in 1837 to the Commencement of the 20th Century*, London, 1906; *Economic History of British India: A Record of Agriculture and Land Settlements, Trade and Manufacturing Industries*, London, 1902.

Duus, Peter, *Feudalism in Japan*, USA, 1976.

Dyson, Tim, 'The Population History of Berar since 1881 and its Potential Wider Significance', *The Indian Economic and Social History Review*, Vol. XXVI, No. 2 (April-June 1989), pp. 167-203; 'On the Demography of South Asian Famines', *Population Studies*, Vol. 45 (1991), pp. 5-25; *India's Historical Demography: Studies in Famine, Disease, and Society*, London, 1989.

Fogel, Robert W. and Stanley L. Engerman, *Time on the Cross: The Economics of American Negro Slavery*, 2 Vols., Boston, 1974.

Ford, Richard I., ed., *Prehistoric Food Production in North America*, Ann

Arbor, 1985; 'Gardening and Farming before AD 1000: Patterns of Prehistoric Culture North of Mexico', *Journal of Ethnobiology* 1 (1), pp. 6-7.

Frykenberg, Robert E., *Land Control and Social Structure in Indian History*, Madison, 1969; 'Privileged Landholding: The Concept Stretched to Cover the Case', in Robert E. Frykenberg, ed., *Land Tenure and Peasant in South Asia*, New Delhi, 1977.

Gallman, Robert E., 'Self-Sufficiency and Cotton Economy of the Antebellum South', *Agricultural History*, XLIV, No. 1 (January 1970), pp. 5-23.

Genovese, Eugene D., *Roll, Jordon, Roll: The World the Slaves Made*, New York, 1974.

Guha, Sumit, *Agrarian Economy of Bombay Deccan, 1818-1941*, Delhi, 1985.

Habib, Irfan, Economic History of the Delhi Sultanate, *Indian Historical Review*, Vol. IV, No. 2 (1981); *The Agrarian System of Mughal India, 1556-1707*, Bombay, 1963; Problems of Marxist Historical Analysis, *Enquiry* 3, No. 2 (1968); Colonization of the Indian Economy, 1757-1900, *Social Scientist* (March 1975); *An Atlas of the Mughal Empire*, Delhi, 1982.

Habib, Mohammad, *Some Aspects of the Foundation of the Delhi Sultanate*, Delhi, 1968.

Hall, John Whitney and Marius Janson, eds., *Studies in the Institutional History of Early Modern Japan*, Princeton, 1968.

Hamadani, Agha Hussain, *Frontier Policy of the Delhi Sultanate*, Islamabad, 1986.

Harnetty, Peter, *Imperialism and Free Trade: Lancashire and India in the mid-Nineteenth Century*, Vancouver, 1972; India and British Commercial Enterprise: The Case of Manchester Cotton Company, 1860-64, *Indian Economic and Social History Review*, Vol. III, No. 4 (Dec. 1966), p. 396; Crop Trends in Central Provinces of India, 1861-1921, *Modern Asian Studies*, Vol. II (1977), pp. 341-78; Cotton Exports and Indian Agriculture, 1861-70, *Economic History Review*, Series 2, Vol. XXIV, No. 3 (1971), pp. 414-29; Landlords and the Raj: The Malguzars of the Central Provinces, 1861-1921, *Studies in History*, Vol. 3, No. 3 (July-Dec. 1987), pp. 187-10; The Cotton Improvement Program in India, 1865-75, *Agricultural History*, Vol. XLIV (1970), pp. 379-92; The Indian Cotton Duties Controversy, 1894-96, *English Historical Review*, Vol. LXXVII (1962), pp. 684-702; Cotton Exports and Indian Agriculture, 1861-1870, *The Economic History Review*, Vol. XXIV (1971), pp. 414-29.

Hauser, Walter, *The Bihar Provincial Kisan Sabha, 1929-1949: A Study of an Indian Peasant Movement*, Doctoral Thesis, Chicago, 1961.

Hawley, John Stratton, *Songs of the Saints of India*, New York, 1988; *Sur Das: Poet, Singer, and Saint*, Seattle, 1984.

Higgs, Robert, *Competition and Coercion: Blacks in the American Economy*,

1865-1914, Cambridge, 1977.

Hilton, Rodney Howard, *English and French Towns in Feudal Society: A Comparative Study*, Cambridge, 1992.

Hutton, James, *Thugs and Dacoits of India*, Delhi, 1981.

Irschick, Eugene F., *Politics and Social Conflict in South India: The Non-Brahman Movement and Tamil Separatism, 1916-1929*, Bombay, 1969.

Jurgensmeyer, Mark, *Religion as Social Vision: The Movement Against Untouchability in 20th Century Punjab*, Berkeley, 1982; Mark and N. Gerald Barrier, eds., *Sikh Studies: Comparative Perspectives on a Changing Tradition*, Berkeley, 1979.

Kautilya, *Arthashastra*, tr. by R. Shamasastry, 5th edn, Mysore, 1956.

Kling, Blair, *The Blue Mutiny: The Indigo Disturbances in Bengal, 1859-1862*, London, 1966.

Kulikoff, Alan, *Tobacco and Slaves: The Development of Southern Cultures in the Chesapeake, 1680-1800*, Chapel Hill, 1986.

Kumar, Ravinder, *Western India in the Nineteenth Century: A Study in the Social History of Maharashtra*, London, 1968; 'The Rise of Rich Peasants in Western India', in D. A. Low., ed., *Soundings in Modern South Asian History*, London, 1968.

Ladurie, Emmanuel LeRoy, *Tithe and Agrarian History from the Fourteenth to the Nineteenth Centuries: An Essay in Comparative History*, New York, 1982; *Times of Feast and Times of Famine: A History of Climate Since the Year 1000*, Doubleday, 1971; *The French Peasantry, 1450-1660*, Berkeley, 1987.

Landes, David, *Unbound Prometheus: Technological Change and Industrial Development in Western Europe from 1750 to the Present*, Cambridge, 1979.

Laslett, Peter, *The World We Have Lost: England Before the Industrial Age*, London, 1984.

Lathrap, Donald W., The Introduction of Maize in Prehistoric Eastern North America: The View from Amazonia and the Santa Elena Peninsula, in William F. Keegan, ed., *The Emergent Horticultural Economies of the Eastern Woodlands*, Carbondale, Illinois (1987), Center for Archaeological Investigations, Occasional Paper 7.

Lefebvre, Georges, *The Great Fear of 1789: Rural Panic in Revolutionary France*, New York, 1973.

Lenin, Vladmir Ilich, *Imperialism, The Highest Stage of Capitalism*, New York, 1939; *The Lenin Anthology*, New York, 1974; *Selected Works*, 3 Vols., New York, 1967; *Collected Works*, 5 Vols., Moscow, 1963.

Leonard, Karen Isaksen, *Social History of an Indian Caste: The Kayasths of Hyderabad*, Berkeley, 1978; The Hyderabad Political System and its Participants, *Journal of Asian Studies* 30, No. 3 (May 1971), pp. 569-82; Banking Firms in Nineteenth Century Hyderabad Politics, *Modern Asian Studies*, Vol. 15 (1981), pp. 177-202.

Lewis, Archibald, *Knights and Samurai: Feudalism in Northern France and Japan*, London, 1974.

Logan, Frenise A., India-Britain's Substitute for American Cotton, 1861-1865, *The Journal of Southern History*, XXIV, No. 4 (Nov. 1958), pp. 472-80.

Malcolm, Thomas, *The Luddites: Machine Breaking in Regency England*, Newton Abbott (England), 1970.

Mandle, Jay, *The Roots of Black Poverty: The Southern Plantation Economy After the Civil War*, Durham, 1978.

Manu, *The Laws of Manu*, tr. with extracts from seven commentaries by George Buhler, New York, 1969.

Martin Jr., Briton, *New India 1885: British Official Policy and the Emergence of the Indian National Congress*, Berkeley, 1969.

Marx, Karl, *The Communist Manifesto* (1848), Samuel H. Beer, ed., Arlington Heights (Illinois), 1955; *Capital: A Critique of Political Economy*, Vol. 1, Introduced by Ernest Mandel, New York, 1977.

McAlpin, Michelle Burge, *Subject to Famine: Food Crisis and Economic Change in Western India, 1860-1920*, New Jersey, 1983.

McLane, John R., *Indian Nationalism and the Early Congress*, New Jersey, 1977.

Mcleod, W. H., *Guru Nanak and the Sikh Religion*, Oxford, 1968.

Metzer, Jacob, 'Rational Management, Modern Business Practices, and Economics of Scale in the Ante-Bellum Southern Plantation', *Exploration in Economic History*, Vol. 12 (1975), pp. 123-50.

Mill, James, *The History of British India*, Abridged, Chicago, 1975.

Moore, Barrington, *Social Origins of Dictatorship and Democracy: Lords and Peasants in the Making of the Modern World*, Boston, 1966.

Naoroji, Dadabhai, *Poverty and Un-British Rule in India*, London, 1901; *Poverty of India: Papers and Statistics*, London, 1888; *Correspondence*, 2 Vols., R. P. Patwardhan, ed., Bombay, 1977.

Orwell, George, *Burmese Days*, San Diego, 1974.

Pandey, Gyanendra, A View of the Observable: A Positivist 'understanding' of Agrarian Society and Political Protest in Colonial India, *Journal of Peasant Studies* 7, No. 3 (April 1980); *The Ascendancy of the Congress in Uttar Pradesh, 1926-34: A Study in Imperfect Mobilization*, Delhi, 1978.

Prasad, G. V. R. and Ashok Sahni, First Cretaceous Mammal from India, *India*, Vol. 332 (No. 14) 14 April 1988.

Prakash, Gyan, *Bonded Histories: Genealogies of Labour Servitude in Colonial India*, Cambridge, 1990; Prakash and Douglas Haynes, eds., *Contesting Power: Resistance in Everyday Social Relations in South Asia*, Berkeley, 1991; *The World of Rural Labour in Colonial India*, New York, 1992; *Production and Reproduction of Bondage: Kamias and Maliks in South Bihar, circa 1300-1930*, Ph.D Thesis: Pennsylvania, 1984.

Prawdin, Michael, *Dschingis-Khan*, Lubbe, 1979.

Quddusi, Mohammed Yaseen, *Berar Under the Mughals, 1595-1724*, Ph.D

Thesis, Nagpur, 1973, in microfilm at National Archives of India, Acc. No. 1891.

Ramaswamy, T. N., tr., *Essentials of Indian Statecraft: Kautilya's Arthasastra for Contemporary Readers*, Bombay, 1962.

Ransom, Roger L. and Richard Sutch, *One Kind of Freedom: The Economic Consequences of Emancipation*, Cambridge, 1977.

Ray, Bharati, *Hyderabad and British Paramountcy, 1858-1883*, Delhi, 1988.

Reid, Robert William, *The Land of Lost Content: The Luddist Revolt, 1812*, London, 1986.

Roy, Mahendra Prakash, *Origin, Growth, and Suppression of the Pindaris*, New Delhi, 1973.

Said, Edward W., *Orientalism*, New York, 1978.

Saran, Kishori Lal, *Twilight of the Sultanate: A Political, Social and Cultural History of the Sultanate from the Invasion of Timur to the Conquest of Babur, 1398-1526*, New York, 1963.

Sawer, Marian, *Marxism and the Question of the Asiatic Mode of Production*, Nijhoff, 1977.

Scott, James, *Weapons of the Weak: Everyday Forms of Peasant Resistance*, New Haven, 1985,

Sen, Amartya Kumar, *Poverty and Famine*, Delhi, 1982; Famine Mortality: A Study of the Bengal Famine of 1943, in E. Hobsbawm *et al.*, eds., *Peasants in History*, Oxford, 1980.

Sen, Surendra Nath, *The Military System of the Marathas*, Calcutta, 1979.

Sethia, Tara, *The Railway and Mining Enterprises in Hyderabad State under the British Raj during the 1870s and 1880s*, Doctoral Dissertation, UCLA, 1986.

Sharma, R. S., *Indian Feudalism, circa A.D. 300-1200*, Delhi, 1980.

Shih, Yuan Chao Pi, *Index to the Secret History of the Mongols*, by Igor de Rachhewiltz, Bloomington, 1872.

Siddiqi, Majid Hayat, *The Agrarian Unrest in North India, 1918-22*, New Delhi, 1978.

Silver, Arthur, *Manchester Men and Indian Cotton, 1847-1872*, Manchester, 1966.

Sinha, Birendra Kumar, *The Pindaris, 1798-1818*, Calcutta, 1971.

Soboul, Albert, *Sans-culottes: The Popular Movement and Revolutionary Government, 1793-1794*, New York, 1972.

Srinivas, M. N., *Social Change in Modern India*, Los Angeles, 1962; *Caste in Modern India and Other Essays*, New York, 1962.

Srivastava, S. K., *Proceedings of Symposium on Cretaceous of India*, Lucknow, 1983.

Stein, Burton, Integration of the Agrarian System in South India, in Robert E. Frykenberg, ed., *Land Control and Social Structure in Indian History*, Madison, 1969.

Stokes, Eric, *The Peasant and the Raj: Studies in Agrarian Society and Peasant Rebellion in Colonial India*, Cambridge, 1980; *The Peasant Armed*, Oxford, 1986; *The English Utilitarians and India*, Oxford, 1959.

Sweezy, Paul, *Transition from Feudalism to Capitalism*, London, 1976.

Thomson, E. P., *The Making of the English Working Class*, New York, 1964.

Trautman, Thomas, *Kautilya and the Arthashastra: A Statistical Investigation of the Authorship and Evolution of the Text*, Leiden, 1971.

Tuker, Ivan Simms, *The Yellow Scarf: The Story of the Life of Thuggee Sleeman*, London, 1961.

Vaudeville, Charlottee, *Kabir-Vani*, Pondicherry, 1982; *Pastorales par Sour-Das*, Paris, 1971.

Vicziany, Marika, 'The Deindustrialization of India in the Nineteenth Century', A Methodological Critique of Amiya Bagchi, *Indian Economic and Social History Review*, XVI, No. 2 (April-June 1979), p. 105.

Vincent, Joan, *Teso in Transformation: The Political Economy of Peasant and Class in Eastern Africa*, Berkeley, 1982.

Washbrook, David A., Progress and Problems: South Asian Economic and Social History, circa 1720-1860, *Modern Asian Studies* 22, pt. 1 (1988): pp. 57-96; *The Emergence of Provincial Politics, 1880-1920*, Delhi, 1977.

Wayne, Michael, *The Reshaping of Plantation Society: The Natchez District, 1860-1880*, Baton Rouge, 1983.

Weiner, Jonathan M., *Social Origins of the New South: Alabama, 1860-1885*, Baton Rouge, 1978.

Wittfogel, Karl, *Oriental Despotism: A Comparative Study of Total Power*, New Haven, 1957.

Woodman, Harold, *King Cotton and His Retainers*, Lexington, 1968.

Wright, Gavin, *The Political Economy of the Cotton South: Households, Markets, and Wealth in the Nineteenth Century*, New York, 1978.

Yazdani, Zubaida, *Hyderabad During the Residency of Henry Russell, 1811-1820*, Oxford, 1976.

ABBREVIATIONS FOR ARCHIVES

APSA	Andhra Pradesh State Archives, Hyderabad
BML	British Museum and Library, London
CSL	Central Secretariat Library, London
CUL	Columbia University Library, New York
HUL	Harvard University Library, Boston
IOLR	India Office Library and Records, London
NAI	National Archives of India, New Delhi
NMML	Nehru Memorial Museum and Library, New Delhi

Index